Handbook of
Marketing Scales

Handbook of Marketing Scales

Multi-Item Measures for Marketing and Consumer Behavior Research

William O. Bearden
Richard G. Netemeyer
Mary F. Mobley

Published in Cooperation With the Association for Consumer Research

SAGE Publications
International Educational and Professional Publisher
Newbury Park London New Delhi

University of
Wisconsin-Madison
Libraries

For information address:

SAGE Publications, Inc.
2455 Teller Road
Newbury Park, California 91320

SAGE Publications Ltd.
6 Bonhill Street
London EC2A 4PU
United Kingdom

SAGE Publications India Pvt. Ltd.
M-32 Market
Greater Kailash I
New Delhi 110 048 India

Printed in the United States of America

Library of Congress Cataloging-in-Publication Data

Bearden, William O., 1954-
    Handbook of marketing scales: multi-item measures for marketing and consumer behavior research / William O. Bearden, Richard G. Netemeyer, Mary F. Mobley.
        p.   cm.
    "Published in cooperation with the Association for Consumer Research."
    Includes bibliographical references.
    ISBN 0-8039-5155-8
    1. Marketing research. 2. Consumer behavior—Research.
I. Netemeyer, Richard G., 1956-   II. Mobley, Mary F.
III. Title.
HF5415.3.B323   1993
658.8′3—dc20

92-45241
CIP

93 94 95 96   10 9 8 7 6 5 4 3 2 1

TABLE OF CONTENTS

Self-Monitoring

Innovativeness

Discontent, Alienation, Assertiveness, and Aggressiveness

Group Influences

Chapter Three: Values

General Values

Specific Consumption Values

Materialism

Chapter Four: Involvement and Information Processing

Involvement Scales

Involvement With a Specific Class of Products

Involvement General to Several Products

Revised Versions of the PII

Other Involvement Measures General to Several Products

Chapter Five: Reactions to Advertising Stimuli

Measures Relating to Ad Emotions and Ad Content

Measures Related to Ad Believability

Measures Related to Children's Advertising

Chapter Six: Attitudes About the Performance of Business Firms, Social Agencies, and the Marketplace

Consumer Attitudes Toward Business Practices

Business Ethics

Business Attitudes Toward the Marketplace

Chapter Seven: Sales, Sales Management, and Inter-Intrafirm Issues

Sales and Sales Management Issues

Job Satisfaction

Role Perceptions and Job Tension

Performance

Leadership

Commitment

Sales Approaches

Inter-Intrafirm Issues

PREFACE

The authors would like to acknowledge several individuals and organizations that were instrumental in bringing this project to publication. As a favor, we asked a number of colleagues to read and critique chapters or parts of chapters of this text. Their comments and insight enhanced both the content and organization of the chapters they read. Lynn Kahle of the University of Oregon and Marsha Richins of the University of Missouri at Columbia reviewed sections of the Values chapter. Specifically, Lynn read the General Values section and Marsha read the Materialism section. They not only alerted us to some useful measures, but provided helpful comments as to chapter organization. Peter Bloch of the University of Missouri at Columbia reviewed the Involvement section of Chapter 4. In addition to commenting on several measures, Peter suggested the product specific, product general, and purchasing involvement categorization. Julie Edell of Duke University provided helpful comments pertaining to the Measures Related to Ad Emotions and Ad Content section of Chapter 5. Jagdip Singh of Case Western Reserve University and Ajay Kohli of the University of Texas at Austin critiqued Chapter 7. Jagdip provided insightful comments and additions with regard to Sales and Sales Management Issues, and Ajay did the same for the Inter-Intra Issues.

Gil Churchill and Paul Peter of the University of Wisconsin at Madison and Terry Shimp and Subhash Sharma of the University of South Carolina at Columbia reacted to initial drafts of our outline and concept. Each was influential in providing guidance for the project. The following Ph.D. students at the University of South Carolina were instrumental in proofing summaries and in providing valuable library assistance: Mike Barone, Brad Brooks, Ken Manning, and Ann Minton. Lastly, we owe a debt of thanks to Keith Hunt of Brigham Young University and Jim Muncy of Clemson University for their assistance throughout the publication of this text. We consistently ran over deadlines that we set, and they patiently waited until we supplied them with drafts of the text.

Most of the measures summarized in this text were originally published in marketing- and consumer-related journals or conference proceedings. In addition, the social psychology and organizational behavior literatures, as well several books, contributed measures to this volume. We would like to thank *all* the publishers that granted us permission to reprint the measures summarized in this text. In particular, we are grateful to the following publishers and their corresponding publications:

American Marketing Association
Journal of Marketing
Journal of Marketing Research
Journal of Public Policy & Marketing
AMA Proceedings
250 South Wacker Drive, Suite 200
Chicago, IL 60606-5819

Association for Consumer Research
ACR Proceedings
63 TNRB
Brigham Young University
Provo, UT 84602

University of Chicago Press
Journal of Consumer Research
5801 South Ellis
Chicago, IL 60637

American Psychological Association
Journal of Personality and Social Psychology
Journal of Applied Psychology
2nd Floor
750 1st St., N.E.
Washington, DC 20002-4242

William O. Bearden, University of South Carolina
Richard G. Netemeyer, Louisiana State University
Mary F. Mobley, Augusta College

1

Introduction

BACKGROUND

This volume provides a summary compilation of multi-item, self-report measures developed and/or frequently used in consumer behavior and marketing research. A driving force behind the compilation of the measures in this volume was our own research experience. Like many others, we have often used paper and pencil measures in various types of research projects. Though at times we were aware that measures existed, we were unaware of the authors, the source, and/or the measure's reliability and validity. Thus, we felt that a handbook of available scale measures of the more widely studied constructs in marketing and consumer behavior would be useful.

There are several other reasons for compiling the measures in this text. First, the book should be helpful in reducing the time it takes to locate instruments for survey research in marketing and consumer behavior, and given that a number of constructs have several measures, the book should provide researchers with options to consider. Second, a number of the measures in this volume have been used in several studies. Therefore, the book should serve as a partial guide to the literature for certain topic areas, and may spur further refinement of existing measures in terms of item reduction, dimensionality, reliability, and validity. This text may also help identify those areas where measures are needed, thus encouraging further development of valid measures of consumer behavior and marketing constructs. Lastly, we hope that the book will serve as an impetus to advance knowledge. By using the same measures across several studies, comparison and integration of results may be enhanced.

Criteria For Measure Selection

The emphasis of this project has been upon compiling and summarizing multi-item scales developed or frequently used in marketing and consumer behavior survey research. For the most part, we have included measures from articles whose major objective (or at least one of the major objectives) was measurement development. We have not attempted the overwhelming task of compiling single-item measures, and, despite our attempt to be thorough, no claim is made that this volume contains every multi-item measure relevant to marketing and consumer behavior. Many studies included multi-item scales as operationalizations of independent and dependent variables. Our intent was to include only those published measures subjected to some minimal developmental procedures. Throughout the search process, "judgment calls" were made with regard to what measures to include and what measures to exclude. However, the general criteria for inclusion and exclusion (as stated below) were followed, and we do feel confident that we have included the majority of higher-quality instruments available. Of course, the list of measures will have to be revised as oversights on our part are brought to our attention and as new scales are developed. We, therefore, invite researchers to send us information about scales we have inadvertently excluded, as well as information about the scales we have included, and newly developed measures.

Criteria for inclusion:
   a) The measure had a reasonable theoretical base and/or conceptual definition.

   b) The measure was composed of several (i.e., at least three) items or questions.

   c) The measure was developed within the marketing or consumer behavior literature or was commonly used in the marketing or consumer behavior literature.

   d) At least some scaling procedures were employed in scale development.

   e) Estimates of reliability and/or validity existed.

What was excluded:
   a) Single-item measures — though important in many studies, the task of compiling them was not a focus of this text.
   b) Multi-item measures that did not meet the above five criteria. For example: 1) multi-item measures based on "face

validity" alone; and 2) multi-item measures included in studies as dependent or independent variables that were not derived through scale development procedures.

SEARCH PROCEDURES

Three procedures were used in the search process for the scales included in this volume: 1) an on-line computer search of publications in marketing and consumer behavior; 2) a visual search of the major publications in marketing and consumer behavior; and 3) a letter was sent to all ACR members on the 1990 ACR mailing list requesting information on scales and measures that they were aware of or currently working on.

The on-line computer searches were performed at the University of South Carolina and Louisiana State University for the following marketing and consumer behavior publications:

Journal of Marketing Research (all issues)
Journal of Consumer Research (all issues)
Journal of Marketing (1964 to present)
Journal of Retailing (1964 to present)
Journal of the Academy of Marketing Science (all issues)
Journal of Advertising (all issues)
Journal of Advertising Research (all issues)
Psychology & Marketing (all issues)
Journal of Public Policy and Marketing (all issues)
Journal of Business Research (all issues)
AMA Summer Educators' Conference Proceedings (1964 to present)
ACR Proceedings (all issues)

The key words and phrases used in the computer search included words and phrases like "measures, measurement, scale, scale development, validity, reliability, and construct measurement." Except where noted, the on-line search included every volume and issue of the above publications. For the *Journal of Marketing*, the *Journal of Retailing*, and the *AMA Summer Educators' Conference Proceedings*, we used "1964 to the present" as limits in the search. The rationale for choosing 1964 as a cutoff year was twofold. First, it was cited as a year in which some of the earliest evidence of concern for construct measurement in marketing and consumer behavior was observed, and second, it was the first year of publication for the *Journal of Marketing Research* (Churchill and Peter 1984).

We also visually inspected the titles and abstracts of these publications, and in many cases, articles were read to determine if other multi-item measures were available. Again, in the Fall of 1990, a letter was sent to every ACR member on the ACR mailing list. We requested any scales or measures of marketing and consumer behavior constructs that they were aware of or were working on. We included most of the measures sent to us.

FORMAT AND PRESENTATION OF MEASURES

This text is organized in a manner similar to Robinson and Shaver's (1973) and Robinson, Shaver, and Wrightsman's (1991) volumes of social and psychological measures. For each scale summarized, we have tried to provide the following information using the outline shown below. *If information from the original source (or other sources) for a particular subheading was not available or applicable,* we noted by stating so or simply listing "N/A."

a) *Construct*: the definition and/or theoretical base of the construct as provided by the authors of the scale.

b) *Description*: the description of the measure including the number of items, scale points, scoring procedures, and dimensionality.

c) *Development*: how the scale was developed (i.e., the general procedures used to derive the scale from the original scale development article).

d) *Samples*: the samples used in scale development and validation.

e) *Validity*: estimates of validity (i.e., reliability, convergent, discriminant, and nomological validity) from development of the scale. In many cases, actual estimates are provided. However, in articles performing numerous tests of validity, a summary of the pattern of results, along with some example findings that provided evidence of validity, was offered.

f) *Scores*: mean and/or percentage scores on the scale from the original scale development article.

g) *Source*: the source(s) of the scale (the authors who developed the scale and the publication[s] the scale first appeared in).

h) *Other evidence*: Other evidence of validity (i.e., reliability, convergent, discriminant, and nomological validity), and scores from applications of the scale other than the original source. In general, we restricted "other evidence" to one to three applications of the scale in the marketing and consumer behavior literature.

i) *Other sources*: Sources from select applications of the scale (e.g., the sources in which "other evidence" was found).

j) *References*: Critical references from articles pertaining to the topic area other than those of the source of the scale and other sources. These references typically involved description of the construct domain or definition.

k) *Scale items*: the actual items in the scale, dimensions to which the items belong, items that require reverse scoring, and where applicable, the directions for using the scale.

CAVEATS AND CAUTIONS

A number of caveats and cautions regarding the development of this text are warranted. For each measure, we have tried to provide a reasonably complete description of the scale itself, the procedures used to develop the scale, and some of the available evidence regarding the reliability and validity of each scale. However, the articles on which the scales are based vary greatly in depth, length, and detail. Consequently, the summaries themselves are dependent upon the characteristics of the original source(s). And, within any one write-up or summary, the information included in the outline categories often required some creative assignment. For example, in some articles it was not always clear when scale development procedures ended and subsequent validation began. Hence, the outlines for each scale are best viewed as a means of organizing the presentation and not as a definitive guide.

There are also a number of important cautions related to the use of this text. This volume is not intended to be a substitute for careful evaluation of available measures or the development of valid measures for use in specific studies. In addition, the inclusion of a scale in the volume does not ensure an acceptable level of quality. In fact, the detail and sophistication of the procedures underlying some of the scales vary dramatically. Prospective users of these measures are encouraged to refer to the original source(s) and to make their own detailed evaluation prior to use of any measure in their research. (See "Evaluation of Measures" in the next several pages.) Lastly, it is hoped that the enhanced availability of the scales in this volume will not lead to the blind inclusion of "additional variables" on data collection instruments without sufficient theoretical justification.

EVALUATION OF MEASURES

In using, evaluating, or developing multi-item scale measures, a number of guidelines and procedures are recommended to help ensure that the measure is as psychometrically sound as possible. These procedures are outlined in the psychometric literature and the discussion that follows borrows heavily from this literature (e.g., American Psychological Association 1985; Bohrnstedt and Borgatta 1981; Carmines and Zeller 1979; Churchill 1979; DeVellis 1991; Nunnally 1979; Peter 1979, 1981; Robinson, Shaver, and Wrightsman 1991). As a general observation, some of the scales in this volume suffer from a developmental perspective regarding the use of nonrepresentative samples, failure to control for the spurious effects of response set bias and social desirability, and limited presentation of normative data such as scale dimensionality, test-retest reliability, means, and standard deviations.

Construct Definition and Domain

First, the scale should be based on a solid theoretical definition with the construct's domain thoroughly delineated and outlined. This definition and attendant description should entail both what is included in the domain of the construct, what is excluded from the construct's domain, and the a priori dimensionality of the construct's domain. The theoretical definition, the domain of the construct, and its dimensionality should be derived from a thorough review of the existing literature and, if available, expert opinion.

Content Validity

The scale items should exhibit "content" or "face" validity. That is, on the surface, they should appear consistent with the theoretical domain of the construct. In development, it is generally recommended that a number of items be generated that "tap the domain of the construct" (some say as high as 250 - see Table 1), that the items be screened by judges with expertise in the literature, and that several pilot tests on samples from relevant populations be conducted to trim and refine the pool of items (e.g., Bearden et al. 1989; Churchill 1979; Robinson, Shaver, and Wrightsman 1991). Furthermore, shorter and simpler items (ones that are easier to process and understand) are generally easier to respond to and are more reliable (Carmines and Zeller 1979; Churchill 1979; Churchill and Peter 1984; Converse and Presser 1986; Robinson et al. 1991; Sudman and Bradburn 1982). Thus, items should be representative of the construct they are proposed to measure, and should be easy to respond to (i.e., avoid jargon or difficult wording, avoid double-barreled items, avoid ambiguous wording).

Scale Dimensionality

A construct's domain can be hypothesized as uni- or multidimensional. Thus, the scale (or subscales) used to operationalize the construct should reflect the hypothesized dimensionality. The fact that a single factor (unidimensionality) underlies a set of items is considered a necessary, but not sufficient, condition for a factor or dimension's validity (Gerbing and Anderson 1988; Hattie 1985; McDonald 1981). Therefore, the scale's empirical factor structure should reflect its theoretical dimensionality.

Though a number of procedures have been employed to check the dimensionality of a scale (i.e., item-analysis, exploratory and confirmatory factor analysis), various approaches regarding the appropriate criteria for assessing unidimensionality exist. The reader is strongly urged to consult the following literature when examining dimensionality of measures (Anderson, Gerbing, and Hunter 1987; Gerbing and Anderson 1988; Kumar and Dillon 1987a, 1987b; Hattie 1985; McDonald 1981, 1985; Nunnally 1979).

Reliability

There are two broad types of reliability referred to in the psychometric literature: 1) test-retest - the correlation between the same person's score on the same set of items at two points in time, and 2) internal consistency - the correlation among items or sets of items in the scale for all who answer the items.

Test-retest. The stability of a respondent's item responses over time has not been assessed in scale use or development as frequently as internal consistency. This has been the case across disciplines (Robinson et al. 1991), and marketing and consumer behavior are no exceptions. Less than half of the scales in this text offer test-retest coefficients, but over 90% offer some estimate of internal consistency reliability. It is unfortunate that test-retest estimates are available for so few of the scales in the marketing and consumer behavior literature, and those planning scale development work should give a priori consideration to assessing test-retest reliability in addition to other procedures of evaluating reliability and validity.

Internal Consistency. Items comprising a scale (or sub-scale) should show high levels of internal consistency. Some commonly used criteria for assessing internal consistency are individual corrected item-to-total correlations, the inter-item correlation matrix for all scale items or items proposed to measure a given scale dimension, and a number of reliability coefficients (Bohrnstedt, Mohler, and Muller 1987; Churchill 1979; Lord and Novick 1973; Nunnally 1979; Peter 1979; Robinson et al. 1991). A recently used rule of thumb for corrected item-to-total correlations is that they should be .50 or greater to retain an item (e.g.,

Bearden et al. 1989; Shimp and Sharma 1987; Zaichkowsky 1985). Rules of thumb for individual correlations in the inter-item correlation matrix vary (i.e., Robinson et al. [1991] recommend levels of .30 or better as exemplary).

The most widely used internal consistency reliability coefficient is Cronbach's (1951) alpha. (Others, such as split-halves and rank order coefficients are available, but given the widespread use of alpha, we will limit our discussion to alpha.) A number of rules of thumb for what constitutes an acceptable level of alpha also exist. Some estimates go as low as .70 (Nunnally 1979) or .60 (Robinson et al. 1991). Regardless, scale length must be considered. As the number of items increases, alpha will tend to increase, and, since parsimony is also a concern in measurement (Carmines and Zeller 1979), an important question is "how many items does it take to measure a construct?" The answer to this question depends partially on the domain and dimensions of the construct. Naturally, a construct with a wide domain and multiple dimensions will require more items to adequately tap the domain/dimensions than a construct with a narrow domain. However, given that most scales are self-administered, and respondent fatigue and/or noncooperation need to be considered, it would seem that scale brevity is often a concern (cf., Bohrnstedt et al. 1987; Carmines and Zeller 1979; Churchill and Peter 1984).

With the advent of structural equation modeling packages such as LISREL (Joreskog and Sorbom 1987) and EQS (Bentler 1985), other tests of internal consistency are available. Composite reliability (Werts, Linn and Joreskog 1974), which is similar to coefficient alpha, can be calculated directly from the LISREL or EQS output (cf., Fornell and Larcker 1981).

A more stringent test of internal stability involves assessing the amount of variance captured by a construct's measure in relation to the amount of variance due to random error. An advocated rule of thumb is that the variance extracted by the construct's measure is $\geq .50$ (Fornell and Larcker 1981).

By using a combination of the criteria above (i.e., item-to-total correlations, examining the inter-item correlation matrix, alpha, composite reliability, and variance extracted estimates), reliable scales can be developed in an efficient manner without sacrificing internal consistency.

Lastly, and as noted recently by Robinson et al. (1991), it is possible to derive a scale with high internal consistency by writing the same items in different ways. Internal consistency of a scale is highly desirable, but must be balanced by sampling of item content, proper item wording, and other validity checks.

Construct Validity

Beyond content validity, dimensionality, and reliability, a number of other validity issues must be considered in scale use and development including convergent, discriminant, nomological, and known group validity. (These types of validity have been collectively referred to as "construct validity.") Again, a number of procedures and rules of thumb exist and should be considered.

Convergent, Discriminant, and Nomological Validity. Convergent validity refers to the degree to which two measures designed to measure the same construct are related. Convergence is found if the two measures are highly correlated. Discriminant validity assesses the degree to which two measures designed to measure similar, but conceptually different, constructs are related. A low to moderate correlation is often considered evidence of discriminant validity. Multi-trait multi-method matrices (MTMM) have traditionally been used to assess convergent and discriminant validity where maximally different measurement methods (i.e., self report vs. observational) are required (Campbell and Fiske 1959; Churchill 1979; Peter 1981). An early advocated rule of thumb for convergent validity is that the correlation between two measures designed to assess the same construct should be statistically significant and "sufficiently large to encourage further examination of validity" (Campbell and Fiske 1959, p. 82). Early advocated criteria for discriminant validity were: 1) entries in the validity diagonal should be higher than the correlations that occupy the same row and column in the heteromethod block; 2) convergent validity coefficients should be higher than the correlations in the heterotrait-monomethod triangles; and 3) the pattern of correlations should be the same in all of the heterotrait triangles (Campbell and Fiske 1959). Though these criteria have been criticized as problematic and vague (Peter 1981), they do offer some guidance as to what constitutes convergent and discriminant validity. Also, our discussion of MTMM here has been extremely brief and over-simplified and the reader is strongly urged to consult the original source (Campbell and Fiske 1959) and a number of critical evaluations and updates (e.g., Bagozzi 1980; Kumar and Dillon Kumar 1992; Peter 1981; Schmitt, Coyle, and Saari 1977; Schmitt and Stults 1986; Widaman 1985).

Nomological validity has been defined as the degree to which predictions from a formal theoretical network containing the concept under scrutiny are confirmed (Campbell 1960). It assesses the degree to which constructs that are theoretically related are actually empirically related (i.e., their measures correlate significantly in the predicted direction). Rules of thumb for nomological validity also exist, but have been criticized as well (Peter 1981).

As with internal consistency, structural equation packages (i.e., LISREL and EQS) have been recently used to assess the convergent, discriminant, and nomological validity of scale measures. MTMM procedures via structural equations are tenable where variance in the measures is partitioned as trait, method, and error variance (e.g., Bagozzi 1980, Bollen 1989; Kumar and Dillon 1992; Schmitt and Stults 1986; Werts and Linn 1970; Widaman 1985). Convergent and discriminant validity is assessed via chi-square maximum likelihood tests and related fit statistics. Similarly, the empirical relationships among theoretically related measures (i.e., nomological validity) can also be assessed with structural equation models. Numerous books (e.g., Bagozzi 1980; Bollen 1989; Hayduk 1987; James, Mulaik, and Brett 1982) and countless articles (e.g., Anderson and Gerbing 1988; Bagozzi 1984; Bagozzi and Phillips 1982; Bentler 1980; Bentler and Chou 1987) illustrate modeling techniques, evaluative criteria, and rules of thumb for what constitutes an acceptable level of validity.

Known Group Validity. Known group validity asks the question "can the measure reliably distinguish between groups of people that should score high on the trait and low on the trait?" As examples, a person who is truly conservative should score significantly higher on a conservatism scale than a person who is liberal, and salespeople in the retail car business and the large computer business should differ in their levels of customer orientation (Saxe and Weitz 1982). Thus, mean score differences on a given scale should be conducted and can be used as evidence of known group validity.

Other Issues to Consider

There are other issues that warrant some discussion regarding the development and evaluation of multi-item scales in marketing and consumer research: 1) representative sampling; 2) normative information; and 3) response set bias.

An often neglected issue in scale development, particularly in the marketing and consumer behavior literature, has been representative sampling. Too many scales have been developed using samples of college students only, and in general, results from student samples are difficult to generalize to other populations. (For an excellent review, see Sears [1986]). We are not advocating the discontinuation of using college student samples. However, we are recommending that scale developers go beyond student samples to those samples more representative of the population as a whole, or a given population of interest. In essence, the prime consideration in scale evaluation, use, and development is the applicability of the scale and scale norms to respondents who are likely to use them in the future (Robinson et al. 1991).

Another area often overlooked by those who develop scales is the reporting of mean and/or percentage scores and variances (i.e., normative information). A raw score on a measurement instrument is not particularly informative about the position of a person on the characteristic being measured because the units in which the scale is expressed are often interval and unfamiliar (Churchill 1979, p. 72). Scale means, individual item means, and standard deviations across different sample groups represent useful information as they offer a frame of reference and comparison points for the potential scale user.

Lastly, increased testing for response set bias is needed in scale development and use in consumer and marketing research. Response set bias refers to a tendency on the part of individuals to respond to attitude statements for reasons other than the content of the statements (Robinson et al. 1991; Paulhus 1991). What can result is a scale score not truly reflective of how the respondent actually stands on the construct. Two sources of response set bias are commonly cited, acquiescence bias and social desirability bias. Acquiescence bias can take the form of responses that reflect an attitude change in accordance with a given situation, or "yeasaying and naysaying" - where respondents are willing to go along with anything that sounds good or are unwilling to look at the negative side of an issue (Robinson et al. 1991). Though there are no easy answers regarding the elimination of acquiescence bias, there are scales and procedures that have been recommended (Paulhus 1991; Robinson et al. 1991).

Trying to make a good impression is the most common form of social desirability bias. That is, respondents may purposefully score low on measures assessing undesirable social characteristics (i.e., selfishness), or purposefully score high on measures assessing desirable social characteristics (i.e., altruism). Again, though truly difficult to detect and control, Robinson et al. (1991) and Paulhus (1991) offer procedures and scales for examining social desirability bias.

Summary

In the preceding few pages, we have tried to delineate those most frequently acknowledged concepts and procedures useful for developing, evaluating, and using self-report scale measures. These procedures include examining the theoretical base of the measure, content validity, dimensionality, reliability, construct validity, and issues relating to sample representativeness, scale norms, and response set bias. We have offered only a brief discussion of each of these procedures, and as we have stated throughout, the reader is strongly urged to consult the more thorough

sources that we have cited. None-the-less, Table 1 offers a useful "snapshot" of what to look for in scale development, evaluation, and use.

CHAPTER OVERVIEWS

As previously stated, this volume is organized by topical area. We have divided the topics into the six general areas, with sub-topics, and have devoted a chapter to each area. The six areas are:

1) *Individual Traits*, covered in Chapter Two;

2) *Values*, covered in Chapter Three;

3) *Involvement and Information Processing*, covered in Chapter Four;

4) *Reactions to Advertising Stimuli*, covered in Chapter Five;

5) *Attitudes About the Performance of Business Firms, Social Agencies, and the Marketplace*, covered in Chapter Six; and

6) *Sales, Sales Management and Inter-Intrafirm Channel Issues*, covered in Chapter Seven.

At the suggestion of colleagues, topic areas were chosen in terms of marketing mix and consumer behavior variables. Still, the placement of certain scales into topic areas involved some subjectivity. For example, many *values* can be considered *individual traits* and vice versa, and several *attitudes about the performance of business* could be viewed as *sales and sales management issues*. Thus, "judgment calls" were made on our part regarding the topical categorization of some of the measures.

For each topic and sub-topic area, scales are presented in chronological order. However, for some constructs, several measures existed. In these cases, all scales relevant to a given construct were presented in chronological order, and then, the chronology of the remaining scales in the chapter was preserved. The following is a brief overview of what is contained in each chapter.

Chapter Two

Chapter Two contains measures of individual traits. In a sense, many of the measures in this text could be labeled as individual traits, but as stated above, judgment calls were made as to categorization. Several of the measures in this chapter were developed outside of the marketing literature [e.g., the I-O Social Preference Scale (Kassarjian 1962), the Self-Monitoring Scale (Snyder 1974), and Cacioppo and Petty's (1982)

TABLE 1
Some General Rating Criteria for Evaluating Attitude Measures

Criterion rating	4. Exemplary	3. Extensive	2. Moderate	1. Minimal	0. None
Theoretical development/ structure	Reflects several important works in the field plus extensive face validity checks	Either reviews several works or has extensive face validity	Reviews more than one source	Reviews one (no sources)	Ad hoc
Pilot testing/ item development	More than 250 items in the initial pool; several pilot studies	100-250 items in initial pool; more than two pilot studies	50-100 items in initial pool; two pilot studies	Some items eliminated; one small pilot study	All initial items included; no pilot study
Means for some available norms	Means and SDs for several subsamples and total sample; extensive information for each item	Means and SDs for total and some groups; some item information	Means for some subgroups; information for some items	Means for total group only; information for 1-2 items	None; no item information
Samples of respondents	Random sample of nation/ community with response rate over 60%	Cross-sectional sample of nation/ community; random national sample of college students	Some representation of noncollege groups; random sample of college students in same departments or colleges	Two or more college classes (some heterogeneity)	One classroom group only (no heterogeneity)
Inter-item correlations	Inter-item correlation average of .30 or better	Inter-item correlation average of .20-.29	Inter-item correlation average of .10-.19	Inter-item correlations below .10	No inter-item analysis reported
Coefficient alpha	.80 or better	.70-.79	.60-.69	< .60	Not reported
Factor analysis	Single factor from factor analysis	Single factor from factor analysis	Single factor from factor analysis	Some items on same factors	No factor structure
Test-retest	Scale scores correlate more than .50 across at least a 1-year period	Scale scores correlate more than .40 across a 3 - 12-month period	Scale scores correlate more than .30 across a 1 - 3-month period	Scale scores correlate more than .20 across less than a 1-month period	No data reported

TABLE 1 (CONTINUED)
Some General Rating Criteria for Evaluating Attitude Measures

Criterion rating	4. Exemplary	3. Extensive	2. Moderate	1. Minimal	0. None
Known groups validity	Discriminate between known groups highly significant; groups also diverse	Discriminate between known groups highly significant	Discriminate between known groups significant	Discriminate between known groups	No known groups data
Convergent validity	Highly significant correlations with more than two related	Significant correlations with more than two related measures	Significant correlations with two related measures	Significant correlations with one related measure	No significant correlations reported
Discriminant validity	Significantly different from four or more unrelated measures	Significantly different from two or three unrelated measures	Significantly different from one unrelated measure	Different from one correlated measure	No difference or no data
Freedom from response set	Three or more studies show independence	Two studies show independence	One study shows independence	Some show independence, others do not	No tests of independence

NOTE: This table was reprinted with permission from John P. Robinson, Phillip R. Shaver, and Lawrence S. Wrightsman (1991), *Measures of Personality and Social Psychological Attitudes*, San Diego, CA: Academic Press, 12-13.

Need for Cognition Scale]. Given their relevance and use to consumer research, they were included in this volume. Most of the remaining measures in this chapter come from the marketing and consumer behavior literature and range from areas as heavily studied as innovativeness (e.g., Leavitt and Walton 1975) to emerging fields such as ethnic studies (i.e., Valencia's [1985] Hispanicness scale) and compulsive buying (Faber and O'Guinn 1989).

Chapter Three
Chapter Three offers various measures that we have labeled as "values." A recurring theme throughout this chapter is "what are the important and satisfying things in one's life related to consumer behavior"? Some scales deal with "general" consumer values [i.e., VALS (Mitchell 1983) and Kahle's (1983) LOV scale], but the majority of the scales pertain to specific value areas. For example, several measures pertaining to materialism (e.g., Belk 1984, 1985; Richins and Dawson 1993; Scott and Lundstrom 1989) are summarized in this chapter, as well as scales related to societal and environmental concerns [i.e.,

socially responsible consumption behavior (Antil 1979), Leonard-Barton's (1981) voluntary simplicity lifestyle scale]. Lastly, most of the scales in this chapter have some theoretical roots in the Rokeach Value Survey (1968), and numerous studies have found relationships between the Rokeach values and consumer behavior. Thus, though developed outside of the marketing and consumer behavior literature, the Rokeach Value Survey was included in Chapter Three under the heading of "general values."

Chapter Four
In the past decade or so, perhaps no other construct has received more attention in terms of measurement than involvement. Chapter Four offers numerous measures of involvement ranging from scales that assess product specific involvement (e.g., fashion involvement [Tigert, Ring, and King 1976], and Bloch's [1981] involvement with automobiles), to measures general to any product category (e.g., a general scale to measure product class involvement [Traylor and Joseph 1984], various versions of

Zaichkowsky's [1985] PII, and Laurent and Kapferer's [1985] involvement profiles), to purchasing involvement [Mittal 1990]).

Chapter Four also offers a number of measures related to information processing. Two of these measures, Zuckerman's (1974) Sensation Seeking Tendency Scale and Mehrabian and Russell's (1978) Arousal Seeking Tendency Scale, are sub-categorized as measures of Optimal Stimulation in consumer behavior. Again, though developed outside the marketing and consumer behavior literature, these two measures have been shown to be related to a number of consumer behaviors. Other measures classified as information processing include a mood scale (Peterson and Sauber 1983), a spousal conflict arousal scale (Seymour and Lessne 1984), visual versus verbal style of processing measure (Childers, Houston, and Heckler 1985), and the attention to social comparison information factor (ATSCI) derived by Lennox and Wolfe (1984). The ATSCI measure is from the social psychology literature, but has been shown to be relevant to consumer behavior (Bearden and Rose 1990).

Chapter Five

The measures in Chapter Five assess consumer views toward some aspect of advertising, hence the *Reactions to Advertising Stimuli* label. Several of these measures assess emotional/ affective reactions to ads or ad content and have been subcategorized as such. Most of the scales in this subcategory owe a great debt to Well's Reaction Profile (1964) and Leavitt's Commercial Profile (1970), as many of the items in the scales were borrowed from these two sources. As such, we have included the original Wells and Leavitt scales and several measures related to them (e.g., relevance, confusion and entertainment scales [Lastovicka 1983], the standardized emotional profile [Holbrook and Batra 1987], and Burke and Edell's [1986] feelings toward the ad scale). Children's views toward advertisements are included as a subcategory (Rossiter's 1977; Macklin and Machleit 1988), as well as a subcategory of scales assessing concepts related to ad believability (Beltramini 1982; Roobian 1990).

Chapter Six

Chapter Six is entitled *Attitudes About the Performance of Business Firms, Social Agencies, and the Marketplace*. This chapter reviews scales measuring concepts related to consumer views of the social role of business. Peters (1972) social responsibility for marketing personnel scale, Klein's (1982) attitudes of consumers and business people toward consumerism scale, Williams' (1982) attitudes toward the social role of the corporation scale, the index of consumer sentiment toward marketing (Gaski and Etzel 1986), the SERVQUAL

scale (Parasuraman, Zeithaml and Berry 1986), and Reis and Gundlach's (1989) satisfaction with social services are all included. This chapter also contains scales measuring business ethics (e.g., Hunt, Wood and Chonko 1989; Reidenbach and Robin 1990), measures assessing corporate attitudes toward the marketplace (Narver and Slater 1990; Sharma, Netemeyer, and Mahajan 1990), and a measure of management conservatism (Sturdivant, Ginter, and Sawyer 1986).

Chapter Seven

The measures offered in the *Sales, Sales Management, and Inter-Intrafirm Issues* chapter have been sub-categorized into two broad areas. The first area, sales and sales management issues, includes several measures used in sales research. Though a number of these measures were developed in the organizational behavior literature, they have seen wide application in a variety of sales-related settings. Furthermore, the measures in the sales and sales management category have been broken down into sub-categories of job satisfaction, role perceptions and job tension, performance and leadership, commitment, and sales approaches.

Several job satisfaction scales are reviewed, including the Job Characteristics Inventory, i.e., the JCI (Sims, Szilagyi, and Keller 1976), INDSALES of Churchill, Ford, and Walker (1974), and a measure developed by Wood, Chonko, and Hunt (1986). The role perception scales measure the level of conflict and ambiguity related to one's job and include the Rizzo, House, and Lirtzman (1970) scales, the Ford, Walker, and Churchill (1975) scales, and the MULTIRAM scale (Singh and Rhoads 1991). Behrman and Perreault's (1982) performance scale and the retail salesperson performance scale (Bush, Bush, Ortineau, and Hair 1990) represent the performance measures reviewed. Two measures of leadership are also included. Two organizational commitment scales are included, Mowday, Steers, and Porter's (1979) measure and Hunt, Chonko, and Wood's (1986) scale. Lastly, the SOCO scale (Saxe and Weitz 1982) and the ADAPTS scale (Spiro and Weitz 1990) are classified as "sales approaches."

The second area in Chapter Seven is labeled "Inter-Intrafirm Issues". Here, several measures of dependence based power and influence within and among organizations are summarized (e.g., Frazier 1983; Swasy 1979; Comer 1984; Kohli and Zaltman 1988). Also included are measures of channel member satisfaction (Ruekert and Churchill 1984) and channel leadership behavior (Schul, Pride, and Little 1983).

REFERENCES

Anderson, James C. and David W. Gerbing (1988), "Structural Equation Modeling in Practice: A Review and Recommended Two-Step Approach," *Psychological Bulletin*, 103, 411-423.

Anderson, James C., David W. Gerbing and John E. Hunter (1987), "On the Assessment of Unidimensional Measurement: Internal and External Consistency, and Overall Consistency Criteria," *Journal of Marketing Research*, 24 (November) 432-437.

American Psychological Association (1985), *Standards for Educational and Psychological Tests*, Washington DC: APA.

Bagozzi, Richard P. (1980), *Causal Models in Marketing*, New York: Wiley.

Bagozzi, Richard P. (1984), "A Prospectus for Theory Construction in Marketing," *Journal of Marketing*, 48 (Winter), 11-29.

Bagozzi, Richard P. and Lynn W. Phillips (1982), "Representing and Testing Organizational Theories: A Holistic Construal," *Administrative Science Quarterly*, 27, 459-489.

Bearden, William O., Richard G. Netemeyer, and Jesse E. Teel (1989), "Measurement of Consumer Susceptibility to Interpersonal Influence," *Journal of Consumer Research*, 15 (March), 473-481.

Bentler, Peter M. (1980), "Multivariate Analysis With Latent Variables: Causal Modeling," *Annual Review of Psychology*, 32, 419-456.

Bentler, Peter M. (1985), *Theory and Implementation of EQS: A Structural Equations Program*, Los Angeles: BMDP Statistical Software.

Bentler, Peter M. and Chih-Ping Chou (1987), "Practical Issues in Structural Modeling," *Sociological Methods & Research*, 16 (August), 78-117.

Bohrnstedt, George and Edgar F. Borgatta (1981), *Social Measurement: Issues*, Newbury Park, CA: Sage.

Bohrnstedt, George, Peter P. Mohler, and W. Muller (1987), *Empirical Study of the Reliability and Stability of Survey Research Items*, Newbury Park, CA: Sage.

Bollen, Kenneth A. (1989), *Structural Equations With Latent Variables*, New York: Wiley.

Campbell, Donald T. (1960), "Recommendations for APA Test Standards Regarding Construct, Trait, or Discriminant Validity," *American Psychologist*, 15, 546-553.

Campbell, Donald T. and Donald W. Fiske (1959), "Convergent and Discriminant Validity by the Multitrait-Multimethod Matrix," *Psychological Bulletin*, 56 (March), 81-105.

Carmines, Edward G. and Richard G. Zeller (1979), *Reliability and Validity Assessment*, Beverly Hills, CA: Sage Publications.

Churchill, Gilbert A. (1979), "A Paradigm for Developing Better Measures of Marketing Constructs," *Journal of Marketing Research*, 16 (February), 64-73.

Churchill, Gilbert A. and J. Paul Peter (1984), "Research Design Effects on the Reliability of Rating Scales: A Meta-Analysis," *Journal of Marketing Research*, 21 (November), 360-375.

Converse, Jean M. and Stanley S. Presser (1986), *Survey Questions: Handcrafting the Standardized Questionnaire*, Newbury Park CA: Sage Publications Inc.

Cronbach, Lee J. (1951), "Coefficient Alpha and the Internal Structure of Tests," *Psychometrika*, 31, 93-96.

DeVellis, Robert F. (1991), *Scale Development: Theory and Applications*, Newbury Park, CA: Sage Publications Inc.

Fornell, Claes and David F. Larcker (1981), "Evaluating Structural Equation Models With Unobservable Variables and Measurement Error," *Journal of Marketing Research*, 18 (February), 39-50.

Gerbing, David W. and James C. Anderson (1988), "An Updated Paradigm for Scale Development Incorporating Unidimensionality and Its Assessment," *Journal of Marketing Research*, 25 (May), 186-192.

Hattie, John (1985), "Methodology Review: Assessing Unidimensionality of Tests and Items," *Applied Psychological Measurement*, 9 (June), 139-164.

Hayduk, Leslie A. (1987), *Structural Equations Modeling With LISREL: Essentials and Advances*, Baltimore: The John Hopkins University Press.

James, Lawrence R., Stanley A. Mulaik, and Jeanne M. Brett (1982), *Causal Analysis: Assumptions, Models, and Data*, Beverly Hills, CA: Sage Publications Inc.

Joreskog, Karl G. and Dag Sorbom (1987), *LISREL 7: A Guide to the Program and Applications*, Chicago: SPSS Inc.

Kumar, Ajith and William R. Dillon (1987a), "The Interaction of Measurement and Structure in Simultaneous Equation Models with Unobservable Variables," *Journal of Marketing Research*, 24 (February), 98-105.

Kumar, Ajith and William R. Dillon (1987b), "Some Further Remarks on Measurement-Structure Interaction and the Unidimensionality of Constructs," *Journal of Marketing Research*, 24 (November), 438-444.

Kumar, Ajith and William R. Dillon (1992), "An Integrative Look at the Use of Additive and Multiplicative Covariance Structure Models in the Analysis of MTMM Data," *Journal of Marketing Research*, 29 (February), 51-64.

Lord, Frederick M. and Melvin R. Novick (1968), *Statistical Theories of Mental Tests Scores*, Reading, MA: Addison-Wesley.

McDonald, Roderick P. (1981), "The Dimensionality of Tests and Items," *British Journal of Mathematical and Statistical Psychology*, 34, 100-117.

McDonald, Roderick P. (1985), *Factor Analysis and Related Methods*, Hillsdale, NJ: Lawrence Earlbaum Associates.

Nunnally, Jum (1979), *Psychometric Theory*, New York: McGraw-Hill.

Paulhus, Delroy L. (1991), "Measurement and Control of Response Bias," in *Measures of Personality and Social Psychological Attitudes*, J. P. Robinson, P. R. Shaver, and L. S. Wrightsman (eds.), San Diego, CA: The Academic Press, 17-59.

Peter, J. Paul (1979), "Reliability: A Review of Psychometric Basics and Recent Marketing Practices," *Journal of Marketing Research*, 16 (February), 6-17.

Peter, J. Paul (1981), "Construct Validity: A Review of Basic Issues and Marketing Practices," *Journal of Marketing Research*, 18 (May), 133-145.

Robinson, John P. and Phillip R. Shaver (1973), *Measures of Social Psychological Attitudes*, University of Michigan, Ann Arbor, MI: Survey Research Center Institute for Social Research.

Robinson, John P., Phillip R. Shaver, Lawrence S. Wrightsman (1991), "Criteria for Scale Selection and Evaluation" in *Measures of Personality and Social Psychological Attitudes*, J. P. Robinson, P. R. Shaver, and L. S. Wrightsman (eds.), San Diego, CA: The Academic Press, 1-15.

Saxe, Robert and Barton A. Weitz (1982), "The SOCO Scale: A Measure of the Customer Orientation of Salespeople," *Journal of Marketing Research*, 19 (August), 343-351.

Schmitt, Neal, Brian W. Coyle, and Bryce B. Saari (1977), "A Review and Critique of Multitrait-Multimethod Matrices," *Multivariate Behavioral Research*, 12, 447-478.

Schmitt, Neal and Daniel M. Stults (1986), "Methodology Review: Analysis of Multitrait-Multimethod Matrices," *Applied Psychological Measurement*, 10, 1-22.

Sears, David O. (1986), "College Sophomores in the Laboratory: Influences of a Narrow Data Base on Social Psychology's View of Human Nature," *Journal of Personality and Social Psychology*, 51, 515-530.

Shimp, Terence A. and Subhash Sharma (1987), "Consumer Ethnocentrism: Construction and Validation of the CETSCALE," *Journal of Marketing Research*, 24 (August), 280-289.

Sudman, Seymour, and Norman M. Bradburn (1982), *Asking Questions*, San Francisco: Jossey-Bass.

Werts, Charles E. and Robert L. Linn (1970), "Cautions in Applying Various Procedures for Determining the Reliability and Validity of Multiple-Item Scales," *American Sociological Review*, 34, 757-759.

Werts, Charles E., Robert L. Linn, and Karl G. Joreskog (1974), "Interclass Reliability Estimates: Testing Structural Assumptions," *Educational and Psychological Measurement*, 34, 25-33.

Widaman, Keith F., (1985), "Hierarchically Nested Covariance Structure Models for Multitrait-Multimethod Data," *Applied Psychological Measurement*, 9, 1-26.

Zaichkowsky, Judith Lynne (1985), "Measuring the Involvement Construct," *Journal of Consumer Research*, 12 (December), 341-352.

2
Individual Traits

GENERAL TRAITS

SOCIAL CHARACTER: I-O SOCIAL PREFERENCE SCALE
(Kassarjian 1962)

Construct: The I-O scale is designed to assess two of the social character types proposed by Riesman (1950) in his book *The Lonely Crowd.* These two types are inner-directed and other-directed people. Inner-directed persons turn to their own inner values and standards for guidance in their behavior while other-directed persons depend upon the people around them to give direction to their actions (Kassarjian 1962, p. 213). Inner-directed persons are thought to be driven by their need for accomplishment while other-directed persons are motivated by the need for approval from others. The I-O Preference Scale (i.e., the preference for inner-versus other-directedness) is designed to place people along a continuum from other- to inner-directedness.

Description: The scale consists of 36 forced-choice items. Each item consists of an incomplete statement and two responses, one inner-directed and one other-directed. Respondents select the response that they agree with most and provide their degree of agreement with each item. (See instructions in Kassarjian [1962, p. 226].) The other-directed answer is assigned a value of -2; the inner- directed answer is assigned a value of +2. A constant of 72 is added to the total score to avoid negative values. Consequently, the scale can range from 0 (complete other-direction) to 144 (complete inner-direction).

Development: Little detail was provided by Kassarjian (1962, pp. 217-217) regarding the development of the 36-item scale. In a preliminary study, first person-worded statements with forced choice response formats were found superior to other procedures. Only those items which consistently elicited varied responses and which contributed to scale internal consistency were retained for the final scale. Item reliability was verified using test-retest procedures. A number of validation procedures was also performed.

Sample(s): UCLA undergraduates served as subjects in all preliminary studies. The validation studies were carried out with both graduate and undergraduate students while the general distribution of scores was examined on a stratified sample of Los Angeles residents. The final test reported by Kassarjian (1962, p. 217) involved 150 undergraduate students.

Validity: Item-to-total correlations ranged from 0.32 to 0.94. A four week test-retest administration on a sample of 52 undergraduates yielded a reliability coefficient of 0.85. Correlations between the I-O scale and an index of behaviors (e.g., hobbies, sports, social activity) ranged from 0.55 to 0.69 across various combinations of the student samples. These behaviors were expected to vary between other- and inner-directed individuals. Evidence of discriminant validity was provided by low correlations with two personality characteristic measures (e.g., the SI-scale of the MMPI) thought similar but different from social character and low correlations with an Asch-type measure of social conformity. A significant difference in means (t=4.98, p<0.05) between two samples of undergraduate students selected from varying majors to represent predictable differences in other-directed individuals (e.g., education, social welfare majors) and inner-directed individuals (e.g., natural sciences, philosophy majors) was also obtained.

While city dwellers were found more other-directed than rural residents, other demographic comparisons were largely nonsignificant. However, additional evidence of validity was provided by lower scores on a 25-item version of the I-O scale for a general population sample (i.e., older and, hence, more inner-directed) as compared to student respondents.

Scores: The average score for the undergraduate sample of 150 was 72.2 (SD = 16.93) (with a range of 22 to 109). A sample of 96 graduate students resulted in a significantly higher mean of 86.97 (SD = 17.85) (i.e., significantly more inner-directed). The undergraduate mean scores for the varying academic majors were 79.4 and 93.9 for the other- and inner-directed groups, respectively.

Source: Kassarjian, Waltraud M. (1962), "A Study of Riesman's Theory of Social Character," *Sociometry*, 25 (September), 213-230.

Other evidence: Additional evidence of the validity of I-O scale as a measure of social character has been provided by its successful application in a number of marketing and consumer contexts by other researchers. (Three of these are cited below; a larger number of successful applications outside of consumer contexts have been reported as well.) This consumer research-related evidence includes the research by Kassarjian (1965) which found that inner- and other-directed individuals show differential preference for advertisements created to appeal to varying character types.

Relationships among social character, innovation proneness, adoption leadership among farmers were studied by Barban, Sandage, Kassarjian, and Kassarjian (1970). Their results (based upon use of a 30-item version of the scale) revealed that social character was normally distributed across the sample of 828 male heads of farm households. In addition, inner-directed subjects were found to be more prone to adopt to innovations. Only weak relationships were found between inner-other directedness and adoption leadership and key demographic variables. Support for these findings was provided by Donnelly (1970) in his research involving a survey of 140 housewives. Specifically, it was concluded that the I-O Social Preference Scale was related to the acceptance of five innovative grocery products. The mean score for the 140 housewives in Donnelly's research was 72.2.

Other sources: Kassarjian, Harold H. (1965), "Social Character and Differential Preference for Mass Communication," *Journal of Marketing Research*, 2 (May), 146-153.

Donnelly, James H., Jr. (1970), "Social Character and Acceptance of New Products," *Journal of Marketing Research*, 7 (February), 111-113.

Barban, Arnold M., C. H. Sandage, Waltraud M. Kassarjian, and Harold H. Kassarjian (1970), "A Study of Riesman's Inner-Other Directedness Among Farmers," *Rural Sociology*, 35 (June), 232-243.

References: Riesman, David (1950), *The Lonely Crowd*, New Haven: Yale University Press.

SOCIAL CHARACTER: I-O SOCIAL PREFERENCE SCALE
(Kassarjian 1962)

1. With regard to partying, I feel
   a. the more the merrier (25 or more people present);
   b. it is nicest to be in a small group of intimate friends (6 or 8 people at most).

2. If I had more time,
   a. I would spend more evenings at home doing the things I'd like to do;
   b. I would more often go out with my friends.

3. If I were trained as an electrical engineer and liked my work very much and would be offered a promotion into an administrative position, I would
   a. accept it because it means an advancement in pay which I need quite badly;
   b. turn it down because it would no longer give me an opportunity to do the work I like and am trained for even though I desperately need more money.

4. I believe that
   a. it is difficult to draw the line between work and play and therefore one should not even try it;
   b. one is better off keeping work and social activities separated.

5. I would rather join
   a. a political or social club or organization;
   b. an organization dedicated to literary, scientific, or other academic subject matter.

6. I would be more eager to accept a person as a group leader who
   a. is outstanding in those activities which are important to the group;
   b. is about average in the performance of the group activities but has an especially pleasing personality.

7. I like to read books about
   a. people like you and me;
   b. great people or adventurers.

8. For physical exercise or as a sport, I would prefer
   a. softball, basketball, volleyball, or similar team sport;
   b. skiing, hiking, horsebackriding, bicycling, or similar individual sport.

9. With regard to a job, I would enjoy more
   a. one in which one can show his skill or knowledge;
   b. one in which one gets contact with many different people.

10. I believe
    a. being able to make friends is a great accomplishment in and of itself;
    b. one should be concerned more about one's achievements rather than making friends.

11. It is more desirable
    a. to be popular and well liked by everybody;
    b. to become famous in the field of one's choice or for a particular deed.

12. With regard to clothing,
    a. I would feel conspicuous if I were not dressed the way most of my friends are dressed;
    b. I like to wear clothes which stress my individuality and which not everybody else is wearing.

13. On the subject of social living,
    a. a person should set up his own standards and then live up to them;
    b. one should be careful to live up to the prevailing standards of the culture.

14. I would consider it more embarrassing
    a. to be caught loafing on a job for which I get paid;
    b. losing my temper when a number of people are around of whom I think a lot.

15. I respect the person most who
    a. is considerate of others and concerned that they think well of him;
    b. lives up to his ideals and principles.

16. A child who has intellectual difficulties in some grade in school
    a. should repeat the grade to be able to get more out of the next higher grade;
    b. should be kept with his age group though he has some intellectual difficulties.

17. In my free time
    a. I'd like to read an interesting book at home;
    b. I'd rather be with a group of my friends.

18. I have
    a. a great many friends who are, however, not very intimate friends;
    b. few but rather intimate friends.

19. When doing something, I am most concerned with
    a. "what's in it for me" and how long will it last;
    b. what impression others will get of me for doing it.

20. As leisure-time activity, I would rather choose
    a. woodcarving, painting, stamp collecting, photography, or a similar activity;
    b. bridge or other card game, or discussion groups.

21. I consider a person most successful, when
    a. he can live up to his own standards and ideals;
    b. be can get along with even the most difficult people.

22. One of the main things a child should be taught is
    a. cooperation;
    b. self-discipline.

23. As far as I am concerned,
    a. I am only happy when I have people around me;
    b. I am perfectly happy when I am left alone.

24. On a free evening,
    a. I like to go and see a nice movie;
    b. I would try to have a television party at my (or a friend's) house.

25. The persons whom I admire most are those who
    a. are very outstanding in their achievements;
    b. have a very pleasant personality.

26. I consider myself to be
    a. quite idealistic and to some extent a "dreamer";
    b. quite realistic and living for the present only.

27. In bringing up children, parents should
    a. look more at what is done by other families with children;
    b. stick to their own ideas on how they want their children brought up regardless of what others do.

28. To me, it is very important
    a. what one is and does regardless of what others think;
    b. what my friends think of me.

29. I prefer listening to a person who
    a. knows his subject matter real well but is not skilled in presenting interestingly;
    b. knows his subject matter not as well but has an interesting way of discussing it.

30. As far as I am concerned
    a. I see real advantages to keeping a diary and would like to keep one myself;
    b. I'd rather discuss my experiences with friends than keep a diary.

31. Schools should
    a. teach children to take their place in society;
    b. be concerned more with teaching subject matter.

32. It is desirable
    a. that one shares the opinions others hold on a particular matter;
    b. that one strongly holds onto his opinions even though they may be radically different from those of others.

33. For me it is more important to
    a. keep my dignity (not make a fool of myself) even though I may not always be considered a good sport;
    b. be a good sport even though I would lose my dignity (and make a fool of myself) by doing it.

34. When in a strange city or foreign country, I should have no great difficulty because
    a. I am interested in new things and can live under almost any new conditions;
    b. people are the same everywhere and I can get along with them.

35. I believe in coffee breaks and social activities for employees because
    a. it gives people a chance to get to know each other and enjoy work more;
    b. people work more efficiently when they do not work for too long a stretch at a time and can look forward to a special event.

36. The greatest influence upon children should be
    a. from outside their own age group and from educational sources outside the family since they can be more objective in evaluating the child's needs;
    b. from the immediate family who should know the child best.

NOTES: As stated above in the *Description* section, scoring procedures for the scale are provided in Kassarjian (1962, p. 226). We have not provided these procedures here because of the complexity of them. Though all statements are dichotomous, they are scored on a four choice basis using columns, where the respondent is asked to choose one column over the others. Thus, the potential user of the scale is referred to Kassarjian (1962) for explicit instructions on scale administration.

INTERPERSONAL ORIENTATION: THE CAD SCALE
(Cohen 1967)

Construct: The CAD scale is designed to measure a person's interpersonal orientation. The instrument was derived from Horney's (1945) tripartite model. Specifically, the scale is designed to assess compliant, aggressive, and detached interpersonal orientations. Compliant oriented persons are those who desire to be a part of the activities of others (i.e., who move toward others). Aggressive persons are those who want to excel, to achieve success, prestige, and admiration. Detached individuals desire to put emotional distance between themselves and others (i.e., those who move away from others) (Cohen 1967, pp. 270-271). The impetus for the scale is based upon the expected effects of varying interpersonal orientations on consumer decision-making.

Description: The scale consists of thirty-five items each operationalized using six-point scales labeled "extremely undesirable" to "extremely desirable." Ten items each are used to represent the compliant and detached factors. The remaining 15 items reflect the aggressive dimension. Total scores for each subscale are formed by summing item scores within each dimension.

Development: The exact procedures used to develop the initial set of items were not described in Cohen (1967). However, a number of separate analyses were conducted in evaluation of the thirty-five item, three-factor scale. In support of the measures, seven expert judges agreed that the items demonstrated face validity and reflected their respective dimensions. Several tests for evidence of convergent and predictive validity were performed.

Sample(s): A series of different undergraduate and graduate student samples was used in the initial development and validation of the CAD scales. For example, the final validation efforts involving the study of a wide range of consumer decisions were based upon the responses of 157 undergraduate business students.

Validity: Evidence of convergent validity was provided by correlations between the CAD scale and an occupational interpersonal relations scale. For example, the correlation between the compliant CAD factor and the occupational compliant factor was 0.48 (p<.05) (Cohen 1967). Differences between groups were also observed between student groups of varying majors (i.e., social welfare, business administration, and geology). For example, the highest factor mean scores for the compliant, aggressive, and detached factors were for the social welfare, business, and geology students, respectively. And, as predicted, less aggressive and more compliant subjects exhibited greater "change" in a study of susceptibility to interpersonal influence (Cohen 1967, p. 273).

In addition to the validity evidence cited above, the CAD scale factors were further examined for differences across a number of product and brand purchase decisions. The results indicate that "some products and brands appear to express either compliant, aggressive, or detached responses to life" (Cohen 1967, p. 277). Some of the specific findings include the following. High aggressive students exhibited differential brand preferences for deodorant, beer, and dress shirts. Both high and low aggressive and high and low detached students differed in their television viewing preferences.

Scores: Cohen (1967) reports a series of mean scores for each factor. However, in his Appendix, it is noted that "Studies reported in this article have used an earlier four-point response format" (Cohen 1967, p. 277). Hence, mean scores from the original article are not reproduced here since the final version reported by Cohen (1967) recommends a wider six-point response format.

Source: Cohen, Joel B. (1967), "An Interpersonal Orientation to the Study of Consumer Behavior," *Journal of Marketing Research*, 4 (August), 270-278.

Other evidence: A number of studies have either employed or reevaluated the CAD scale(s). Three of these are cited below.

Ryan and Becherer (1976) reported internal consistency reliability estimates for the three factors as follows: compliant, 0.72; aggressive, 0.68; and detached, 0.51. Though the results of a factor analysis with varimax rotation produced a four-factor solution, most of the items did load on three factors that appeared to represent aggressive, compliant, and detached orientations. In addition, these were the first three factors of the four-factor solution.

Tyagi (1983) reported coefficient alpha estimates of internal consistency of 0.72, 0.62 and 0.63 for the compliant, aggressive, and detached factors. Intercorrelations among the three factors ranged from -0.31 to 0.25. The results of an MTMM analysis using measures of nurturance, aggression, and autonomy provided mixed but generally positive support for the convergent and discriminant validity of the measures.

Noerager (1979) provided less supportive results. Specifically, the coefficient alpha estimates of internal consistency reliability for the compliant, aggressive, and detached factors were 0.60, 0.36, and 0.43, respectively. And, the results of a factor analysis of the 35 items did not reveal a pattern of simple structure along the lines predicted by the theoretical justification for the measures (i.e., a three-factor model).

Other sources: Noerager, Jon P. (1979), "An Assessment of CAD: A Personality Instrument Developed Specifically for Marketing Research," *Journal of Marketing Research*, 16 (February), 53-59.

Ryan, Michael J. and Richard C. Becherer (1976), "A Multivariate Test of CAD Instrument Construct Validity," in *Advances in Consumer Research*, Vol. 3, Beverly B. Anderson, (ed.), Cincinnati, OH: Association for Consumer Research, 149-154.

Tyagi, Pradeep K. (1983), "Validation of the CAD Instrument: A Replication," in *Advances Consumer Research*, Vol. 10, Richard P. Bagozzi and Alice M. Tybout, (eds.), Ann Arbor, MI: Association for Consumer Research, 112-114.

References: Horney, Karen (1945), *Our Inner Conflicts*, New York: W. W. Norton & Company, Inc.

INTERPERSONAL ORIENTATION: THE CAD SCALE
(Cohen 1967)

1. Being free of emotional ties with others is:
2. Giving comfort to those in need of friends is:
3. The knowledge that most people would be fond of me at all times would be:
4. To refuse to give in to others in an argument seems:
5. Enjoying a good movie by myself is:
6. For me to pay little attention to what others think of me seems:
7. For me to be able to own an item before most of my friends are able to buy it would be:
8. Knowing that others are somewhat envious of me is:
9. To feel that I like everyone I know would be:
10. To be able to work hard while others elsewhere are having fun is:
11. Using pull to get ahead would be:
12. For me to have enough money or power to impress self-styled "big-shots" would be:
13. Basing my life on duty to others is:
14. To be able to work under tension would be:
15. If I could live all alone in a cabin in the woods or mountains it would be:
16. Pushing those who insult my honor is:
17. To give aid to the poor and underprivileged is:
18. Standing in the way of people who are too sure of themselves is:
19. Being free of social obligations is:
20. To have something good to say about everybody seems:
21. Telling a waiter when you have received inferior food is:
22. Planning to get along without others is:
23. To be able to spot and exploit weaknesses in others is:

24. A strong desire to surpass others' achievements seems:
25. Sharing my personal feelings with others would be:
26. To have the ability to blame others for their mistakes is:
27. For me to avoid situations where others can influence me would be:
28. Wanting to repay others' thoughtless actions with friendship is:
29. Having to compete with others for various rewards is:
30. If I knew that others paid very little attention to my affairs it would be:
31. To defend my rights by force would be:
32. Putting myself out to be considerate to others' feelings is:
33. Correcting people who express an ignorant belief is:
34. For me to work alone would be:
35. To be fair to people who do things which I consider wrong seems:

NOTES: The items belonging to the factors are arranged as follows:
           Compliant: 2, 3, 9, 13, 17, 20, 25, 28, 32, 35;
           Aggressive: 4, 7, 8, 11, 12, 14, 16, 18, 21, 23, 24, 26, 29, 31, 33;
           Detached: 1, 5, 6, 10, 15, 19, 22, 27, 30, 34.

CONSUMER SELF-ACTUALIZATION TEST: CSAT
(Brooker 1975)

Construct: Based upon Maslow's (1970) description of the self-actualizing person, this measure attempts to assess consumer self-actualization. The self-actualizing person may be described as one who achieves the full use and exploitation of talents, capacities, and potential. Specifically, the following 16 characteristics were assumed to underlie the construct and were used as the basis for developing the consumer-related item pairs: comfortable perceptions with reality; acceptance of self and others; spontaneity, simplicity, and naturalness; problem-centering; detached; autonomy; freshness of appreciation; feeling for mankind; interpersonal relations; democratic; discrimination between means and ends; philosophical sense of humor; creativeness; resistance to enculturation; resolution of dichotomies; and peak experiences.

Description: The test contains 20 items of the A vs. B variety. Each item receiving a self-actualizing response receives a score of one, zero otherwise. Scores are then summed to form an overall index which can range from 0 to 20 (Brooker 1975, p. 567).

Development: An initial set of over 150 pairs of actualizing and nonactualizing items were developed. Items were written for all traits except "peak experience." A panel of four faculty judges evaluated the items for self-actualizing content. Three hundred and nineteen subjects responded to the items, varied in order to address respondent fatigue. Items were selected using a combination of corrected item-to-total correlations balanced with the need to have items reflecting the various dimensions. The final scale contains items representing 14 of the 16 traits identified by Maslow (1970). Test-retest reliability was also assessed.

Sample(s): A convenience sample of 319 subjects (186 females) responded to the initial set. The average of age of respondents was 30.6 years. Thirty-five MBA students participated in the first test-retest administration. Another sample of 24 was also used.

Validity: Item-to-total correlations ranged from 0.12 to 0.40. Based on the responses of 35 MBA students, the Spearman test-retest correlation, as an estimate of reliability, was 0.57. A similar test using a more heterogeneous sample of 24 respondents resulted in an estimate of 0.67.

Evidence of content validity was said to be provided by the representation of the various traits (i.e., 14 of the 16 traits) in the final 20-item set. Evidence of concurrent validity was provided by differences in CSAT scores and those using or not using ecologically beneficial products (i.e., certain types of gasoline and detergents). Higher scores for females and older subjects were also cited as evidence of known group validity. And, differences between those scoring high and low on the CSAT measure in terms of several personal characteristics were also argued to represent support for the measure. For example, those scoring above the median were found to be "more relaxed, more outdoorsy, more secure, happier, more outgoing, more homebodyish, more natural, and non-drinkers" (Brooker 1975, p. 573).

Scores: For the sample used to develop the test (n=319), test scores ranged from 2 to 19 with a mode of ten and a median of 10.4.

Source: Brooker, George (1975), "An Instrument to Measure Consumer Self-Actualization," in *Advances in Consumer Research*, Vol. 2, Mary Jane Schlinger (ed.), Ann Arbor, MI: Association for Consumer Research, 563-575.

Other evidence: N/A.

Other sources: N/A.

References: Maslow, Abraham H. (1970), *Motivation and Personality*, 2nd Edition, New York: Harper and Row.

CONSUMER SELF-ACTUALIZATION TEST: CSAT
(Brooker 1975)

(Detached)
1.   *a. Information from publications such as *Consumer Reports* is quite valuable to me in deciding on costly purchases.
     b. I find publications of little use to me; I prefer personal recommendations for expensive purchases.

(Accepting of Self, Others)
2.   *a. Usually, I am not upset when products fail to meet my expectations.
     b. I am often upset when products fail to meet my expectations.

(Feeling for Mankind)
3.   *a. When one helps a friend make a purchase, it's enough to know the assistance was needed.
     b. When one helps a friend make a purchase, I think it's only proper that one is thanked for the help.

(Democratic Character Structure)
4.   *a. All people are worthy of respect.
     b. Some people are not worthy of respect.

(Resolution of Dichotomies)
5.   a. It is more fun to give a gift than to decide what to give.
     *b. Deciding what to give for a gift is as much fun as giving it.

(Spontaneity, Simplicity)
6.   a. I usually feel more confident when I know I am dressed in the latest fashion.
     *b. I am at ease regardless of how I am dressed.

(Detached)
7.   *a. When I am shopping for myself, I make my decisions without help from others.
     b. I often look to people I know for help when buying something for myself.

(Freshness of Appreciation)
8.   a. I like advertisements I see often more than those I have seen only a few times.
     *b. I find myself trying to avoid advertisements I have seen before.

(Means-End Relationships)
9.   a. Money may not be everything, but it's got a big lead over whatever is second.
     *b. It's true, money can't buy happiness.

(Autonomy; Independence)
10. *a. The things I desire for the good life are often different from those chosen by others in my economic class.
     b. The things I would choose for the good life are similar to the choices of others in my economic class.

(Freshness of Appreciation)
11. a. I am often bored.
     *b. I am seldom bored.

(Sense of Humor)
12. a. I like jokes that are slightly off-color.
     *b. I like jokes that make me think.

(Problem Centered)
13. *a. Activities like charity work and community service attract me.
     b. I am so busy doing day-to-day things I can't be bothered thinking about volunteer work.

(Sense of Humor)
14. a. I prefer comedians who imitate famous people.
     *b. I prefer comedians who comment on the present time.

(Accepting of Self, Others)
15. a. When I go on a buying spree, I often regret it later.
   *b. I seldom regret a buying spree.

(Resistance to Enculturation)
16. *a. Being fashionable or chic holds no interest for me.
   b. It is important to me to be fashionable or chic.

(Perceptions of Reality)
17. *a. When I am nervous or anxious, I usually try to avoid buying things.
   b. When I am nervous or anxious, I often find buying something new helps me feel better.

(Interpersonal Relationships)
18. a. It is usually wise to present yourself to people in such a way that they will like you.
   *b. It is unwise to present anything but your true self to people.

(Perceptions of Reality)
19. a. I am reluctant to try new products until I can find out if they are good.
   *b. I often try new things just because they look interesting or good.

(Resistance to Enculturation)
20. *a. I could probably live under any economic system and be just as happy.
   b. I can imagine myself being happy living only in one kind of economic system.

NOTES: (Parentheses represent Characteristics, Trait)
        * indicates the self-actualizing response.

SELF-CONCEPTS, PERSON CONCEPTS, AND PRODUCT CONCEPTS
(Malhotra 1981)

Construct: Measures are derived for evaluating self-concepts, person concepts, and product concepts. The specific concepts chosen for study were automobiles and actors. [The objective of the research on which the measures are based was to describe the construction of the scales rather than the development of a generalized scale for measuring self-concepts, person concepts, and product concepts (Malhotra 1981, p. 456).] The measure is said to be applicable for coordinating the image of a product with the self-concept(s) of a target market and image of a spokesperson that might be used in testimonial for that product.

Description: The final scale includes fifteen semantic differential items anchoring seven-place response formats. The scale is multi-dimensional and, hence, summed scores are not appropriate. Item scores can be summed within dimensions.

Development: A beginning pool of 70 items was developed from pretest data generated from free associations, repertory grid procedures and the studies of Osgood, Suci, and Tannenbaum (1957). A panel of four judges was used to reduce the item pool to 27. These items included at least two semantic differential scales for eight factors: evaluative, potency, activity, stability, tautness, novelty, receptivity, and aggressiveness. Based on analysis of the two student surveys described below, the 15-item final scale was developed as follows. First, a series of factor analyses (i.e., principal factoring with iterations followed by varimax rotation) was conducted and examined for stability, loading patterns, uniqueness, and explained variance. Second, hierarchical clustering procedures supported the factor analysis results. As summarized by Malhotra (1981, p. 460), the 15 items were selected using the following criteria: high loadings on the factor they represent, high correlations with other items representing the same factor or cluster, low correlations with items representing other factors or clusters, high stability across self-concepts, auto brands, or actors, uniqueness in the cluster solutions, and high coefficients of multiple correlation with multidimensional space coordinates.

Six of the factors are represented by two items each. The tautness and aggressiveness factors are not reflected in the final scale.

Sample(s): Two surveys were used in the development of the measures. The first survey involved 167 student subjects for three self-concepts (i.e., "ideal," "actual," and "social") and nine brands of automobiles. The second survey involved 187 students (of which 135 had participated in the first survey) for the same three self-concepts and nine actors (i.e., "persons").

Validity: Test-retest estimates were obtained from 135 subjects over a four week delay for the ideal, actual and social self ratings. All correlations were significant. Evidence of stability was also provided through individual level correlations. Coefficient alpha estimates for appropriate factor subscales ranged from .50 to .70 (with a single exception).

Evidence provided by the expert panel judgments was cited as support for face validity. Evidence of convergent and discriminant validity was provided from a multitrait-multimethod analysis in which the actors and brands served as traits and the semantic differentials and similarity ratings served as methods. For example, validity coefficients for the autos and actors were .38 and .49, respectively (Malhotra 1981, p. 463).

Scores: Neither overall nor item mean scores were reported.

Source: Malhotra, Naresh K. (1981), "A Scale to Measure Self-Concepts, Person Concepts, and Product Concepts," *Journal of Marketing Research*, 16 (November), 456-464.

Other evidence: N/A.

Other sources: N/A.

References: Osgood, C. E., George J. Suci, and Percy M. Tannenbaum (1957), *Measurement of Meaning*, Urbana,IL: The University of Illinois Free Press.

SELF-CONCEPTS, PERSON CONCEPTS, AND PRODUCT CONCEPTS
(Malhotra 1981)

1. Rugged .... delicate

2. Excitable .... calm

3. Uncomfortable .... comfortable

4. Dominating .... submissive

5. Thrifty .... indulgent

6. Pleasant .... unpleasant

7. Contemporary .... noncontemporary

8. Organized .... unorganized

9. Rational .... emotional

10. Youthful .... mature

11. Formal .... informal

12. Orthodox .... liberal

13. Complex.. simple

14. Colorless .... colorful

15. Modest .... vain

NOTES: Though considered multidimensional, items belonging to specific dimensions were not explicitly given nor was the directionality of the items (i.e., the specification of reverse coding) stated by Malhotra (1981).

NEED FOR COGNITION: NFC
(Cacioppo and Petty 1982)

Construct: Need for cognition (NFC) represents the tendency for individuals to engage in and enjoy thinking (Cacioppo and Petty 1982). Cohen, Stotland and Wolfe (1955) originally described the need for cognition as a need to structure relevant situations in meaningful, integrated ways and a need to understand and make reasonable the experiential world. The scale has been frequently used in consumer research in examining the effects of persuasive arguments. Among these applications, the concept has been shown to be useful in understanding how argument strength and endorser attractiveness in advertisements may influence consumer attitudes (e.g., individuals high in need for cognition are more influenced by the quality of arguments in an advertisement) (Haugtvedt, Petty, Cacioppo, and Steidley 1988). In addition, it has been shown that low need for cognition individuals react to the simple presence of a price promotion signal whether or not the price of the promoted brand is reduced (Inman, McAlister, and Hoyer 1990).

Description: The original scale is comprised of 34 items each scored -4 to +4 as follows: +4, very strong agreement; +3, strong agreement; +2, moderate agreement; +1, slight agreement; 0, neither agreement nor disagreement; -1, slight disagreement; -2, moderate disagreement; -3, strong disagreement; and, -4, very strong disagreement. An 18-item short form for assessing need for cognition has been proposed by Cacioppo, Petty, and Kao (1984). The items included in both versions are presented here. Some of the items are varied in direction to inhibit response bias. Item scores are summed for an overall index.

Development: An unspecified pool of items was edited (i.e., deleted or revised) for ambiguity. The remaining pool of 45 items was administered to the faculty of a large mid-Western university (i.e., a high need for cognition group) and a group of factory line workers from the same community (Cacioppo and Petty 1982, p. 118). The initial sample (combining both groups) included a total of 96 respondents; eighty-four of the respondents were included in these initial analyses. A series of 2x2 (gender by high and low cognition) (i.e., gender by faculty/factory line worker) analysis of variance tests were used to delete items that did not discriminate between the high and low groups. Tests for the overall sum for the initial 45 items and the final 34 items revealed a significant main effect for need for cognition but nonsignificant effects for gender and the interaction. Remaining items that failed to correlate significantly with the total score were also eliminated.

Sample(s): As explained above, 84 university professors and factory workers were used in the Study One development of the 34-item NFC measure. The sample was comprised of approximately equal numbers of males and females. Four hundred and nineteen introductory psychology students participated in Study Two. Study Three involved 104 (35 males and 69 females) students from the University of Iowa; 97 student subjects participated in Study Four.

Validity: A single dominant factor from a principal components analysis was interpreted as support for a unidimensional scale comprised of 34 items. The correlation between factor loadings in Studies 1 and 2 was 0.76 (n=34, p<0.01).

Multiple sources of validity evidence are described in Cacioppo and Petty (1982). For example, evidence of discriminant validity was found in Study 2 from low correlations with measures of cognitive style and test anxiety. In Study 3, correlations with intelligence (r=0.39), social desirability (r=0.08), and dogmatism (r=-.27) were provided as evidence of the scale's validity. In Study 4, a significant hypothesized interaction revealed that high NFC subjects reported enjoying a complex task more than a simple task while low NFC subjects enjoyed a simple task more than a complex task. Also in Study 4, a modest negative correlation with dogmatism was found (r=-0.23); however, a significant correlation with a measure of social desirability was revealed (r=0.21).

Scores: Means and standard deviations were not provided in the cited manuscripts.

Source: Cacioppo, John T. and Richard E. Petty (1982), "The Need for Cognition," *Journal of Personality and Social Psychology*, 42 (1), 116-131.

Other evidence: In the development of the short form, Cacioppo et al. (1984) reported coefficient alpha estimates of internal consistency reliability of 0.90 and 0.91 for the 18-item and 34-item versions, respectively.

Substantial evidence of the validity of the construct and the measures described here has been provided by a number of studies which have successfully used the Cacioppo and Petty (1982) need for cognition scale. As recent examples, the two studies by Haugtvedt et al. (1988) showed, as predicted from the theory underlying the construct, that individuals high in need for cognition were more influenced by the quality of arguments in advertisements and that individuals low in NFC were influenced more by the peripheral cue endorser attractiveness. Similarly, Inman et al. (1990) used the NFC measure to successfully predict the effects of price signals (i.e., price messages without actual price information).

Other sources: Cacioppo, John T., Richard E. Petty, and Kao Feng Chuan (1984), "The Efficient Assessment of Need for Cognition," *Journal of Personality Assessment*, 48 (3), 306-307.

Haugtvedt, Curt, Richard E. Petty, John T. Cacioppo, and Theresa Steidley (1988), "Personality and Ad Effectiveness: Exploring the Utility of Need for Cognition," in *Advances in Consumer Research*, Vol. 15, Michael. J. Houston, (ed.), Provo, UT: Association for Consumer Research, 209-212.

Inman, J. Jeffrey, Leigh McAlister, and Wayne D. Hoyer (1990), "Promotion Signal: Proxy for a Price Cut," *Journal of Consumer Research*, 17 (June), 74-81.

References: Cohen, A. R., E. Stotland, and D. M. Wolfe (1955), "An Experimental Investigation of Need for Cognition," *Journal of Abnormal and Social Psychology*, 51, 291-294.

NEED FOR COGNITION
(Cacioppo and Petty 1982)

1. I really enjoy a task that involves coming up with solutions to problems. (b)

2. I would prefer a task that is intellectual, difficult, and important to one that is somewhat important but does not require much thought. (b)

3. I tend to set goals that can be accomplished only by expending considerable mental effort.

4. I am usually tempted to put more thought into a task than the job minimally requires.

5. Learning new ways to think doesn't excite me very much.(a,b)

6. I am hesitant about making important decisions after thinking about them. (a)

7. I usually end up deliberating about issues even when they do affect me personally. (b)

8. I prefer to let things happen rather than try to understand why they turned out that way. (a)

9. I have difficulty in thinking in new and unfamiliar situations. (a)

10. The idea of relying on thought to get my way to the top does not appeal to me. (a,b)

11. The notion of thinking abstractly is not appealing to me. (a,b)

12. I am an intellectual.

13. I only think as hard as I have to. (a,b)

14. I don't reason well under pressure. (a)

15. I like tasks that require little thought once I've learned them. (a,b)

16. I prefer to think about small daily projects to long-term ones. (a,b)

17. I would rather do something that requires little thought than something that is sure to challenge my thinking abilities. (b)

18. I find little satisfaction in deliberating hard and for long hours. (a,b)

19. I more often talk with other people about the reasons for and possible solutions to international problems than about gossip of tidbits of what famous people are doing.

20. These days, I see little chance for performing well, even in "intellectual" jobs, unless one knows the right people. (a)

21. More often than not, more thinking just leads to more errors. (a)

22. I don't like to have the responsibility of handling a situation that requires a lot of thinking. (a,b)

23. I appreciate opportunities to discover the strengths and weaknesses of my own reasoning.

24. I feel relief rather than satisfaction after completing a task that required a lot of mental effort. (a,b)

25. Thinking is not my idea of fun. (a,b)

26. I try to anticipate and avoid situations where there is a likely chance I'll have to think in depth about something.(a,b)

27. I prefer watching educational to entertainment programs.

28. I think best when those around me are very intelligent.

29. I prefer my life to be filled with puzzles that I must solve. (b)

30. I would prefer complex to simple problems. (b)

31. Simply knowing the answer rather than understanding the reasons or the answer to a problem is fine with me. (a)

32. It's enough for me that something gets the job done; I don't care how or why it works. (a,b)

33. Ignorance is bliss. (a)

34. I enjoy thinking about an issue even when the results of my thoughts will have no outcome on the issue.

NOTES: "a" denotes items requiring reverse scoring; "b" denotes items included in short form. There were slight wording variations for some items in both versions.

AN INDEX TO MEASURE "HISPANICNESS"
(Valencia 1985)

Construct: The term "Hispanicness" refers to the rate or degree of acculturation of Hispanic consumers living in the USA (Valencia 1985, p. 118). Acculturation is defined as the process of learning a culture other than the one to which one is born. The impetus for the research is based upon the recognition that the degree of identification the individual feels with a given ethnic group may largely determine the level of commitment regarding cultural norms and the degree of influence exerted by a particular culture (Hirschman 1981). Consequently, differences in consumption preferences should be observed.

Description: The index has six indicators that are summed and range from 6 to 23. The English language ability item is reverse scored. Item scoring procedures for the six questions are shown below. The measure is designed to include the following attributes: strength of ethnic identification, understanding of the English language, extent of Spanish language maintenance, length of time lived in the American culture, and marital relationships (i.e., miscegenation).

Development: The items comprising the scale were developed to reflect the attributes of Hispanicness reviewed in the manuscript's introduction. More traditional item generation procedures were not employed in the development of the scale. However, a series of multiple bilingual translations were used to ensure consistent meaning and interpretation of the items and the survey used to test the index.

Sample(s): The index was tested on a sample of respondents to a mail survey of residents of New York, Los Angeles, Miami, and San Antonio (i.e., cities with high concentrations of Hispanic residents and including 42 percent of America's Hispanic population). After excluding responses from inappropriate ethnic groups and incomplete responses, data were available from 178 Hispanic and 288 white respondents (Valencia 1985, p. 119).

Validity: An unspecified reliability estimate of .73 was provided. The correlation between the Hispanic Index and a six-item measure of consumer acculturation was 0.17 ($p<.05$). The Spearman correlation between the scale and place of birth (i.e., outside or within the U.S.) was 0.54 ($p<.01$). In addition, mean differences in shopping opinions and behaviors between whites and low and high Hispanic groups were cited as further evidence of the scale's validity.

Scores: In an earlier study, index scores ranged from 6 to 19. Other data regarding means were not provided in Valencia (1985).

Source: Valencia, Humberto (1985), "Developing an Index to Measure 'Hispanicness'," in *Advances in Consumer Research*, Vol. 12, Elizabeth C. Hirschman and Morris Holbrook, (eds.), Provo, UT: Association for Consumer Research, 118-121.

Other evidence: N/A.

Other sources: N/A.

References: Hirschman, Elizabeth C. (1981), "American Jewish Ethnicity: Its Relationship to Some Selected Aspects of Consumer Behavior," *Journal of Marketing*, 45 (Summer), 102-110.

AN INDEX TO MEASURE "HISPANICNESS"
(Valencia 1985)

1. *Strength of ethnic identification*

> "How strongly do you identify yourself with the ethnic or racial group you mentioned above?
> 1) Very strongly, 2) Strongly, 3) More or less, 4) Weak, 5) Very weak.

2. *English language ability*

> "As you may know, some people in the U.S. are bilingual. If you speak Spanish, please answer the next three questions. Would you say you speak English:
> 1) Very well, 2) Well, 3) Not well, 4) Not at all.

3. *Spanish language spoken at home*

> "Would you say your family speaks Spanish at home?"
> 1) All of the time, 2) Most of the time, 3) Sometimes, 4) Not at all.

4. *Language preference*

> "If you had the chance to communicate with someone just as well in English or Spanish, which would you prefer to converse with them?
> 1) Spanish, 2) Either Spanish or English, 3) English.

5. *Ratio of length of residence in the U.S.*

> "How long have you lived in the U.S.? ____ Years."
> Note: Number of years is divided by age and weighted by 4.

6. *Miscegenation*

> "If married, with which ethnic or racial group does your spouse identify with?
> 1) Hispanic/Hispanic spouse or Hispanic single, 2) Hispanic/Anglo spouse, 3) Anglo/Hispanic spouse, 4) Anglo/Anglo spouse or Anglo single.

NOTES: For higher scores to reflect higher levels of Hispanicness, item 1, and items 3 through 6 require reverse coding.

PROPENSITY TO PROVIDE MARKETPLACE AND SHOPPING INFORMATION: THE MARKET MAVEN SCALE
(Feick and Price 1987)

Construct: The "market maven" refers to individual consumers with a propensity to provide general shopping and marketplace information. Market mavens are defined formally as "individuals who have information about many kinds of products, places to shop, and other facets of markets, and initiate discussions with consumers and respond to requests from consumers for market information" (Feick and Price 1987, p. 85). The definition is comparable with the definition of opinion leaders in that influence derives from knowledge and expertise, but differs in that the expertise is not product specific (i.e., a more general knowledge of markets). Mavens obtain information because they think it will be useful to others or because it will provide a basis for conversations.

Description: The scale consists of six statements, five of which are operationalized as seven-place scales labeled strongly disagree to strongly agree. The sixth item has a 7-point response format of "the description does not fit me well at all—the description fits me very well." Items scores are summed to form an overall score and the range of the scale is from 6 to 42. All items are worded such that greater agreement results in a larger total score (i.e., a greater propensity to provide marketplace information).

Development: An initial pool of 40 items was generated based on the concept definition. This set was reduced to 19 by a panel of marketing academics and practitioners. The responses of a pilot sample of 265 MBA's, factor analysis, item-to-total correlations, and coefficient alpha were used to reduce the final scale to six items.

Sample(s): The main study for which the final instrument was administered involved nation-wide telephone interviews (selected by random digit dialing) with 1,531 adult household heads. Sixty-four percent of the sample was female. Subjects were randomly assigned to subsamples; 771 were in the food and 760 in the drug subsamples (Feick and Price 1987, p. 87). In addition, 265 part-time MBA students participated in an earlier scale development study. A probability sample of 303 heads of households from a large Northeastern city also participated in a study of the discriminant validity of the scale in relation to measures of opinion leadership.

Validity: For the pilot study, coefficient alpha was 0.84; item-to-total correlations ranged from 0.51 to 0.67. For the main study, the estimate of internal consistency reliability was 0.82, and item-to-total correlations ranged from 0.48 to 0.65.

Validity evidence regarding the concept was provided from responses to queries regarding knowledge of individuals fitting the market maven description (46%), and the importance of those persons in making purchase decisions. Discriminant validity was examined (and supported) through factor analysis of the market maven items and a series of opinion leadership items. The correlation between the maven scale and a measure of opinion leadership was 0.22. Correlations between the market maven measure and a series of innovativeness variables were positive and significant. For example, the correlations for the food sample ranged from 0.31 to 0.34. Discriminant validity evidence was also provided from confirmatory factor analysis of the main study sample.

Substantial correlational evidence of the scale's validity was provided by a series of proposition tests in which the scale was used to form low, medium, and high groups across which a series of difference tests were performed. In addition, the market maven scale was found correlated as predicted with a series of shopping and individual characteristics. These results confirm expectations regarding the construct and, hence, support the validity of the measure. For example, Feick and Price (1987, p. 94) conclude: market mavens exist, consumers can identify them, and they use them in making purchase decisions. Further, the concept was found related to: early awareness of new products, provision of information, extensive use of information sources, and market activities such as couponing and reading advertising.

Scores: The mean score and standard deviation based on the sample of 1,531 interviews were 25.6 and 8.5, respectively.

Source: Feick, Lawrence F. and Linda L. Price (1987), "The Market Maven: A Diffuser of Marketplace Information," *Journal of Marketing*, 51 (January), 83-97.

Other evidence: 213 subjects were interviewed by telephone (Price et al. 1988). Difference tests across groups revealed evidence for the scale's validity as mavens were more likely to engage in smart shopping behaviors (i.e., use of coupons, designing grocery budgets) than non-mavens.

Other sources: Price, Linda L., Lawrence F. Feick, and Audrey Guskey-Federouch (1988), "Couponing Behaviors of the Market Maven: Profile of a Super Shopper," in *Advances in Consumer Research*, Vol. 15, Michael J. Houston, (ed.), Provo, UT: Association for Consumer Research, 354-359.

References: N/A.

PROPENSITY TO PROVIDE MARKETPLACE AND SHOPPING INFORMATION: THE MARKET MAVEN SCALE
(Feick and Price 1987)

1. I like introducing new brands and products to my friends.

2. I like helping people by providing them with information about many kinds of products.

3. People ask me for information about products, places to shop, or sales.

4. If someone asked where to get the best buy on several types of products, I could tell him or her where to shop.

5. My friends think of me as a good source of information when it comes to new products or sales.

6. Think about a person who has information about a variety of products and likes to share this information with others. This person knows about new products, sales, stores, and so on, but does not necessarily feel he or she is an expert on one particular product. How well would you say this description fits you?

NOTES: Item six is scored from "the description does not fit me well at all" to "the description fits me very well."

CONSUMER ETHNOCENTRISM: THE CETSCALE
(Shimp and Sharma 1987)

Construct: The CETSCALE is designed to measure consumers' ethnocentric tendencies (i.e., disposition to act in a consistent fashion) related to purchasing foreign-versus American made products. Consumer ethnocentrism represents the beliefs held by consumers about the appropriateness, indeed morality of purchasing foreign-made products (Shimp and Sharma 1987, p. 280). The purchase of foreign made products, in the minds of ethnocentric consumers, is wrong because it hurts the domestic economy, causes loss of jobs, and is unpatriotic.

Description: The scale consists of 17 items scored on 7-point Likert-type formats (strongly agree = 7, strongly disagree = 1). Item scores are summed to form an overall score ranging 17 to 119. In its original form, the scale was designed for use on American subjects, as most items contain reference to America or the U.S. (A shortened ten-item version using 5-place response format was also tested in the national consumer goods study described below.) Both versions are considered unidimensional.

Development: Recommended scaling procedures were used in scale development. The CETSCALE was developed using an initial pool of 180 nonredundant items based upon the common wording of responses from an open-ended elicitation study of 800 consumers. Following a judgmental screening of items by a panel of six academics, two purification studies were conducted to develop the final form of the scale. Initially, the development phase addressed seven facets of consumers' orientations toward foreign products. Common factor analysis of the data obtained in the first purification study reduced the item pool to 25 items reflecting the ethnocentrism dimension. From the second purification study, 17 items consistently demonstrated satisfactory reliability in a series of confirmatory factor analyses.

Sample(s): The respondents were 407 households in the first study. The second study included approximately 320 households from each of three metropolitan areas (Detroit, Denver, Los Angeles) and 575 households from the Carolinas. Using some of these same data, four additional studies were conducted to assess reliability and validity of the scale: (1) a four areas study, n=1535; (2) Carolinas study, n=47; (3) national consumer goods study, n=2000+; and (4) crafted-with-pride study, n=145 involved. Only the crafted-with-pride study involved student subjects.

Validation: The assessment of reliability and validity of the CETSCALE in the original article was stringent and extensive. Only a brief summary is provided here. Interested readers are advised to refer to Shimp and Sharma (1987) for details. Internal consistency estimates of reliability ranged from 0.94 to 0.96; test-retest was estimated at 0.77. Evidence of convergent and discriminant validity was provided by significant and positive correlations of the CETSCALE and measures of patriotism and political-economic conservatism. Extensive tests of nomological validity (in one instance over a two year delay) were also presented in support of the scale. Briefly, scale scores were found, as predicted, negatively correlated with varying measures of consumers' beliefs, attitudes, and intentions toward foreign made products. Other data revealed that origin of manufacturer was more important for high scorers and that higher scorers were biased in favor of American products and in opposition to European and Asian products. Lastly, tests of mean differences revealed that scores were highest among individuals whose quality of life and economic situation (and hardships) are threatened by foreign competition (i.e., lower social classes, Detroit respondents).

Scores: Mean scores and standard deviations for the CETSCALE for the four geographic areas followed a predicted pattern: (1) Detroit, 68.58 (25.96); (2) Carolinas, 61.28 (24.41); (3) Denver, 57.84 (26.10); (4) Los Angeles, 56.62 (26.37). The mean scores for the two phase student sample used in the crafted-with-pride study resulted in mean scores of 51.92 (16.37) and 53.39 (16.52). Scores also were found to decline predictably across three social classes: upper-lower, 73.63; lower-middle, 64.01; and upper-middle, 51.91.

Source: Shimp, Terence A. and Subhash Sharma (1987), "Consumer Ethnocentrism: Construction and Validation of the CETSCALE," *Journal of Marketing Research*, 24 (August), 280-289.

Other evidence: In a validation study, Netemeyer, Durvasula, and Lichtenstein (1991) used student samples of 71, 73, 70, and 76 from colleges in the U.S., Germany, France and Japan, respectively. Netemeyer et al. (1991) reported alpha levels ranging from 0.91 to 0.95 across the four countries studied. In addition, the CETSCALE was correlated with a number of behavioral measures reflecting a consumer ethnocentric bias. Across countries, these correlations offered evidence of nomological validity for the scale.

Other sources: Netemeyer, Richard G., Srinivas Durvasula, and Donald R. Lichtenstein (1991), "A Cross-National Assessment of the Reliability and Validity of the CETSCALE," *Journal of Marketing Research*, 28 (August), 320-327.

References: N/A.

CONSUMER ETHNOCENTRISM: THE CETSCALE
(Shimp and Sharma 1987)

1. American people should always buy American-made products instead of imports.

2. Only those products that are unavailable in the U.S. should be imported.

3. Buy American-made products. Keep America working.

4. American products, first, last and foremost.

5. Purchasing foreign-made products is un-American.

6. It is not right to purchase foreign products.

7. A real American should always buy American-made products.

8. We should purchase products manufactured in America instead of letting other countries get rich off us.

9. It is always best to purchase American products.

10. There should be very little trading or purchasing of goods from other countries unless out of necessity.

11. Americans should not buy foreign products, because this hurts American business and causes unemployment.

12. Curbs should be put on all imports.

13. It may cost me in the long run but I prefer to support American products.

14. Foreigners should not be allowed to put their products on our markets.

15. Foreign products should be taxed heavily to reduce their entry into the U.S.

16. We should buy from foreign countries only those products that we cannot obtain within our own country.

17. American consumers who purchase products made in other countries are responsible for putting their fellow Americans out of work.

NOTES: Items composing the ten item reduced version are items 2, 4 through 8, 11, 13, 16, and 17.

THE SEXUAL IDENTITY SCALE: SIS
(Stern, Barak, and Gould 1987)

Construct: The SIS assesses the degree to which one identifies with a given gender. That is, the measure assesses the degree to which individuals view themselves as more masculine or more feminine regardless of their actual gender (Stern et al. 1987).

Description: The SIS is a four-item measure scored on five-point scales from "very masculine" to "very feminine." (See Appendix for scoring details.) The scale is unidimensional and scores range from a low of 100 for very masculine to a high of 500 for very feminine.

Development: Based on a thorough review of the sex role and age research literatures, four items were generated to measure four aspects of sex role identity. A large sample composed of both men and women was used in assessing the reliability and validity of the SIS.

Samples: A sample of 380 adult men and 380 adult women from the New York/New Jersey area were used in scale reliability and validity analyses.

Validity: Reliability via coefficient alpha was .85 for women, .87 for men, and .96 for the total sample combined. SIS correlations with biological sex ranged from -.70 to -.81, and was -.81 for the total SIS. Correlations of the SIS with a femininity index were .35 for women and -.05 for men. Correlations of the SIS with a masculinity index were -.21 for men and -.07 for women. A confirmatory factor analysis via LISREL also showed evidence of discriminant and convergent validity for the SIS when compared to the femininity and and masculinity indices. Lastly, a series of mean tests between the male and female samples showed the expected SIS differences between men and women (i.e., men more strongly identified with masculinity than women and vice-versa).

Scores: Mean scores were reported for both men and women for the overall SIS and each SIS item. The mean of the overall SIS for females was 399.54 (sd = 60.13), and the mean for males was 188.62 (sd = 55.08). These two means were significantly different (t = 50.42, $p < .01$).

Source: Stern, Barbara B., Benny Barak, and Stephen J. Gould (1987), "Sexual Identity Scale: A New Self-Assessment Measure," *Sex Roles*, 17, 503-519.

Other evidence: In a study of gender schema and fashion, Gould and Stern (1989) reported an alpha of .97 for the SIS. Furthermore, the SIS exhibited correlations of .38 with fashion consciousness, .42 with an index of femininity and -.26 with an index of masculinity, providing evidence for SIS validity.

Other sources: Gould, Stephen J., and Barbara B. Stern (1989), "Gender Schema and Fashion Consciousness," *Psychology & Marketing*, 6 (Summer), 129-145.

References: Barak, Benny (1987), "Cognitive Age: A New Multi-dimensional Approach to Measure Age Identity," *The International Journal of Aging and Human Development*, in press.

THE SEXUAL IDENTITY SCALE: SIS
(Stern, Barak, and Gould 1987)

Please specify—for each of the following—how MASCULINE or FEMININE you consider yourself to be.

1) I FEEL as though I am . . .

2) I LOOK as though I am . . .

3) I DO most things in a manner typical of someone who is . . .

4) My INTERESTS are mostly those of a person who is . . .

APPENDIX
   1 = very masculine
   2 = masculine
   3 = neither masculine nor feminine
   4 = feminine
   5 = very feminine

Sexual Identity is a composite measure. The scoring system is derived from the summation/division scoring system used by the Cognitive Age Scale. (See Barak [1987] for scoring procedures.) Scores range from a low of 100 for *very masculine* to a high of 500 for *very feminine*. The SIS index is computed by averaging the midpoints of the measure's four items: (FEEL/age + LOOK/age + DO/age + INTEREST/age)/4.

A DIAGNOSTIC TOOL FOR CLASSIFYING COMPULSIVE CONSUMERS
(Faber and O'Guinn 1989)

Construct: This abnormal form of consumer behavior is typified by chronic buying episodes of a somewhat stereotyped fashion in which the consumer feels unable to stop or significantly moderate the behavior(s). Although compulsive buying may produce some short-term positive feelings for the individual, it ultimately is disruptive to normal life functioning and produces significant negative consequences (Faber and O'Guinn 1988, 1989). As such, compulsive buying shares similarities with other types of compulsive and addictive behaviors. Items in the measure include consumer behaviors exemplified by the following: buying items only because they are on sale, buying in order to feel better, and buying items that really can't be afforded.

Description: The measure is a screening instrument designed to identify compulsive consumers. The instrument is composed of the unweighted sum of scores to 14 items. Each item is operationalized using five-point Likert type scales. The range of the measure is 14 to 70. Lower scores reflect greater agreement or compulsivity.

Development: The development began with an initial set of 32 variables which assessed psychological, motivational, and behavioral aspects of buying. These items were developed from the literature on other compulsive behaviors, the authors' previous experiences, and a pilot test with a small group of compulsive consumers.

Those 14 items discriminating (p<.10) between the two groups (i.e., the two samples described below) were selected for inclusion in the measure. Using the general population sample, factor analysis of these 14 items revealed "only one viable and interpretable factor."

Sample(s):   A compulsive sample of 386 respondents to a mail survey was derived from individuals in contact (but not in therapy) with a self-help group for problem consumers. A comparison sample of 285 individuals was obtained after three mailings to a sample of 800 drawn from three Illinois cities of varying sizes.

Validity: The coefficient alpha estimate of internal consistency reliability was 0.83.

In the ensuing analyses, the distributions of the screening measure were examined for both groups. The intersections of the distributions were examined to determine a threshold score (i.e., two standard deviations below the mean for the general distribution) or 42 which also was the modal value for the compulsive sample. Approximately six percent of the general sample was identified as compulsives. Test of mean differences between the 16 compulsives in the general sample were compared with 16 individuals drawn randomly from the compulsive group. These comparisons revealed that the screener measure is capable of identifying compulsives in the general population similar to individuals in the compulsive group but quite different from other members of the general population. Differences were examined for measures of self-esteem, payments for past purchases, general compulsivity, envy, and fantasy.

Scores: Mean scores are reported for both a "comparison strata" and "a compulsive strata." (See Table 2.) The mean scores (and standard deviations) were 37.44 (10.74) and 57.33 (7.51) for the compulsive and comparison strata, respectively. The corresponding modal values were 42 and 58.

Source: Faber, Ronald J. and Thomas C. O'Guinn (1989), "Classifying Compulsive Consumers: Advances in the Development of a Diagnostic Tool," in *Advances in Consumer Research*, Vol. 16, Thomas K. Srull, (ed.), Provo, UT: Association for Consumer Research, 738-744.

Other evidence: N/A.

Other sources: N/A.

References: Faber, Ronald J. and Thomas C. O'Guinn (1988), "Compulsive Consumption and Credit Abuse," *Journal of Consumer Policy*, 11, 97-109.

A DIAGNOSTIC TOOL FOR CLASSIFYING COMPULSIVE CONSUMERS
(Faber and O'Guinn 1989)

1.   Bought things even though I couldn't afford them.

2.   Felt others would be horrified if they knew of my spending habits.

3.   If I have any money left at the end of the pay period, just have to spend.

4.   Made only the minimum payments on my credit cards.

5.   Bought something in order to make myself feel better.

6.   Wrote a check when I knew I didn't have enough money in the bank to cover it.

7.   Just wanted to buy things and didn't care what I bought.

8.   I often buy things simply because they are on sale.

9.   Felt anxious or nervous on days I didn't go shopping.

10. Shopping is fun.

11. Felt depressed after shopping.

12. Bought something and when I got home I wasn't sure why I had bought it.

13. Went on a buying binge and wasn't able to stop.

14. I really believe that having more money would solve most of my problems.

NOTES: The items above are as they originally appeared in Faber and O'Guinn (1989). Some of the items may require a slight wording change to reflect the meaning intended.

COUNTRY-OF-ORIGIN SCALE
(Pisharodi and Parameswaran 1991)

Construct: According to Pisharodi and Parameswaran (1991), country-of-origin is an evolving construct which states that people attach stereotypical "made in" perceptions to products from specific countries and this influences purchase and consumption behaviors in multi-national markets. Furthermore, the construct encompasses perceptions of a sourcing country's economic, political, and cultural characteristics, as well as specific product image perceptions (i.e., in this study automobiles was the focal product).

Description: The final version of the scale is composed of 24 items scored on 10-point scales ranging from "not at all appropriate" (1) to "most appropriate" (10). The scale has six factors: 3 relating to general product attitudes (GPA); 2 relating to general country attitudes (GCA); and 1 relating to specific product attributes (SPA). The first five factors are applicable across product attitudes and country attitudes (i.e., the GPA and GCA factors), and the last factor (SPA) is specific to automobiles. Items scores can be summed within factors to form factor indices. The scale is considered multi-dimensional, but items within the factors reflect unidimensional measurement.

Development: Via an extensive review of the literature, 40 items were generated to reflect the GPA, GCA, and SPA factors. Initially, it was felt that the construct would be best represented by just a three-factor solution (i.e., one factor each for GPA, GCA, and SPA). Responses from a large sample were then used to trim the number of items and assess dimensionality and internal consistency. Using confirmatory factor analysis (via LISREL) and the ITAN package (Gerbing and Hunter 1988), an iterative process that examines inter-item correlations, item factor loadings and dimensionality, the final form of the scale was derived. The final form reflected three factors relating to GPA. Two of the GPA factors stress positive attributes (i.e., labeled GPA2 and GPA3), and one reflects negative attributes (i.e., labeled GPA1). The final form of the scale also contains one factor relating to SPA (positive car attributes).

Samples(s): A total of 678 adults from a large midwestern metropolitan area responded to the 40 items in the original questionnaire.

Validity: The fit of the six-factor model, representing the final form of the scale, indicated unidimensionality of items in each of the six factors. Coefficient alpha estimates for the factors were .872, .849 .918 .735, .796, and 819 for GCA1, GCA2, GPA1, GPA2, GPA3, and SPA, respectively.

Scores: Neither mean nor percentage scores were reported.

Source: Pisharodi, R. Mohan, and Ravi Parameswaran (1991), "Confirmatory Factor Analysis of a Country-of-Origin Scale: Initial Results," *Advances in Consumer Research*, Vol. 19, John Sherry and Brian Sternthal (eds.), in press.

Other evidence: N/A.

Other sources: N/A.

References: Gerbing, David W., and John E. Hunter (1988), *ITAN: A Statistical Package for Item Analysis With Correlational Data Including Multiple Groups Factor Analysis*, Portland State University, Portland, OR.

COUNTRY-OF-ORIGIN SCALE
(Pisharodi and Parameswaran 1991)

GCA1 Items
1) Well educated
2) Hard-working
3) Achieving high standards
4) Raised standards of living
5) Technical skills

GCA2 Items
1) Similar political views
2) Economically similar
3) Culturally similar

GPA1 Items
1) Unreasonably expensive
2) Imitations
3) Not attractive
4) Frequent repairs.
5) Cheaply put together

GPA2 Items
1) Sold in many countries
2) Intensely advertised
3) Advertising information
4) Easily available

GPA3 Items
1) Long lasting
2) Good value
3) Prestigious products

SPA Items
1) Workmanship good
2) Handles well
3) Little maintenance
4) Made to last

NOTES: Though not specified by the authors, the GPA1 items require recoding to reflect positive scores on the GPA1 factor.

OPINION LEADERSHIP

OPINION LEADERSHIP
(King and Summers 1970; Childers 1986)

Construct: The King and Summers' measure of opinion leadership summarized here is actually an adaptation of an earlier measure presented by Rogers and Cartano (1962). A more recent revision of the scale by Childers (1986) is also summarized. In King and Summers' (1970) original study of opinion leadership generalization across product categories, a product or issue specific seven-item opinion leadership scale was offered. As originally conceptualized, opinion leadership reflects the extent to which individuals give information about a topic and the extent to which information is sought by others from those individuals. Opinion leadership is thought to be a critical determinant of word-of-mouth communication and interpersonal influences affecting the diffusion of new products, concepts, and services.

Description: The original King and Summers scale consists of seven items—five are operationalized using a dichotomous response format while the remaining items have three response possibilities. The total range of the scale is from seven to sixteen. The items are worded such that alternative product categories can be inserted into each statement. For example, the first item reads as follows: "In general, do you like to talk about _____ with your friends? Yes ___ - 1 No ___ - 2"

The revised Opinion Leadership Scale (Childers 1986) also contains seven items adaptable to different product categories. However, the revised measure contains a modified set of items which are each operationalized via five-place bipolar response formats. Item scores are summed to form a range of 7 to 35. (Both the King and Summers' and the Childers' versions are included below.) Childers eventually recommends that item #5 be deleted, resulting in a potential range of 6 to 30.

Development: The scale was developed by modifying an already existing self-designating measure of opinion leadership (Rogers 1961; Rogers and Cartano 1962). The modifications to the Rogers' measure included: (1) omitting the word "new" in each of six questions to remove bias in favor of innovators; (2) adding an additional question; and (3) changing the order of questions (King and Summers 1970, p. 46).

Childers (1986) reported two studies in his efforts to investigate the King and Summers' measure. The first was designed to evaluate the original scale. His second study was designed to evaluate a revised version in which the response format for all items was changed to 1 to 5 place scales anchored by bipolar adjectives or adjective sets.

Sample(s): The data on which the King and Summers' (1970) measure were evaluated reflected the responses of 1000 housewives interviewed in 1967. Participants were residents of Marion County, Indiana. Responses were obtained for six product categories (i.e., packaged food products, women's clothing, household cleansers and detergents, cosmetics, large appliances, and small appliances). Respondents were categorized as leaders or nonleaders in a proportion designed to achieve comparability with the opinion leader categorizations of Katz and Lazarfield (1965). Childers (1986) initial analysis of the King and Summers' scale was based upon the responses of 110 respondents to a mail survey. His second study, conducted to examine the revised scale, involved the responses of 176 households either adopting or refusing subscription to a cable service.

Validity: Little evidence of validity was offered in the original King and Summers' (1970) article. Childers (1986), however, offers several estimates of reliability and validity. An internal consistency reliability estimate of 0.66 was reported by Childers as well as an average item-to-total correlation of 0.43. (Deletion of item seven increased the reliability estimate to 0.68.) The Childers' version was found to correlate with measures of product ownership, product specific risk, multiple use potential, and creativity/curiosity and to differ as expected across known groups (Childers 1986). For example, a correlation of 0.28 with a product specific measure of perceived risk was found.

Other results revealed an internal consistency estimate of 0.83 after deletion of item #5. The average item-to-total correlation improved to 0.62 (after an r to z transformation). Correlations with four of five validity measures were significant as predicted. And, mean scores were found to differ across groups as expected (i.e., the means for premium cable subscribers, basic-only subscribers, and refusers were 20.0, 19.5, and 15.2, respectively).

Scores: Means and standard deviations were not reported in King and Summers (1970). The means for premium cable subscribers, basic-only subscribers, and refusers in Childers' second study were 20.0, 19.5, and 15.2, respectively.

Source: King, Charles W. and John O. Summers (1970), "Overlap of Opinion Leadership Across Product Categories," *Journal of Marketing Research*, 7 (February), 43-50.

Childers, Terry L. (1986), "Assessment of the Psychometric Properties of An Opinion Leadership Scale," *Journal of Marketing Research*, 23 (May), 184-188.

Other evidence: A number of studies have used and/or evaluated some form of the opinion leadership scale. Three of these are briefly described here.

Darden and Reynolds' (1972) administration of a modified (5 item) instrument assessed the opinion leadership of suburban males (n=104) in addition to fraternity (n=76) and nonfraternity (n=102) undergraduate students. They report a split-half reliability estimate of .79. Riecken and Yavas (1983) report KR-20 estimates of reliability ranging from .50 to .82 across five samples for the King and Summers' version. Their mean scores ranged from 11.59 to 14.99.

Goldsmith and Desborde (1991) provide the most recent and extensive tests for the revised scale (cf. Childers 1986) (based on the responses of 187 undergraduate business students). Record albums were the domain of study. Goldsmith and Desborde (1991) found significant correlations between the revised scale and measures of awareness (r=0.46), purchase (r=0.32), and innovativeness (0.22). The overall mean reported by Goldsmith and Desborde (1991) was 19.3 (sd=5.66) for Childers' version. The means for males and females were 20.8 and 17.6, respectively.

Other sources: Darden, William R. and Fred D. Reynolds (1972), "Predicting Opinion Leadership for Men's Apparel Fashions," *Journal of Marketing Research*, 9 (August), 324-328.

Goldsmith, Ronald E. and Rene Desborde (1991), "A Validity Study of a Measure of Opinion Leadership," *Journal of Business Research*, 22, 11-19.

Riecken, Glen and Ugur Yavas (1983), "Internal Consistency of King and Summers' Opinion Leadership Scale: Further Evidence," *Journal of Marketing Research*, 20 (August), 325-326.

References: Katz, Elihu and Paul Lazarfield (1965), *Personal Influence*, Glencoe: Free Press.

Rogers, Everett and David G. Cartano (1962), "Methods of Measuring Opinion Leadership," *Public Opinion Quarterly*, 26 (Fall), 435-441.

Rogers, Everett (1961), *Characteristics of Agricultural Innovators and Other Adopter Categories*, Wooster Ohio: Ohio Experiment Station, *Research Bulletin 882*.

OPINION LEADERSHIP
(King and Summers 1970)

1. In general, do you like to talk about _____ with your friends?

   Yes _____ -1   No _____ -2

2. Would you say you give very little information, an average amount of information, or a great deal of information about
   _____ to your friends?

   You give very little information ...._____ -1
   You give an average amount of information ..._____ -2
   You give a great deal of information ...._____ -3

3. During the past six months, have you told anyone about some _____ ?

   Yes _____ -1   No _____ -2

4. Compared with your circle of friends, are you less likely to be asked, about as likely to be asked, or more likely to be asked about _____ ?

   Less likely to be asked ...._____ -1
   About as likely to be asked ......_____ -2
   More likely to be asked ...._____ -3

5. If you and your friends were to discuss _____ , what part would you be most likely to play? Would you mainly listen to your friend's ideas or would you try to convince them of your ideas?

   You mainly listen to your friends ideas ...._____ -1
   You try to convince them of your ideas ...._____ -2

6. Which of these happens more often? Do you tell your friends about some _____ , or do they tell you about some _____ ?

   You tell them about ...._____ -1
   They tell you about some ...._____ -2

7. Do you have the feeling that you are generally regarded by your friends and neighbors as a good source of advice about _____ ?

   Yes _____ -1   No _____ -2

NOTES: Though not explicitly stated in the original article, it appears that items 1, 3, 6, and 7 require recoding.

OPINION LEADERSHIP
(Childers 1986)

1. In general, do you talk to your friends and neighbors about cable television:

very often				never
5	4	3	2	1

2. When you talk to your friends and neighbors about cable television do you:

give a great deal of information				give very little information
5	4	3	2	1

3. During the past six months, how many people have you told about cable television?

told a number of people				told no one
5	4	3	2	1

4. Compared with your circle of friends, how likely are you to be asked about cablevision?

very likely to be asked				not at all likely to be asked
5	4	3	2	1

5. In a discussion of cablevision, would you be most likely to:

listen to your friend's ideas				convince your friends of your ideas
5	4	3	2	1

6. In discussions of cable television, which of the following happens most often?

you tell your friends about cable				your friends tell you about cable
5	4	3	2	1

7. Overall in all of your discussions with friends and neighbors, are you:

often used as a source of advice				not used as a source of advice
5	4	3	2	1

NOTES: Childers (1986) recommends deletion of item #5 (which also apparently requires reverse coding).

OPINION LEADERSHIP AND INFORMATION SEEKING
(Reynolds and Darden 1971)

Construct: Reynolds and Darden's (1971) view of opinion leadership is similar to that of King and Summers' (1970) conceptualization in that opinion leadership is felt to reflect the extent to which individuals give information about a topic and the extent to which information is sought by others from those individuals. In operationalizing opinion leadership though, Reynolds and Darden measured an information seeking factor as well because it is thought to be a critical determinant of word-of-mouth communication and interpersonal influences affecting the diffusion of new products, concepts, and services. Reynolds and Darden used clothing as the focal product in their study.

Description: Reynolds and Darden's opinion leadership scale is composed of five 5-point Likert items scored from strongly disagree to strongly agree. Items scores are summed to form an index of opinion leadership. Their information seeking scale is composed of three 5-point Likert items, and scores on these items are also summed to form an overall index of information seeking.

Development: Items for both scales were generated from other published sources. The appropriateness of these items was then examined through factor, reliability, and validity analyses on a large sample.

Sample(s): A sample of 300 housewives was used in the study.

Validity: Split-halves reliability was .79 and .73 for the opinion leadership and information seeking scales, respectively. Factor analysis revealed that the hypothesized two-factor structure (opinion leadership and information seeking) was confirmed. A number of chi-square tests showed support for the validity of both scales.

Source: Reynolds, Fred D. and William R. Darden (1971), "Mutually Adaptive Effects of Interpersonal Communication," *Journal of Marketing Research*, 8 (November), 449-454.

Other evidence: N/A.

Other sources: N/A.

References: N/A.

OPINION LEADERSHIP AND INFORMATION SEEKING
(Reynolds and Darden 1971)

Opinion leadership

1) My friends and neighbors often ask my advice about clothing fashions.

2) I sometimes influence the types of clothes my friends buy.

3) My friends come to me more often than I go to them for information about clothes.

4) I feel that I am generally regarded by my friends and neighbors as a good source of advice about clothing fashions.

5) I can think of at least two people whom I have told about some clothing fashion in the last six months.

Information seeking

1) I often seek out the advice of my friends regarding which clothes I buy.

2) I spend a lot of time talking with my friends about clothing fashions.

3) My friends or neighbors usually give me good advice on what brands of clothes to buy.

SELF-MONITORING

SELF-MONITORING SCALE
(Snyder 1974)

Construct: Self-monitoring of expressive behavior and self-presentation were defined originally by Snyder (1974) as self-observation and self-control guided by situational cues to social appropriateness. An instrument was designed to discriminate individual differences in concern for social appropriateness, sensitivity to the expression and self-presentation of others in social situations as cues to social appropriateness of self-expression, and use of these cues as guidelines for monitoring and managing self-presentation and expressive behavior (Snyder 1974). The self-monitoring scale has generated a substantial body of research that continues to develop. The research includes a number of evaluations of the scale that include both supportive and critical evaluations. The scale has been used successfully in a number of consumer behavior studies (e.g., Becherer and Richard 1978) and has implications for salesperson behavior as well.

Description: The scale consists of twenty-five true-false items. Negatively worded items are reversed scored such that higher scores reflect higher self-monitoring. Labels for each item or situation were: True or Mostly True; and, False or Not Usually True. Five factors were assumed to underlie the original development of items: a) concern with the social appropriateness of one's self-presentation; b) attention to social comparison information as cues to appropriate self-expression; c) the ability to control and modify one's self-presentation and expressive behavior; d) the use of this ability in particular situations; and e) the extent to which the person's self-presentation is cross-situationally consistent or variable (Snyder 1974, p. 529). Items are scored 0 or 1 and summed such that scores range from 0 to 25.

Development: A beginning set of forty-one true-false items was first administered to 192 Stanford undergraduates. This set included items designed to reflect the above five factors. Items in the final scale were selected based upon their contribution to internal consistency and their ability to discriminate between low and high scorers on the original set.

Sample(s): Student samples of 192 and 146 from Stanford and Minnesota were used in the initial development of the scale. Subsamples of actors (n = 24) and psychiatric patients (n = 31) were also used in validity testing.

Validity: The KR-20 and test-retest estimates of reliability were 0.70 and 0.83, respectively. The KR-20 estimate reliability for a separate sample of 146 undergraduates was 0.63. Evidence of discriminant validity was provided by a -0.19 (p <. 05) correlation with the Marlowe-Crowne Social Desirability Scale. Modest correlations with measures of Machiavellianism (r=-0.09) and inner-other directedness (r=-0.19), among others, were also cited as evidence of discriminant validity.

A series of other studies was conducted to validate the measure. First, 16 fraternity members participated in a peer rating study of other fraternity members which found the SM measure to be related to external peer ratings of self-monitoring (r=0.45, p<.05). Second, differences in mean scores were obtained between a sample of actors, the Stanford student sample, and a sample of psychiatric patients. Third, in a study of taped expressions, high self-monitors were better able than low self-monitors to express arbitrary emotional states in facial and vocal behavior. And, in a study in which subjects were allowed to look or not to look at social comparison information (i.e., normative social comparison information) prior to an anticipated task, high self-monitors were more likely than low self-monitors to seek out social comparison information.

Scores: The mean scores for the actor and psychiatric patient samples were 18.41 and 10.19, respectively. These means were also said to be significantly above and below the Stanford student sample.

Source: Snyder, Mark (1974), "Self-Monitoring of Expressive Behavior," *Journal of Personality and Social Psychology*, 30 (4), 526-537.

Other evidence: Snyder and Gangestad (1986) also offer an eighteen-item reduced version of Snyder's (1974) original scale. This version exhibited alpha estimates in excess of .70, and the first unrotated factor accounted for 62% of the scale variance.

As noted above, the research stimulated by Snyder's (1974) self-monitoring concept, measure, and related work has been extensive. For an excellent review of this work see Snyder and Gangestad (1986). For consumer behavior purposes, only the manuscript by Becherer and Richard (1978), which reproduces the original scale in their *JCR* article, is referenced here. In that research, self-monitoring was shown to moderate the effects on consumer decisions. Specifically, as expected from the theory underlying the self-monitoring construct, situational factors (as opposed to personal dispositions or personality traits) were suggested as being most related to consumption for high self-monitors. In addition, the data indicated that, among the low self-monitoring group, the relationship between a series of personality measures (e.g., tolerance) and private brand proneness was significant for both social and nonsocial products.

Other sources: Becherer, Richard C. and Lawrence M. Richard (1978), "Self-Monitoring as a Moderating Variable in Consumer Behavior," *Journal of Consumer Research*, 5 (December), 159-162.

Snyder, Mark and Steve Gangestad (1986), "On the Nature of Self-Monitoring: Matters of Assessment, Matters of Validity," *Journal of Personality and Social Psychology*, 51, 125-139.

References: N/A.

SELF-MONITORING SCALE
(Snyder 1974)

1. I find it hard to imitate the behavior of other people.
2. My behavior is usually an expression of my true inner feelings, attitudes, and beliefs.
3. At parties and social gatherings, I do not attempt to do or say things that others will like.
4. I only argue for ideas which I already believe.
5. I can make impromptu speeches on topics about which I have almost no information.
6. I guess I put on a show to impress or entertain people.
7. When I am uncertain how to act in a social situation, I look to the behavior of others for cues.
8. I would probably make a good actor.
9. I rarely need the advice of my friends to choose books, movies, or music.
10. I sometimes appear to others to be experiencing deeper emotions than I am.
11. I laugh more when I watch a comedy with others than I do when I watch alone.
12. In a group of people, I am rarely the center of attention.
13. In different situations with different people, I often act like very different people.
14. I am not particularly good at making other people like me.
15. Even if I am not enjoying myself, I often pretend to be having a good time.
16. I am not always the person I appear to be.
17. I would not change my opinions (or the way I do things) in order to please someone else or to win their favor.

18. I have considered being an entertainer.

19. In order to get along and be liked, I tend to be what people expect me to be rather than anything else.

20. I have never been good at games like charades or improvisational acting.

21. I have trouble changing my behavior to suit different people and different situations.

22. At a party I let others keep the jokes and stories going.

23. I feel a bit awkward in company and do not show up quite so well as I should.

24. I can look anyone in the eye and tell a lie with a straight face (if for a right end).

25. I may deceive people by being friendly when I really dislike them.

NOTES: A "TRUE" response for items 5 through 8, 10, 11, 13, 15, 16, 18, 19, 24, and 25 reflects high self-monitoring. A "FALSE" response for items 1 through 4, 9, 12, 14, 17, and 20 through 23 also reflects high self-monitoring.

Items 1, 3, 4, 5, 6, 8, 12, 13, 14, 16, 17, 18, and 20 through 25 represent Snyder and Gangestad's 18-item version.

REVISED SELF-MONITORING SCALE
(Lennox and Wolfe 1984)

Construct: Lennox and Wolfe (1984) restrict the concept of self-monitoring to the ability to modify self-presentation and sensitivity to the expressive behavior of others. This more narrow definition of the construct is felt to be more reflective of the forte of the high self-monitor (Lennox and Wolfe 1984).

Description: The Lennox and Wolfe version of the scale is composed of 13 items each scored on six-point scales. Subjects are asked to indicate the degree to which each item is reflective of their own behavior: "0" = certainly, always false; "1" = generally false; "2" = somewhat false, but with exception; "3" = somewhat true, but with exception; "4" = generally true; "5" = certainly, always true. Seven items represent ability to modify self-presentation, and six items represent sensitivity to the expressive behavior of others. Item scores can be summed within these two factors to form factor indices, or overall to form an overall measure of self-monitoring (Lennox and Wolfe 1984).

Development: Over four studies, Lennox and Wolfe administered and factor analyzed Snyder's original scale and items they generated to measure the construct. In Study One, they factor analyzed the original scale and found that several items did not load as hypothesized. In Study Two, they retained 19 of Snyder's original items, added 28 of their own and factor analyzed them using the previously described six-point scoring system. From these 28 items, a four-factor structure was retained. Studies Three and Four further analyzed the scale and resulted in the final two-factor scale to measure self-monitoring. Coefficient alpha and a number of validity checks were performed on the final scale.

Sample(s): The four samples used for the four studies were all composed of student subjects. Sample sizes were 179, 128, 224, and 201 for the four studies, respectively.

Validity: The final scale had a coefficient alpha of .75 for the total scale (all 13 items), .77 for the seven-item ability to modify self presentation factor, and .70 for the six-item sensitivity to the expressive behavior of others (n = 201). Correlations with related constructs revealed evidence of construct validity. For example, the overall scale had a correlation of .30 with a measure of individuation, and .17 with private self-consciousness.

Scores: Mean scores for the total scale and subscales were not provided. Table 9 of Lennox and Wolfe (1984, p. 1361) provides item means and standard deviations.

Source: Lennox, Richard D. and Raymond N. Wolfe (1984), "Revision of the Self-Monitoring Scale," *Journal of Personality and Social Psychology*, 46, 1349-1364.

Other evidence: N/A.

Other sources: N/A.

References: Snyder, Mark (1974), "The Self-Monitoring of Expressive Behavior," *Journal of Personality and Social Psychology*, 30 (4), 526-537.

REVISED SELF-MONITORING SCALE
(Lennox and Wolfe 1984)

Ability to Modify Self-Presentation

1) In social situations, I have the ability to alter my behavior if I feel that something else is called for.

2) I have the ability to control the way I come across to people, depending on the impression I wish to give them.

3) When I feel that the image I am portraying isn't working, I can readily change it to something that does.

4) I have trouble changing my behavior to suit different people and different situations.*

5) I have found that I can adjust my behavior to meet the requirements of any situation I find myself in.

6) Even when it might be to my advantage, I have difficulty putting up a good front.*

7) Once I know what the situation calls for, it's easy for me to regulate my actions accordingly.

Sensitivity to the Expressive Behaviors of Others

1) I am often able to read people's true emotions correctly through their eyes.

2) In conversations, I am sensitive to even the slightest change in the facial expression of the person I'm conversing with.

3) My powers of intuition are quite good when it comes to understanding others' emotions and motives.

4) I can usually tell when others consider a joke to be in bad taste, even though they may laugh convincingly.

5) I can usually tell when I've said something inappropriate by reading it in the listener's eyes.

6) If someone is lying to me, I usually know it at once from that person's manner of expression.

NOTES: * denotes items that require reverse coding.

INNOVATIVENESS

INNOVATIVENESS: OPENNESS OF INFORMATION PROCESSING
(Leavitt and Walton 1975, 1988)

Construct: Innovativeness is assumed to be a personality trait underlying the adoption of innovations. The construct, as involved in the research on which the following measures are based, has lately been redefined to be termed "openness of information processing" (Leavitt and Walton 1975, 1988). Innovators are described as individuals open to new experiences and novel stimuli, as possessing the ability to transform information about new concepts, ideas, products or services for their own use, and as having a low threshold for recognizing the potential application of new ideas. (NOTE: This scale is still under refinement and interested users are encouraged to contact the authors for additional details regarding these measures. Only the information provided in the most recent faculty working paper is summarized here.)

Description: The 1975 version of the measure(s) consisted of two forms each containing 30 items (24 scale items with 6 filler items). Each statement is evaluated in terms of "how well it fits the respondent's own views." The five place scales associated with each statement are labeled as follows: 1, "not well at all"; 2, "not very well"; 3, "fairly well"; 4, "very well"; and 5, "extremely well". In its original form, item scores are summed to form an overall index. Both positively and negatively worded statements along with several social desirability filler items can be included in each form. (The filler items are discarded in computation of overall scores. Only a few of the items refer directly to the purchase of products and services.)

Development: An initial pool of 144 items was developed from the original definition by a group of three "experts" (Leavitt and Walton 1975, p. 549). Twenty-nine positive items were selected from this group based upon item-to-total correlations and consideration of social desirability bias. Next, the 29 items were included in a second study with 33 negative items and a series of psychological scales. Again, two parallel forms were developed using both positive and negative statements and a series of item-to-total correlations.

Sample(s): The initial set of items was administered to a sample of 300 undergraduate women. The exact nature of the sample was not provided. A second sample involved the responses from 299 women.

Validity: Estimates of internal consistency reliability were 0.74 and 0.72 for forms A and B, respectively. The correlation between the two forms was 0.72. Correlations between the two forms and an index of innovation were 0.35 and 0.38. Differences in means scores between users and nonusers of a new food service provided some evidence of known group validity. The results of a factor analysis for both males and females provided some evidence for the validity of the expected loadings.

Scores: Based on one of the original samples using intercept interviews, the mean scores for noninnovators and innovators were 76.5 and 84.1, respectively. Mean scores for Form A for 796 users of a new service and 266 nonusers of a service who were aware of the service were 84.3 and 79.1 (Leavitt and Walton 1988).

Source: Leavitt, Clark and John Walton (1975), "Development of a Scale for Innovativeness," in *Advances in Consumer Research*, Vol. 2, Mary Jane Schlinger (ed.), Ann Arbor, MI: Association for Consumer Research, 545-554.

Leavitt, Clark and John R. Walton (1988), "Openness of Information Processing as a Moderator of Message Effects on Behavior," *Faculty Working Paper*, College of Business of Administration, Ohio State University.

Other evidence: Goldsmith (1984) reported an internal consistency reliability estimate of 0.78 for Form B of the scale. Evidence of the nomological validity of the scale was provided by significant correlations with dogmatism (r=-.38), empathy (r=.62) and self-esteem (r=.69) (Goldsmith 1984, p. 63). However, nonsignificant results were obtained for social character and cosmopolitanism.

Craig and Ginter (1975) factor analyzed Leavitt and Walton's (1975) version and found seven factors: new is wasteful, social desirability, novelty seeking, risk aversion, style consciousness, satisfaction with status quo, and other directedness (see the following pages). Three of these factors were found to discriminate between innovative and non-innovative samples.

Other sources:	Craig, C. Samuel and James L. Ginter (1975), "An Empirical Test of a Scale for Innovativeness," in *Advances in Consumer Research*, Vol. 2, Mary Jane Schlinger (ed.), Ann Arbor, MI: The Association for Consumer Research, 555-562.
	Goldsmith, Ronald E. (1984), "Some Personality Correlates of Open Processing," *Journal of Psychology*, 116, 59-66.
References:	N/A.

INNOVATIVENESS: OPENNESS OF INFORMATION PROCESSING
(Leavitt and Walton 1975, 1988)

Form A

1. I like to take a chance.
2. I don't like to talk to strangers.
3. The unusual gift is often a waste of money.
4. I enjoy looking at new styles as soon as they come out.
5. Buying a new product that has not yet been proven is usually a waste of time and money.
6. Often the most interesting and stimulating people are those who don't mind being original and different.
7. I would like a job that requires frequent changes from one kind of task to another.
8. If people would quit wasting their time experimenting, we would get more accomplished.
9. If I got an idea, I would give a lot of weight to what others think of it.
10. I like to try new and different things.
11. In hunting for the best way to do something, it is usually a good idea to try the obvious way first.
12. I like to wait until something has been proven before I try it.
13. When it comes to taking chances, I would rather be safe than sorry.
14. I like people who are a little shocking.
15. When I see a new brand on the shelf, I often buy it just to see what it is like.
16. I feel that too much money is wasted on new styles.
17. I often try new brands before my friends and neighbors do.
18. I enjoy being with people who think like I do.
19. At work, I think everyone should work on only one thing, thereby becoming more of an expert.
20. I like to experiment with new ways of doing things.
21. In the long run, the usual ways of doing things are the best.
22. Some modern art is stimulating.

23. I like to fool around with new ideas even if they turn out later to be a total waste of time.

24. Today is a good day to start a new project.

Form B

1. I like to experiment.

2. I like to try new products to see what they are like.

3. The changing styles, especially in clothes, are a waste of money.

4. I like a great deal of variety.

5. I don't like to take chances if I don't have to.

6. Sometimes original and different people make me uneasy.

7. Unless there is good reason for changing, I think we should continue doing things the way they are being done now.

8. I start up conversations with strangers.

9. I feel that the tried and true ways of doing things are the best at work and in my life.

10. I like to spend money on unusual gifts and toys.

11. New products are usually gimmicks.

12. I generally like to try new ideas at work and in my life.

13. I like to see what my friends and neighbors think of a product before I try it.

14. I like new styles in clothes, especially those that are reallydifferent.

15. I dread having to start another new project.

16. I take chances more than others do.

17. I can enjoy being with people whose values are very different from mine.

18. People who are shocking are usually trying to impress someone.

19. In hunting for the best way of doing something, it is usually a good idea to look at the situation from a completely different angle—one that wouldn't occur to someone.

20. I would like a job that doesn't require me to keep learning new tasks.

21. I like to look at strange pictures.

22. When I see a new brand on the shelf, I usually pass right by.

23. I would not risk my position at work by putting into effect some new idea that might not work.

24. I'm the kind of person who is always looking for an exciting, stimulating, active life.

NOTES: Though not specified by the original authors, items requiring reverse coding apparently are items 2, 3, 5, 8, 9, 11, 12, 13, 16, 18, 19, and 21 of Form A, and items 3, 5, 6, 7, 9, 11, 13, 15, 18, 20, 22, and 23 of Form B. Recoding these items would reflect a higher level of innovativeness. Also, the "filler" items are not included in the above scales.

INNOVATIVENESS FACTORS
(Craig and Ginter 1975)

FACTOR ANALYSIS OF THE LEAVITT AND WALTON ITEMS BY CRAIG AND GINTER (1975)

Factor 1 (New is Wasteful)

1. The unusual gift is often a waste of money.
2. Some modern art is stimulating.
3. I would rather not waste my time with some new idea.
4. Buying a new product that has not yet been proven is usually a waste of time and money.
5. I would like a job that doesn't require me to keep learning new tasks.
6. The changing styles, especially in clothes, are a waste of money.

Factor 2 (Social Desirability)

1. I am always courteous even to people who are disagreeable.
2. I have never been irked when people express ideas very different from my own.
3. No matter who I am talking to, I am always a good listener.
4. I am always willing to admit when I make a mistake.
5. I have never felt that I was punished without cause.

Factor 3 (Novelty Seeking)

1. I like to experiment with new ways of doing things.
2. I like to fool around with new ideas even if they turn out to be a waste of time.
3. I like to try new and different things.
4. When I see a new brand on the shelf, I often buy it just to see what it's like.

Factor 4 (Risk Aversion)

1. I like to take a chance.
2. When it comes to taking chances, I'd rather be safe than sorry.
3. I like people who are a little shocking.

Factor 5 (Style Consciousness)

1. I enjoy looking at new styles as soon as they come out.
2. The changing styles, especially in clothes, are a waste of money.

Factor 6 (Satisfaction with Status Quo)

1. I believe in leaving well enough alone.
2. If people would quit wasting their time experimenting, we would get more accomplished.
3. When I see a brand on the shelf, I often buy it just to see what it's like.

Factor 7 (Other Directedness)

1. If I got an idea, I would give a lot of thought to what others think.
2. I like to see what my friends and neighbors think of a product before I try it.

NOTES: Many of these items are not part of the scale published by Leavitt and Walton. Apparently, several of these items (particularly the social desirability items) come from an earlier version (possibly item generation stage) of their scale. In the Craig and Ginter paper, item 2 of the "new is wasteful" factor loaded negatively, items 1 and 3 of the "risk aversion" factor loaded negatively on that factor, and item 2 of the "style consciousness" loaded negatively on that factor (Craig and Ginter 1975, p. 557-558).

USE INNOVATIVENESS
(Price and Ridgeway 1983)

Construct: Use innovativeness (or variety seeking in product use) involves the use of previously adopted products in novel ways (Price and Ridgeway 1983, p. 679). The concept was initially introduced by Hirschman (1980). As conceptualized by Price and Ridgeway, use innovativeness encompasses five factors: creativity/curiosity, risk preferences, voluntary simplicity, creative reuse, and multiple use potential.

Description: The scale consists of 44 items designed to reflect the five factors. Each item was operationalized using a seven-place, Likert-type format. The factor labels and corresponding number of items are as follows: 1) creativity/curiosity, 13; 2) risk preferences, 9; 3) voluntary simplicity, 5; 4) creative reuse, 10; 5) multiple use potential, 7. Item scores can be summed within factors for factor indices and can be summed overall for an overall use innovativeness measure.

Development: An initial set of 70 items was generated to reflect the five factors assumed to underlie use innovativeness. This set also included five voluntary simplicity items from Leonard-Barton (1981). The set of 70 items was reduced to 60 "based on the judgment of several experts." These 60 items were administered to 358 student subjects along with six questions about calculator usage. The final 44 items were selected using the following criteria: high loadings on the anticipated factor; high item-to-total correlations for each subscale or factor; and high item-to-total correlations for the combined scale. These analyses resulted in four items being reassigned to another factor and 16 items (predominantly risk-taking and multiple use measures) being eliminated.

Sample(s): The developmental and validation analyses were performed on a sample of 358 undergraduate student subjects.

Validity: Factor analysis was performed to verify the structure of the scale. A four-factor solution was said to be superior; however, five factors are reported. The inclusion of the five items as a voluntary simplicity factor may have accounted for the inconsistency between the reported results and the final scale depicted in Table 1 (Price and Ridgeway 1983, pp. 681-682). Estimates of internal consistency for the subscales were .86 for creativity/curiosity; .70 for risk preferences; .64 for voluntary simplicity; .82 for creative re-use; and .56 for multiple-use potential. Intercorrelations among the factors range from 0.14 to 0.65. Using scores for the total scale, the sample was partitioned into upper, middle and lower thirds. Analysis of variance tests of mean differences across groups revealed that the calculator usage scores behaved in a predictable pattern. That is, subjects scoring higher on the scale exhibited greater variety in their use of calculators.

Scores: The mean use innovativeness score for the entire scale summed as a whole was 199, varying from a low of 112 to a high of 299 (Price and Ridgeway 1983, p. 681).

Source: Price, Linda L. and Nancy M. Ridgeway (1983), "Development of a Scale to Measure Use Innovativeness," in *Advances in Consumer Research*, Vol. 10, Richard P. Bagozzi and Alice M. Tybout, (eds.), Ann Arbor, MI: Association for Consumer Research, 679-684.

Other evidence: N/A.

Other sources: N/A.

References: Hirschman, Elizabeth C. (1980), "Innovativeness, Novelty Seeking, and Consumer Creativity," *Journal of Consumer Research*, 7 (December), 283-295.

Leonard-Barton, Dorothy (1981), "Voluntary Simplicity Lifestyles and Energy Conservation," *Journal of Consumer Research*, 8 (June), 243-252.

USE INNOVATIVENESS
(Price and Ridgeway 1983)

Creativity/Curiosity

1. Knowing how a product works offers almost as much pleasure as knowing that the product works well.
2. I am very creative when using products.
3. I am less interested in the appearance of an item than in what makes it tick.
4. As a child, I really enjoyed taking things apart and putting them back together again.
5. As long as a product works well, I don't really care how it works.
6. Curiosity is one of the permanent and certain characteristics of a vigorous intellect.
7. I am very curious about how things work.
8. I like to build things for my home.
9. If I can't figure out how something works, I would rather tinker with it than ask for help.
10. I never take anything apart because I know I'll never be able to put it back together again.
11. I like to fix things around the house.
12. I have gotten instruction in self-reliance skills (e.g.,carpentry, car tune-up, etc.).
13. I would rather fix something myself than take it to someone to fix.

Risk Preferences

1. When I try to do projects on my own, I'm afraid I will make a worse mess of them than if I had just left them alone.
2. I always follow manufacturer's warnings against removing the backplates on products.
3. When I try to do projects on my own, without exact directions, they usually work out really well.
4. I find very little instruction is needed to use a product similar to one I'm already familiar with.
5. I'm afraid to buy a product I don't know how to use.
6. I'm uncomfortable working on projects different from types I'm accustomed to.
7. I always follow manufacturer's warnings regarding how to use a product.
8. If a product comes in an assembled and an unassembled form, I always buy the assembled form, even though it costs a little more.
9. I like to improvise when I cook.

Voluntary Simplicity

1. I like to make clothing or furniture for myself and my family.
2. I often buy clothing at second hand stores.
3. I often make gifts instead of buying them.
4. When building something, it is better to use things already around the house than to buy materials.
5. I often buy items such as furniture at garage sales.

Creative Reuse

1. I save broken appliances because I might fix them someday.
2. I save broken appliances because I might be able to use the parts from them.

3. I enjoy thinking of new ways to use old things around the house.

4. I find myself saving packaging on products to use in other ways (e.g., egg cartons, L'eggs eggs, plastic shopping bags, etc.).

5. When I build something, I can often make do with things I've already got around the house.

6. Even if I don't have the right tool for the job, I can usually improvise.

7. I never throw something away that I might use later.

8. I take great pleasure in adapting products to new uses that the manufacturer never intended.

9. In general, I would rather alter an old product to work in a new situation than purchase a new product specifically for that purpose.

10. After the useful life of a product, I can often think of ways to use the parts of it for other purposes.

Multiple Use Potential

1. I do not enjoy a product unless I can use it to its fullest capacity.

2. I use products in more ways than most people.

3. I often buy a food item for a particular recipe but end up using it for something else.

4. A product's value is directly related to the ways that it can be used.

5. It's always impossible to improve upon a project by adding new features.

6. After purchase of a product such as a stereo or camera, I try to keep track of new accessories that come out into the market.

7. I enjoy expanding and adding onto projects that I'm involved in on a continuing basis.

NOTES: Though not explicitly stated by the authors, it would seem that items 5 and 10 of the "creativity/curiosity" would require recoding to reflect a higher level of this factor. It would also seem that items 3, 4, and 9 of the "risk preference" require recoding to reflect a risk aversion preference, and item 5 of the multiple use potential requires recoding to reflect a higher level of multiple use potential.

COGNITIVE AND SENSORY INNOVATIVENESS
(Venkatraman and Price 1990)

Construct: Cognitive (sensory) innovativeness is the preference for engaging in new experiences with the objective of stimulating the mind (senses). Venkatraman and Price (1990) assume that consumer innovativeness is not an undifferentiated construct and that cognitive and sensory innovativeness are differentiated by unique demographic and personality profiles and are related differently to adoption behaviors. Cognitive innovators enjoy thinking for its own sake and have a propensity to devote a great deal of mental energy to solve problems they encounter. Sensory innovators enjoy fantasy and daydreaming and adventurous activities such as sky diving.

Description: The final form of the measure(s) includes eight items for both the cognitive and sensory innovativeness scales. Each scale also includes four internal and four external items. The scores are computed by averaging the scores across the internal and external items within each scale.

Development: The scales included here represent refinement of the 80 item Novelty Experiencing Scale (NES) (Pearson 1970). Details regarding the specifics of item deletion and selection were not presented. The developmental procedures included tests of alternative factor structures (for the final sets of two eight-item scales) using confirmatory factor analysis. (In the second validity study involving nonstudent subjects, a higher-order factor model provided the best fit to the data.) Prior to these LISREL analyses, item correlations with measures of sensation seeking cognition seeking were apparently used to select items for the final scale versions (Venkatraman and Price 1991). Several other estimates of reliability and validity were gathered.

Sample(s): The NES items were first examined using a sample of 200 undergraduate students. Three hundred and twenty-six undergraduate students participated in the first validation study. Two hundred and forty respondents to a mail survey (from an initial sample of 450) participated in the product innovation and demographic characteristic validation study. Fifty-nine percent of this sample were male; the average age was 37.2 years. The average income was $41,440.

Validity: Coefficient alpha estimates of reliability (based upon the initial sample of 200) were 0.73 and 0.69 for the cognitive and sensory scales, respectively.

Two follow-up studies were conducted to evaluate the validity of the measures. In the first study (n=326), the two scales were correlated with a series of related measures. Evidence for support of the hypothesized relationships was found. For example, a significant positive correlation (r=0.26, p<.01) was found between the cognitive innovativeness measure and need for cognition (Cacioppo and Petty 1982). Other correlations in support of the measures include: r=0.41 (p<.01) between sensory innovativeness and arousal-seeking tendency (Mehrabian and Russell 1974); and, r=0.22, (p<.01) between a measure of impulsivity and sensory innovativeness.

A second validity study (n=245) was conducted to demonstrate that cognitive and sensory innovators differ in their responses to innovations and demographically. The alpha coefficients of reliability for this study were 0.64 and 0.70 for the cognitive and sensory scales, respectively. Hypothesized differences with product purchase behavior across products selected to vary in hedonic value were not found. However, partial support for the demographic predictions were observed: men scored higher on sensory innovativeness; younger respondents scored higher on sensory innovativeness; and, higher education was associated with higher cognitive scores.

Scores: Some scale mean scores were presented in Table 6 across demographic groups (Venkatraman and Price 1991, p. 309).

Source: Venkatraman, Meera P. and Linda L. Price (1990), "Differentiating Between Cognitive and Sensory Innovativeness: Concepts, Measurement, and Implications," *Journal of Business Research*, 20, 293-315.

Other evidence: N/A.

Other sources: N/A.

References: Pearson, Pamela H. (1970), "Relationships Between Global and Specific Measures of Novelty Seeking," *Journal of Consulting and Clinical Psychology*, 34, 199-204.

Cacioppo, John T. and Richard E. Petty (1982), "The Need for Cognition," *Journal of Personality and Social Psychology*, 42, 116-131.

Mehrabian, Albert and James A. Russell (1974), *An Approach to Environmental Psychology*, Cambridge, MA: The MIT press.

COGNITIVE AND SENSORY INNOVATIVENESS
(Venkatraman and Price 1990)

Cognitive Innovativeness

1. Finding out the meaning of words I don't know.

2. Trying to figure out the meaning of unusual statements.

3. Thinking about different ways to explain the same thing.

4. Figuring out the shortest distance from one city to another.

5. Analyzing my own feelings and reactions.

6. Discussing unusual ideas.

7. Thinking about why the world is in the shape it is in.

8. Figuring out how many bricks it would take to build a fireplace.

Sensory Innovativeness

1. Being on a raft in the middle of the Colorado River.

2. Having a vivid dream with strange colors and sounds.

3. Riding the rapids in a swift moving stream.

4. Having a strange new feeling as I awake in the morning.

5. Steering a sled down a steep hill covered with trees.

6. Dreaming that I was lying on the beach with the waves running all over me.

7. Walking across a swinging bridge over a deep canyon.

8. Having vivid and unusual daydreams as I was riding along.

NOTES: Reprinted by permission of the publisher from Venkatraman, Meera P. and Linda L. Price (1990), "Differentiating Between Cognitive and Sensory Innovativeness: Concepts, Measurement, and Implications," *Journal of Business Research*, 20, 293-315. Copyright 1992 by Elsevier Science Publishing Co., Inc.

DOMAIN SPECIFIC INNOVATIVENESS: DSI
(Goldsmith and Hofacker 1991)

Construct: Domain or product category specific innovativeness reflects the tendency to learn about and adopt innovations (new products) within a specific domain of interest (Goldsmith and Hofacker 1991, p. 211). This definition is consistent with the contention that innovativeness must be identified and characterized on a product category or domain basis (Gatignon and Robertson 1985).

Description: The DSI is a six-item scale where the items are scored on 5-point disagree-agree formats. Item scores are summed to form an overall DSI score, and the DSI is considered unidimensional. There are two versions of the DSI. Each version has three positively worded items and three negatively worded items. Therefore, versions can be used interchangeably, and are considered applicable to a wide number of product domains.

Development: Six studies were used in the development and validation of the DSI. In Study One, an initial pool of 11 items was generated based on the construct's definition and a literature review. (Rock music records/tapes was used as the product of interest.) After pretesting the items on a small sample, a larger sample responded to the items. Via item analysis, coefficient alpha, and preliminary criterion validity checks, the final 6 items representing the two versions of the DSI were derived. Study Two further examined the reliability, validity, and factor structure of the two versions of the DSI (again with rock music as the domain). Studies Three and Four used fashion and household entertainment equipment as domains and again looked at the scales' psychometric properties. Study Five examined the scale's test- retest reliability, predictive validity, and possible confounds (again with rock music). Lastly, Study Six assessed convergent and discriminant validity using cologne, perfume, and aftershave as the product categories.

Samples: The samples from each of the above six studies were composed of the following: The pretest sample of Study One was 27 students and the large sample of Study One was composed of 309 students. Study Two was composed of 274 students, and Study Three used 97 female students. Four-hundred and sixty two nonstudent adults were used in Study Four. A sample of 70 students was used in Study Five, and a sample of 306 (students and nonstudents) was used in Study Six.

Validity: In Study One, the correlations of the six items with four measures of criterion validity ranged from .26 to .40 across items. Coefficient alpha for Study Two was .86, and confirmatory factor analysis (via LISREL) supported the scales' unidimensionality. Correlations of the DSI with seven criterion validity measures ranged from .07 to .78. In Study Three, alpha for the scale was .82, and the positive and negative halves of the scale had a correlation of -.71. Unidimensionality again was confirmed and the correlations between the DSI and seven criterion measures ranged from .11 to .80. Study Four reported an alpha of .81, a unidimensional factor structure and predictive validity correlations of .41 and .46. Test-retest reliability in in Study Five was .86 (over 15 weeks), and the internal consistency, dimensionality, and predictive validity of the scale was supported. Also, the scale exhibited low correlations with a measure of social desirability bias (i.e., -.13 to .12). Lastly, MTMM analysis supported the convergent and discriminant validity of the DSI, and alpha was reported to be .85, .83, and .83 across three different product categories.

Scores: Mean scores were reported for several of the studies. In Study Two, the overall mean was 15.8 (sd = 5.20). In Study Three, the mean score was 19.4 (sd = 4.64). In Study Four, means of 16.5 (sd = 4.80) and 17.3 (sd = 4.80) were reported for two product categories.

Source: Goldsmith, Ronald E. and Charles Hofacker (1991), "Measuring Consumer Innovativeness," *Journal of the Academy of Marketing Science*, 19 (Summer), 209-221.

Other evidence: N/A.

Other sources: N/A.

References: Gatignon, Hubert, and Thomas R. Robertson (1985), "A Propositional Inventory for New Diffusion Research," *Journal of Consumer Research*, 11 (March), 849-867.

DOMAIN SPECIFIC INNOVATIVENESS: DSI
(Goldsmith and Hofacker 1991)

1) In general, I am among the first (last) in my circle of friends to buy a new _____ when it appears.

2) If I heard that a new _____ was available in the store, I would (not) be interested enough to buy it.

3) Compared to my friends I own a few of (a lot of) _____ .

4) In general, I am the last (first) in my circle of friends to know the titles/brands of the latest _____ .

5) I will not buy a new _____ if I haven't heard/tried it yet. (I will buy a new _____ if I haven't heard/tried it yet.)

6) I (do not) like to buy _____ before other people do.

NOTES: Items 1, 3, and 4 comprise the negative items in Version 1, and items 2, 5, and 6 comprise the positive items in Version 1. Conversely, Items 1, 3, and 4 comprise the positive items in Version 2, and items 2, 5, and 6 comprise the negative items in Version 2. Words/sentences in parentheses denote the positive and negative wording for individual items.

DISCONTENT, ALIENATION, ASSERTIVENESS, AND AGGRESSIVENESS

CONSUMER DISCONTENT SCALE
(Lundstrom and Lamont 1976)

Construct: The scale is designed to measure consumers' attitudes toward marketing and marketing-related practices of the business system. Consumer discontent is defined to include the collection of attitudes held by consumers toward: (1) the product strategies of business; (2) business communications and information; (3) the impersonal nature of business and retail institutions; (4) and the broader socioeconomic forces which are linked with the business system (Lundstrom and Lamont 1976, p.374).

Description: The final scale consists of 82 statements operationalized using six-point scales from "strongly agree," "agree," "agree a little," "disagree a little," "disagree" to "strongly disagree." Individual scores for each statement are summed to form an aggregate measure. Twenty-five of the items are worded as "pro-business." The range of the scale is from 82 to 492.

Development: A beginning pool of 173 items was generated from the literature underlying the four aspects of the construct definition (i.e., product strategies of business, business communications and information, the impersonal nature of business and retail institutions, and socioeconomic and political forces). This initial pool was edited to eliminate ambiguous and redundant items. Ten judges then evaluated the remaining 118 items in an effort to classify the items as either pro- or anti-business. This process eliminated an additional 19 items.

The remaining 99 items were administered to a sample of 309 Denver, Colorado residents. The set of 99 items was reduced to 84 by deleting those items that did differ significantly ($p<0.10$) between the high and low quartiles determined by the total scores to the preliminary set of 99 items. A student sample of 226 students was used to evaluate the reliability of the remaining 84 items and test-retest reliability.

Two additional items were deleted from the scale based on item-to-total correlations using the responses to 280 subjects comprising a third sample. In addition, this sample was split into two groups hypothesized to differ in discontent (i.e., a discontented group and a contented group).

Sample(s): Four samples were used in various stages of the development. Initial item analysis was conducted on a sample of 309 Denver residents (from an initial sample of 600). A convenience sample of 226 university students was used in a series of reliability tests. From this group, 154 participated in a test-retest administration. A contented group of 100 business members of Rotary and Kiwanis clubs and a discontented group of 180 consumers were involved in the known group test validation. The latter group was selected from members of the Arizona Consumers Council and complainers to the Denver Better Business Bureau.

Validity: The split-half reliability coefficient for the 84 item version was 0.94 (corrected for scale length). The results of a six week test-retest (n=154) revealed a coefficient of reliability of .79. In addition, correlations with measures of agreement response tendency and social desirability bias were not significant. For example, the Spearman rank order correlation between a measure of social desirability bias and the combined scale was -0.03.

As described above, cited evidence of validity was provided by the face validity of the items, the multiple estimates of reliability, and the known group analyses (cf. Lundstrom and Lamont 1976).

Scores: The mean for a contented group (n = 100) was 247; the mean for a discontented group (n = 180) was 354 (z = 28.2, p < .01).

Source: Lundstrom, William J. and Lawrence M. Lamont (1976), "The Development of a Scale to Measure Consumer Discontent," *Journal of Marketing Research*, 13 (November), 373-381.

Other evidence:	N/A.
Other sources:	N/A.
References:	N/A.

CONSUMER DISCONTENT SCALE
(Lundstrom and Lamont 1976)

This is a survey to find out what the consumer thinks about business. Below are some statements regarding consumer issues. Please give your own opinion about these statements, i.e., whether you agree or disagree. A simple checkmark in the space provided is all that is necessary.

1. The business community has been a large influence in raising a country's standard of living. (P)

2. Business profits are too high. (A)

3. Styles change so rapidly a person can't afford to keep up. (A)

4. People who sell things over the telephone are always trying to jip you. (A)

5. Advertising is a good source of information. (P)

6. Credit makes things too easy to buy. (A)

7. Many times I need assistance in a store and I'm just not able to get it. (A)

8. Warranties would not be necessary if the manufacturer made the product right in the first place. (A)

9. Salesmen really take an interest in the consumer and make sure he finds what he wants. (P)

10. Products that last a long time are a thing of the past. (A)

11. Business takes a real interest in the environment and is trying to improve it. (P)

12. Food which is not nutritious is another example of business trying to make a buck and not caring about the consumer. (A)

13. People rate other people by the value of their possessions. (A)

14. Business firms usually stand behind their products and guarantees. (P)

15. When a product is advertised as "new" or "improved" it is the same old thing only in a different package. (A)

16. Industry has an obligation to clean up the waste they have been dumping but they aren't doing it. (A)

17. Chain stores are getting so big that they really don't treat the customer personally. (A)

18. Permanent price controls are the only way to end inflation. (A)

19. The quality of goods has consistently improved over the years. (P)

20. Many times the salesman says one thing to the shopper but he knows it's just the opposite. (A)

21. Many times it's easier to buy a new product rather than trying to fix the old one. (A)

22. The only person who cares about the consumer is the consumer himself. (A)

23. The actual product I buy is usually the same as advertised. (P)

24. It is hard to make a buying decision because of all the products to choose from. (A)

25. The small business has to do what big business says, or else! (A)

26. Most companies have a complaint department which backs up their products and handles consumer problems. (P)

27. Business is the one using up our natural resources (oil, gas, trees, etc) but it does nothing to replace what has been taken. (A)

28. Many companies listen to consumer complaints but they don't do anything about them. (A)

29. Generally speaking, products work as good as they look. (P)

30. Products fall apart before they have had much use. (A)

31. Products are only as safe as required by government standards, but no more. (A)

32. Stores advertise "special deals" just to get the shopper into the store to buy something else. (A)

33. Companies are helping minorities and the under privileged by providing them with jobs. (P)

34. The information on most packages is enough to make a good decision. (P)

35. Most salesman who call at home try to force the consumer into buying something. (A)

36. All business really wants to do is to make the most money it can. (A)

37. The business community is actively involved in solving social problems. (P)

38. Most people know that advertising lies a "little." (A)

39. Companies encourage the consumer to buy more than he really needs. (A)

40. The government should enforce ethical business practices. (A)

41. The consumer knows exactly what he is buying with food products because the ingredients are on the package. (P)

42. Companies aren't willing to listen or do anything about consumer gripes. (A)

43. Recycling of products is one way business is cleaning up the environment. (P)

44. Business does not help local residents because it's not profitable. (A)

45. When the consumer is unsure of how good a product is, he can get the correct information from the salesman. (P)

46. The consumer is usually the least important consideration to most companies. (A)

47. Salesman are "pushy" just so they can make a sale. (A)

48. If all advertising were stopped, the consumer would be better off. (A)

49. Sales clerks in stores just don't care about the consumer anymore. (A)

50. Most products are safe when they are used right. (P)

51. Advertised "specials" aren't usually in the store when the shopper goes there. (A)

52. Service departments "pad" the bill by charging for unneeded work. (A)

53. The price I pay is about the same as the quality I receive. (P)

54. Companies try to take a personal interest in each consumer rather than treating him as a number. (P).

55. As soon as they make the sale, most businesses forget about the buyer. (A)

56. Commercials make a person unhappy with himself because he can't have everything he sees. (A)

57. Health and safety warnings on packages are not adequate enough to inform the consumer of possible danger. (P)

58. Service manuals aren't provided for products because the company wants to make money servicing products as well as selling them. (A)

59. What is seen on the outside of a package is many times not what you get on the inside. (A)

60. There are too many of the same types of products which is a waste of money. (A)

61. In general, companies are honest in their dealings with the consumer. (P)

62. Prices of products are going up faster than the incomes of the ordinary consumer. (A)

63. Advertising tempts people to spend their money foolishly. (A)

64. Business profits are high yet they keep on raising their prices. (A)

65. Companies generally offer what the consumer wants. (P)

66. Business has commercialized many meaningful holidays, such as Christmas. (A)

67. The main reason a company does things for society is to make more sales. (A)

68. An attractive package many times influences a purchase that isn't necessary. (A)

69. A large variety of products allow the consumer to choose the one that he really wants. (P)

70. Self-service stores leave the consumer at the mercy of how the product looks. (A)

71. Companies "jazz up" a product with no real improvement, just to get a higher price or sell more. (A)

72. Most of the things I buy are overpriced. (A)

73. Prices are reasonable given the high cost of business. (P)

74. Promotional or "junk" mail is just a waste. (A)

75. Repairs take too long because the right part is not in stock. (A)

76. Advertising tells the shopper about things he would not ordinarily hear about. (P)

77. A warranty or guarantee may be a good one but the service department is often unable to do the work correctly. (A)

78. Repair work is usually done right the first time. (P)

79. Business takes advantage of poor people or minorities by charging higher than normal prices. (A)

80. The stock market is controlled by big financial institutions. (A)

81. Consumer activists, like Ralph Nader, do more harm than good to business. (P)

82. Companies try to influence the government just to better themselves. (A)

NOTES: Items are scored on a six point Likert-type scale from "strongly disagree" to "strongly agree." (P) indicates a pro-business statement, (A) an anti-business statement.

CONSUMER ALIENATION FROM THE MARKETPLACE
(Pruden, Shuptrine, and Longman 1974)

Construct: Pruden, Shuptrine, and Longman (1974) use Seeman's (1959) theoretical base to define their construct of consumer alienation from the marketplace. The concept encompasses five facets:

Powerlessness - the expectancy held by the individual that his own behavior cannot determine the occurrence of the outcomes of reinforcements that he seeks.

Meaninglessness - the individual is unclear as to what he ought to believe—when his minimal standards for clarity in decision-making have not been met.

Normlessness - situation in which social norms regulating behavior are no longer effective rules for individual behavior.

Social isolation - isolation or a sense of estrangement from society and its culture.

Self-estrangement - a person who experiences himself as an alien and can relate more easily to others than he can to himself.

Description: Pruden et al.'s (1974) alienation index is composed of ten 6-point Likert items (strongly agree to strongly disagree). Though the scale was designed to tap the five facets above, item scores are summed to form an overall index of alienation.

Development: Four items for each facet were initially generated based on facet definitions and existing literature. A pretest was then used to reduce this pool of 20 items to the final 10 item scale. Reliability and validity checks were then performed over two samples.

Sample(s): A sample of 140 (mostly housewives) and a sample of 35 students were used to examine reliability and validity.

Validity: For the sample of 35, the Spearman rank order correlation reliability coefficient was .79. For the sample of 140, the five facets of alienation showed levels of intercorrelations ranging from .14 to .45, and correlations of each facet to the total scale ranged from .16 to .55. No other evidence of validity was offered.

Score(s): Neither mean nor percentage scores were reported.

Source: Pruden, Henry, O., F. Kelly Shuptrine, and Douglas S. Longman (1974), "A Measure of Alienation from the Marketplace," *Journal of the Academy of Marketing Science*, 2, 610-619.

Other evidence: Shuptrine et al. (1977) found that business executive were less alienated than consumers. No other estimates (reliability and validity) were provided.

Other sources: Shuptrine, F. Kelly, Henry O. Pruden, and Douglas S. Longman (1977), "Alienation from the Marketplace," *Journal of the Academy of Marketing Science*, 5, 233-148.

References: Seeman, Melvin (1959), "On the Meaning of Alienation," *American Sociological Review*, 24 (December), 783-791.

CONSUMER ALIENATION FROM THE MARKETPLACE
(Pruden, Shuptrine, and Longman 1974)

1) There is little use in writing complaint letters to company officials because usually they won't do anything to satisfy and individual consumer.

2) There is little that people like myself can do to improve the quality of the products they sell.

3) Any satisfaction i get from trying new products vanishes a short time after they are purchased.

4) Sometimes, when I look at new products, I wonder if any of them are worth while.

5) Many people with fine homes, new cars and other nice things get them only by going over their heads in debt.

6) I sometimes buy products that I really shouldn't buy.

7) The whole idea of fashion and the creation of new styles is not for me.

8) I really like to own things that have well known brand names.

9) The products and services I buy and use (for example eating, dressing, entertaining, furnishing my house and so on) allow me to really be myself.

10) The way the world is, I have to buy things that other people expect me to rather than to satisfy myself.

NOTES: Items 1 and 2 represent the powerlessness facet; items 3 and 4 represent the meaninglessness facet; items 5 and 6 represent the normlessness facet; items 7 and 8 represent the social isolation facet; and items 9 and 10 represent the self-estrangement facet.

CONSUMER ALIENATION FROM THE MARKETPLACE
(Allison 1978)

Construct: Consumer alienation from the marketplace was defined as feelings of separation from the norms and values of the marketplace. Such a state was said to include a lack of acceptance of or identification with market institutions, practices, and outputs as well as feelings of separation from the self when one is involved in the consumption role. The marketplace was defined to include the entire spectrum of channels of distribution from the producer to the seller as well as any support services such as advertising or credit (Allison 1978, p. 570). Alienation from the marketplace was also conceptualized using consumer adapted definitions for the four sociological constructs of powerlessness, normlessness, social isolation, and self-estrangement. Powerlessness was defined as feelings held by consumers that they are unable to help determine market practices, an inability to control the market environment or events within the marketplace. Normlessness within the market system is represented by a distrust of business and market practices, often manifested in unclear standards for buyer behavior. Social isolation is characterized by feelings of estrangement from the practices and outputs of market systems, and feelings of self-estrangement arise from an inability to identify with behavior traditionally associated with the consumption role (Allison 1978).

Description: The scale consists of 35 statements, each operationalized using five-place Likert scale response formats ranging from "strongly agree" to "strongly disagree." Four of the items are positively worded and require reverse scoring. The range of the summed scores is from 35 to 165.

Development: The four sociological constructs of alienation were used to develop a set of 115 attitudinal statements. Approximately half the items were worded positively. This pool of items was reduced to 50 by a panel of 35 undergraduate student judges. These remaining items satisfied two criteria: (1) 75 percent or more of the judges agreed that the item would differentiate between alienated and nonalienated consumers; and (2) 60 percent attributed the item to the same alienation dimension. Several pretest interviews in neighborhoods varying in socioeconomic class were used to revise and clarify the wording of the remaining 50 items.

Factor analysis of the data (n=368) revealed that a four-factor solution was most meaningful; however, the factor loadings did not support the validity of the theoretical structure as anticipated (Allison 1978, p. 568). Subsequent coefficient alpha estimates were interpreted as support for a unidimensional scale. Consequently, the original theoretical definition was revised to the definition provided above (i.e., at the beginning of this summary). Additional item-to-total correlation and internal consistency estimates were used to reduce the number of items to the final set comprising the 35-item scale.

Sample(s): Personal interviews were conducted with 400 respondents selected as part of a stratified-by-area sampling procedure. Of these, 386 were usable (Allison 1978). These procedures provided a random sample that was representative of the local population (i.e., Austin, Texas) in terms of gender, age, income, and ethnic origin. The 50 items were, however, self-administered. A convenience sample of 123 graduate business students participated in the test-retest study.

Validity: The 3 week test-retest reliability correlation was 0.75 (p<.05). A series of correlation and mean difference tests were used to examine the validity of the scale. The correlation between the 35-item consumer alienation scale and a general measure of social alienation was 0.61 (p<.01). The correlation between the consumer alienation scale and a measure of belief in government intervention was 0.45 (p<.01). A series of mean difference tests across ethnic and income groups also supported the validity of the scale. Using the responses to the 386 survey respondents, lower income groups and minority segments were associated with higher average alienation scores as predicted.

Scores: An analysis of covariance test in which the effects of ethnic origin on alienation scores controlling for income resulted in the following adjusted mean scores across groups: white, 108.67; Black, 112.20; and Mexican-American, 116.84. Similar analyses across income groups controlling for ethnic origin resulted in adjusted mean scores ranging from 115.45 for individuals with incomes below $4,000 to 104.51 for individuals with incomes over $16,000.

Source: Allison, Neil K. (1978), "A Psychometric Development of a Test for Consumer Alienation from the Marketplace," *Journal of Marketing Research*, 15 (November), 565-575.

Other evidence: The dimensionality, internal consistency, and nomological validity of the scale were evaluated in a follow-up study by Bearden, Lichtenstein, and Teel (1983). Factor analysis of mail survey responses to 748 members of a two state university consumer panel revealed a three-factor solution for 22 of the 35 items. These factors were subsequently labeled as business ethics, informed choice, and personal norm. Construct reliability estimates for these factors were .83, .67, and .61, respectively. The estimate of internal consistency for the total scale (i.e., for the reduced set of 22 items), allowing for multiple dimensions, was 0.84. A series of correlations between each of the three factors and measures of life satisfaction, general consumer satisfaction, powerlessness, and satisfaction with four services (e.g., electric and gas) provided modest support for the validity of the three revised consumer alienation factors (Bearden et al. 1983, p. 38).

Other sources: Bearden, William O., Donald R. Lichtenstein, and Jesse E. Teel (1983), "Reassessment of the Dimensionality, Internal Consistency, and Validity of the Consumer Alienation Scale," in *1985 American Marketing Association Summer Educators' Conference Proceedings*, in Patrick E. Murphy et al. (eds.), Chicago, IL: American Marketing Association, 35-40.

References: N/A.

CONSUMER ALIENATION FROM THE MARKETPLACE
(Allison 1978)

1. Most companies are responsive to the demands of the consumer.*

2. It seems wasteful for so many companies to produce the same basic products.

3. Unethical practices are widespread throughout business.*

4. Stores do not care why people buy their products just as long as they make a profit.

5. Shopping is usually a pleasant experience.

6. People are unable to help determine what products will be sold in the stores.

7. Advertising and promotional costs unnecessarily raise the price the consumer has to pay for a product.

8. What a product claims to do and what it actually does are two different things.

9. Mass production has done away with unique products.

10. Misrepresentation of product features is just something we have to deal with.

11. Harmful characteristics of a product are often kept from the consumer.*

12. It is embarrassing to bring a purchase back to the store.

13. I tend to spend more than I should just to impress my friends with how much I have.*

14. Even with so much advertising, it is difficult to know what brand is best.*

15. A sale is not really a bargain but a way to draw people into the store.

16. It is difficult to identify with current trends and fads in fashion.*

17. I often feel more for buying so many unnecessary products.*

18. Most brands are the same with just different names and labels.

19. A product will usually break down as soon as the warranty is up.*

20. Business is responsible for unnecessarily depleting our natural resources.*

21. It is difficult to identify with business practices today.*

22. One must be willing to tolerate poor service from most stores.*

23. It is difficult to know what store has the best buy.*

24. Business' prime objective is to make money rather than satisfy the consumer.*

25. I often feel frustrated when I fail to find what I want in the store.

26. After making a purchase, I often find myself wondering "why."*

27. It is hard to understand why some brands are twice as expensive as others.*

28. It is not unusual to find out that business has lied to the public.*

29. Buying beyond one's means is justifiable through the use of credit.*

30. It is often difficult to understand the real meaning of most advertisements.

31. Products are designed to wear out long before they are sold.*

32. Most claims of product quality are true.*

33. I am often dissatisfied with a recent purchase.

34. The wide variety of competing products makes intelligent buying decisions more difficult.

35. Advertisements usually present a true picture of the product.*

NOTES: * denotes the 22 items identified by Bearden et al. (1983) as possessing stability and simple structure. Items 1, 5, 32, and 35 require reverse coding. In addition, items 1, 3, 4, 11, 19, 20, 21, 24, 28, 31, 32, and 35 comprise the "business ethics" factor. Items 14, 16, 23, 27, and 34 comprise the "informed choice" factor, and items 13, 17, 22, 26, and 29 comprise the "personal norm" factor of the Bearden et al. (1983) three factor structure.

ASSERTIVENESS, AGGRESSIVENESS, AND COMPLAINING BEHAVIOR
(Fornell and Westbrook 1979)

Construct: Assertive behavior was defined by Galassi and Galassi (1977) as a complex set of behaviors emitted by a person in an interpersonal context which expresses that person's feelings, attitudes, wishes, opinions or rights directly, firmly, and honestly while respecting the feelings, attitudes, wishes, opinions, and rights of other persons. Using this model, Fornell and Westbrook (1979) developed measures of both assertiveness and aggressiveness. The aggressive person does not recognize the potential consequences of his or her actions and does not assume responsibility for them. The person who impels his desire for self-assertion to excessive proportions by expressing opinions in a hostile, threatening or assaultive manner is aggressive (Fornell and Westbrook 1979, p. 106). The assertive individual stands up for his or her rights without violating the rights of others.

Description: The measures include 19 items each operationalized using six-point agree-disagree response format. Eighteen of the items loaded on seven factors. The last item (see Fornell and Westbrook 1979, p. 108) did not load highly on any factor.

The seven factors were labeled by Fornell and Westbrook (1979) as follows: F1, submissiveness; F2, vociferousness; F3, congeniality; F4, aggression with undertones of violence; F5, one item favoring enforcement of all laws; F6, tolerance versus intolerance; and F7, shyness. The scores to the items within each factor are summed to form factor indices.

Development: The items were taken from Alberti and Emmons (1974) and Evans (1977). A minimum eigenvalue criterion of one led to a seven-factor solution which explained 61.9 percent of the variance. Intercorrelations among the factors ranged from under 0.10 to 0.20. As shown above, some of the factors include high or low levels of both traits—the two behaviors, then, do not represent manifestations of completely different personality traits. (Note: this research was clearly described by the authors as exploratory and the measures provided were said to be in need of further validation [Fornell and Westbrook 1979].)

Sample(s): One hundred nineteen undergraduate students responded to a self-administered questionnaire.

Validity: Using the factor scores as independent variables, a series of regression analyses was conducted in which the assertiveness and aggressiveness variables were used to predict a series of grocery shopping, self-reports of complaining behavior. The explained variance estimates ranged from 0.08 to 0.16. Evidence of predictive validity was provided for factors: F1, submissiveness; F4, aggressive self-assertion; and, F6, tolerance. In general, evidence that non-assertive consumers are less likely to resort to complaint actions as a means of reducing frustration is supported by the data.

Scores: Mean scores and standard deviations were not provided.

Source: Fornell, Claes and Robert A. Westbrook (1979), "An Exploratory Study of Assertiveness, Aggressiveness, and Complaining Behavior," in *Advances in Consumer Research*, Vol. 6, William L. Wilkie, Ed., Ann Arbor, MI: Association for Consumer Research, 105-110.

Other evidence: N/A.

Other sources: N/A.

References: Galassi, M. D. and J. P. Galassi (1977), *Assert Yourself—How To Be Your Own Person*, New York: Human Sciences Press.

Alberti, R. E. and M. L. Emmons (1974), *Your Perfect Right: A Guide to Assertive Behavior*, 2nd Edition, San Luis Obispo, CA: Impact.

Evans, C. (1977), *Understanding Yourself*, New York: A&W Visual Library.

ASSERTIVENESS, AGGRESSIVENESS, AND COMPLAINING BEHAVIOR
(Fornell and Westbrook 1979)

1. I often avoid people or situations for fear of embarrassment.

2. When a salesman makes an effort, I find it hard to say no.

3. I find no difficulty in maintaining eye contact, keeping my head upright in a personal conversation.

4. I am openly critical of others' ideas, opinions, and behavior.

5. When a person is highly unfair, I call it to his/her attention.

6. I sometimes show my anger by name-calling or obscenities.

7. I speak out in protest when someone takes my place in line.

8. I find it difficult to compliment or praise others.

9. People who watch bullfights ought to be given a taste of the suffering the bull has to experience.

10. There should be a gun in every home.

11. Man is a dangerous and aggressive animal who is slowly becoming civilized.

12. Sometimes I can feel so angry or annoyed at a person that I feel I could hit him/her.

13. I am in favor of very strict enforcement of all laws.

14. Slow drivers are more of a menace on the roads than fast drivers.

15. The U.S. would be better off if there were no freaks.

16. I am reluctant to speak up in a discussion or a debate.

17. When I meet a stranger, I am usually the first to begin a conversation.

18. I feel uncomfortable stating my views to an authority figure.

19. I dislike arguing with people.

NOTES: The seven factors as labeled by Fornell and Westbrook (1979) are as follows: F1, submissiveness; F2, vociferousness; F3, congeniality; F4, aggression with undertones of violence; F5, one item favoring enforcement of all laws; F6, tolerance versus intolerance; and F7, shyness. Factors to which items belong and scoring procedures were presented by Fornell and Westbrook as follows (no other detail as to scoring was provided): Items 1, 2 and 3 loaded highly on F1. Items 4 through 7 loaded highly on F2. Items 3, 8, and 9 loaded highly on F3. Items 10 through 12 loaded highly on F4. Item 13 loaded highly on F5. Items 14 and 15 loaded highly on F6. Items 16 through 18 loaded highly on F7. (Item 19 did not load highly on any factor.

Factor	Items	Aggressiveness	Assertiveness
F1	1,2,3	—	Low
F2	4,5,6,7	High	High
F3	3,8,9	Low	Medium
F4	10,11,12	High	—
F5	13	—	—
F6	14,15	Low	Fairly high
F7	16,17,18	Low	Low

CONSUMER ASSERTIVENESS AND AGGRESSIVENESS
(Richins 1983)

Construct: Assertiveness and aggressiveness represent two consumer interaction styles in the market-place — behaviors to maintain one's rights in the marketplace. Interaction style refers to relatively consistent behavior patterns that individuals employ in interpersonal interactions with retail employees (Richins 1983, p. 73). Assertiveness involves standing up for one's rights without infringing upon those of others, whereas aggression involves the use of verbal and nonverbal noxious stimuli to maintain rights (Richins 1983). The research by Richins develops two validated measures — one for each construct. In her research, three interaction situations (i.e., requesting information or assistance, resisting requests for compliance, and seeking remedy for dissatisfaction) and four interaction styles were identified: assertive, nonassertive, aggressive, and resort-to-aggressive. These interaction styles or strategies were based upon both a review of existing measures and a series of in depth personal interviews.

Description: The assertiveness scale consists of three subscales each containing five items. These subscales are labeled as follows: resisting requests for compliance, requesting information or assistance, and seeking redress. The aggressiveness scale consists of six items. The response format for each item was a five-point Likert scale, where "strongly agree" was scored 5 and "strongly disagree" was scored 1 (Richins 1983, p.81). Nine of the assertiveness items require reverse coding. Hence, higher scores represent greater assertiveness or aggressiveness. Item scores are summed within subscales (15 items for assertiveness and six items for aggressiveness) to form subscale indices.

Development: Seventy-nine items reflecting aggressive and assertive behaviors across the three situations were developed. Initial editing of redundant and ambiguous items in addition to those with strong potential for social desirability bias were deleted. Analysis for each factor separately using item-to-total correlations and principal components resulted in the final 15-item assertiveness scale and the 6-item aggressiveness measure.

Sample(s):   An initial administration for the edited pool of 59 items was given to 118 undergraduate and graduate students. Validation data were collected from a general population mailing and two consumer active groups (i.e., members of a consumer protection group and complainers to a government agency). These efforts resulted in a usable set of 356 respondents.

Validity: Estimates of coefficient alpha (adjusted for dimensionality) for the two measures were 0.73 for the aggression scale and 0.87 for the assertiveness measure. Corresponding test-retest estimates were 0.82 and 0.83 for the student sample of n = 112.

Using the responses of 83 college students to the present scales and a series of general assertion and aggression measures, evidence of convergent and discriminant validity was provided from a MTMM matrix analysis. For example, correlations of 0.68 and 0.42 were provided as evidence of convergent validity for the assertiveness and aggressiveness measures, respectively. Based upon the responses of 93 college students to the present measures and a shortened form of the Crowne Marlowe Social Desirability Scale (1964), corresponding correlations of 0.13 and -0.28 were cited as evidence of limited social desirability bias. Estimates of internal consistency reliability based upon the adult validation sample were 0.80 and 0.89 for the assertiveness and aggressiveness items, respectively.

Extensive additional evidence was provided by Richins (1983, pp. 77-80). Only some of those results are cited here. More aggressive individuals had more negative attitudes toward business and were more likely to report enjoying making a complaint than nonaggressive individuals as predicted; the resort-to-aggression group reported the greatest number of complaints; and, individuals lowest in both variables took the longest to get off the phone in a follow-up solicitation involving the telephone purchase of craftkits. The assertiveness scale was correlated (modestly) with education and income. Aggressive individuals tended to be younger and male.

Scores: Mean scores were provided for both scales as part of a known group validation. For the mail survey sample, the general population sample was significantly different in terms of assertiveness from the rest of the sample. Mean scores for the general population, consumer protection, and third-party complainer subsamples were 56.5, 58.9, and 58.1, respectively. The means also differed for the aggressiveness factor: third-party complainers, 16.5; general population, 14.5; and consumer protection group, 14.7.

Source: Richins, Marsha L. (1983), "An Analysis of Consumer Interaction Styles in the Marketplace," *Journal of Consumer Research*, 10 (June), 73-82.

Other evidence: Data were collected in a follow-up validation research effort from two American samples (i.e., 122 general respondents and 234 consumer active respondents) and 304 residents of the Netherlands. (See Richins and Verhage [1987] for details.) Briefly, for the Dutch sample, the estimates of internal consistency reliability were 0.72 and 0.77 for the aggressiveness and assertiveness scales, respectively. Corresponding estimates for the American sample were 0.76 and 0.80. Confirmatory factor analysis generally supported the factor structure using the data for both countries. However, the factor analysis results were somewhat stronger in support of the measures for the American data. Scalar equivalence was examined using a series of regression equations in which the scales were used to predict a series of dependent variables and/or behaviors (i.e., seeking redress) for each country. An acceptable level of equivalence was obtained for the aggressiveness measure.

Other sources: Richins, Marsha L. and Bronislaw J. Verhage (1987), "Assertiveness and Aggression in Marketplace Exchanges," *Journal of Cross Cultural Psychology*, 18 (1), 93-105.

References: N/A.

CONSUMER ASSERTIVENESS AND AGGRESSIVENESS
(Richins 1983)

ASSERTIVENESS ITEMS

Resisting Requests For Compliance

1. I have no trouble getting off the phone when called by a person selling something I don't want.

2. I really don't know how to deal with aggressive salespeople.(*)

3. More often than I would like, I end up buying something I don't want because I have a hard time saying no to the salesperson. (*)

4. If a salesperson comes to my door selling something I don't want, I have no trouble ending the conversation.

5. If a salesperson has gone to a lot of trouble to find an item for me, I would be embarrassed not to buy it even if it isn't exactly right. (*)

Requesting Information or Assistance

6. I sometimes don't get all the information I need about a product because I am uncomfortable bothering salespeople with questions. (*)

7. I am uncomfortable asking store employees where products are located in the store. (*)

8. In signing a sales contract or credit agreement, I am reluctant to ask for an explanation of everything I don't understand. (*)

9. If a store doesn't have the size or color of an item I need, I don't mind asking the salesperson to check for the item at other store locations.

10. If a cashier is talking with friends while I am waiting to be waited on, it would not bother me to interrupt the conversation and ask for assistance.

Seeking Redress

11. If a defective product is inexpensive, I usually keep it rather than put up a fuss or complain. (*)

12. I'd rather do almost anything than return a product to the store. (*)

13. I am probably more likely to return an unsatisfactory product than most people I know.

14. I often procrastinate when I know I should return a defective product to the store. (*)

15. I would attempt to notify store management if I thought service in a store was particularly bad.

AGGRESSIVENESS ITEMS

16. I have on occasion told salespeople I thought they were too rude.

17. On occasion, I have tried to get a complaint taken care of by causing a stir which attracts the attention of customers.

18. I get a certain amount of satisfaction from putting a discourteous salesperson in his place.

19. Sometimes being nasty is the best way to get a complaint taken care of.

20. I'll make a scene at the store if necessary to get a complaint handled to my satisfaction.

21. Salespeople need to be told off when they are rude.

NOTES: * denotes items requiring reverse coding.

GROUP INFLUENCES

CONSUMER SUSCEPTIBILITY TO REFERENCE GROUP INFLUENCE
(Park and Lessig 1977)

Construct: Reference group influence is defined as the influence from an actual or imaginary individual or group conceived of having significant relevance upon an individual's evaluations, aspirations, or behavior. Furthermore, reference group influence has three motivational components (Park and Lessig 1977, p. 102):

Informational - influence accepted from others for its informational content because it enhances the individual's knowledge of his/her environment or his/her ability to cope with some aspect of the environment, e.g., a product purchase.

Utilitarian - influence based on compliance with others. An individual complies because he/she perceives that significant others can mediate rewards or punishments, because the individual's behavior is known or visible to others, or because the individual is motivated to realize a reward or avoid punishment.

Value expressive - influence relating to the individual's desire to enhance his/her self-concept in the eyes of others (i.e., the individual identifies with positive referents and dissociates him/herself with negative referents).

Description: The reference group scale is composed of 14 statements each measured along 4 point scales (i.e., highly relevant = 4, medium relevance = 3, low relevance = 2, and not relevant = 1 to one's consumer behavior). There are 5 items each for the informational and value expressive dimensions, and 4 items for the utilitarian dimension. Items scores are summed within dimensions and then divided by the number of items within each dimension to form indices for each dimension.

Development: Informal interviews and author judgment were used to generate 18 items that tapped the three dimensions of reference group influence. These items were pretested with a student sample and then trimmed to the final 14-item scale. A number of reliability and validity tests were then performed on new samples over 20 different product categories.

Samples: A sample of 22 students was used to trim the pool of 18 statements down to 14. A sample of 42 consumers was used in a validity check study, and samples of 100 housewives and 51 and 37 students also participated in validation studies.

Validity: Test-retest reliabilities for the three dimensions ranged from .43 to .78 (for a subsample of 20 of the housewife sample of 100) and .56 to .96 (for a subsample of 13 from one of the student samples). MTMM analyses supported the convergent and discriminant validity of the measures as across products, the correlations among measures of the same trait were high, and correlations with different traits were low. (Beyond this, little detail was provided by Park and Lessig on their MTMM analyses). Also, a number of mean difference tests between the housewife and student samples supported the scale's validity. That is, students were more susceptible to reference group influence for products like beer and cigarettes, and housewives were more susceptible to influence for products like furniture.

Scores: A number of mean scores are reported by Park and Lessig (1977, Tables 1, 2, 3, and 4, pp. 106-108). Across the 20 products studied, mean scores ranged from 2.46 to 4.00 for informational influence, 2.33 to 3.95 for utilitarian influence, and 1.93 to 3.97 for value expressive influence.

Source: Park, C. Whan and V. Parker Lessig (1977), "Students and Housewives: Differences in Susceptibility of Reference Group Influence," *Journal of Consumer Research*, 4 (September), 102-110.

**Other
evidence:** Bearden and Etzel (1982) used a slightly modified version of the Park and Lessig measures. Thirteen of the items were used with slight wording changes and measures on 6-point disagree-agree statements (i.e., 4 items for informational, 5 for value expressive, and 4 for utilitarian). Across several product decisions, alpha for the dimensions were .63, .88, and .71 for the informational, value expressive, and utilitarian subscales, respectively. Across several brand decisions, alphas were .70, .80, and .77 for the three dimensions. Average test-retest reliabilities over a three week period ranged from .53 to .68 for the dimensions. A number of mean difference tests showed hypothesized differences between the three influence types.

**Other
sources:** Bearden, William O. and Michael J. Etzel (1982), "Reference Group Influence on Product and Brand Purchase Decisions," *Journal of Consumer Research*, 9 (September), 183-194.

References: N/A.

CONSUMER SUSCEPTIBILITY TO REFERENCE GROUP INFLUENCE
(Park and Lessig 1977)

Informational influence

1) The individual seeks information about various brands and products from an association of professionals or independent group of experts.

2) The individual seeks information from those who work with the product as a profession.

3) The individual seeks brand related knowledge and experience (such as how Brand A's performance compares to Brand B's) from those friends, neighbors, relatives, or work associates who have reliable information about the brands.

4) The brand which the individual selects is influenced by observing a seal of approval of an independent testing agency (such as Good Housekeeping).

5) The individual's observation of what experts do influences his choice of a brand (such as observing the type of car which police drive or the brand of TV which repairmen buy).

Utilitarian influence

6) To satisfy the expectations of fellow work associates, the individual's decision to purchase a particular brand is influenced by their preferences.

7) The individual's decision to purchase a particular brand is influenced by the preferences of people with whom he has social interaction.

8) The individual's decision to purchase a particular brand is influenced by the preferences of family members.

9) The desire to satisfy the expectations that others have of him has an impact on the individual's brand choice.

Value expressive influence

10) The individual feels that the purchase or use of a particular brand will enhance the image which others will have of him.

11) The individual feels that those who purchase or use a particular brand possess the characteristics which he would like to have.

12) The individual sometimes feels that it would be nice to be like the type of person which advertisements show using a particular brand.

13) The individual feels that the people who purchase a particular brand are admired or respected by others.

14) The individual feels that the purchase of a particular brand helps him show others what he is, or would like to be (such as an athlete, successful businessman, good mother, etc.).

CONSUMER SUSCEPTIBILITY TO INTERPERSONAL INFLUENCE
(Bearden, Netemeyer, and Teel 1989)

Construct: Consumer susceptibility to interpersonal influence is assumed to be a general trait that varies across individuals and is related to other individual traits and characteristics. The construct is defined as the need to identify with or enhance one's image in the opinion of significant others through the acquisition and use of products and brands, the willingness to conform to the expectations of others regarding purchase decisions, and/or the tendency to learn about products and services by observing others or seeking information from others (Bearden, Netemeyer, and Teel 1989, p. 474). That is, the construct is multidimensional in that both normative influences (e.g., value expressive and utilitarian) and informational influences are considered (e.g., Deutsch and Gerard 1955; Burnkrant and Cousineau 1975).

Description: The scale consists of twelve items each operationalized as a bipolar, seven-place rating scale ranging from "strongly agree" to "strongly disagree." All items are positively worded. The 12 items reflect two correlated dimensions of susceptibility to interpersonal influence. Item scores are summed within each dimension to form normative and informational indices, and can be summed overall for an overall susceptibility to interpersonal influence score ranging from 12 to 84.

Development: An original pool of 166 items was developed from a review of prior research. The number was reduced to 135 after deletion of ambiguous items and items with essentially identical meaning. Five judges were then used to assign items to categories based upon definitions provided for the three factors. Items that did not receive consistent classification by four of the five judges were eliminated. This process reduced the number of items to 86. The pool of items was further reduced to 62 using a second judgmental procedure. That is, those items not classified as clearly representative of each of the three factors by four marketing faculty judges were eliminated.

The remaining 62 items were interspersed across the three factors and then administered to a convenience sample of 220 adults. Corrected item-to-total correlations for each factor and oblique factor analysis (restricting the solution to three factors) were used to reduce the set of items to 18. Those items with item-to-total correlations below 0.50 were first deleted. Items not exhibiting simple structure were then eliminated.

The remaining 18 items were examined using confirmatory factor analysis which revealed 3 items with low reliabilities. For the five items remaining as indicators of informational, utilitarian, and value expressiveness influences, the respective construct reliabilities were 0.86, 0.87, and 0.83. Subsequent tests of convergent and discriminant validity revealed, however, that the value expressiveness and utilitarian factors were not discrete. This finding resulted then in a 10-item normative factor. Estimates of construct reliability and shared variance for this factor were 0.91 and 0.52.

These 15 items were subsequently examined on a student sample of 141 subjects. Confirmatory factor analysis then supported (after the deletion of 3 additional items) a 12-item scale reflecting informational (4 items) and normative influences (8 items).

Sample(s): The first administration obtained responses from a convenience sample of 220 adult (non-student) subjects. The second administration involved a survey of 141 student subjects. The validity of the scale was then evaluated on separate samples of 47 students in a correlational study involving measures of self-esteem and attention-to-social-comparison-information, 35 and 43 students in a two phase behavioral index study, 72 fraternity and sorority subjects in the external judges study, and a group of 143 students in a study of motivations-to-comply.

Validity: Coefficient alpha estimates for the informational and normative factors were 0.82 and 0.88 (n = 220). A small sample of 35 subjects resulted in corresponding test-retest estimates of 0.75 and 0.79. Confirmatory factor analysis tests of invariant structure across the two samples also supported the stability of the measures.

The validity of the measures were further examined in five separate studies. (See Bearden et al. 1989, pp. 477-479, for details.) First, correlations between the two factors and measures of self-esteem and attention-to-social-comparison-information provided some evidence of construct validity in that the correlations were in the direction and pattern as expected. The evidence here was strongest for the normative factor. Second, the correlations between the informational factor and the normative factor and a series of self-reported behavioral indices were 0.37 (p<.05) and 0.15, respectively. Third and fourth, two external judgmental rating procedures also supported the ability of the scale to explain susceptibility to interpersonal influences. Lastly, the normative and informational factor measures were correlated with measures of motivations-to-comply as predicted. These estimates were 0.39 and 0.59 for the informational and normative scales, respectively.

Scores: Mean scores were not reported in the studies cited below. The authors did find that students scored significantly higher than nonstudents.

Source: Bearden, William O., Richard G. Netemeyer, and Jesse E. Teel (1989), "Measurement of Consumer Susceptibility to Interpersonal Influence," *Journal of Consumer Research*, 15 (March), 473-481.

Other evidence: The dimensionality and validity of the scales were further examined by the same authors (Bearden, Netemeyer, and Teel 1990) in a series of follow-up tests on new data and reanalyses of the data presented above. The results of correlating the susceptibility to interpersonal influence measures with a number of personality traits were reported. For the normative factor, example measures and significant correlations include the following: consumer confidence, r=-0.53; interpersonal orientation, r=0.38; inner-other directedness, r=0.37; and extroversion, r=0.16. In addition, the SUSCEP measures were shown to be more highly correlated with ATSCI and self-esteem than comparable measures developed from Park and Lessig (1977).

Confirmatory factor analyses revealed that the two-factor solution was superior to both null and single factor model solutions in terms of model fit and that the construct reliabilities were similar to those reported by Bearden et al. (1989).

Other sources: Bearden, William O., Richard G. Netemeyer, and Jesse E. Teel (1990), "Further Validation of the Consumer Susceptibility to Interpersonal Influence Scale," in *Advances in Consumer Research*, Vol. 17, Marvin E. Goldberg, Gerald Gorn, and Richard W. Pollay, (eds.), Provo, UT: The Association for Consumer Research, 770-776.

References: Park, C. Whan and Parker V. Lessig (1977), "Students and Housewives: Differences in Susceptibility to Reference Group Influence," *Journal of Consumer Research*, 4 (September), 102-110.

Deutsch, Morton and Harold B. Gerard (1955), "A Study of Normative and Informational Influence Upon Individual Judgment," *Journal of Abnormal and Social Psychology*, 7 (November), 1-15.

Burnkrant, Robert E. and Alain Cousineau (1975), "Informational and Normative Influence in Buyer Behavior," *Journal of Consumer Research*, 2 (December), 206-215.

CONSUMER SUSCEPTIBILITY TO INTERPERSONAL INFLUENCE
(Bearden, Netemeyer, and Teel 1989)

1. I often consult other people to help choose the best alternative available from a product class.

2. If I want to be like someone, I often try to buy the same brands that they buy.

3. It is important that others like the products and brands I buy.

4. To make sure I buy the right product or brand, I often observe what others are buying and using.

5. I rarely purchase the latest fashion styles until I am sure my friends approve of them.

6. I often identify with other people by purchasing the same products and brands they purchase.

7. If I have little experience with a product, I often ask my friends about the product.

8. When buying products, I generally purchase those brands that I think others will approve of.

9. I like to know what brands and products make good impressions on others.

10. I frequently gather information from friends or family about a product before I buy.

11. If other people can see me using a product, I often purchase the brand they expect me to buy.

12. I achieve a sense of belonging by purchasing the same products and brands that others purchase.

NOTES: Normative factor items are 2, 3, 5, 6, 8, 9, 11, and 12; informational factor items are 1, 4, 7, and 10.

SOURCES FOR CHAPTER TWO

Allison, Neil K. (1978), "A Psychometric Development of a Test for Consumer Alienation from the Marketplace," *Journal of Marketing Research*, 15 (November), 565-575; Appendix, pp. 573-574.

Bearden, William O., Richard G. Netemeyer, and Jesse E. Teel (1989), "Measurement of Consumer Susceptibility to Interpersonal Influence," *Journal of Consumer Research*, 15 (March), 473-481; Table 2, p. 477.

Brooker, George (1975), "An Instrument to Measure Consumer Self-Actualization," in *Advances in Consumer Research*, Vol. 2, Mary Jane Schlinger, (ed.), Ann Arbor, MI: Association for Consumer Research, 563-575; Figure 2, pp. 568-569.

Cacioppo, John T. and Richard E. Petty (1982), "The Need for Cognition," *Journal of Personality and Social Psychology*, 42 (1), 116-131; Table 1 pp. 120-121.

Childers, Terry L. (1986), "Assessment of the Psychometric Properties of An Opinion Leadership Scale," *Journal of Marketing Research*, 23 (May), 184-188; Table 2, p. 186.

Cohen, Joel B. (1967), "An Interpersonal Orientation to the Study of Consumer Behavior," *Journal of Marketing Research*, 4 (August), 270-278; Appendix, p. 278.

Craig, C. Samuel and James L. Ginter (1975), "An Empirical Test of a Scale for Innovativeness," in *Advances in Consumer Research*, Vol. 2, Mary Jane Schlinger (ed.), Ann Arbor, MI: The Association for Consumer Research, 555-562.

Faber, Ronald J. and Thomas C. O'Guinn (1989), "Classifying Compulsive Consumers: Advances in the Development of a Diagnostic Tool." in *Advances in Consumer Research*, Vol. 16, Thomas K. Srull, (ed.), Provo, UT: Association for Consumer Research, 738-744; Table 1, p. 741.

Feick, Lawrence F. and Linda L. Price (1987), "The Market Maven: A Diffuser of Marketplace Information," *Journal of Marketing*, 51 (January), 83-97; Appendix, p. 95.

Fornell, Claes and Robert A. Westbrook (1979), "An Exploratory Study of Assertiveness, Aggressiveness, and Complaining Behavior," in *Advances in Consumer Research*, Vol. 6, William L. Wilkie, (ed.), Ann Arbor, MI: Association for Consumer Research; 105-110, Table 1 p. 108.

Goldsmith, Ronald E. and Charles Hofacker (1991), "Measuring Consumer Innovativeness," *Journal of the Academy of Marketing Science*, 19 (Summer), 209-221; Table 1 p. 212.

Kassarjian, Waltraud M. (1962), "A Study of Riesman's Theory of Social Character," *Sociometry*, 25 (September), 213-230; Appendix pp. 226-230.

King, Charles W. and John O. Summers (1970), "Overlap of Opinion Leadership Across Product Categories," *Journal of Marketing Research*, 7 (February), 43-50; Figure, p. 45.

Leavitt, Clark and John R. Walton (1975), "Development of a Scale for Innovativeness," in *Advances in Consumer Research*, Vol. 2, Mary Jane Schlinger, (ed.), Ann Arbor, MI: Association for Consumer Research, 545-554; Table 1, pp. 557-558.

_____ and _____ (1988), "Openness of Information Processing as a Moderator of Message Effects on Behavior," *Faculty Working Paper*, College of Business of Administration, Ohio State University.

Lennox, Richard D., and Raymond N. Wolfe (1984), "Revision of the Self-Monitoring Scale," *Journal of Personality and Social Psychology*, 46, 1349-1364; Table 10, part 2, p. 1362.

Lundstrom, William J. and Lawrence M. Lamont (1976), "The Development of a Scale to Measure Consumer Discontent," *Journal of Marketing Research*, 13 (November), 373-381; Appendix A, pp 379-381.

Malhotra, Naresh K. (1981), "A Scale to Measure Self-Concepts, Person Concepts, and Product Concepts," *Journal of Marketing Research*, 18 (November), 456-464; Table 3, p. 462.

Park, C. Whan and V. Parker Lessig (1977), "Students and Housewives: Differences in Susceptibility to Reference Group Influence," *Journal of Consumer Research*, 4 (September), 102-110; Exhibit, p. 105.

Pisharodi, R. Mohan and Ravi Parameswaran (1991), "Confirmatory Factor Analysis of a Country-of-Origin Scale: Initial Results," in *Advances in Consumer Research*, Vol., 19, John Sherry and Brian Sternthal, (eds.), Provo, UT: The Association for Consumer Research, (in press); Table 1.

Price, Linda L., and Nancy M. Ridgeway (1983), "Development of a Scale to Measure Use Innovativeness," in *Advances in Consumer Research*, Vol. 10, Richard. P. Bagozzi and Alice. M. Tybout, (eds.), Ann Arbor, MI: Association for Consumer Research, 679-684; Table 1, pp. 681-682.

Pruden, Henry O., F. Kelly Shuptrine, and Douglas S. Longman (1974), "A Measure of Alienation from the Marketplace," *Journal of the Academy of Marketing Science*, 2, 610-619; Table 2, p. 612.

Reynolds, Fred D. and William R. Darden (1971), "Mutually Adaptive Effects of Interpersonal Communication," *Journal of Marketing Research*, 8 (November), 449-454; Appendix, p. 453.

Richins, Marsha L. (1983), "An Analysis of Consumer Interaction Styles in the Marketplace," *Journal of Consumer Research*, 10 (June), 73-82; Appendix, p. 81.

Shimp, Terence A. and Subhash Sharma (1987), "Consumer Ethnocentrism: Construction and Validation of the CETSCALE," *Journal of Marketing Research*, 24 (August), 280-289; Table 1, p. 282.

Snyder, Mark (1974), "Self-Monitoring of Expressive Behavior," *Journal of Personality and Social Psychology*, 30 (4), 526-637; Table 1, p. 531.

Stern, Barbara B., Benny Barak, and Stephen J. Gould (1987), "Sexual Identity Scale: A New Self-Assessment Measure," *Sex Roles*, 17, 503-529; Appendix A and B, pp. 517-518.

Valencia, Humberto (1985), "Developing an Index to Measure 'Hispanicness,'" in *Advances in Consumer Research*, Vol. 12, Elizabeth C. Hirschman and Morris Holbrook, (eds.), Provo, UT: Association for Consumer Research, 118-121; Appendix, p. 120.

Venkatraman, Meera P. and Linda L. Price (1990), "Differentiating Between Cognitive and Sensory Innovativeness: Concepts, Measurements, and Implications," *Journal of Business Research*, 20, 293-315; Table 1, p. 297.

3

Values

GENERAL VALUES

THE ROKEACH VALUE SURVEY: RVS
(Rokeach 1968, 1973)

Construct: A value is defined as an enduring prescriptive or proscriptive belief that a specific end state of existence or specific mode of conduct is preferred to an opposite end state or mode of conduct (Rokeach 1968, 1973). These values are considered the important principles guiding one's behavior throughout life.

The Rokeach Value Survey (RVS) is designed to measure two sets of values. One set is composed of 18 terminal values or desired end states of existence (e.g., an exciting life, national security), and the other set is composed of 18 instrumental values, or preferable modes of behavior (e.g., being ambitious, independent).

The importance of values and, specifically, the Rokeach value survey to marketing/consumer research can not be understated. Two reviews of the relevance of values to consumer behavior can be found in Kahle (1985) and Prakash and Munson (1985).

Description: The 18 values within each category (terminal and instrumental) are alphabetically listed on two separate pages (Form D). Then, subjects are asked to rank order each value as to its importance as a guiding principle in living their life. A "1" indicates the most important value and an "18" the least important. Scale responses are considered ordinal.

Development: The original development of the scale is described in Rokeach (1968, 1973). At first, 12 values were initially selected to represent each set of values, but due to the omission of salient values and low reliability estimates, both sets of values were expanded to 18 in each category. For the terminal values, an extensive literature review, the author's own judgement, and interviews with students (n = 30) and nonstudents (n = 100) produced an initial pool of values in the hundreds. Then, through further judgement by the authors, and empirical analysis examining similarity among items, 18 items were retained.

For the instrumental values, Anderson's (1968) checklist of 555 personality-trait words was used as a base. This list was trimmed to about 200, and then the 18 instrumental values were chosen according to the following criteria: 1) by retaining only one word from a group of synonyms; 2) by retaining those judged to be maximally different or minimally intercorrelated with one another; 3) by retaining those judged representative of important American values; 4) by retaining those that would maximally discriminate across demographic variables; 5) by retaining those values judged to be meaningful in all cultures; and 6) by retaining those items that respondents could admit to without appearing to be immodest or vain.

Initial estimates of predictive validity are offered by Rokeach (1968, 1973), and results and comments pertaining to other applications of the scale outside of marketing/consumer behavior can also be found in Rokeach (1973) and Robinson and Shaver (1973). In fact, the scale has undergone numerous reliability and validity checks across various samples.

Sample(s): Various samples were used by Rokeach throughout the derivation of the value survey instrument. Some of these samples include 50 policemen, 141 unemployed whites and 28 unemployed blacks, 298 students, and 75 Calvinest students. Other applications of the scale outside the marketing/consumer behavior literature are numerous and have employed a wide range of samples encompassing all types of demographic classifications.

Validity: Test-retest reliability (over a 7-week period) has been in the .70 range and above for RVS. Other estimates of test-retest reliability for applications of the scale outside of marketing/ consumer behavior have been in the .70 to .79 range for Form D. In most of these applications, the values were ranked as originally prescribed by Rokeach, thus more traditional estimates of internal consistency (i.e., coefficient alpha) are rarely reported. As mentioned above, estimates of predictive validity can be found in Rokeach (1968, 1973). For example, the value "salvation" was found to be predictive of religious affiliation and church attendance, and the values of "equality" and "freedom" were predictive of participation in civil rights demonstrations.

Scores: Since the Rokeach survey is a rank order scale, mean scores have generally not been reported. However, a comprehensive table of the frequencies for all 36 values across select demographic characteristics is available in Rokeach (1973, pp. 363-419).

Source(s):   Rokeach, Milton (1968), *Beliefs, Attitudes and Values*, San Francisco: Jossey-Bass Inc., pp. 156-178.

Rokeach, Milton (1973), *The Nature of Human Values*, New York: Free Press.

Other evidence: In the marketing/consumer behavior literature, samples have been comprised of both student (Munson and McQuarrie 1988; Reynolds and Jolly 1980; Shrum et al. 1990; Vinson et al. 1977) and non- student groups (e.g., Beatty et al. 1985; McQuarrie and Langmeyer 1985; Munson and McQuarrie 1988). These applications of the scale have used all 18 terminal and all 18 instrumental values, as well as shortened versions of the scale where 12 instrumental and 12 terminal values are evaluated (Rokeach 1968, 1973). In addition, many of these applications have used various scoring formats including Rokeach's original ranking procedure, anchored endpoint scoring, and Likert-type interval scoring. Several of these applications are briefly discussed below.

Based on the difficulty subjects have had in ranking all 18 terminal and 18 instrumental values, many marketing researchers have attempted alternative scaling formats for the Rokeach values. Vinson et al. (1977) had subjects evaluate the 36 values on an interval scaling format ranging from important to not important. They report that two distinct dimensions were found (i.e., the terminal and instrumental value dimensions as espoused by Rokeach). However, within the two dimensions, several sub-dimensions were found. Six factors for the terminal values were found including social harmony, personal gratification, self-actualization, security, love and affection, and personal contentedness. Four factors were found for the instrumental dimension including competence, compassion, sociality, and integrity. Estimates of internal consistency were not reported.

Munson and McIntyre (1979) compared three different scaling formats of the Rokeach values. The three formats were the original format proposed by Rokeach, Likert statements for each of the 36 values ranging from extremely important to extremely unimportant, and an anchored scaling format. Over a two-week period, test-retest reliability was estimated via Spearman's rho for each format. For Rokeach's rank order format rho = .82 and .76 for the terminal and instrumental values, respectively. For the Likert format rho = .76 and .74 for the terminal and instrumental values, and for the anchored scaling, rho = .73 and .68 for the terminal and instrumental values. Munson and McIntyre concluded that the Likert format was an appropriate alternative to Rokeach's rank order format.

Reynolds and Jolly (1980) also compared three scaling formats including Rokeach's rankings, a Likert-type format, and a paired comparison format for the 18 terminal values and a 12 value subset of the terminal values. Over a two-week period, test-retest reliability was computed across the formats via Spearman's rho and Kendall's tau. They concluded that the Likert format may not be appropriate based on the following results:

	Rokeach		Likert		Paired	
	18	12	18	12	18	12
Rho	.78	.76	.66	.75	.67	.77
Tau	.62	.62	.62	.69	.57	.66

Using Rokeach's ranking procedure, Kahle et al. (1985) found the 18 terminal values to have convergent/discriminant validity when compared to corresponding values from the LOV survey (Kahle 1983).

In a special issue of *Psychology & Marketing* (1985, Vol. 2, No.4), a number of papers examined the Rokeach value survey. For example, McQuarrie and Langmeyer used a 15 value subset of the Rokeach values in studying attitudes toward personal computers. The 15 items were evaluated in relation to home computers using 5-point agree-disagree Likert statements (alpha = .90). Evidence of discriminant validity between the 15 item value measure and related constructs was also reported. Prakash and Munson used the Rokeach ranking procedure for the 36 values, but found seven factors underlying the values (i.e., fun and enjoyment, workplace ethics, sapience, autonomy, aesthetics, security, and love).

Munson and McQuarrie (1988) attempted to reduce the Rokeach value survey to values most relevant to consumer behavior. In one sample, subjects were asked to identify the 12 values most irrelevant to consumer behavior. In a subsequent sample, subjects evaluated the 24 remaining values on the degree to which they were related to consumer behavior on 3-point scales (i.e., not related, weakly related, strongly related). Coefficient alpha was .94. In another sample, these 24 values were again evaluated on the degree to which they were related to consumer behavior on 5-point scales (i.e., no, weak, some, definite, or strong relation), with a coefficient alpha of .95. Furthermore, 3 factors were found to underlie the 24 consumer behavior relevant values—a values to help fulfill adult responsibilities factor, a values to help fulfill lifestyle goals factor, and a values to help relieve tension factor.

In one study though, all 36 values were assessed on 7-point Likert scales and mean scores are reported for various subsamples (Vinson et al. 1977, p. 251). The mean scores ranged from a low of 4.5 for "social recognition" to a high of 6.6 for "honesty" and "self-respect."

Lastly, Crosby et al. (1990) had a sample of 418 rank, then rate on 7-point scales the 18 instrumental and 18 terminal values. Confirmatory factor analysis found three dimensions for the instrumental values: 1) self-direction (9 items), conformity (5 items), and virtuousness (4 items) with composite reliability estimates of .81, .57, and .65, respectively. Correlations among these dimensions ranged from .08 to .59 Three dimensions were also found for the terminal values: 1) self-actualization/hedonism (12 items), idealism (3 items), and security (3 items) with composite reliabilities of .62, .58, and .67, respectively. Correlations among these dimensions ranged from -.44 to .77.

Other Sources:

Beatty, Sharon E., Lynn R. Kahle, Pamela Homer and Shekhar Misra (1985), "Alternative Measurement Approaches to Consumer Values: The List of Values and the Rokeach Value Survey," *Psychology & Marketing*, 2 (Fall), 181-200.

Crosby, Lawrence A., Mary Jo Bitner, and James D. Gill (1990), "Organizational Structure of Values," *Journal of Business Research*, 20 (March), 123-134.

Kahle, Lynn R. (1985), "Social Values in the Eighties: A Special Issue," *Psychology & Marketing*, 2 (Winter), 231-237.

McQuarrie, Edward F. and Daniel Langmeyer (1985), "Using Values to Measure Attitudes Toward Discontinuous Innovations," *Psychology & Marketing*, 2 (Winter), 239-252.

Munson, J. Michael, and S. H. McIntyre (1979), "Developing Practical Procedures for the Measurement of Personal Values in Cross-Cultural Marketing," *Journal of Marketing Research*, 16 (February), 48-52.

Munson, J. Michael, S. H. McIntyre and Edward F. McQuarrie (1988), "Shortening the Rokeach Value Survey for Use in Consumer Behavior," in *Advances in Consumer Research*, Michael J. Houston (ed.), Vol. 15, Provo, UT: The Association for Consumer Research, 381-386.

Prakash, Ved and J. Michael Munson (1985), "Values, Expectations from the Marketing Systems and Product Expectations," *Psychology & Marketing*, 2 (Winter), 279-298.

Reynolds, Thomas J. and James P. Jolly (1980), "Measuring Personal Values: An Evaluation of Alternative Methods," *Journal of Marketing Research*, 17 (November), 531-536.

Shrum, L. J., John A. McCarty, and Tamara L. Loeffler (1990), "Individual Differences in Value Stability: Are We Really Tapping True Values," in *Advances in Consumer Research*, Marvin E. Goldberg, Gerald Gorn, and Richard W. Pollay (eds.), Vol. 17, Provo, UT: The Association for Consumer Research, 609-615.

Vinson, Donald E., J. Michael Munson, and Masao Nakanishi (1977), "An Investigation of the Rokeach Value Survey for Consumer Research Applications," in *Advances in Consumer Research*, William E. Perreault (ed.), Vol. 4, Provo, UT: The Association for Consumer Research, 247-252.

References:
Anderson, N. H. (1968), "Likableness Ratings of 555 Personality-Trait Words," *Journal of Personality and Social Psychology*, 9, 272-279.

Robinson, J. P. and R. P. Shaver (1973), *Measures of Social Psychological Attitudes*, Ann Arbor, MI: Survey Research Center, Institute for Social Research.

Rokeach, Milton J. (1968), "The Role of Values in Public Opinion Research," *Public Opinion Quarterly*, 32 (Winter), 547-549.

THE ROKEACH VALUE SURVEY: RVS
(Rokeach 1968, 1973)

Value Survey Instructions

Listed below are 18 values in alphabetical order. Your task is to arrange them in order of importance to YOU, as guiding principles in YOUR life. Study the list very carefully and then rank all 18 in terms of their importance to you. Place a "1" next to the value that is the most important as a guiding principle in your life, a "2" next to the second most important value as a guiding principle in your life, a "3" to the third most important value as a guiding principle in your life, and so on. Again, it is important that you rank all values from 1 to 18.

Work slowly and think carefully. If you change your mind, feel free to change your answers. The end result should truly show how you really feel.

<u>Value</u>   <u>Rank</u>

1. A comfortable life (i.e., a prosperous life)   _____
2. An exciting life (i.e., a stimulating, active life)   _____
3. A sense of accomplishment (i.e., a lasting contribution)   _____
4. A world at peace (i.e., free of war and conflict)   _____
5. A world of beauty (i.e, beauty of nature and the arts)   _____
6. Equality (i.e., brotherhood, equal opportunity for all)   _____
7. Family security (i.e., taking care of loved ones)   _____
8. Freedom (i.e., independence, free choice)   _____
9. Happiness (i.e., contentedness)   _____

10. Inner harmony (i.e., freedom from inner conflict)   ———
11. Mature love (i.e., sexual and spiritual intimacy)   ———
12. National security (i.e., protection from attack)   ———
13. Pleasure (i.e., an enjoyable, leisurely life)   ———
14. Salvation (i.e., saved, eternal life)   ———
15. Self-respect (i.e., self-esteem)   ———
16. Social recognition (i.e., respect, admiration)   ———
17. True friendship (i.e., close companionship)   ———
18. Wisdom (i.e., a mature understanding of life)   ———

When you have finished go to the next page.

Please rank these 18 values in order of importance, the same as before.

Value   Rank

19. Ambitious (i.e., hard working, aspiring)   ———
20. Broadminded (i.e., open minded)   ———
21. Capable (i.e., competent, effective)   ———
22. Cheerful (i.e., lighthearted, joyful)   ———
23. Clean (i.e., neat, tidy)   ———
24. Courageous (i.e, standing up for your beliefs)   ———
25. Forgiving (i.e., willing to pardon others)   ———
26. Helpful (i.e., working for the welfare of others)   ———
27. Honest (i.e., sincere, truthful)   ———
28. Imaginative (i.e., daring, creative)   ———
29. Independent (i.e., self-reliant, self-sufficient)   ———
30. Intellectual (i.e., intelligent, reflective)   ———
31. Logical (i.e., consistent, rational)   ———
32. Loving (i.e., affectionate, tender)   ———
33. Obedient (i.e., dutiful, respectful)   ———
34. Polite (i.e., courteous, well-mannered)   ———
35. Responsible (i.e., dependable, reliable)   ———
36. Self-controlled (i.e., restrained, self-disciplined)   ———

NOTES: Items 1-18 are terminal and items 19-36 are instrumental values.

Values 4, 6, 8, 12 and 14 comprise a social harmony factor; values 1, 2, 3, 13 and 16 comprise a personal gratification factor; values 3, 5, 10, 15 and 18 comprise a self-actualization factor; values 7 and 14 comprise a security factor; values 2, 11 and 17 comprise a love and affection factor; values 8 and 9 a personal contentedness factor; values 19, 21, 24, 28, 29, 30 and 31 a competence factor; values 22, 25, 26 and 32 a compassion factor; values 23, 33 and 34 a sociality factor; values 27, 34, 35 and 36 an integrity factor (Vinson et al. 1977).

Values 6, 13, 14, 17 and 33 comprise a fun and enjoyment factor; values 1, 3, 21, 19, 27 and 34 a workplace ethics factor; values 1, 2, 10, 15, 17 and 18 a sapience factor; values 25, 26, 29 and 30 an autonomy factor; values 4 and 5 an aesthetics factor; values 4, 9 and 12 a security factor; values 11 and 32 a mature love factor. Only values with loadings $\geq \pm .30$ were reported (Prakash and Munson 1985).

Values 3, 6, 7, 8, 10, 13, 15, 16 and 18 represent the reduced set of terminal values, and values 19, 21, 28, 29, 30 and 36 represent a reduced set of instrumental values (McQuarrie and Langmeyer 1985).

Values 1, 2, 3, 5 through 10, 13, 15, 16 and 18 represent the reduced set of terminal values relevant to consumer behavior, and values 19 through 23, 28, 29, 30, 32, 35, and 36 represent the reduced set of instrumental values relevant to consumer behavior. Furthermore, values 6,

7, 18, 19, 21, 30, 31, 35 and 36 comprise an adult responsibilities factor; values 1, 2, 3, 8, 9, 13 and 16 comprise a lifestyle goals factor; and 5, 10, 15, 20, 22, 23 and 28 comprise a remove tension factor (McQuarrie and Munson 1988).

Values 3, 10, 11, 14, 15, 17, 18 represent the self-actualization aspect, and values 1, 2, 9, 13, and 16 represent the hedonism aspect of the self actualization/hedonism dimension of the terminal values. Values 5, 6, and 8 represent the idealism dimension, and values 4, 7, and 12 represent the security dimension of the terminal values (Crosby et al. 1990). Values 1 - 3, 5, 10 - 13, and 18 represent the self-direction dimension of the instrumental values. Values 4, 5, and 15 - 17 represent the conformity dimension, and values 7 - 9, and 14 represent the virtuousness dimension of the instrumental values identified by Crosby et al. (1990).

THE VALUES AND LIFESTYLE TYPOLOGY: VALS
(Mitchell 1983)

Construct: VALS provides a systematic classification of American Adults into nine value and lifestyle typologies that have been useful for developing marketing strategy and predicting consumer behaviors. The lifestyle types in the U.S. include survivors (4%), sustainers (7%), belongers (35%), emulators (9%), achievers (22%), I-am-me (5%), experiential (7%), societally conscious (9%), and integrated (2%). The preceding typologies also present a rank ordering of these groups based from worst lifestyle typology to best (i.e., survivor is the most undesirable category to be in because of its poverty stricken, need driven characteristics, and integrated is considered the most desirable category to be in due to its inner-outer directed view of life). Character and personality profiles, as well as likely demographic profiles for each of these typologies, can be found in Mitchell (1983) and Hawkins, Best and Coney (1983).

Description: The items used in the original VALS survey were 40 attitude (i.e., value) statements scored on a 6-point disagree strongly agree strongly basis, and 15 more questions assessing various views on politics, finances, job satisfaction and the like (Mitchell 1983, pp. 242-268). In addition, the original VALS survey asked a number of demographic, media habits, activities, financial issues, household inventory, and product usage questions. The original VALS study contained over 800 questions (Mitchell 1983).

A reduced version comprising the VALS algorithm is also offered (Mitchell 1983) and this reduced version is reported here. Though the weights and scoring procedures for the algorithm are not directly reported, a consistency score between the full VALS and the condensed algorithm was reported to be 86%. Thus, for empirical purposes, both versions should provide essentially the same information.

Also, it should be noted that a revised versions of VALS, VALS II, has been developed.

Development: The development of VALS started from the theoretical base of Maslow's (1954) hierarchy of needs and the concept of social character. Through statistical and theoretical means, Mitchell identified values and demographic questions useful for classifying individuals into the nine typologies.

Samples: The original study was a national probability sample of 1,635 American adults (i.e., 18 or over) and their spouses/mates (1,078).

Validity: In terms of traditional methods of assessing reliability (i.e., coefficient alpha, test-retest reliability) and validity (i.e., correlations with theoretically related constructs) little published information exists for VALS. However, both the full and reduced versions exhibited internal reliability. Both versions classified individuals into the same typologies, and both versions exhibited external reliability (i.e., both versions classified individuals into the same typologies as the VALS staff. These reliability checks were accomplished via discriminant analysis (Mitchell 1983, pp. 269-272).

Much of the validity of VALS rests on its ability to correctly classify individuals into the nine lifestyle typologies and predictive ability in terms of relating the typologies to various consumer related behaviors. In this respect, the VALS typology has been very useful to practitioners (Mitchell 1983)

Scores: Scores on VALS have been traditionally reported as the percentage of respondents falling into each category. In the original study the lifestyle types in the U.S. include survivors (4%), sustainers (7%), belongers (35%), emulators (9%), achievers (22%), I-am-me (5%), experiential (7%), societally conscious (9%), and integrated (2%).

Source: Mitchell, Arnold (1983), *The Nine American Lifestyles: Who We Are and Where We're Going*, New York: MacMillan.

Other evidence: Kahle et al. (1986) examined the VALS algorithm with a student sample of n = 193 to determine if the percentage of respondents falling into the respective VALS categories in the original study would be replicated with students. Beatty et al. (1988) also used a student sample (n = 167) for purposes similar to those of Kahle et al. (1986). These studies also provide evidence for the ability of VALS to classify people into the nine typologies, as both studies found that the percentage of their sample falling into each VALS algorithm category differed very little from that of Mitchell's categorization (1983).

As previously stated, VALS scores have been reported as the percentage of respondents falling into each category. Below is a Table that summarizes these scores across the studies discussed above:

Typology	Mitchell	Kahle et al.	Beatty et al.	
Survivor	4%	3%	3.0%	(6.6%)
Sustainers	7%	8%	8.4%	(.6%)
Belongers	35%	9%	10.2%	(9.6%)
Emulators	9%	5%	5.4%	(5.4%)
Achievers	22%	10%	3.0%	(4.2%)
I-am-me	5%	58%	62.3%	(55.4%)
Experiential	7%	5%	4.8%	(12.6%)
Societally cons.	9%	2%	3.0%	(6.6%)
Integrated	2%	—	—	—

Scores in parentheses are from a demographically adjusted empirical mirror method (Beatty et al. 1988, p. 378).

Other sources: Beatty, Sharon E., Pamela M. Homer, and Lynn R. Kahle (1988), "Problems with VALS in International Marketing Research: An Example from an Application of the Empirical Mirror Technique," in *Advances in Consumer Research*, Vol. 15, Michael J. Houston (ed.), Ann Arbor, MI: Association for Consumer Research, 375-380.

Kahle, Lynn R., Sharon E. Beatty, and Pamela Homer (1986), "Alternative Measurement Approaches to Consumer Values: The List of Values (LOV) and Values and Life Style (VALS)," *Journal of Consumer Research*, 13 (December), 405-409.

References: Hawkins, Del, I., Roger Best, and Kenneth A. Coney, (1983) *Consumer Behavior: Implications for Marketing Strategy*, Plano, TX: Business Publications INC.

Maslow, Abraham H. (1954), *Motivation and Personality*, New York: Harper.

THE VALUES AND LIFESTYLE TYPOLOGY: VALS
(Mitchell 1983)

The VALS Algorithm

ATTITUDES

In this part of the survey, we are interested in your attitudes about a number of social and economic issues.

1) Following is a series of statements. Please indicate how much you agree or disagree with each one by checking the box which comes closest to how you feel.

c) I'd say I'm rebelling against the way I was brought up.
g) In general, it's more important to understand my inner self than to be famous, powerful, or wealthy.
h) My greatest achievements are ahead of me.
i) I believe a woman can work outside the home even if she has small children and still be a good mother.

m) It's very important to me to feel I am a part of a group.
o) Overall, I'd say I'm very happy.
s) I would rather spend a quite evening at home than go out to a party.
w) A woman's life is fulfilled only if she can provide a happy home for her family.
cc) Air pollution is a major worldwide danger.
dd) I often feel left out of things going on around me.
ff) It is wrong for an unmarried man or an unmarried woman to have sexual relations.
gg) Women should take care of running their homes and leave running the country up to men.
hh) It would be best for the future of this country if the United States continues to take an active part in world affairs.
jj) The purchase and use of marijuana should be legalized.
nn) I think we are spending to much money on military armaments.

2) During the last three years would you say your financial situation has been getting worse, stayed the same, or has it been getting better? (Please check *one* box.)

        _____ 1. Getting worse
        _____ 2. About the same

3) How satisfied are you with your present financial situation? (Please check *one* box.)

        _____ 1. Very dissatisfied
        _____ 2. Mostly dissatisfied
        _____ 3. Mostly satisfied
        _____ 4. Very satisfied

4) How much satisfaction do you get from each of the following in your life? (Please check *one* box for *each* item.)

Level of Satisfaction

	not much	some	a great deal	an extreme amount	doesn't apply
a) Your job (whether you work, keep house, or go to school).					
b) Nonwork activities such as hobbies.					
c) Your friends.					

5) About how much confidence would you say you have in the following groups in our country? (Please check *one* box for *each* group.)

Level of Confidence

	no confidence	a small amount	some	a fair amount	a great deal
b) Leaders of major companies					
c) Leaders of the military					

BACKGROUND INFORMATION

The following background information questions are included only to help us interpret your responses on other questions. Your responses here and throughout the questionnaire will be held *strictly* confidential.

1) What is your marital status? (Please check *one* box)

    _____ 1. first marriage   _____ 5. widowed
    _____ 2. second or later marriage   _____ 6. separated
    _____ 3. living together, not married   _____ 7. single, never married
    _____ 4. divorced

2) What is your current age? (Please check *one* box)

_____ 1. 18 - 24
_____ 2. 25 - 29
_____ 3. 30 - 34
_____ 4. 35 - 44

_____ 5. 45 - 54
_____ 6. 55 - 64
_____ 7. 65 and over

3) What is the highest level of formal education you have completed? (Please check *one* box)

_____ 1. grades 1 - 8
_____ 2. grade 9
_____ 3. grade 10
_____ 4. grade 11
_____ 5. graduated high school
_____ 6. technical school

_____ 7. first year of college
_____ 8. second year of college
_____ 9. third year of college
_____ 10. graduated college (4 yrs)
_____ 11. attended or completed graduate school

4) What is the highest level of formal education *your father* completed? (Please check *one* box)

_____ 1. grades 1 - 8
_____ 2. grade 9
_____ 3. grade 10
_____ 4. grade 11
_____ 5. graduated high school
_____ 6. first year of college

_____ 7. second year of college
_____ 8. third year of college
_____ 9. graduated college (4 yrs)
_____ 10. attended or completed graduate school
_____ 11. don't know

5) What ethnic group do you consider yourself to be a member of? (Please check *one* box)

_____ 1. Caucasian or white
_____ 2. Black
_____ 3. Hispanic or Spanish origin
_____ 4. Other (please specify)

9) Generally speaking, do you usually think of yourself as a Republican, a Democrat or an Independent? (please check *one* box)

_____ 1. Republican (Please answer question 9a)
_____ 2. Democrat (Please answer question 9a)
_____ 3. Independent (Please answer question 9b)

9a) IF YOU ARE A REPUBLICAN OR DEMOCRAT, would you call yourself a strong or not very strong Republican or Democrat? (Please check *one* box)
_____ 1. strong Republican
_____ 2. not very strong Republican
_____ 3. not very strong Democrat
_____ 4. strong Democrat

9b) IF YOU ARE AN INDEPENDENT, do you think of yourself as closer to the Republican or Democratic party? (Please check *one* box)
_____ 1. closer to the Republican party
_____ 2. not close to either party
_____ 3. closer to the Democratic party

10) In terms of your political outlook, do you usually think of yourself as: (Please check *one* box)

_____ 1. very conservative
_____ 2. somewhat conservative
_____ 3. middle of the road

_____ 4. somewhat liberal
_____ 5. very liberal

20) What was your *major* activity during the last week? (Please check *one* box)

     _____ 1. working full time (30 hours or more)
     _____ 2. working part time (less than 30 hours) (please answer question 21)
     _____ 3. have a job but not at work due to illness, vacation, strike, etc.
     _____ 4. looking for work, unemployed, laid off
     _____ 5. attending school
     _____ 6. retired   *(please skip to question 22)*
     _____ 7. keeping house
     _____ 8. other (please specify)

21) Which one of the following categories best describes your occupation? (Please check *one* category)

     _____ 1. professional or technical (e.g., accountant, artist, computer specialist, dentist, engineer, lawyer, librarian, nurse, physician, scientist, teacher, technician, writer, etc.)
     _____ 2. manager or administrator (except on a farm)
     _____ 3. sales worker (e.g., insurance salesman, realtor, sales clerk, stockbroker, etc.)
     _____ 4. clerical worker (e.g., bank teller, bookkeeper, cashier, office clerk, postman, secretary, teacher's aide, telephone operator, etc.)
     _____ 5. crafts worker (e.g., baker, carpenter, electrician, foreman, jeweler, mechanic, painter, plumber, tailor, etc.)
     _____ 6. machine operator (e.g., bus driver, conductor, factory worker, truck driver, operator of other kinds of machines)
     _____ 7. laborer (except on a farm) (e.g., carpenter's helper, fisherman, garbage collector, stock handler, teamster, warehouseman, etc.)
     _____ 8. farmer or farm manager
     _____ 9. farm foreman or farm laborer
     _____ 10. service worker (except in a private household) (e.g., barber, bartender, cook, dental assistant, dishwasher, firefighter, janitor, nursing aide, police officer, usher, waiter, etc.)
     _____ 11. private household worker
     _____ 12. government or military worker
     _____ 13. other (please specify your job title and briefly describe what you do):

22) If you were asked to use one of the following terms to describe your social class, which would you choose? (Please check *one* box)

     _____ 1. lower class   _____ 4. upper-middle class
     _____ 2. lower-middle class   _____ 5. upper class
     _____ 3. middle class

23) What is your total *household* income in 19— from all sources before taxes? (Please include here *all* income received by *anyone* in your household.) (Please check *one* box)

     _____ 1. less than $5,000   _____ 7. $25.000 - $29,999
     _____ 2. $5,000 - $7,499   _____ 8. $30,000 - $39,999
     _____ 3. $7,500 - $9,999   _____ 9. $40,000 - $49,999
     _____ 4. $10,000 - $14,999   _____ 10. $50,000 - $74,999
     _____ 5. $15,000 - $19,999   _____ 11. $75,000 - $99,999
     _____ 6. $20,000 - $24,999   _____ 12. $100,000 and over

Size of residence area (coded from ZIP codes)

     _____ 1. large central city (250,000 or more)
     _____ 2. medium central city (50,000 - 250,000)
     _____ 3. suburb of large central city
     _____ 4. suburb of medium size central city
     _____ 5. not within an SMSA (Standard Metropolitan Statistical Area) and open country within large civil divisions, e.g., township division, small city, town, or village.

NOTES: Items in questions are scored on 6-point disagree strongly-agree strongly statements. The lettering of each item in question one reflects the lettering used in the reduced VALS algorithm.

As noted by Kahle et al (1986), there seems to be some controversy as to the exact number of questions used in the original VALS study by Mitchell (1983). The questions comprising the algorithm presented above are taken directly form the reduced version offered by Mitchell (1983).

Reprinted with the permission of MacMillan Publishing Company from *The Nine American Lifestyles: Who We Are and Where We're Going* by Arnold Mitchell. Copyright 1983 by Arnold Mitchell.

THE LIST OF VALUES: LOV
(Kahle 1983)

Construct: The term "value" has been defined as an enduring prescriptive or proscriptive belief that a specific end state of existence or specific mode of conduct is preferred to an opposite end state or mode of conduct for living one's life (cf., Kahle 1983; Rokeach 1968, 1973).

The LOV typology draws a distinction between external and internal values, and notes the importance of interpersonal relations in value fulfillment, as well as personal factors, (i.e., self-respect, self-fulfillment), and apersonal factors (i.e., fun, security, excitement) in value fulfillment. In essence, the LOV measures those values that are central to people in living their lives, particularly the values of life's major roles (i.e., marriage, parenting, work, leisure and daily consumptions). The LOV is most closely tied to social adaptation theory (Kahle, Beatty and Homer 1986) and many studies suggest that the LOV is related to and/or predictive of consumer behavior and related activities (e.g., Homer and Kahle 1988; Kahle 1983; Kahle et al. 1986; Kahle and Kennedy 1988).

Description: The LOV is composed of 9 values which can be scored in a number of ways. Each value can be evaluated on 9 or 10 point scales (very unimportant to very important), or the values can be rank ordered from most to least important. Also, some combination of the two methods can be used where each value is rated on 9 or 10 point scales and then subjects are asked to circle the one or two values that are most important to them in living their daily lives (e.g., Kahle 1983; Kahle et al. 1986; Kahle and Kennedy 1988).

Development: The LOV was developed from a theoretical base of values proposed by Feather (1975), Maslow's (1954) hierarchy of values, Rokeach's (1973) 18 terminal values, and various other contemporaries in values research. The LOV items were derived by culling the values from the above sources from a much larger pool of values to the 9 LOV items. For a more detailed discussion of the scale development procedures see Kahle (1983, 1986) and Kahle et al. (1986).

Sample(s): The major study on the LOV was conducted with a probability sample of n = 2,264 Americans. The study was conducted by the Survey Research Center of the Institute for Social Research at the University of Michigan (Kahle 1983, 1986; Kahle and Kennedy 1988).

Validity: The original study found the LOV to be significantly correlated with various measures of mental health, well-being, adaptation to society, and self (Kahle 1983). Thus, evidence for the nomological validity of the LOV exists.

Scores: Mean scores for the nine values were not directly reported by Kahle (1983). However, the percentage of respondents selecting the one value that is most important to them is available in Kahle (1983). (See also Kahle, Liu, and Watkins [1992] below.)

Source: Kahle, Lynn R. (1983), *Social Values and Social Change: Adaptation to Life in America*, New York: Praeger Publishers.

Other evidence: The LOV was also tested with a student sample of 193 (of which 122 were foreign students) in terms of predictive ability of consumer related trends (Kahle et al. 1986), a convenience sample of 356 in terms of comparing it to the Rokeach Value survey (Beatty et al. 1985), and a sample of 831 food shoppers for predictive validity purposes (Homer and Kahle 1988).

Beatty et al. (1985) found that 92% and 85% of respondents who picked any given first value ranked it first or second one month later, offering support for the LOV's consistency over time. In one study, using 10-point scales to evaluate each of the nine LOV items, a three-factor representation of the values was found with composite reliability estimates (via LISREL) of .69 for a factor representing internal individual values, .68 for an external values factor, and .58 for an internal interpersonal values factor (Homer and Kahle 1988).

Most studies employing the LOV have focused on the distribution of values across the U.S. (e.g., Kahle 1986), the predictive validity of the LOV toward consumer behaviors, and/or the relationship of the LOV with other psychological constructs (e.g., Homer and Kahle 1988; Kahle 1983; Kahle et al. 1986). These studies indicate that the LOV was found to be significantly correlated with various measures of mental health, well-being, adaptation to society and self (Kahle 1983), and predictive of a number of consumer behaviors (Homer and Kahle 1988; Kahle et al 1986). Furthermore, the hypothesized dispersion of values across areas of the U.S. was supported (Kahle 1986). In sum, evidence for the nomological and predictive validity of the LOV exists.

In the Homer and Kahle (1988) study, means of the LOV items by various discriminant groups are also reported.

In yet another study, LOV rankings from 997 respondents in the U.S. were compared to LOV rankings from Kahle's (1983) original LOV study (Kahle, Poulos, and Sukhdial 1988). A Spearman rank-order correlation between the ranks of the values (i.e., in terms of the percentage of people endorsing the value as the primary value) across the two studies revealed stability in importance placed on different values by the American people over a decade. The correlation for males was .91; for females was .79; and for the sample combined, the correlation was .83. Kahle et al. (1988) offer numerous breakdowns of the LOV values by gender and age groups.

Mean scores for eight LOV values across four U.S. geographic regions are reported in Kahle, Liu, and Watkins (1992). These means scores are based on 7-point scales (not at all important to me—extremely important to me) and are reproduced below:

Value	Region Order	Mean1	Mean2	Mean3	Mean4
Self-respect	w,e,m,s	6.37	6.55	6.55	6.72
Security	e,m,w,s	6.29	6.29	6.31	6.43
Warm relations with others	e,w,m,s	6.03	6.29	6.31	6.39
Self of fulfillment	m,w,e,s	5.82	5.91	6.03	6.16
Sense of accomplishment	m,w,e,s	6.04	6.14	6.17	6.31
Being well respected	w,e,m,s	5.72	5.97	6.01	6.20
Sense of belonging	w,e,m,s	5.52	5.77	5.81	6.02
Fun and enjoyment in life	m,e,w,s	5.53	5.60	5.67	5.81

e=east, m=midwest, s=south, w=west; total n = 442

Other sources:

Beatty, Sharon E., Lynn R. Kahle, Pamela Homer and Shekhar Misra (1985), "Alternative Measurement Approaches to Consumer Values: The List of Values and the Rokeach Value Survey," *Psychology & Marketing*, 2 (Fall), 181-200.

Homer, Pamela and Lynn R. Kahle (1988), "A Structural Equation Analysis of the Value-Attitude-Behavior Hierarchy," *Journal of Personality and Social Psychology*, 54 (April), 638-646.

Kahle, Lynn (1985), "Social Values in the Eighties: A Special Issue," *Psychology & Marketing*, 2 (Winter), 231-237.

Kahle, Lynn (1986), "The Nine Nations of North America and the Values Basis of Geographic Segmentation," *Journal of Marketing*, 50 (April), 37-47.

Kahle, Lynn and Patricia Kennedy (1988), "Using the List of Values (LOV) to Understand Consumers," *The Journal of Services Marketing*, 2 (Fall), 49-56.

Kahle, Lynn, Ruiming Liu, and Harry Watkins (1992), "Psychographic Variation Across United States Geographic Regions," in *Advances in Consumer Research*, Vol. 18, John F. Sherry and Brian Sternthal (eds), Provo, UT: The Association for Consumer Research, (in press).

Kahle, Lynn, Basil Poulos, and Ajay Sukhdial (1988), "Changes in Social Values in the United States During the Past Decade," *Journal of Advertising Research*, 28 (February/March), 35-41.

References: Feather, Norman T. (1975), *Values in Education and Society*, New York: Free Press.

Maslow, Abraham H. (1954), *Motivation and Personality*, New York: Harper.

Rokeach, Milton J. (1968), "The Role of Values in Public Opinion Research," *Public Opinion Quarterly*, 32 (Winter), 547-549.

Rokeach, Milton J. (1973), *The Nature of Human Values*, New York: Free Press.

THE LIST OF VALUES: LOV
(Kahle 1983)

The following is a list of things that some people look for or want out of life. Please study the list carefully and then rate each thing on how important it is in your daily life, where 1 = very unimportant, and 9 = very important.

	Very Unimportant					Very Important				%	M
1) Sense of belonging	1 2 3 4 5 6 7 8 9									8.8%	7.05
2) Excitement	1 2 3 4 5 6 7 8 9									—	7.08
3) Warm relationships with others	1 2 3 4 5 6 7 8 9									16.2%	8.76
4) Self-fulfillment	1 2 3 4 5 6 7 8 9									9.6%	8.62
5) Being well respected	1 2 3 4 5 6 7 8 9									8.8%	7.55
6) Fun and enjoyment of life	1 2 3 4 5 6 7 8 9									4.5%	8.08
7) Security	1 2 3 4 5 6 7 8 9									20.6%	7.75
8) Self-respect	1 2 3 4 5 6 7 8 9									21.1%	8.97
9) A sense of accomplishment	1 2 3 4 5 6 7 8 9									11.4%	8.59

Now reread the items and *circle the one thing that is most important to you in your daily life.*

NOTES: The above scoring format is but one possible format. As indicated earlier, the values can be rank ordered, or respondents can be asked to indicate their top two values, and/or use 10-point scales and/ or a combination of scoring methods.

In the original study (n = 2,264), only .2% of the sample endorsed "excitement" as their top value. Subsequently, excitement was collapsed into the "fun and enjoyment in life" category. The percentages presented above reflect the percentage of respondents who ranked the value as the most important in living their daily lives. The percent reported for "fun and enjoyment in life" reflects the 2% added to it for those respondents endorsing "excitement" as their top value (Kahle 1983).

The mean values (M) are based on 10-point items and were calculated by averaging the values reported in Table 7 of Homer and Kahle (1988). Also values 2, 4, 8, and 9 represent the internal individual values factor; values 1, 5, and 7 represent the external dimension values factor; and values 3 and 6 represent the internal interpersonal values factor (Homer and Kahle 1988).

APPENDIX TO GENERAL VALUES

Another value assessment technique has been proposed by Hofstede (1980). Through a lengthy survey of work-related values over 53 cultures (similar in form to VALS), Hofstede identified four value dimensions related to basic anthropological/societal issues (Hofstede and Bond 1984, pp. 419-420):

Power distance - the extent to which less powerful members of institutions and organizations accept that power is distributed unequally. The basic anthropological/societal issue "power distance" relates to is social inequality and the amount of authority of one person over others.

Uncertainty avoidance - the extent to which people feel threatened by ambiguous situations, and have created beliefs and institutions that try to avoid these. This dimension is related to the way a society deals with conflicts and aggression, and, as the last resort, with life and death.

Individualism vs. collectivism - individualism is viewed as a situation in which people are supposed to look after themselves and their immediate family only, and collectivism is viewed as a situation in which people belong to in-groups and are supposed to look after them in exchange for loyalty. This dimension reflects a bipolar continuum, and is related to the individual's dependence on the group, his or her self-concept as "I" or "we."

Masculinity vs. Femininity - masculinity is defined as a situation in which the dominant values in society are success, money, and things. Its opposite, femininity is defined as a situation in which the dominant values in society are caring for others and the quality of life. The anthropological/societal issue this dimension relates to is the choice of social sex roles and its effects on one's self-concept. These value dimensions show correspondence with the Rokeach values. Though not extensively used in the U.S. marketing/consumer behavior literature, the Hofstede values have seen use in the cross-cultural psychology literature. The interested reader is referred to the following sources:

Source(s): Hofstede, Geert (1980), *Culture's Consequences: International Differences in Work-Related Values*, Beverly Hills, CA: Sage.

Hofstede, Geert and Michael H. Bond (1984), "Hofstede's Culture Dimensions: An Independent Validation Using Rokeach's Value Survey," *Journal of Cross-Cultural Psychology*, 15 (December), 417-433.

Though not a specific personality assessment procedure, a "laddering" technique that ranks the values associated with product attributes has also been proposed. Specifically, laddering refers to an in-depth, one-on-one interviewing technique used to develop an understanding of how consumers translate the attributes of products into meaningful associations with respect to self, following Means-End Theory (e.g., Guttman 1982; Reynolds and Guttman 1988). For example, a typical laddering format employs a series of direct probes such as "Why is that (attribute, product) important to you?", where the goal is to determine linkages between key perceptual elements across the range of product attributes, consequences of purchase, and values. The networks or "ladders" constructed represent combinations of elements that serve as the basis for distinguishing between and among products in a given product class. The above description is an overly simplistic and brief one. The interested reader is referred to the following sources:

Source(s): Guttman, Jonathan (1982), "A Means-End Chain Model Based on Consumer Categorization Processes," *Journal of Marketing*, 46 (April), 60-72.

Guttman, Jonathan (1984), "Analyzing Consumer Orientations Toward Beverages Through Means-End Chain Analysis," *Psychology & Marketing*, 3/4, 23-43.

Reynolds, Thomas J. and Jonathan Guttman (1988), "Laddering Theory, Method, Analysis, and Interpretation," *Journal of Advertising Research*, 28 (February/March), 11-31.

SPECIFIC CONSUMPTION VALUES

SOCIALLY RESPONSIBLE CONSUMPTION BEHAVIOR: SRCB
(Antil and Bennett 1979; Antil 1984)

Construct: Socially responsible consumption is defined as those consumer behaviors and purchase decisions which are related to environmental and resource-related problems and are motivated not only by a desire to satisfy personal needs, but also by a concern for the welfare of society in general (Antil 1978; Antil and Bennett 1979).

Description: The SRCB is composed of 40 Likert items (agree-disagree) scored on a five-point basis. Scores on the items are summed to form an overall SRCB index. Thus, the scale is considered unidimensional and the possible range of scores is 40 to 200.

Development: An initial pool of 138 items was developed from a number of relevant sources based on the definition of the construct. Using recommended scaling procedures that included item analysis, coefficient alpha, and factor analysis (across numerous samples described below), the final scale was derived.

Sample(s):   A number of samples were used in the scale development process (Antil and Bennett 1978). An initial student sample (n = 444) was used for deleting ambiguous and redundant items. Item analysis based on this sample resulted in trimming the initial pool of 138 to 59 items. A second student sample (n = 321) was used to assess initial reliability and item-to-total correlations resulting in 42 items being retained. A third non-student sample (n = 98) was used for reliability and item analysis, resulting in the final 40 item scale. Lastly, two non-student samples to examine the dimensionality, reliability, and validity of the final scale (n = 690 and n = 98 Sierra Club members) were collected.

Validity: The reliability, dimensionality, and validity of the final 40 item scale were assessed with the last two non-student samples as follows. Two measures of internal consistency were used to assess the scale's reliability. Guttman's Lambda 3 and Cronbach's alpha were .93 and .92, respectively.

Factor analysis indicated that a single factor underlies the dimension of the scale. The first factor accounted for 78.3% of the variance in a three-factor solution using the eigenvalue greater-than-one rule for retaining factors. Thus, evidence for the unidimensionality of the SRCB was found.

In addition, the SRCB demonstrated convergent and discriminant validity (via MTMM) when correlated with measures of traditional social responsibility and ecological concern. For example, the correlation between SRCB and social responsibility was .29, and the correlation between SRCB and ecological concern was .73.

Mean score differences also offered evidence of known group validity. The mean score for the n = 736 sample was 144.30, and the mean score for the Sierra Club sample was 168.50. The difference between these two means was statistically significant.

Scores: Mean scores for the final two validation samples were reported. For combined samples (n = 690 and n = 98), the overall mean of the scale was 144.50 (sd = 24.3). The mean score for the n = 736 sample was 144.30, and the mean score for the Sierra Club sample was 168.50. As stated above, the difference between these last two means was statistically significant.

Source(s):   Antil, John A, and Peter D. Bennett (1979), "Construction and Validation of a Scale to Measure Socially Responsible Consumption Behavior," in *The Conserver Society*, Karl H. Henion II and Thomas C. Kinnear (eds.), Chicago: The American Marketing Association, 51-68.
Antil, John A. (1984), "Socially Responsible Consumers: Profile and Implications for Public Policy," *Journal of Macromarketing*, (Fall), 18-39.

Other
evidence: N/A.

Other
sources: N/A.

References: N/A.

SOCIALLY RESPONSIBLE CONSUMPTION BEHAVIOR: SRCB
(Antil and Bennett 1979; Antil 1984)

1) People should be more concerned about reducing or limiting the noise in our society.

2) Every person should stop increasing their consumption of products so that our resources will last longer.

3) The benefits of modern consumer products are more important than the pollution which results from their production and use.*

4) Pollution is presently one of the most critical problems facing this nation.

5) I don't think we're doing enough to encourage manufacturers to use recyclable packages.

6) I think we are just not doing enough to save scarce natural resources from being used up.

7) Natural resources must be preserved even if people must do without some products.

8) All consumers should be interested in the environmental consequences of the products they purchase.

9) Pollution is not personally affecting my life.*

10) Consumers should be made to pay higher prices for products which pollute the environment.

11) It genuinely infuriates me to think that the government doesn't do more to help control pollution of the environment.

12) Nonreturnable bottles and cans for soft drinks and beer should be banned by law.

13) I would be willing to sign a petition or demonstrate for an environmental cause.

14) I have often thought that if we could just get by with a little less there would be more left for future generations.

15) The Federal government should subsidize research on technology for recycling waste products.

16) I'd be willing to ride a bicycle or take a bus to work in order to reduce air pollution.

17) I would probably never join a group or club which is concerned solely with ecological issues.*

18) I feel people worry too much about pesticides on food products.*

19) The whole pollution issue has never upset me too much since I feel it's somewhat overrated.*

20) I would donate a day's pay to a foundation to help improve the environment.

21) I would be willing to have my laundry less white or bright in order to be sure that I was using a nonpolluting laundry product.

22) Manufacturers should be forced to use recycled materials in their manufacturing and processing operations.

23) I think that a person should urge his/her friends not to use products that pollute or harm the environment.

24) Commercial advertising should be forced to mention the ecological disadvantages of products.

25) Much more fuss is being made about air and water pollution than is really justified.*

26) The government should provide each citizen with a list of agencies and organizations to which citizens could report grievances concerning pollution.

27) I would be willing to pay a 5% increase in my taxes to support greater governmental control of pollution.

28) Trying to control water pollution is more trouble than it is worth.*

29) I become incensed when I think about the harm being done to plant and animal life by pollution.

30) People should urge their friends to limit their use of products made from scarce resources.

31) I would be willing to pay one dollar more each month for electricity if it meant cleaner air.

32) It would be wise for the government to devote much more money toward supporting a strong conservation program.

33) I would be willing to accept an increase in my family's total expenses of $120 next year to promote the wise use of natural resources.

34) Products which during their manufacturing or use pollute the environment should be heavily taxed by the government.

35) People should be willing to accept smog in exchange for the convenience of automobiles.*

36) When I think of the ways industries are polluting I get frustrated and angry.

37) Our public schools should require all students to take a course dealing with environmental and conservation problems.

38) I would be willing to stop buying products from companies guilty of polluting the environment even though it might be inconvenient.

39) I'd be willing to make personal sacrifices for the sake of slowing down pollution even though the immediate results may not seem significant.

40) I rarely ever worry about the effects of smog on myself and family.*

NOTE: * denotes items that are reversed coded.

VOLUNTARY SIMPLICITY SCALE: VSS
(Leonard-Barton 1981)

Construct: Voluntary simplicity is defined as the degree to which an individual selects a lifestyle intended to maximize his/her control over daily activities and to minimize his/her consumption and dependency (Leonard-Barton 1981). Five basic values underlie a voluntary simplicity lifestyle:

Material simplicity - non-consumption oriented patterns of use.

Self-determination - desire to assume greater control over personal destiny.

Ecological awareness - recognition of the interdependency of people and resources.

Human scale - a desire for smaller scale institutions and technology.

Personal growth - a desire to explore and develop the inner life.

Description: The VSS is a multi-dimensional scale comprised of 18 statements that assess the degree to which respondents engage in voluntary simplicity behaviors. Fourteen of the items provided by Leonard-Barton are scored on a 5 point basis on the degree to which a behavior is performed. Two of the items offer six response alternatives, and two are dichotomous (yes-no). Though exact scoring procedures are not offered, scores on the VSS can range up to a high of 90 (Leonard-Barton 1981).

Several versions of the scale are tenable, including 6, 9 and 14-item scales (Leonard-Barton 1981), and a version proposed by Cowles and Crosby (1986).

Development: Initially, the scale consisted of nine items. It was subsequently expanded to 19 items, and then reduced to an 18-item format (Leonard-Barton 1982). Via a number of scaling procedures, including factor analysis and internal consistency reliability across several studies, the 9- and 19-item versions of the scale were derived. The samples and studies used to arrive at these versions are described below.

Sample(s): A number of samples were used in the scale development and validation process. The original 9-item version was tested on a sample from Palo Alto, California (n not reported). The expanded 19-item version was tested on data collected by Elgin and Mitchell (1977) with a sample of 423. This 19-item version was also tested on another sample (n = 215) of homeowners in California. (Half of this sample were users of solar energy in their home.) Lastly, the 18-item version was administered to 812 California homeowners (see Leonard-Barton 1981).

Validity: Reliability estimates of the 9- and 19-item versions of the scale ranged from alpha of .52 to alpha of .70. (These were the only reliability estimates reported by Leonard-Barton (1981)). It should be noted that these alpha estimates should be viewed with caution as the VSS is composed of six factors and the alphas reported above represent reliability estimates for the summed 9- and 19-item versions.

In the original paper (Leonard-Barton 1981), factor analysis was used to determine the dimensionality of the scale, and across samples, a six-factor structure was found. The six factors underlying the five simplicity lifestyle values were labeled as: 1) conservation through biking; 2) self-sufficiency in services; 3) recycling of resources; 4) self-sufficiency through making goods; 5) recycling of durable goods; and 6) closeness with nature. Leonard-Barton did not report direct estimates of factor internal consistency, but provided factor loadings ranging from a low of .31 to a high of .87 across factors (Leonard-Barton 1981, p. 245).

The 18-item VSS was found to be positively related to education (r =.16) and negatively related to age (n = 812). The VSS was positively correlated with "mechanical ability" to do one's own repairs (r = .15 to .22 across the three versions), investment in energy conserving equipment (beta = .40 in a regression equation), personal conviction to conserve energy (r = .27), and other energy conserving practices like weather stripping and caulking doors and windows (r = .21) (n = 812), thus providing evidence for the validity of the scale (Leonard-Barton 1981).

Scores:	Mean scores on the 18-item version were reported by income level only. For families with a 1978 reported household income of less then $15,000, M = 35.9; for families with 1978 income between $16,000 - $35,000, M = 38.2; and for families with income $46,000 or more, M = 35.9. These mean values were not statistically different from each other (n = 812, Leonard-Barton 1981).
Source(s):	Leonard-Barton, Dorothy (1981), "Voluntary Simplicity Lifestyles and Energy Conservation," *Journal of Consumer Research*, 8 (December), 243-252.
Other evidence:	In a more recent study, Cowles and Crosby (1986) also examined the VSS with a sample of California and Colorado household consumer panel members (n = 412).

Cowles and Crosby (1986) reported composite reliability estimates (via LISREL) for each of the six factors originally found by Leonard-Barton, and for a three-factor model they proposed. These estimates are presented below:

Factor	Leonard-Barton	Crosby and Cowles
Biking	.880	—
Self-sufficiency/services	.898	—
Recycling resources	.775	—
Recycling durable goods	.827	—
Self-sufficiency/goods	.777	—
Closeness to nature	.865	—
Material simplicity	—	.779
Self-determination	—	.938
Ecological awareness	—	.892

The three factors proposed by Cowles and Crosby are also labeled in the above table. Cowles and Crosby found that the two factor structures fit the data equally well and suggested that their proposed three-factor measure of the VSS was an appropriate alternative to the 18-item, six-factor measure of Leonard-Barton.

Other sources:	Cowles, Deborah and Lawrence A. Crosby (1986), "Measure Validation in Consumer Research: A Confirmatory Factor Analysis of the Voluntary Simplicity Lifestyle Scale," in *Advances in Consumer Research*, Vol. 13, Richard Lutz (ed.), Provo, UT: The Association for Consumer Research, 392-397.
References:	Elgin, Duane and Arnold Mitchell (1977), "Voluntary Simplicity," *The Co-Evolution Quarterly*, Summer, 5-18.

VOLUNTARY SIMPLICITY SCALE: VSS
(Leonard-Barton 1981)

Please indicate the degree to which you engage in each of the following behaviors by circling the appropriate response.

1) Make gifts instead of buying
   a) never
   b) occasionally
   c) frequently
   d) usually
   e) always

2) Ride a bicycle for exercise or recreation
   a) never
   b) once or twice a year
   c) once a month
   d) once a week
   e) everyday

3) Recycle newspapers used at home
   a) never recycle newspapers
   b) recycle some
   c) recycle many
   d) recycle most
   e) recycle all newspapers

4) Recycle glass jars/bottles used at home
   a) never recycle jars/bottles
   b) recycle some
   c) recycle many
   d) recycle most
   e) recycle all jars/bottles

5) Recycle cans used at home
   a) never recycle cans
   b) recycle some
   c) recycle many
   d) recycle most
   e) recycle all cans

6) Family members or friends change the oil in the family car
   a) never
   b) sometimes
   c) frequently
   d) usually
   e) always

7) Have gotten instructions in skills to increase self-reliance, for example, in carpentry, car tune-up and repair, or plumbing
   a) never
   b) occasionally (informally from friends)
   c) frequently (informally from friends)
   d) have taken a class
   e) have taken more than one class

8) Intentionally eat meatless main meals
   a) never
   b) occasionally
   c) frequently
   d) usually
   e) always

9) Buy clothing at a second hand store
   a) none of my clothes
   b) a few items
   c) many items
   d) most of my clothes
   e) all of my clothes

10) Buy major items of furniture or clothing at a garage sale (over $15)
   a) never
   b) rarely
   c) sometimes
   d) fairly often
   e) very often

11) Make furniture or clothing for the family
   a) none
   b) a few small items
   c) some items
   d) many items
   e) most of the clothing or most of the furniture

12) Have exchanged goods or services with others in lieu of payment with money, e.g., repairing equipment in exchange for other skilled work
   a) never
   b) have once
   c) have several times
   d) have many times
   e) do so whenever possible

13) Have a compost pile
   a) yes
   b) no

14) Contribute to ecologically oriented organizations
   a) never have
   b) did contribute once; do not now
   c) occasionally contribute now
   d) contribute regularly to one organization
   e) contribute regularly to two or more organizations
   f) do not know

15) Belong to a cooperative
   a) yes
   b) no

16) Grow the vegetables the family consumes during the summer season
   a) none
   b) some
   c) many
   d) most
   e) all

17) Ride a bicycle for transportation to work
   a) never
   b) occasionally
   c) frequently
   d) usually
   e) always
   f) do not know

18) Ride a bicycle on errands within two miles of home
   a) never
   b) occasionally
   c) frequently
   d) usually
   e) always

NOTES: The reduced six-item scale proposed by Leonard-Barton is comprised of items 5, 6, 9, 11, 14, and 18. Leonard-Barton's proposed nine-item version is comprised of items 3, 4, 5, 8, 9, 10, 12, 15, and 16. Her 14-item version includes all items *except* 8, 9, 17, and 18.

The items comprising the six factors found by Leonard-Barton are as follows: conservation through biking is composed of items 2, 17, and 18; self-sufficiency in services is composed of items 6, 7, and 12; recycling of resources is composed of items 3, 4, and 5; self-sufficiency through making goods is composed of items 1 and 11; recycling durable goods is composed of items 9 and 10; and closeness to nature is composed of items 4, 8, 13, 14, and 16. Item 15 did not load above .30 on any factor (Leonard-Barton 1981).

The three-factor structure proposed by Cowles and Crosby (1981) is as follows: material simplicity is composed of items 2, 9, 10, 17, and 18; self-determination is composed of items 1, 6, 7, 11, 12, 13, and 16; ecological awareness is composed of items 3, 4, 5, 13, and 14. (Items 9 and 10 were allowed to load on the self-determination factor and the composite reliabilities previously reported reflect the cross-loadings.)

SUBJECTIVE LEISURE SCALES: SLS
(Unger and Kernan 1983)

Construct: In their research, Unger and Kernan (1983) measure leisure from a subjective perspective. Most definitional discussions of leisure from this perspective relate leisure to free time, recreation, and play. From this theoretical base, Unger and Kernan (1983) propose six determinants of leisure:

Intrinsic satisfaction - leisure is seen as an end unto itself rather than a means to an end.

Perceived freedom - leisure is viewed as free, i.e., perceived as voluntary, without coercion or obligation.

Involvement - true leisure means total absorption in an activity, such that it is an escape from daily life.

Arousal - arousal (i.e., novelty seeking, exploration, and risk taking) is present in leisure pursuits.

Mastery - one has the opportunity to test oneself or to conquer the environment through leisure pursuits (i.e., mastery of the activity, mental or physical, is present).

Spontaneity - unlike obligatory events, leisure activities are not routine, planned, or anticipated.

Description: The SLS is a six-factor measure designed to assess the six determinants of leisure discussed above. A total of 26 items are used to measure the six determinants and all items are scored on six point formats from strongly disagree (1) to strongly agree (6). Scores on items within each dimension can be summed to form indices of each dimension.

Development: Forty-two items were generated to reflect the six determinants of leisure. The items were checked for face validity by a panel of 10 marketing professors and Ph.D students, resulting in 36 items retained. Various tests for reliability, validity, and factor structure were then performed on the remaining items to derive the final scales over two samples and six leisure scenarios.

Sample(s):   Two samples were used in scale development. (Two other samples were also used to generate the leisure scenarios for validity testing but did not respond to the leisure items.) The first sample consisted of 132 students and the second sample consisted of 160 nonstudent adults. Three other samples (n = 10, 200, and 123) were also used in preliminary stages (i.e., item editing and pretesting).

Validity: Using the student sample, responses to the 36 items were examined for internal consistency. Two items that decreased internal consistency (on the respective factors) were deleted. Principal components analysis was also used to trim the number of items. Items with loadings lower than .40 on any factor in three or more of the scenarios were deleted, resulting in the final 26-item, six-factor SLS. In the nonstudent sample, the SLS was checked for dimensionality and validity. With this sample, factor analysis revealed that the intrinsic satisfaction and perceived freedom dimensions were not distinct, and the arousal and mastery dimensions were not distinct, suggesting that the hypothesized dimensionality of the SLS requires further testing. Though reliability estimates were performed (i.e., coefficient alpha, split-halves), they were not reported in the paper (Unger and Kernan 1983). Numerous concurrent, construct, and nomological validity tests, however, did show support for the validity of the SLS. For example, using the SLS factors as predictors across six different leisure scenarios produced multiple Rs ranging from .05 to .56, with most multiple Rs in the .30 and above range. (See Table 1, p. 389.)

Scores: Mean or percentage scores were not reported.

Source:	Unger, Lynette and Jerome B. Kernan (1983), "On the Meaning of Leisure: An Investigation of Some Determinants of the Subjective Experience," *Journal of Consumer Research*, 9 (March), 381-392.
Other evidence:	N/A.
Other sources:	N/A.
References:	N/A.

SUBJECTIVE LEISURE SCALES: SLS
(Unger and Kernan 1983)

Following are statements concerning the situation described below. For each statement, indicate whether you strongly agree, agree, somewhat agree, somewhat disagree, disagree, or strongly disagree *as the statement pertains to the way you feel about the situation.*

[SOME LEISURE RELATED SITUATION IS DESCRIBED HERE]

1) It is its own reward.

2) "Not because I have to but because I want to" would characterize it.

3) I feel like I'm exploring new worlds.

4) I feel I have been thoroughly tested.

5) I could get so involved that I would forget everything else.

6) I wouldn't know the day before that it was going to happen.

7) I enjoy it for its own sake, not for what it will get me.

8) I do not feel forced.

9) There is novelty in it.

10) I feel like I'm conquering the world.

11) It helps me forget about the day's problems.

12) It happens without warning or pre-thought.

13) Pure enjoyment is the only thing in it for me.

14) It is completely voluntary.

15) It satisfies my sense of curiosity.

16) I get a sense of adventure or risk.

17) It totally absorbs me.

18) It is a spontaneous occurrence.

19) I do not feel obligated.

20) It offers novel experiences.

21) I feel like a real champion.

22) It is like "getting away from it all."

23) It happens "out of the blue."

24) Others would not have to talk me into it.

25) It makes me feel like I'm in another world.

26) It is a "spur-of-the-moment" thing.

NOTES: Items 1, 7, and 13 are designed to measure intrinsic satisfaction. Items 2, 8, 14, 19, and 24 are designed to measure perceived freedom. Items 3, 9, 15, and 20 are designed to measure arousal. Items 4, 10, 16, and 21 are designed to measure mastery. Items 5, 11, 17, 22, and 25 are designed to measure involvement. Items 6, 12, 18, 23, and 26 are designed to measure spontaneity.

MOTIVATIONAL TENDENCIES OF DRINKING-DRIVING BEHAVIORS: MTDD
(Lastovicka, Murray, Joachimsthaler, Bhalla, and Scheurich 1987)

Construct: Drinking-driving behaviors are posited to be related to several motivational tendencies and AIOs (Lastovicka, Murray, Joachimsthaler, Bhalla, and Scheurich 1987). The MTDD was derived to determine if it can characterize young males most likely to drink and drive.

Description: The MTDD scales are composed of five measures that tap related dimensions of the propensity to drink and drive. Each measure is composed of three 4-point Likert items scored from strongly disagree to strongly agree (a total of 15 items). Items can be summed within factors to form indices of each factor.

Development: The procedures used to develop the measures generally followed guidelines found in the psychometric scaling literature. Preliminary data from convenience samples was used to select the 15 items. Then, via a phone survey of 703 18-24-year-old males, the factor structure, reliability, and validity of the measures were assessed.

Samples: As stated above, convenience samples were used to develop the the items. Then, a sample of 703 18-24-year-old males was used to examine the scales psychometric properties and relationship to the likelihood of drinking and driving.

Validity: Via factor analysis and a cross-validation procedure, the dimensionality and reliability of the items were examined. A five-factor solution established a 1) Problem behaviors factor, 2) a Partying factor, 3) a Sensation-Seeking factor, 4) a Macho factor, and 5) a Dissatisfaction with life factor. Each factor was composed of 3 items. The Kaiser-Caffrey alpha estimates of the representativeness of the sampling domain of items were .78, .70, .74, .55, and .88 for factors 1 through 5, respectively. A cross validation procedure (i.e., the stability of the factor solution across splits in the sample) showed coefficients ranging from .88 to .97 across the five factors.

Means on the lifestyle factors and percentages of respondents reporting drinking and driving behaviors indicated relationships between the measures and drinking-driving behaviors (Lastovicka et al. 1987, Table 2, p. 260).

Scores: Means on the lifestyle factors by various behavioral-based clusters are reported in Table 2. These means are based on a K-means clustering solution (Lastovicka et al. 1987, p. 260).

Source: Lastovicka, John L., John P. Murray Jr., Erich A. Joachimsthaler, Gaurav Bhalla, and Jim Scheurich (1987), "A Lifestyle Typology to Model Young Male Drinking and Driving," *Journal of Consumer Research*, 14 (September), 257-263.

Other evidence: N/A.

Other sources: N/A.

References: N/A.

MOTIVATIONAL TENDENCIES OF DRINKING-DRIVING BEHAVIORS: MTDD
(Lastovicka, Murray, Joachimsthaler, Bhalla, and Scheurich 1987)

1) I frequently skipped classes in high school.

2) I have been suspended from school for fighting on more than one occasion.

3) Except for times when I was sick, I hardly ever missed a day of school.*

4) It seems like no matter what my friends do on a weekend, we almost always end up at a bar getting smashed.

5) A party wouldn't be a party without some liquor.

6) I've been drunk at least five times this month.

7) Taking chances can be fun.

8) I would like to drive a race car.

9) I like to speed in my car.

10) If someone gives me a hard enough time, I'll punch him.

11) It's important for me to act and dress like I'm a tough guy.

12) There should be a gun in every home.

13) My life appears to be coming apart at the seams.

14) I feel like I'm getting a raw deal out of life.

15) Overall, I'd say I'm very happy.*

NOTES: * denotes reverse scoring.

Items 1 to 3 comprise the "problem behaviors" factor; items 4 to 6 comprise the "partying" factor; items 7 to 9 comprise the "sensation-seeking" factor; items 10 to 12 comprise the "macho" factor; and items 13 to 15 comprise the "dissatisfaction with life" factor.

VALUE CONSCIOUSNESS AND COUPON PRONENESS: VC AND CP
(Lichtenstein, Netemeyer, and Burton 1990)

Constructs: Value consciousness is defined as a concern for paying lower prices, subject to some quality constraint, and coupon proneness is defined as an increased propensity to respond to a purchase offer because the coupon form of the purchase offer positively affects purchase evaluations (Lichtenstein, Netemeyer, and Burton 1990). Based on these two conceptual definitions and a distinction between the two constructs grounded in transaction utility theory, the VC and CP scales were developed.

Description: The VC and CP scales are composed of 7 and 8 Likert items, respectively (strongly agree - strongly disagree). All of the items are scored on a 7-point basis. Scores on the items are summed within each scale to form overall VC and CP scores.

Development: Consistent with the psychometric scaling literature, a pool of 66 items (33 for each construct) was generated based on the definitions of VC and CP and existing literature. Two expert judge panels were used to screen ambiguous and redundant items and check for content validity. This trimmed the initial pool of items to 15 for VC and 25 for CP. Factor analysis and various estimates of reliability were then used to further purify the scales and assess the dimensionality and internal consistency of the scales. This resulted in the final 7-item VC and 8-item CP scales.

Sample(s): Two samples were used in the scale development process. The first consisted of 263 students. The second sample consisted of 350 nonstudent adults from a southeastern SMSA.

Validity: Based on the student sample, the composite reliability estimates for the VC and CP scales were .80 and .88, respectively. Via confirmatory factor analysis, tests of discriminant validity revealed that VC and CP measures were related yet distinct measures. The correlation between VC and CP was .36 for the student sample.

With the nonstudent sample, composite reliability estimates again were .80 and .88 for the VC and CP scales, and tests of discriminant validity also revealed that the two measures were distinct, supporting the scale's discriminant validity. The VC-CP correlation was .24 for the nonstudent sample. In addition, the VC and CP measures were correlated with a number of cognitive and behavioral measures theoretically related to VC and CP. The pattern of correlations suggest that the VC and CP measures exhibited nomological validity (Lichtenstein et al. 1990). For example, CP explained between 15.5% and 24.4% of the variance in measures of coupon redemption. VC was significantly correlated with measures of enduring product involvement (.26), product knowledge (.43), price knowledge (.41), and information from *Consumer Reports* (.20).

Scores: No mean or percentage scores were reported.

Source: Lichtenstein, Donald R., Richard G. Netemeyer, and Scot Burton (1990), "Distinguishing Coupon Proneness From Value Consciousness: An Acquisition-Transaction Utility Theory Perspective," *Journal of Marketing*, 54 (July), 54-67.

Other evidence: N/A.

Other sources: N/A.

References: N/A.

VALUE CONSCIOUSNESS AND COUPON PRONENESS: VC AND CP
(Lichtenstein, Netemeyer, and Burton 1990)

VC:

1) I am very concerned about low prices, but I am equally concerned about product quality.

2) When grocery shopping, I compare the prices of different brands to be sure I get the best value for the money.

3) When purchasing a product, I always try to maximize the quality I get for the money I spend.

4) When I buy products, I like to be sure that I am getting my money's worth.

5) I generally shop around for lower prices on products, but they still must meet certain quality requirements before I will buy them.

6) When I shop, I usually compare the "price per ounce" information for brands I normally buy.

7) I always check prices at the grocery store to be sure I get the best value for the money I spend.

CP:

1) Redeeming coupons makes me feel good.

2) I enjoy clipping coupons out of the newspaper.

3) When I use coupons, I feel that I am getting a good deal.

4) I enjoy using coupons regardless of the amount I save by doing so.

5) I have favorite brands, but most of the time I buy the brand I have a coupon for.

6) I am more likely to buy brands for which I have a coupon.

7) Coupons have caused me to buy products I normally would not buy.

8) Beyond the money I save, redeeming coupons gives me a sense of joy.

MATERIALISM

A number of scales have been designed to measure materialism or aspects of materialism. Seven of these scales are presented here in chronological order.

MEASURE OF MATERIALISTIC ATTITUDES: MMA
(Moschis and Churchill 1978)

Construct:	Materialistic attitude is defined as orientations emphasizing possessions and money for personal happiness and social progress (Moschis and Churchill 1978, p. 607).
Description:	The MMA is composed of 6 Likert-type items scored on a 5-point disagree-agree basis. Items scores are summed to form an overall MMA index.
Development:	The selection of items for the MMA was done by summing appropriate items, using item-to-total correlations to purify the measure, and coefficient alpha to assess the resultant reliability of the measure (Moschis and Churchill 1978). These items were largely adapted from earlier research assessing racial differences in response to advertising to adolescents (Wackman, Reale, and Ward 1972).
Sample(s):	The scale was developed and tested using a sample of 806 adolescents (ages 12 to 18).
Validity:	The coefficient alpha reliability of the scale was reported to be .60. In addition, the MMA was significantly related to measures of social utility in regression analysis (beta = .16) as well as peer communication (beta = .12), and gender (-.20) (i.e., males held stronger materialistic attitudes).
Scores:	Scores (i.e., mean scores or percentages) were not reported.
Source:	Moschis, George P. and Gilbert A. Churchill, Jr. (1978), "Consumer Socialization: A Theoretical and Empirical Analysis," *Journal of Marketing Research*, 15 (November), 599 - 609.
Other evidence:	N/A.
Other sources:	N/A.
References:	Wackman, Daniel B., Greg Reale, and Scot Ward (1972), "Racial Differences in Response to Advertising among Adolescents," in *Television in Day-to-Day Life*, Eli P. Rubenstein, George A. Comstock, and John P. Murray (eds.), Rockville, MD: U.S. Department of Health, Education, and Welfare, 543-551.

MEASURE OF MATERIALISTIC ATTITUDES: MMA
(Moschis and Churchill 1978)

1) It is really true that money can buy happiness.

2) My dream in life is to be able to own expensive things.

3) People judge others by the things they own.

4) I buy some things that I secretly hope will impress other people.

5) Money is the most important thing to consider in choosing a job.

6) I think others judge me as a person by the kinds of products and brands I use.

MATERIALISM-POST MATERIALISM SCALE
(Inglehart 1981)

Construct: Inglehart (1981) delineates materialism from post materialism as follows: materialism gives top priority to physical sustenance and safety, while post materialism emphasizes belonging, self-expression and the quality of life. This delineation is based on a value shift from materialism to post materialism from World War II to the early eighties. This value shift has conceptual roots in two key hypotheses (Inglehart 1981, p. 881):

Scarcity hypothesis: an individual's priorities reflect the socioeconomic environment - one places the greatest subjective value on those things that are in relatively short supply.

Socialization hypothesis: the relationship between socioeconomic environment and value priorities is not one of immediate adjustment - a substantial time lag is involved, for, to a large extent, one's basic values reflect the conditions that prevailed during one's preadult years.

Description: The materialism-post materialism scale is composed of 12 items, 6 designed to tap materialism (as defined above) and 6 designed to tap post materialism. Scoring procedures for the items are sketchy. Respondents are asked what they personally consider the most important goals among the 12 items and then are classified as exclusively materialist, exclusively post materialist, or a "mixed" type (a combination of the two). Scores are then reported as the percentage of respondents falling into each category across a number of cross-classification variables. In one sample, respondents were asked to rank-order their priorities as to the 12 items. Thus, it seems that a rank order scoring procedure is also tenable. A reduced, 4-item version of the scale also has seen use.

Development: Little information as to scale development was provided. Statements were generated to tap the materialism-post materialism construct and administered to several cross-cultural samples over numerous time periods. Validity for the measure is offered via several cross-classification variables and percentage scores on the scale.

Sample(s): Samples included representative samples from several western nations including Japan, Britain, France, West Germany, Belgium, Italy, Netherlands, Luxembourg, Ireland, Denmark, and the U.S. Longitudinal data was collected across several time periods including 1970-1979, 1974-1976, and 1976-1979. Also, a sample of 742 candidates for seats in the European parliament were included. Other sample sizes are reported in Tables 4, 6, and 8 of Inglehart (1981). For example, pooled data from 9 European Community nations classified 18,292 respondents as materialists, 26,694 respondents as "mixed," and 6,098 respondents as post materialists (Inglehart 1981, p. 891, Table 4).

Validity: Though few classic estimates of reliability (i.e., test-retest correlations, coefficient alpha) were offered, the materialism-post materialism scale showed evidence of discriminant validity. First, for the sample of 742 parliament candidates, a principal components analysis revealed two distinct a priori dimensions as the 6 items to tap materialism loaded on one factor and the 6 items designed to measure post materialism loaded on another factor. Second, across most of the cross-classification variables, those respondents who gave top priority to one materialist goal also gave top priority to other materialist items, and likewise, those respondents who gave top priority to one post materialist goal also gave top priority to other post materialist items.

Numerous cross-classifications of the scale with a number of demographic and personality variables show evidence for the scale's validity. These cross-classification variables include age, country, support for and resistance to social change, protest potential, occupation, and support for nuclear power.

Scores: Scores are primarily reported as the percentage of respondents categorized as materialists, post materialists, and "mixed" across numerous cross-classification variables and numerous time periods. Table 4 (p. 891) shows pooled data from 9 European Community nations that classified 18,292 respondents as materialists, 26,694 respondents as "mixed," and 6,098 respondents as post materialists. Several other tables offer breakdowns across other variables.

Source:	Inglehart, Ronald (1981), "Post-Materialism in an Environment of Insecurity," *American Political Science Review*, 75 (December), 880-900.
Other evidence:	N/A
Other sources:	N/A
References:	N/A

MATERIALISM-POST MATERIALISM SCALE
(Inglehart 1981)

a. Maintain order in the nation.

b. Give people more say in the decisions of the government.

c. Fight rising prices.

d. Protect freedom of speech.

e. Maintain a high rate of economic growth.

f. Make sure the country has strong defense forces.

g. Give people more say in how things are decided at work and in their community.

h. Try to make our cities and countryside more beautiful.

i. Maintain a stable economy.

j. Fight against crime.

k. Move toward a friendlier, less impersonal society.

l. Move toward a society where ideas count more than money.

NOTES: Items a, c, e, f, i, and j tap materialism while the remaining items measure post materialism. Items a though d comprise the 4-item version of the scale.

BELIEF IN MATERIAL GROWTH SCALE: BIMG
(Tashchian, Slama, and Tashchian 1984)

Construct: Belief in material growth states that certain individuals place a high value on material comforts and conveniences, value economic effort, and may view actions taken for the common good as working against them (Slama and Tashchian 1984). The BIMG was designed to measure these beliefs in relation to energy consumption.

Description: The BIMG consists of 12 statements. (Scoring procedures were not mentioned, but it appears that the statements can be scored on a strongly disagree - strongly agree 5- or 7-point basis and then summed to form an overall BIMG index.) The measure is considered unidimensional (Tashchian et al. 1984).

Development: The BIMG was developed as part of a larger project investigating attitude toward energy conservation (Tashchian et al. 1984). In this study, three scales were developed, a scale to measure cynicism toward the mid 70s energy crisis, a scale to measure belief in technology to solve energy problems, and the BIMG. The procedures just for the BIMG are described below.

The procedures used to develop the BIMG generally adhere to the scale development process outlined in the psychometric literature. A pool of 50 items was generated to reflect the construct. Then, judges were asked to indicate the degree to which they felt each item was relevant to the definition of the construct on a four-point scale (i.e., highly relevant, moderately relevant, somewhat relevant and not relevant at all). Items which 75% of the judges agreed were either highly or moderately relevant to the construct were retained. Another measure of interjudge reliability indicated a high level of agreement among judges toward what items should be retained. Item-to-total correlations were used to trim the remaining items in such a fashion as to obtain a short 12-item scale. The 12 remaining items were assessed for reliability and validity within a larger study.

Sample(s): A focus group of 25 student judges was used to trim the original pool of 50 items to a more manageable number. A sample of 365 adults was used to assess the reliability and validity of the scale using a systematic area sampling method.

Validity: The overall coefficient alpha for the final 12-item BIMG was .82 (based on the sample of 365).

The nomological validity of the scale was assessed by correlating it with a measure of environmental concern, and by examining mean differences on BIMG for high and low energy conservation groups. Results show that BIMG was negatively correlated with environmental concern ($r = -.509$), and mean differences show that the low conservation group scored higher on BIMG than the high conservation group. These results support the scale's validity (Tashchian et al. 1984).

Scores: Mean or percentage scores for the scale were not reported. (Only ANOVA F-values were reported for the high and low conservation groups.)

Source: Tashchian, Armen, Mark E. Slama, and Roobian Tashchian (1984), "Measuring Attitudes Toward Energy Conservation: Cynicism, Belief in Material Growth, and Faith in Technology," *Journal of Public Policy & Marketing*, 3 (2), 134-148.

Other evidence: N/A.

Other sources: N/A.

References: N/A.

BELIEF IN MATERIAL GROWTH SCALE: BIMG
(Tashchian, Slama, and Tashchian 1984)

1) I always buy the best.

2) Material growth has an irresistible attraction for me.

3) Material growth makes for happier living.

4) Growth in material consumption helps raise the level of civilization.

5) Ownership and consumption of material goods has a high value for me.

6) More is better.

7) Increases in the amount of goods and services produced is not essential to my well being.*

8) I am reluctant to conserve material goods and services when it affects my daily life.

9) I would rather be perfectly comfortable in my home (neither warm nor cold) than be slightly comfortable to conserve.

10) I have worked hard to get where I am - and am entitled to the "good things in life."

11) People should heat and cool their homes to the most comfortable temperatures regardless of what the government says.

12) The only way to let everyone know about my high status is to show it.

NOTE: * denotes items that are reverse scored.

BELK'S MATERIALISM SCALES
(Belk 1984, 1985)

Construct: Materialism is defined as the importance a consumer attaches to worldly possessions. At the highest level of materialism, such possessions assume a central place in a person's life and are believed to provide the greatest sources of satisfaction and dissatisfaction (Belk 1984, 1985). Furthermore, Belk identifies three subtraits of materialism:

Possessiveness - which is defined as the inclination and tendency to retain control or ownership of one's possessions.

Nongenerosity - which is defined as an unwillingness to give possessions or share possessions with others.

Envy - which is defined as the displeasure and ill will at the superiority of another person in happiness, success, reputation, or the possession of anything desirable.

Description: The Belk materialism scale is composed of 24 statements designed to measure the three subtraits alluded to above. The items are scored on 5-point Likert scales from agree to disagree. Items are summed within each subtrait to form an overall score for each subtrait, and all 24 items can be summed to form an overall index of materialism. The scales consist of 9 items for possessiveness, 7 items for nongenerosity, and 8 items for envy.

Development: Based on the conceptual domains identified for materialism and its subtraits, initial pools of 30 to 35 items were generated for each subtrait. Through factor analysis, item-to-total correlations and other measures of internal consistency, 7 to 9 items were selected for each subtrait (based on a student sample of 237 [Belk 1984]).

Sample(s): Two samples were used by Belk (1984) to initially examine the reliability and validity of the scales. For developing the scales, a student sample of 237 was used. Through a number of statistical procedures, the final measures were derived. Belk (1984) also used another larger sample composed of both students and nonstudents (n = 338) to validate the scale.

Using another sample to assess mean differences in materialism by generation, 99 subjects from 33 different families responded to the scales (Belk 1985).

Validity: A number of reliability and validity estimates are reported for the scales. In the Belk (1984) study, coefficient alpha estimates for the possessiveness, nongenerosity, and envy subscales were .68, .72, and .80, respectively, for the student sample (n = 237). The overall summed scale (24 items) had an alpha of .73. For the larger sample (n = 338), these estimates were .57 for possessiveness, .58 for nongenerosity, .64 for envy, and .66 for the overall summed 24-item scale. Based on a subsample of 48 students (from the 338 sample), test-retest reliability estimates were .87 for possessiveness, .64 for nongenerosity, .70 for envy, and .68 for the overall scale. By using MTMM, behavioral and photo indices of materialism were correlated with the materialism scales. In this analyses, Belk (1984) found the scales to have adequate levels of convergent and discriminant validity. Also, all three materialism measures were found to be negatively correlated with measures of happiness and satisfaction in life (i.e., -.26 and -.24, respectively). In sum, the original Belk study showed support for the validity of the scale.

Scores: Mean scores for the summed 24-item scale and the original three subtraits are reported for the n = 338 sample (Belk 1984, 1985). The mean for the overall scale was 73.4. The means for the possessiveness, nongenerosity, and envy subtraits were 32.86, 18.74, and 21.74, respectively. (Mean scores are further broken down by occupation in Belk [1984, p. 294].) Belk (1985, p. 271) also reports mean scores for the overall scale and the three original subtraits by family generation.

Source(s): Belk, Russell W. (1984), "Three Scales to Measure Constructs Related to Materialism: Reliability, Validity, and Relationships to Measures of Happiness," in *Advances in Consumer Research*, Vol. 11, Thomas C. Kinnear (ed.), Provo, UT: The Association for Consumer Research, 291-297.

Belk, Russell W. (1985), "Materialism: Trait Aspects of Living in the Material World," *Journal of Consumer Research*, 12 (December), 265-280.

Other evidence: In a cross-cultural context, Ger and Belk (1990) sampled of 405 students from several different countries (i.e., Germany, England, France, the U.S., and Turkey). Ger and Belk (1990) modified and administered the scale cross-culturally, and based on factor analyses, found a fourth dimension, tangiblization. Coefficient alpha estimates for the four subscales and total scale were reported for the combined sample and by country subsample. For the combined sample (n = 405) alpha estimates were .67 for possessiveness, .69 for nongenerosity, .52 for envy, .56 for tangiblization, and .58 for the overall scale. (See Ger and Belk [1990, p. 188] for alpha estimates by country.) Furthermore, the 4 subscales were correlated with an index assessing the degree to which 20 products/services were viewed as necessities vs. luxury items. The pattern of correlations supported the validity of the scales. For example, correlations of the possessiveness, nongenerosity, envy, and tangiblization factors with the number of items viewed as necessities were .18, -.13, .25, and .10, respectively. Ger and Belk (1990, p. 189) also report mean scores by country for the entire scale and all 4 subtraits.

In another study, Ellis (1992) examined the dimensionality of Belk's scale by estimating numerous competing factor structures based on a sample of 148 respondents. Ellis concluded that a 3-factor structure (i.e., possessiveness, nongenerosity, and envy) appeared to offer the best specification of the materialism items. Though internal consistency estimates were not provided, individual item-to-factor loadings were (see Table 2), and the correlations among the three factors ranged from -.032 to .431.

Other sources: Ger, Guliz and Russell W. Belk (1990), "Measuring and Comparing Materialism Across Countries," in *Advances in Consumer Research*, Vol. 17, Marvin E. Goldberg, Gerald Gorn and Richard W. Pollay (eds.), Provo, UT: Association for Consumer Research, 186-192.

Ellis, Seth R. (1992), "A Factor Analytic Investigation of Belk's Structure of the Materialism Construct," in *Advances in Consumer Research*, Vol. 19, John F, Sherry (ed.), Provo, UT: Association for Consumer Research, in press.

References: N/A.

BELK'S MATERIALISM SCALES
(Belk 1984, 1985)

POSSESSIVENESS:

1) Renting or leasing a car is more appealing to me than owning one.*

2) I tend to hang on to things I should probably throw out.

3) I get very upset if something is stolen from me, even if it has little monetary value.

4) I don't get particularly upset when I lose things.*

5) I am less likely than most people to lock things up.*

6) I would rather buy something I need than borrow it from someone else.*

7) I worry about people taking my possessions.

8) When I travel, I like to take a lot of photographs.

9) I never discard old pictures or snapshots.

NONGENEROSITY:

10) I enjoy having guests stay in my home.*

11) I enjoy sharing what I have.*

12) I don't like to lend things, even to good friends.

13) It makes sense to buy a lawnmower with a neighbor and share it.*

14) I don't mind giving rides to those who don't have a car.*

15) I don't like to have anyone in my home when I'm not there.

16) I enjoy donating things to charity.*

ENVY:

17) I am bothered when I see people who buy anything they want.

18) I don't know anyone whose spouse or steady date I would like to have as my own.*

19) When friends do better than me in competition, it usually makes me happy for them.*

20) People who are very wealthy often feel they are too good to talk to average people.

21) There are certain people I would like to trade places with.

22) When friends have things I can not afford it bothers me.

23) I don't seem to get what is coming to me.

24) When Hollywood stars or prominent politicians have things stolen, I really feel sorry for them.*

NOTES: * denotes reverse scoring.

Items 1, 3 through 6, 9, and 15 comprise the Ger and Belk (1990) scale for possessiveness. In addition, the phasing for item 1 was changed from "a car" to "a place to live."

Items 7, 10, 11, 12, 16, and 19 make up the Ger and Belk nongenerosity scale. In addition, the phrasing for item 10 was changed from "guests" to "people I like."

Items 17, 20, 21, and 23 make up the Ger and Belk envy scale with an additional item that reads as follows:

"If I have to choose between buying something for myself versus someone I love, I would prefer buying for myself,"

Ger and Belk's tangiblization measure is composed of items 2 and 8, and the following three statements:

1) I have a lot of souvenirs.

2) I would rather give someone a gift that lasts than take them to dinner.

3) I like to collect things.

RICHINS' MATERIALISM MEASURE
(Richins 1987)

Construct: Richins (1987, p. 352) describes materialism in terms of its role in consumer culture as ". . . the idea that goods are a means to happiness; that satisfaction in life is not achieved by religious contemplation or social interaction, or a simple life, but by possession and interaction with goods." This view is consistent with extant writings on materialism (e.g., Belk 1984, 1985).

Description: The scale is a 6-item, 2-factor measure. The items are scored on a 7-point Likert format from strongly disagree to strongly agree. Item scores are summed within factors to form indices for each factor.

Development: Scale development procedures consisted of generating 7 items that tapped the content domain of the construct. Then, based on factor analysis and coefficient alpha, the final 6 items were derived.

Sample(s): The sample consisted of a quota sample of 252 adults.

Validity: Factor analysis revealed that four items tapped a personal materialism factor (alpha = .73) and two items tapped a general materialism factor (alpha = .61).

The two materialism factors were correlated with measures of perceived realism of TV ads, media exposure, and life satisfaction. The resulting correlations show modest support for the validity of the measure.

Scores: Mean and/or percentage scores were not reported.

Source: Richins, Marsha L. (1987), "Media, Materialism, and Human Happiness," in *Advances in Consumer Research*, Vol. 14, Melanie Wallendorf and Paul Anderson (eds.), Provo, UT: The Association for Consumer Research, 352-356.

Other evidence: N/A.

Other sources: N/A.

References: Belk, Russell W. (1984), "Three Scales to Measure Constructs Related to Materialism: Reliability, Validity, and Relationships to Measures of Happiness," in *Advances in Consumer Research*, Vol. 11, Thomas C. Kinnear (ed.), Provo, UT: The Association for Consumer Research, 291-297.

Belk, Russell W. (1985), "Materialism: Trait Aspects of Living in the Material World," *Journal of Consumer Research*, 12 (December), 265-280.

RICHINS' MATERIALISM MEASURE
(Richins 1987)

1) It is important to me to have really nice things.

2) I would like to be rich enough to buy anything I want.

3) I'd be happier if I could afford to buy more things.

4) It sometimes bothers me quite a bit that I can't afford to buy all the things I want.

5) People place too much emphasis on material things.*

6) It's really true that money can buy happiness.

NOTES: * denotes reverse scoring.

        Items 1 through 4 comprise the personal materialism factor, and items 5 and 6 the general materialism factor.

POSSESSION SATISFACTION INDEX: PSI
(Scott and Lundstrom 1990)

Construct: The idea of possession satisfaction is derived from the constructs of materialism and attitude toward money. It is felt that possession satisfaction is composed of aspects of these two concepts (Scott and Lundstrom 1990). (No formal definition of the construct is offered.)

Description: The PSI is composed of 20 Likert-type statements scored on 5-point strongly disagree - strongly agree formats. The scale is further composed of five factors assessing various aspects of possession satisfaction. Scores on the factors are derived by summing individual item scores within factors. An overall PSI score can be obtained by summing across all 20 items.

Development: Based on expert opinion, 9 items relating to money and 11 items relating to material possessions were generated. These items were pretested for discrimination on a student sample, and an adult sample was used to examine the factor structure and reliability of the measure.

Sample(s): A student sample (n not given) was used to pretest the 20 items. The main sample was drawn from a mall intercept approach using a quota sampling technique such that the sample would be representative of the geographic area considered in terms of demographic characteristics (n = 150).

Validity: Based on an initial factor analysis and a multi-trait matrix analysis, it was found that the 9 items relating to money and the 11 items relating to material possessions were not distinct. Thus, all 20 items were combined to form one overall scale (PSI). A second factor analysis on the 20 items revealed 5 factors: 1) what possessions can do, 2) what possessions cannot do, 3) public image, 4) success equals possessions, and 5) more is better. Overall coefficient alpha for the scale was .80. (Alphas for the five factors were not reported.) No other estimates of validity were offered.

Scores: No mean or percentage scores were reported.

Source: Scott, Cliff and William J. Lundstrom (1990), "Dimensions of Possession Satisfactions: A Preliminary Analysis," *Journal of Satisfaction, Dissatisfaction and Complaining Behavior*, Vol. 3, Keith Hunt (ed.), 100-104.

Other evidence: N/A.

Other sources: N/A.

References: N/A.

POSSESSION SATISFACTION INDEX: PSI
(Scott and Lundstrom 1990)

1) Money makes life a lot easier.

2) I would rather own property than rent.

3) People with a lot of charge cards are important.

4) Wealthy people are respected.

5) Business has commercialized many meaningful holidays, such as Christmas.

6) Happiness is more important than money.*

7) When I shop, I usually make a purchase.

8) Money isn't everything.*

9) The more I have, the better I feel.

10) Given a choice between a well known brand and a store brand, I would take the store brand.*

11) It isn't important to own a nice car.*

12) It is very important to me how people perceive me.

13) I would take a job for less money if it were more self satisfying.*

14) People enjoy showing others their new possessions.

15) People rate other people by the value of their possessions.

16) Being a success means making a lot of money.

17) It is really true that money can buy happiness.

18) Most of the people I look up to are wealthy.

19) The more I have, the more I want.

20) In general, wealthier people are happier than poor people.

NOTES: * denotes reverse scoring.

Items 1 through 4 comprise the what possessions can do factor; items 5 through 10 comprise the what possessions can not do factor; items 11 through 14 comprise the public image factor; items 15 through 18 comprise the success equals possessions factor; and items 19 and 20 make up the more is better factor.

MATERIAL VALUES
(Richins and Dawson 1992)

Construct: Richins and Dawson (1992) view materialism as a consumer value in that it involves beliefs and attitudes so centrally held that they guide the conduct of one's life. Based on a review of the materialism literature in a variety of disciplines and on popular notions concerning materialism (Fournier and Richins 1991), three important themes concerning materialism were identified. These themes reflect the values consumers place on material goods and the roles these goods play in their lives:

Possessions as defining "success" - the extent to which one uses possessions as indicators of success and achievement in life, both in judging themselves and others.

Acquisition "centrality" - the extent to which one places possession acquisition at the center of one's life (i.e., this lends meaning to life and guides daily endeavors).

Acquisitions as the pursuit of "happiness" - the belief that possessions are essential to satisfaction and well-being in life.

Description: The scale consists of 18 items encompassing the 3 factors above (6 items for "success," 7 for "centrality" and 5 for "happiness"). The items are scored on a 5-point Likert format from strongly agree to strongly disagree. Item scores are summed within dimensions to form indices for each dimension, and can be summed overall to form an overall materialism score.

Development: The development of the scale closely followed recommended psychometric scaling procedures. First, a convenience sample of 11 consumers was asked to describe the characteristics of materialistic people they knew in an open-ended format. Items were then generated based on these responses. Items were also generated from previously developed materialism scales and the materialism literature (Belk 1984, 1985; Richins 1987). Over 120 items were generated. These items were then screened for ambiguity and redundancy, resulting in further development samples examining either 50 or 66 potential materialism statements (Richins and Dawson 1992). From these, a pool of 48 items was retained for further analysis. This pool was trimmed to 30 items via exploratory factor analysis, reliability analysis, and social desirability testing. Through a number of other scaling procedures (i.e., factor analysis, reliability analysis, and validity checks) across several samples, the final scale consisted of 18 items.

Sample(s): As stated above, a convenience sample of 11 consumers was used for item generation. Three samples of students (n = 448, 191, 194) were used in preliminary tests of the scale (Richins and Dawson 1990). Four consumer samples were used in scale development, reliability, and validity checks. Samples sizes were 144, 250, 235, 205. A sample of 58 students was also used to assess test-retest reliability.

Validity: Through factor analyses and reliability analysis, three factors emerged. Over the last three samples, coefficient alpha estimates for the factors ranged from .71 to .75 for centrality, .74 to .78 for the success factor, and .73 to .83 for the happiness factor (Richins and Dawson 1991). Alpha for the overall 18-item scale ranged between .80 to .88. Test-retest reliability over a 3 week interval (n = 58) was .82, .86., .82., and .87 for the centrality, happiness, success, and overall scales, respectively.

Numerous tests of validity were performed. First, the scales were examined for social desirability bias. The correlations between social desirability and the subscales and overall materialism scale ranged form -.03 to -.13, indicating virtually no contamination from social desirability bias.

The materialism factors were also correlated with measures of life satisfaction, values, self-esteem, self-centeredness, and voluntary simplicity in some or all of the samples to examine the validity of the scales. Across samples, the patterns of correlations showed that the materialism factors exhibited construct validity (Richins and Dawson 1992). For example, the correlation between the overall scale and an item assessing voluntary simplicity was -.21; the correlation between the overall scale and Belk's (1985) nongenerosity scale was .25; and the correlation between the scale and a measure of self-esteem was -.12. These correlations support a priori hypotheses about the materialistic individual. A number of other mean difference tests also add support for the scale's validity.

Scores: Mean scores were reported for three samples for each subscale and the overall scale. For the centrality component, mean scores ranged from 19.3 (sd = 4.0) to 19.8 (sd = 4.2). For the happiness component, mean scores ranged from 12.8 (sd = 4.1) to 13.3 (sd = 4.2). For the success component, mean scores ranged from 13.8 (sd = 4.1) to 14.7 (sd = 3.9), and for the overall combined scale, mean scores ranged from 45.9 (sd = 9.8) to 47.9 (sd = 10.2).

Source: Richins, Marsha L. and Scott Dawson (1992), "Materialism as a Consumer Value: Measure Development and Validation," *Journal of Consumer Research*, forthcoming.

Other evidence: N/A.

Other sources: N/A.

References: Belk, Russell W. (1984), "Three Scales to Measure Constructs Related to Materialism: Reliability, Validity, and Relationships to Measures of Happiness, " in *Advances in Consumer Research*, Vol. 11, Thomas C. Kinnear (ed.), Provo, UT: The Association for Consumer Research, 291-297.

Belk, Russell W. (1985), "Materialism: Trait Aspects of Living in the Material World," *Journal of Consumer Research*, 12 (December), 265-280.

Fournier, Susan and Marsha L. Richins (1991), "Some Theoretical and Popular Notions Concerning Materialism," *Journal of Social Behavior and Personality*, 6, 403-414.

Richins, Marsha L. (1987), "Media, Materialism, and Human Happiness," in *Advances in Consumer Research*, Vol. 14, Melanie Wallendorf and Paul Anderson (eds.), Provo, UT: The Association for Consumer Research, 352-356.

Richins, Marsha L. and Scott Dawson (1990), "Measuring Material Values: A Preliminary Report on Scale Development," in *Advances in Consumer Research*, Vol. 17, Marvin E. Goldberg, Gerald Gorn, and Richard W. Pollay, (eds.), Provo, UT: The Association for Consumer Research, 169-175.

MATERIAL VALUES
(Richins and Dawson 1992)

Success

1) I admire people who own expensive homes, cars, and clothes.

2) Some of the most important achievements in life include acquiring material possessions.

3) I don't place much emphasis on the amount of material objects people own as a sign of success.*

4) The things I own say a lot about how well I'm doing in life.

5) I like to own things that impress people.

6) I don't pay much attention to the material objects other people own.*

Centrality

1) I usually buy only the things I need.*

2) I try to keep my life simple, as far as possessions are concerned.*

3) The things I own aren't all that important to me.*

4) I enjoy spending money on things that aren't practical.

5) Buying things gives me a lot of pleasure.

6) I like a lot of luxury in my life.

7) I put less emphasis on material things than most people I know.*

Happiness

1) I have all the things I really need to enjoy life.*

2) My life would be better if I owned certain things I don't have.

3) I wouldn't be any happier if I owned nicer things.*

4) I'd be happier if I could afford to buy more things.

5) It sometimes bothers me quite a bit that I can't afford to buy all the things I'd like.

NOTE: * denotes items that are reversed scored.

APPENDIX TO MATERIALISM

A scale related to materialism is the Money Attitude Scale - the MAS (Yamauchi and Templer 1982). Given its copyrighted and proprietary nature, only a summary of the MAS is offered here. Questions regarding the use of the MAS items should be directed to Dr. Kent Yamauchi, P.O. Box 20022, South Lake Tahoe, CA 95706.

MONEY ATTITUDE SCALE: MAS
(Yamauchi and Templer 1982)

Construct: The psychological aspects of money are felt to encompass three broad content areas (Yamauchi and Templer 1982):

Security - which concerns optimism, confidence, comfort, and its reverse, pessimism, insecurity and dissatisfaction associated with having or not having money.

Retention - which includes parsimony, hoarding, and obsessive personality traits.

Power-prestige - which comprises aspects of status, importance, superiority, and acquisition through money.

The MAS was designed to measure these content areas of attitude toward money.

Description: The MAS is comprised of 29 Likert statements utilizing "always" and "never" as endpoints (7-point items). Though originally designed to assess the three broad content areas described above, the MAS is considered a four dimensional scale where scores on items within each dimension are summed to form indices of each dimension. On overall MAS score can also be derived by summing responses to all 29 items.

Development: Sixty-two items were originally generated to reflect the three content domains described above. Through factor analyses, this original pool of items was trimmed to 34 items reflecting five substantive factors. Items with loadings of .40 or above on a given factor were retained and the five factors accounted for 33.6% of the variance. These five factors were: 1) a power-prestige factor, 2) a retention-time factor, 3) a distrust factor, 4) a quality factor, and 5) an anxiety factor. Due to theoretical overlap with the power-prestige factor, the quality factor was deleted. Thus, the final scale consists of 29 items reflecting four factors. Coefficient alpha was used to assess the internal consistency of the MAS, and a number of validity estimates were also performed (Yamauchi and Templer 1983).

Sample(s):   Two samples were used in scale development and validation. The first sample consisted of 300 adults from two California cities. With this sample, the final 29-item scale was derived from the original pool of 62 items. This sample was used to determine the factor structure, internal consistency, and test-retest reliability of the scale. A second sample of 125 students was used to further examine the reliability and test the validity of the scale.

Validity: Internal consistency estimates of the four factors comprising the final scale were .80, .78, .73, and .69 for the power-prestige, retention-time, distrust, and anxiety factors, respectively. Corresponding test-retest reliability estimates for a subsample of 31 (from the original 300) were .88, .95, .87, and .88.

To examine the validity of the scale, the MAS, along with a number of other scales, was administered to a student sample of 125. The four factors of the MAS were found to be correlated with measures of Machiavellianism (.13 to .44), status concern (.23 to .48), time competence (-.04 to -.33), obsessional personality (.04 to .40), and anxiety (-.12 to .55), all in the predicted directions. Thus, evidence for the nomological validity of the MAS was found.

Scores: Mean scores for the total scale and the four factors were reported for the first sample (n = 300). For the total 29-item scale the mean was 97.69 (15.54). For the four factors, the mean scores were 21.35 (7.45) for the power-prestige factor, 28.83 (8.10) for the retention-time factor, 24.71 (6.08) for the distrust factor, and 22.80 (5.51) for the anxiety factor. (Standard deviations are in parentheses.)

Source:	Yamauchi, Kent T., and Donald I. Templer (1982), "The Development of a Money Attitude Scale," *Journal of Personality Assessment*, 46, 522-528.
Other evidence:	N/A.
Other sources:	N/A.
References:	N/A.

SOURCES FOR CHAPTER THREE

Antil, John A. (1984), "Socially Responsible Consumers: Profile and Implications for Public Policy," *Journal of Macromarketing*, (Fall), 18-39; Appendix B, p. 35.

Antil, John A. and Peter D. Bennett (1979), "Construction and Validation of a Scale to Measure Socially Responsible Consumption Behavior," in *The Conserver Society*, Karl H. Henion II and Thomas C. Kinnear (eds.), Chicago: American Marketing Association, 51-68; pp. 64-65.

Belk, Russell W. (1984), "Three Scales to Measure Constructs Related to Materialism: Reliability, Validity, and Relationships to Measures of Happiness," in *Advances in Consumer Research*, Vol. 11, Thomas C. Kinnear (ed.), Provo, UT: The Association for Consumer Research, 291-297; Table 1, p. 292.

Belk, Russell W. (1985), "Materialism: Trait Aspects of Living in the Material World," *Journal of Consumer Research*, 12 (December), 265-280; Exhibit 1, p. 270.

Guttman, Jonathan (1982), "A Means-End Chain Model Based on Consumer Categorization Processes," *Journal of Marketing*, 46 (April), 60-72.

Hofstede, Geert (1980), *Culture's Consequences: International Differences in Work-Related Values*, Beverly Hills, CA: Sage.

Inglehart, Ronald (1981), "Post-Materialism in an Environment of Insecurity," *American Political Science Review*, 75 (December), 880-900, p. 884.

Kahle, Lynn R. (1983), *Social Values and Social Change: Adaptation to Life in America*, New York: Praeger Publishers; p. 63.

Lastovicka, John L., John P. Murray, Jr., Erich A. Joachimsthaler, Gaurav Bhalla, and Jim Scheurich (1987), "A Lifestyle Typology to Model Young Male Drinking and Driving," *Journal of Consumer Research*, 14 (September), 257-263; Table 1, p. 259.

Leonard-Barton, Dorothy (1981), "Voluntary Simplicity Lifestyles and Energy Conservation," *Journal of Consumer Research*, 8 (December), 243-252; Appendix, pp. 250-251.

Lichtenstein, Donald R., Richard G. Netemeyer, and Scot Burton (1990), "Distinguishing Coupon Proneness From Value Consciousness: An Acquisition-Transaction Utility Theory Perspective," *Journal of Marketing*, 54 (July), 54-67; Appendix A, pp. 64-65.

Mitchell, Arnold (1983), *The Nine American Lifestyles: Who We Are and Where We're Going*, New York: MacMillan; pp. 273-279.

Moschis, George P., and Gilbert A. Churchill, Jr. (1978), "Consumer Socialization: A Theoretical and Empirical Analysis," *Journal of Marketing Research*, 15 (November), 599-609; Appendix, p. 607.

Richins, Marsha L. (1987), "Media, Materialism, and Human Happiness," in *Advances in Consumer Research*, Vol. 14, Melanie Wallendorf and Paul Anderson (eds.), Provo, UT: Association for Consumer Research, 352-356; Table 2, p. 354.

_____ and Scott Dawson (1992), "Materialism as a Consumer Value: Measurement Development and Validation," *Journal of Consumer Research*, forthcoming; Table 2.

Rokeach, Milton (1973), *The Nature of Human Values*, New York, NY: Free Press; Appendix A, 359-360.

Scott, Cliff and William J. Lundstrom (1990), "Dimensions of Possession Satisfactions: A Preliminary Analysis," *Journal of Satisfaction, Dissatisfaction and Complaining Behavior*, Vol. 3, Keith Hunt (ed.), 100-104; Tables 1, 2, and 4, pp. 101-102.

Tashchian, Armen, Mark E. Slama, and Roobian Tashchian (1984), "Measuring Attitudes Toward Energy Conservation: Cynicism, Belief in Material Growth, and Faith in Technology," *Journal of Public Policy & Marketing*, 3 (2), 134-148; Table 4, p. 142.

Unger, Lynette and Jerome B. Kernan (1983), "On the Meaning of Leisure: An Investigation of Some Determinants of the Subjective Experience," *Journal of Consumer Research*, 9 (March), 381-392; Exhibit 3, p. 387.

Yamauchi, Kent T. and Donald I. Templer (1982), "The Development of a Money Attitude Scale," *Journal of Personality Assessment*, 46, 522-528; Tables 1-5, pp. 523-525.

4

Involvement and Information Processing

INVOLVEMENT SCALES

A number of scales have been designed to measure involvement. In general, these scales assess 1) involvement with a specific class of products; 2) involvement general to several products; and 3) purchasing involvement. In this chapter, several involvement scales are presented and summarized according to the above classification in chronological order.

INVOLVEMENT WITH A SPECIFIC CLASS OF PRODUCTS

THE FASHION INVOLVEMENT INDEX (FII) AND THE FASHION INVOLVEMENT FACTOR (FIF)
(Tigert, Ring, and King 1976)

Constructs: A fashion involvement continuum can be defined based on the aggregate effect of a variety of important fashion behavioral activities. These activities pertain to five dimensions which make up the FII (Tigert, Ring, and King 1976):

Fashion innovativeness and time of purchase - a continuum ranging from the early adopter and experimental consumer to the late buying conservative consumer.

Fashion interpersonal communication - a continuum which describes the relative communicative and influential power of the consuming population at conveying fashion involvement.

Fashion interest - a continuum ranging from the highly interested to the totally noninterested in fashion.

Fashion knowledgeability - a continuum ranging from very knowledgeable about fashion, styles, and trends to having no insight into the fashion arena.

Fashion awareness and reaction to changing fashion trends - a continuum ranging from the consumer who actively monitors style trends to the totally nonaware individual.

The Fashion Involvement Factor (FIF) also measures aspects of the above five dimensions, yet is believed to be distinct from the FII. All items are positively worded.

Description: The FII is composed of one three-point question to measure each of the first four dimensions described above, and a five-point scale to measure the fifth dimension described above. Thus, scores on this overall measure can range from 5 to 17.

The FIF is composed of five 6-point Likert items (strongly agree - strongly disagree) that are summed to form an overall score for FIF that can range from 6 to 30.

Development: The final FII was derived using tested measurement technology and earlier field tests, (cf., Tigert, Ring, and King 1976). The six FIF items were derived from an original pool of 24 AIO/lifestyle statements pertaining to various aspects of fashion. Through principal components analysis, the final six statements were chosen from the 24 items.

Samples: The primary sample was composed of 1,000 husband and wife pairs that were part of a special panel from the Toronto Retail Fashion Market Segmentation Research Program.

Validity: In terms of traditional estimates of internal consistency (i.e., coefficient alpha), none was reported. However, factor loadings for the six FIF items ranged from .32 to .60 for females, and .39 to .66 for males. In addition, the correlations between the FII and the FIF were .63 for males and .57 for females.

Several cross-classification analyses revealed that the more highly involved fashion consumers (based on the FII) were heavier buyers of clothes fashions in terms of both volume and price per unit than less fashioned involved individuals. This offers support for the validity of the FII.

Scores: Mean scores on the FII were 9.7 for females and 8.4 for males. The two means were significantly different at the .01 level. Though mean scores were not reported, the mean for females on the FIF was 6.5% higher than the mean for males (p < .01). Other scores broken down by cross-classification are also reported (Tigert, Ring, and King 1976, pp. 50-51).

Source: Tigert, Douglas J., Lawrence R. Ring, and Charles W. King (1976), "Fashion Involvement and Buying Behavior: A Methodological Study," in *Advances in Consumer Research*, Vol. 3, Beverly B. Anderson (ed.), Provo, UT: The Association for Consumer Research, 46-52.

Other evidence: N/A.

Other sources: N/A.

References: N/A.

THE FASHION INVOLVEMENT INDEX (FII) AND THE FASHION INVOLVEMENT FACTOR (FIF)
(Tigert, Ring, and King 1976)

The FII

1) In general, would you say you buy men's (women's) clothing fashions *earlier* in the season, *about the same time*, or *later* in the season than most other men (women)?

   a) Earlier in the season than most other men (women)
   b) About the same time as most other men (women)
   c) Later in the season than most other men (women)

2) Would you say you give *very little information, an average amount of information*, or a *great deal of information* about new men's (women's) clothing fashions to your friends?

   a) I give very little information to my friends.
   b) I give an average amount of information to my friends.
   c) I give a great deal of information to my friends.

3) In general, would you say you are *less interested, about as interested,* or *more interested* in mens's (women's) clothing fashions than most other men (women)?

   a) Less interested than most other men (women)
   b) About as interested as most other men (women)
   c) More interested than most other men (women)

4) Compared with most other men (women), are you *less likely, about as likely,* or *more likely* to be asked for advice about new men's (women's) clothing fashions?

   a) Less likely to be asked than most other men (women)
   b) About as likely to be asked as most other men (women)
   c) More likely to be asked than most other men (women)

5) Which one of the statements below best describes *your reaction to changing fashions in men's (women's) clothes*? (Even though there may be no statement listed which exactly describes how you feel, make the best choice you can from the answers listed.)

   a) I read the fashion news regularly and try to keep my wardrobe up to date with the fashion trends.
   b) I keep up to date on all the fashion changes although I don't always attempt to dress according to those changes.
   c) I check to see what is currently fashionable only when I need to buy some new clothes.
   d) I don't pay much attention to fashion trends unless a major change takes place.
   e) I am not at all interested in fashion trends.

NOTES: Questions 1 through 5 measure fashion innovativeness and time of purchase, fashion interpersonal communication, fashion interest, fashion knowledgeability, and fashion awareness and reaction to changing fashion trends, respectively. Also, questions 1 and 5 require reverse coding to reflect a higher interest in fashion.

The FIF

1) I usually have one or more outfits of the very latest style.

2) An important part of my life and activities is dressing smartly.

3) I like to shop for clothes.

4) I like to think I'm a bit of a swinger.

5) For my fashion needs, I am increasingly shopping at boutiques or fashion specialty stores rather than department stores.

6) When I must choose between the two, I usually dress for fashion, not comfort.

INVOLVEMENT WITH A PRODUCT CLASS - AUTOMOBILES: IPCA
(Bloch 1981)

Construct: Product involvement has been viewed as a long-term interest in a product which is based on the centrality of the product to important values, needs, or the self-concept, and is primarily a function of individual differences. Consistent with this conceptualization, Bloch (1981) views product involvement as a construct which affects consumer behavior on an ongoing basis and varies across individuals (ranging from minimal to extremely high levels). Based on this view, a scale to measure involvement with automobiles was developed (Bloch 1981).

Description: The IPCA is composed of 17 Likert items (strongly agree - strongly disagree) scored on a six-point format. These items are self-administered and can be summed to form an overall score. Furthermore, the IPCA has been found to encompass six factors: 1) Enjoyment of driving and usage of cars; 2) Readiness to talk to others about cars; 3) Interest in car racing activities; 4) Self-expression through one's car; 5) Attachment to one's car; and 6) Interest in cars (Bloch 1981).

Development: The development of the IPCA closely adhered to recommended psychometric procedures found in the scaling literature. Based on the specification of the domain of the construct and a comprehensive literature search, 66 items were initially developed. These items were analyzed by a group of six judges to trim redundant and/or irrelevant statements, resulting in 44 retained items. The 44 items were then purified using a student sample (n = 381) via coefficient alpha and item-to-total correlations, resulting in the final 17-item measure. Factor analysis further revealed that the scale could be broken down into six factors. Reliability and validity of the scale were assessed with three more samples.

Sample(s): Four samples were used throughout the scale development process. The first was a student sample (n = 381) for initial purification purposes. The second and third samples were also students (n = 57 and n = 90), and were used to assess reliability and validity. The fourth sample was composed of 52 members of a sports car club. This sample was used to assess the mean level of involvement for a relevant population.

Validity: A number of reliability tests were performed on the 17-item IPCA. Coefficient alpha internal consistency estimates were reported for two of the student samples. For the first student sample (n = 381), alpha was .83, and for the second student sample (n = 57), alpha was .79. Test-retest reliability was also assessed for the second student sample after a two week interval. Test-retest reliability was .78.

Validity of the scale was assessed by correlating the IPCA with a number of behavioral measures assessing interest in automobiles (using the student sample of 90). The IPCA was significantly correlated with all eight measures of car interest, providing support for the validity of the scale (Bloch 1981). For example, the correlations of the IPCA with measures of purchasing name brand auto supplies, visiting car dealers to see new car models, attending auto races and shows, and performing car repairs were .40, .36, .36, .28, respectively.

Scores: Mean scores were reported for the third student sample (n = 90), and the sports car club sample (n = 52). The mean for the student sample was 59.01, and the mean for the sports car club sample was 37.39. The difference in these two means was significant (p<.01).

Source: Bloch, Peter H. (1981), "An Exploration Into the Scaling of Consumers' Involvement With a Product Class," in *Advances in Consumer Research*, Vol. 8, Kent B. Monroe (ed.), Provo, UT: The Association for Consumer Research, 61-65.

Other evidence: Shimp and Sharma (1983) factor-analyzed the IPCA with a sample of 696 adult nonstudent respondents to test the dimensionality of the scale.

Shimp and Sharma (1983) compared the six-factor solution of Bloch with a number of other factor structures. Through an exploratory factor analysis, Shimp and Sharma found that a three-factor solution accounted for 93.5% of the variance, suggesting that Bloch's six-factor structure may be simplified. Then, Shimp and Sharma estimated 12 confirmatory factor models and found that two- and three-factor models also offered a better fit than the 6-factor model. Shimp and Sharma also offered reduced versions of the scale. A 13-item, three-factor version had construct reliabilities of .84, .76, and .67 for factors 1, 2, and 3, respectively. An 8-item, two-factor version had construct reliability estimates of .84 and .76 for an emotional/personal involvement and a social status factor, respectively. It was concluded that the 8-item two-factor version was a reasonable alternative to Bloch's 17-item, six-factor scale.

These two factors were also correlated with a number of automobile attribute evaluations as a check on validity. For example, the emotional/personal factor had correlations of .12 and .10 with "status" and "looks." Corresponding correlations with the social status factor were .20 and .18.

Other sources: Shimp, Terence and Subhash Sharma (1983), "The Dimensionality of Involvement: A Test of the Automobile Involvement Scale," in the *American Marketing Association Winter Educator's Conference: Research Methods and Causal Models in Marketing*, William R. Darden, Kent B. Monroe, and William R. Dillon (eds.), Chicago: The American Marketing Association.

References: N/A.

INVOLVEMENT WITH A PRODUCT CLASS - AUTOMOBILES: IPCA
(Bloch 1981)

1) It is worth the extra cost to drive an attractive and attention-getting car.

2) I prefer to drive a car with a strong personality of its own.

3) I have sometimes imagined being a race driver.

4) Cars offer me relaxation and fun when life's pressures build up.

5) Sometimes I get too wrapped up in my car.

6) Cars are nothing more than appliances.*

7) I generally feel a sentimental attachment to the cars I own.

8) Driving my car is one way I often use to relieve daily pressure.

9) I do not pay much attention to car advertisements in magazines or on TV.*

10) I get bored when other people talk to me about their cars.*

11) I have little or no interest in car races.*

12) Driving along an open stretch of road seems to "recharge" me in body, mind and spirit.

13) It is natural that young people become interested in cars.

14) When I'm with a friend, we often end up talking about cars.

15) I don't like to think of my car as being ordinary.

16) Driving my car is one of the most satisfying and enjoyable things I do.

17) I enjoy discussing cars with my friends.

NOTES: * denotes items that are reverse scored.

Items 4, 8, 12, and 16 loaded highly (.50 and above) on the "Enjoyment of driving and usage of cars" factor. Items 10, 14, and 17 loaded highly on the "Readiness to talk to others about cars" factor. Items 3 and 11 loaded highly on the "Interest in car racing activities" factor. Items 1, 2, and 13 loaded highly on the "Self-expression through one's car" factor. Items 5, 7, and 15 loaded highly on the "Attachment to one's car" factor, and items 6. 9, and 10 loaded highly on the "Interest in cars" factor (Bloch 1981).

Items 4, 5, 8, 12, and 16 comprise factor one of Shimp and Sharma's 13-item, 3-factor solution. Items 1, 2, and 15 comprise factor 2 of Shimp and Sharma's 13-item, 3-factor solution, and items 9, 10, 11, 14 and 17 comprise factor 3 of Shimp and Sharma's 13-item, 3-factor solution.

Items 4, 5, 8, 12, and 16 comprise the emotional/personal factor of Shimp and Sharma's 8-item, two-factor structure, and items 1, 2, and 15 comprise the social status factor of Shimp and Sharma's 8-item, two-factor structure.

INVOLVEMENT GENERAL TO SEVERAL PRODUCTS

COMPONENTS OF INVOLVEMENT: CP
(Lastovicka and Gardner 1979)

Construct: Lastovicka and Gardner (1979) view involvement as having two major components: normative importance and commitment. Normative importance refers to how connected or engaged a product class is to an individual's values. Commitment refers to the pledging or binding of an individual to his/her brand choice.

Description: The CP is composed of 22 Likert statements (strongly disagree to strongly agree), all on 7-point scales. The original CP is composed of three factors that encompass the two major components. These factors have been labeled familiarity, commitment and normative importance. The items can be summed within each factor to derive an index for each factor.

Development: The items in the CP were chosen such that they reflect the three factors of involvement discussed above. Each item was evaluated across 14 different product categories. Via Tucker's (1963) 3-mode factor analysis, the dimensionality of the CP was determined. This procedure uses an eigenvalue plot to derive the number of factors. The three-factor solution accounted for 72% of the variance in the data.

Sample(s): A sample of 40 graduate and undergraduate students was used in the scale development process. Each subject rated the 22 items across 14 different product categories resulting in 560 observations.

Validity: Traditional estimates of reliability (i.e., coefficient alpha, test-retest) were not reported by Lastovicka and Gardner (1979). However, the pattern of factor loadings suggests that three distinct orthogonal factors did exist (Lastovicka and Gardner 1979, pp. 62-63). Though no formal statistical tests for validity were performed, it was also concluded that the CP possessed adequate levels of content, convergent and discriminant validity.

Scores: Mean and/or percentage scores were not reported for the product classes. However, Lastovicka and Gardner (1979, pp. 66-67) do provide "transformed core matrix" scores across the three factors by high, low, and special interest involvement.

Source: Lastovicka, John L. and David M. Gardner (1979), "Components of Involvement," in *Attitude Research Plays for High Stakes*, J.C. Maloney and B. Silverman (eds.), Chicago: American Marketing Association, 53-73.

Other evidence: In another study using 421 undergraduate students, Jenson, Carlson, and Tripp (1988) used three product categories to further examine the dimensionality of the CP. Jenson et al. (1988) do not provide estimates of reliability and validity. However, they do report that the CP was best represented by a correlated four-factor solution using LISREL. The four factors they found were labeled importance, knowledge, brand preference, and commitment. They also concluded that involvement may be multi-dimensional both between and across products.

Other sources: Jenson, Thomas D., Les Carlson, and Carolyn Tripp (1988), "The Dimensionality of Involvement: An Empirical Test," in *Advances in Consumer Research*, Vol. 16, Melanie Wallendorf and Paul Anderson (eds.), Provo, UT: The Association for Consumer Research, 680-689.

References: Tucker, L. (1963). "Implications of Factor Analysis of Three-Way Matrices for Measurement of Change," in *Problems in Measuring Change*, C. Harris (ed.), Madison, WI: University of Wisconsin Press.

COMPONENTS OF INVOLVEMENT: CP
(Lastovicka and Gardner 1979)

1) This is a product that I could talk about for a long time.

2) I understand the features well enough to evaluate the brands.

3) This is a product that interests me.

4) I have a preference for one or more brands in this product class.

5) This is a product for which I have no need whatsoever.*

6) I am not at all familiar with this product.*

7) I usually purchase the same brand within this product class.

8) If I had made a brand choice in this product class before actually making the purchase, I might easily change my intended choice upon receiving discrepant information.*

9) If I received information that was contrary to my choice in this product class, I would - at all costs - keep my choice.

10) I can protect myself from acknowledging some basic truths about myself by using this product.*

11) If my preferred brand in this product class is not available at the store, it makes little difference to me if I must choose another brand.*

12) My use of this product allows others to see me as I would ideally like them to see me.

13) This product helps me attain the type of life I strive for.

14) I can make many connections or associations between experiences in my life and this product.

15) I definitely have a "wanting" for this product.

16) If evaluating brands in this class, I would examine a very long list of features.

17) I use this product to define and express the "I" and "me" within myself.

18) I rate this product as being of the highest importance to me personally.

19) Because of my personal values, I feel that this is a product that *ought* to be important to me.

20) Use of this product helps me behave in the manner that I would like to behave.

21) Because of what others think, I feel that this is a product that should be important to me.

22) Most of the brands in this product class are all alike.*

NOTES: * denotes items that are reversed scored.

Items 1 through 7 comprise the familiarity factor; items 8 through 11 comprise the commitment factor; and items 12 through 22 comprise the normative importance factor (Lastovicka and Gardner 1979).

Items 10, 12 through 15, and 17 through 21 comprise the importance factor; items 1 through 3, 16, and 22 comprise the knowledge factor; items 4 through 6 comprise the brand preference factor; and items 7 through 9, and 11 comprise the commitment factor (Jenson et al. 1988).

A GENERAL SCALE TO MEASURE INVOLVEMENT WITH PRODUCTS: GSMI
(Traylor and Joseph 1984)

Construct: Traylor and Joseph (1984) conceptualize involvement as a consumer response to a product, message, medium or situation. Furthermore, involvement is a response that reflects an individual's sense of self or identity, and is activated by external stimuli.

Description: The GSMI is a six-item scale composed of Likert statements scored on a seven-point basis (disagree-agree). The scale is considered applicable to a wide range of products, and is also considered unidimensional. An overall GSMI score can be derived by summing the scores on the items.

Development: After a review of the involvement literature and previously developed measures of involvement, 48 items were generated to reflect the construct. These items were checked for face validity and subsequently trimmed to 22 items. The 22 items were then administered to a sample of consumers over three product categories per consumer (65 different products in all). Items with factor loadings of .50 or above on the first factor extracted across all products were retained, resulting in 10 items. A second sample was then used to derive the final 6-item scale where items with factor loadings of .50 or above were retained over 12 different products. This second sample was also used to assess the reliability and validity of the scale.

Samples: Two samples were used in actual scale development. (Twenty focus groups were also used to generate the 65 product categories examined with the first sample.) The first sample consisted of 200 consumers randomly selected in a walk-by traffic district of a large midwestern city. The second sample consisted of a combination of 280 graduate and undergraduate students.

Validity: Coefficient alpha for the six item GSMI was .92 (n = 280). In addition, factor loadings across 12 product categories on the first factor are also reported (Table 1, p. 71). Initial estimates of concurrent and predictive validity show modest support for the scales's overall validity, as the GSMI was related to brand selectivity and frequency of purchase over numerous product categories. For example, there was a correlation of -.24 between the scale and purchase frequency of the 12 products as a group.

Scores: Neither mean nor percentage scores were reported.

Source: Traylor, Mark B. and W. Benoy Joseph (1984), "Measuring Consumer Involvement with Products: Developing a General Scale," *Psychology & Marketing*, 1 (Summer), 65-77.

Other evidence: N/A.

Other sources: N/A.

References: N/A.

A GENERAL SCALE TO MEASURE INVOLVEMENT WITH PRODUCTS: GSMI
(Traylor and Joseph 1984)

1) When other people see me using this product, they form an opinion of me.

2) You can tell a lot about a person by seeing what brand of this product he uses.

3) This product helps me express who I am.

4) This product is "me."

5) Seeing somebody else use this product tells me a lot about that person.

6) When I use this product, others see me the way I want them to see me.

CONSUMER INVOLVEMENT PROFILES: CIP
(Laurent and Kapferer 1985)

Construct: Laurent and Kapferer (1985) view involvement as a multi-faceted construct along five dimensions (i.e., antecedents). Depending upon these five antecedents, consequences on consumer behavior will differ across individuals. The five dimensions can be combined to form an overall involvement profile applicable to any product class. The five antecedents are briefly described below (see Laurent and Kapferer 1985, pp. 43-44):

The perceived importance and risk of the product class - its personal meaning and relevance, and the perceived importance of the consequences of a mispurchase.

The subjective probability of making a mispurchase - the probability of a poor brand choice.

The symbolic or sign value attributed - by the consumer to the product class, its purchase, or its consumption. This differentiates functional risk from psycho-social risk.

The hedonic value of the product class - its emotional appeal; its ability to provide pleasure and affect.

Interest - an enduring relationship with the product class.

Description: The CIP is a five-facet measure currently composed of 16 Likert-type statements (totally disagree - totally agree) all scored on a five-point basis. The items in each facet are summed to form an overall measure of each facet. The CIP was originally drafted in French and then translated into English.

Development: The development of the CIP followed the recommended scaling procedures found in the psychometric literature. Based on the construct's domain and a comprehensive literature review, a pool of items was generated for each facet. Three preliminary samples were used to purify the measure using 14 different product categories. In the first two samples, items were rejected if they had a significant number of nonresponses or "don't know" answers across product categories. Furthermore, to make the CIP amenable for commercial research, each facet was limited to a maximum of five and a minimum of three items. In the third sample, coefficient alpha was used as a criterion in retaining items. From these samples, the final 16 items comprising the CIP were obtained. The third sample was also used to assess validity and dimensionality.

Sample(s):   The first two samples were composed of approximately 100 housewives each, where each person was asked about several products. The third and final sample was composed of 207 housewives recruited on the basis of age, socio-economic quotas, and usage of at least two of the fourteen products examined. Face-to-face, in-home interviewing was conducted for two product categories per subject with a systematic rotation of product categories by interviewee.

Validity: Internal consistency reliability was assessed via coefficient alpha (n = 207). These estimates were .80, .90, .88, .82, and .72 for perceived importance of the product, symbolic or sign value, hedonic value, perceived importance of the negative consequences of a poor choice, and probability of making a poor choice (mispurchase), respectively.

Laurent and Kapferer (1985) also ran a factor analysis and found that perceived importance of the product and perceived risk of the negative consequences of a poor choice were not distinct facets. Thus, they were combined to form a single facet of product/risk importance with an alpha of .87. Furthermore, the four facets (i.e., product/risk importance, symbolic or sign value, hedonic value, and probability of a mispurchase) accounted for 66% of the total variance in the CIP. (Since the "interest" facet had not been added to the CIP at the time of its appearance in *JMR*, a reliability estimate was not reported.)

Discriminant validity among the facets of the CIP and trait validity for the CIP facets were reported. The correlations among the four facets ranged from .15 to .53, suggesting evidence of discriminant validity. Further correlational analyses of the four facets with various behavioral consequences associated with product class involvement showed evidence of construct validity for the CIP. For example, the facets of the CIP explained 71% of the variance in "extensive decision process" relating to product purchase, and 28% of the variance in "keeping informed" about a given product class.

Scores: Mean scores for the four facets (i.e., product/risk importance, symbolic or sign value, hedonic value, and probability of a mispurchase) across each of the 14 product categories are reported in Table 3 of Laurent and Kapferer (1985, p. 45). These scores were based on an average product scoring system of 100, and were shown to vary widely across product categories, which further supports the validity of the CIP.

Source: Laurent, Gilles and Jean-Noel Kapferer (1985), "Measuring Consumer Involvement Profiles," *Journal of Marketing Research*, 22 (February), 41-53.

Other evidence: In two more studies Kapferer and Laurent (1985a, 1986) further examined the reliability and validity of the CIP. From a sample of 1,568 observations over 20 products, a five-item "interest" factor, a three-item "pleasure" factor, a three-item "sign" factor, a three-item "risk importance" factor and a two-item "risk probability" factor had alphas of .76, .83, .81, .72, and .54, respectively. Factor correlations ranged from .10 to .55 (Kapferer and Laurent 1985a). Correlations with various consequences of involvement (i.e., extensive decision making, brand commitment, and reading articles) supported the CIP's nomological validity. For example, as predictor variables, the involvement facets explained 54% of the variance in extensiveness of the decision process, 10% of the variance in brand commitment, and 21% of the variance in readership of articles related to the product category. Kapferer and Laurent (1986) also report mean scores (on the same 100-point scale alluded to above) across the 20 products that support the scale's validity.

See also "NOTES" below for the Jain and Srinivasan items (1990).

Other sources: Jain, Kapil and Narasimhan Srinivasan (1990), "An Empirical Assessment of Multiple Operationalizations of Involvement," in *Advances in Consumer Research*, Vol. 17, Marvin Goldberg, Gerald Gorn, and Richard Pollay (eds.), Provo, UT: The Association for Consumer Research, 594-602.

Kapferer, Jean-Noel and Gilles Laurent (1985a), "Consumer's Involvement Profile: New Empirical Results," in *Advances in Consumer Research*, Vol. 12, Elizabeth Hirschman and Morris Holbrook (eds.), Provo, UT: The Association for Consumer Research, 290-295.

Kapferer, Jean-Noel and Gilles Laurent (1986), "Consumer Involvement Profiles: A New Practical Approach to Consumer Involvement," *Journal of Advertising Research*, 25 (December-January), 49-56.

References: N/A.

CONSUMER INVOLVEMENT PROFILES: CIP
(Laurent and Kapferer 1985)

1) When you choose _____, it is not a big deal if you make a mistake.*

2) It is really annoying to purchase _____ that are not suitable.

3) If, after I bought _____, my choice(s) prove to be poor, I would be really upset.

4) Whenever one buys _____, one never really knows whether they are the ones that should have been bought.

5) When I face a shelf of _____, I always feel a bit at a loss to make my choice.

6) Choosing _____ is rather complicated.

7) When one purchases _____, one is never certain of one's choice.

8) You can tell a lot about a person by the _____ he or she chooses.

9) The _____ I buy gives a glimpse of the type of man/woman I am.

10) The _____ you buy tells a little bit about you.

11) It gives me pleasure to purchase _____ .

12) Buying _____ is like buying a gift for myself.

13) _____ is somewhat of a pleasure to me.

14) I attach great importance to _____ .

15) One can say _____ interests me a lot.

16) _____ is a topic which leaves me totally indifferent.*

NOTES: * denotes items reverse scored.

Items 1 through 3 represent the "perceived product importance/risk" facet. Items 4 through 7 represent the "probability of a mispurchase" facet. Items 8 through 10 represent the "perceived symbolic/sign" facet. Items 11 through 13 represent the "hedonic/pleasure" facet, and items 14 through 16 represent the "interest" facet.

It should be noted that the 16 items above are from an updated version (circa 1989) of the CIP. The reliability and validity estimates reported on the previous pages pertain to an original 19-item CIP reported in Laurent and Kapferer (1985). Furthermore, the "interest" facet of the CIP was not included in the original Laurent and Kapferer article. As stated before, Laurent and Kapferer originally hypothesized five facets as follows:

1) The perceived importance of the product - its personal meaning and relevance.

2) The perceived importance of negative consequences in case of a poor choice (i.e., one facet of perceived risk).

3) The perceived probability of making such a mistake (the other facet of perceived risk).

4) The symbolic or sign value attributed by the consumer to the product, its purchase, or its consumption. This differentiates functional risk from psycho-social risk.

5) The hedonic value of the product, its emotional appeal, its ability to provide pleasure and affect.

However, their factor analysis retained four factors (i.e., product/risk importance, symbolic or sign value, hedonic value, and probability of a mispurchase), and more recently, a fifth facet (interest) was added. To our knowledge, the scale is currently represented by the 16 items above encompassing the five facets below:

1) The perceived importance and risk of the product class - its personal meaning and relevance, and the perceived importance of the consequences of a mispurchase.

2) The subjective probability of making a mispurchase.

3) The symbolic or sign value attributed by the consumer to the product class, its purchase, or its consumptions. This differentiates functional risk from psychosocial risk.

4) The hedonic value of the product class, its emotional appeal, its ability to provide pleasure and affect.

5) Interest - an enduring relationship with the product class.

In a more recent study, Jain and Srinivasan (1990) reported coefficient alphas of .76, .57, .72, .82, and .78 for interest, probability of making a mispurchase, hedonic/pleasure, sign/symbol, and perceived importance/risk facets of the CIP. These estimates are based on the current 16 item CIP. It should be noted though, that Jain and Srinivasan (1990) translated the items using a semantic differential format, rather than the Likert format originally used by Laurent and Kapferer. The Jain and Srinivasan items are listed below.

The Jain and Srinivasan CIP items.

With regard to the following product category. . .

1) It is not a big deal if I make a mistake in choosing it - It is a big deal if I make a mistake in choosing it.

2) It is really annoying to make an unsuitable purchase - It is not annoying to make an unsuitable purchase.*

3) A poor choice wouldn't be upsetting - A poor choice would be upsetting.

4) I never know if I am making the right purchase - I know for sure that I am making the right purchase.*

5) I feel a bit at a loss in choosing it - I don't feel at a loss in choosing it.*

6) Choosing it isn't complicated - Choosing it is complicated.

7) In purchasing it, I am certain of my choice - In purchasing it, I am uncertain of my choice.

8) It tells something about a person - It doesn't tell anything about a person.*

9) What I buy doesn't reflect the kind of person I am - What I buy reflects the kind of person I am.

10) What I buy says something about me - What I buy doesn't say anything about me.*

11) I enjoy buying it for myself - I do not enjoy buying it for myself.*

12) Buying it feels like giving myself a gift - Buying it doesn't feel like giving myself a gift.*

13) I do not find it pleasurable - I find it pleasurable.

14) I attach great importance to it - I attach no importance to it.*

15) I am not at all interested in it - I am very interested in it.

16) I am indifferent to it - I am not indifferent to it.

* denotes items reverse scored.

> Items 1 through 3 represent the "perceived product importance/risk" facet. Items 4 through 7 represent the "probability of a mispurchase" facet. Items 8 through 10 represent the "perceived symbolic/sign" facet. Items 11 through 13 represent the "hedonic/pleasure" facet, and items 14 through 16 represent the "interest" facet.

PERSONAL INVOLVEMENT INVENTORY: PII
(Zaichkowsky 1985)

Construct: Zaichkowsky (1985, p. 342) defines involvement as a person's perceived relevance of the object based on inherent needs, values, and interests. This definition recognizes past definitions of involvement, and the corresponding scale, the PII, is applicable to advertisements, products or purchase decisions.

Description: The PII is composed of 20 semantic differential items scored on seven-point scales. Scores on the items are summed to form an overall measure of involvement ranging from a low score of 20 to a high score of 140. As originally developed, the scale was felt to be unidimensional.

Development: Development of the PII closely followed recommended scaling procedures found in the psychometric literature. Based on the construct's definition, 168 word pairs were initially generated to tap the domain of involvement. These items were then judged for content validity by two panels of expert judges and the author, resulting in 30 semantic differential pairs retained. The remaining items were checked for reliability and content validity over a number of samples, resulting in 20 items retained for the final scale. The final version of the PII was then examined again for reliability and construct validity over several samples.

Sample(s): Several samples were used at the various stages of scale development. Along with the author's judgment, two samples of expert judges (n = 3 and n = 5) rated the content validity of the 168 items, trimming this initial pool to 30 items. A sample of 152 undergraduate students were then used to assess the internal consistency of the 30 items over two products. Adjective pairs with item-to-total correlations of $\geq$ .50 were retained, resulting in 26 items. Based on a factor analysis, 2 more adjective pairs were dropped, with the resulting 24 items explaining 70% of the variance in the data (Zaichkowsky 1985). A second sample comprised of 68 undergraduate and 45 MBA students was used to assess test-retest reliability and internal consistency over four product categories (2 for the undergraduates and 2 for the MBAs). (Of this total sample of 113, 32 were lost to attrition, resulting in 81 for the estimates of reliability.) After deleting 4 more items with low item-to-total correlations, the final 20-item scale was formed. (The sample of 45 MBAs was also used to further assess content validity.)

Two more samples were used to assess the criterion validity of the 20-item PII. One sample (n = 68 undergraduates) was used to elicit the product categories used, and the other sample (n = 47 undergraduates) responded to the PII across the products elicited. A final sample used to assess construct validity was composed of 57 clerical/administrative staff members at a major university. In all, 4 data sets over numerous product categories were used in the development process (not including the expert judges).

Validity: Several estimates of reliability were obtained by Zaichkowsky. For the second sample (n = 81), test-retest reliability was .88, .89, .88, and .93 for the four products studied over a three week period. Internal consistency for this sample ranged from alpha = .95 to .97. Internal consistency was also assessed with the clerical/administrative sample (n = 57) over three products with alphas of .97, .99, and .97, and with purchase scenarios via a subsample (n = 41) of the clerical/administrative sample over two more products with alphas of .97 and .98.

Several criterion and construct validity tests were also offered by Zaichkowsky. The pattern of means for products to be hypothesized as high, medium, and low involvement supported the PII's criterion validity over two samples (i.e., the n = 47 undergraduate students and the n = 57 clerical/administrative sample). Furthermore, the correlations of the PII with a number of behavioral measures relating to product involvement showed that the PII possessed adequate levels of construct validity (n = 57). For example, the correlations of the PII with a measure of reading about how a product is made ranged from .14 to .37 across three product categories. The correlations of the PII with a measure of comparing product characteristics across brands ranged from .23 to .52 across three product categories, and the correlations of the PII with a measure of having a most preferred brand in a product category ranged from .42 to 68.

Scores: Mean scores across samples and the various products examined were reported (cf., Zaichkowsky 1985, pp. 345-351). An overall grand mean score was reported to be 89.55. In addition, those subjects deemed as low involvement across the products studied scored in the 20 - 69 range, medium involvement in the 70 - 110 range, and high involvement in the 111 - 140 range.

Source:	Zaichkowsky, Judith Lynne (1985), "Measuring the Involvement Construct," *Journal of Consumer Research*, 12 (December), 341-352.
Other evidence:	Mean scores across 8 different product categories are reported in Zaichkowsky (1986). A sample of 230 students rated each product category. Automobiles had the highest mean rating on the PII of 131, and cigarettes had the lowest mean rating of 49. Mean scores were also broken down by gender, and many of the differences on the PII between males and females were significant in a direction that supports the PII's validity. See also the next several pages (i.e., revised versions of the PII).
Other sources:	Zaichkowsky, Judith Lynne (1986), "The Emotional Aspect of Product Involvement," in *Advances in Consumer Research*, Vol. 14, Melanie Wallendorf and Paul Anderson (eds.), The Association for Consumer Research, Provo, UT: 32-35.
References:	N/A.

PERSONAL INVOLVEMENT INVENTORY: PII
(Zaichkowsky 1985)

PII Instructions

The purpose of this study is to measure a person's involvement or interest in (product category). To take this measure, we need you to judge (product category) against a series of descriptive scales according to how YOU perceive the product you will be shown. Here is how you are to use these scales.

If you feel that the (product) is *very closely related* to one end of the scale, you should place your check mark as follows:

Unimportant _X_:___:___:___:___:___   Important
                            or
Unimportant ___:___:___:___:___:_X_   Important

If you feel that the (product) is *quite closely related* to one or the other end of the scale (but not extremely), you should place your check mark as follows:

Appealing ___:___:___:___:_X_:___   Unappealing
                          or
Appealing ___:_X_:___:___:___:___   Unappealing

If you feel that the (product) seems *only slightly related* to one or the other end of the scale (but not really neutral), you should place your check mark as follows:

Uninterested ___:___:_X_:___:___:___   Interested
                            or
Uninterested ___:___:___:___:_X_:___   Interested

IMPORTANT:

1) Be sure that you check every scale for every (product); do not omit any.
2) Never put more than one check mark on a single scale.

Make each item a separate and independent judgment. Work at fairly high speed through this questionnaire. Do not worry or puzzle over individual items. It is your first impressions, the immediate feelings about the items, that we want. On the other hand, please do not be careless, because we want your true impressions.

The PII Items

1) important - unimportant*
2) of no concern - of concern to me
3) irrelevant - relevant
4) means a lot to me - means nothing to me*
5) useless - useful
6) valuable - worthless*
7) trivial - fundamental
8) beneficial - not beneficial*
9) matters to me - doesn't matter*
10) uninterested - interested
11) significant - insignificant*
12) vital - superfluous*
13) boring - interesting
14) unexciting - exciting
15) appealing - unappealing*
16) mundane - fascinating
17) essential - nonessential*
18) undesirable - desirable
19) wanted - unwanted*
20) not needed - needed

NOTE: *denotes items that are reversed scored.

REVISED VERSIONS OF THE PII

Several revisions of Zaichkowsky's PII have been made. Four of these versions follow in chronological order.

RPII AND OPII
(McQuarrie and Munson 1986)

Construct: McQuarrie and Munson (1986) argue that involvement is a multidimensional construct. They also feel that the PII was contaminated with "attitudinal" variables and, thus, some interpretational confounding was evident. Their conceptual view of involvement is somewhat similar to Zaichkowsky's, but tries to incorporate risk and sign components into the involvement construct.

Description: The RPII is a multi-dimensional measure of involvement that includes the dimensions of importance, pleasure, and risk. It is composed of 14 semantic differential items, many of which are derived from Zaichkowsky's original PII. The items are scored on seven-point scales. Items can be summed within dimensions to form indices for each dimension, or all 14 items can be summed to form an overall RPII score.

The OPII is another involvement measure derived from Zaichkowsky's PII. It is composed of 16 items and may or may not be unidimensional (cf., McQuarrie and Munson 1986, p. 37). The 16 items can be summed to form an overall OPII score.

Development: Four pairs of adjectives from the original PII were deleted because they were considered inappropriate for a noncollege educated population (i.e., superfluous-vital, mundane-fascinating, significant-insignificant, and fundamental-trivial). The remaining 16 items form the OPII. Factor analysis, reliability, and validity estimates were used to examine the OPII.

The RPII was derived by adding 8 new adjective pairs to the OPII. Then, via reliability and factor analysis, the final 14-item RPII was derived. Though four factors were hypothesized (i.e., importance, risk, pleasure, and sign value), three factors were retained (importance, pleasure, and risk).

Sample(s): One hundred and thirty six student subjects (80 undergraduates and 56 MBAs) responded to 24 adjective pairs (the OPII items and the 8 new RPII items), over 12 stimulus objects. (See footnote 1 of McQuarrie and Munson, 1986, p. 37).

Validity: McQuarrie and Munson (1986) report reliability estimates for both the OPII and the RPII. The OPII (16 items) had an alpha of .95. The 14-item RPII (though considered multidimensional) had a coefficient alpha of .93. A factor analysis of the RPII revealed that the scale had three factors, labeled importance (5 items), pleasure (6 items), and risk (3 items) with alphas of .85, .90, and .67, respectively. Correlations among the three factors ranged from .41 to .60.

Estimates of validity also indicated that both the OPII and the RPII showed evidence of construct validity when correlated with measures reflecting the consequences of involvement (i.e., brand commitment and differentiation, and information search). For example, using the three involvement factors as predictor variables resulted in multiple Rs of .36, .22, and .57 for the prediction of brand commitment, brand differentiation, and information search, respectively.

Lastly, given its fewer items and multidimensional nature, McQuarrie and Munson (1986) concluded that the RPII is a more parsimonious measure of enduring involvement than the OPII or the PII.

Scores: No mean or percentage scores were reported.

Source: McQuarrie, Edward F. and J. Michael Munson (1986), "The Zaichkowsky Personal Involvement Inventory: Modification and Extension," in *Advances in Consumer Research*, Vol.

14, Paul Anderson and Melanie Wallendorf (eds.), Provo, UT: Association for Consumer Research, 36-40.

Other evidence: See the next several pages (i.e., more revisions of the PII).

Other sources: See the next several pages (i.e., more revisions of the PII).

References: Zaichkowsky, Judith Lynne (1985), "Measuring the Involvement Construct," *Journal of Consumer Research*, 12 (December), 341-352.

RPII AND OPII
(McQuarrie and Munson 1986)

1) important - unimportant*
2) of no concern - of concern to me
3) irrelevant - relevant
4) means a lot to me - means nothing to me*
5) valuable - worthless*
6) beneficial - not beneficial*
7) matters to me - doesn't matter*
8) uninterested - interested
9) boring - interesting
10) unexciting - exciting
11) appealing - unappealing*
12) mundane - fascinating
13) essential - nonessential*
14) undesirable - desirable
15) wanted - unwanted*
16) not needed - needed
17) fun - not fun*
18) says nothing about me - says something about me
19) tells me about a person - shows nothing*
20) easy to go wrong - hard to go wrong*
21) not risky - risky
22) easy to choose - hard to pick

NOTES: * denotes items that are reversed scored.

Items 1 through 16 comprise the OPII.

Items 1 through 4 and 7 comprise the RPII importance factor. Items 9 through 11, and 17 through 19 comprise the RPII pleasure factor. Items 20 through 22 comprise the RPII risk factor.

ENDURING INVOLVEMENT SCALE: EIS
(Higie and Feick 1988)

Construct: Higie and Feick (1988) view enduring involvement as an individual difference variable representing an arousal potential of a product or activity that causes personal relevance. Enduring involvement is intrinsically motivated by the degree to which the product or activity is related to the individual's self-image or the pleasure received from thoughts about or use of the product or engaging in the activity (see also Richins and Bloch 1986).

Description: The EIS is a 10-item scale composed of semantic differential pairs from Zaichkowsky's (1985) PII and McQuarrie and Munson's (1986) RPII, as well as items developed by the authors (7-point items). The scale has two factors, a hedonic and a self-expression factor, each composed of 5 items. Scores on items can be summed within dimensions to form hedonic and self-expression indices, or summed overall to form a measure of enduring involvement.

Development: In an initial study, items were chosen from the PII and RPII. Additional items deemed to have face validity were generated by the authors to reflect two hypothesized factors, hedonism and self-expression. Through item analysis and coefficient alpha, five- and four-item subscales for hedonism and self-expression were retained. In a second study, three additional items were generated for the self-expression subscale. Based on reliability and factor analysis results, the final 5-item EIS subscales were derived.

Sample(s): In the first study, a combination of 255 undergraduate and MBA students was used. In the second study, 180 MBA students were used. Personal computers (PCs) and/or lawnmowers were used as the products examined in the two studies.

Validity: In the first study, coefficient alpha for the 5-item hedonic subscale was .88 (for PCs with n = 255). In study two, the corresponding alpha for this measure was .93. Also, the alpha for the final five-item self-expression subscale was .91 for PCs. The combined ten-item hedonic and self-expression measure for PCs had an alpha of .89.

For lawnmowers (study two), the alphas for the hedonic and self-expressive subscales were .92 and .93, respectively, and the combined 10-item scale had an alpha of .92.

The five-item subscales of the EIS, as well the overall EIS, were correlated with a number of measures pertaining to validity (i.e., information search and provision, and opinion leadership). The pattern of correlations ranged from .18 to .46 and suggests that the EIS possessed adequate levels of discriminant and predictive validity.

Scores: Neither mean nor percentage scores were reported.

Source: Higie, Robin A. and Lawrence F. Feick (1988), "Enduring Involvement: Conceptual and Methodological Issues," in *Advances in Consumer Research*, Vol. 16, Thomas Srull (ed.), Provo, UT: Association for Consumer Research, 690-696.

Other evidence: See the next several pages for additional revisions of the PII.

Other sources: See the next several pages for additional revisions of the PII.

References: McQuarrie, Edward F. and J. Michael Munson (1986), "The Zaichkowsky Personal Involvement Inventory: Modification and Extension," in *Advances in Consumer Research*, Vol. 14, Paul Anderson and Melanie Wallendorf (eds.), Provo, UT: Association for Consumer Research, 36-40.

Richins, Marsha and Peter H. Bloch (1986), "After the New Wears Off: The Temporal Context of Product Involvement," *Journal of Consumer Research*, 13 (September), 280-285.

Zaichkowsky, Judith Lynne (1985), "Measuring the Involvement Construct," *Journal of Consumer Research*, 12 (December), 341-352.

ENDURING INVOLVEMENT SCALE: EIS
(Higie and Feick 1988)

1) not fun - fun
2) unappealing - appealing
3) boring - interesting
4) unexciting - exciting
5) dull - fascinating
6) shows nothing - tells me about a person
7) others won't use to judge me - others use to judge me
8) not part of my self-image - part of my self-image
9) doesn't tell others about me - tells others about me
10) does not portray an image of me to others - portrays an image of me to others

NOTES: Items 1 through 5 comprise the hedonic factor, and items 6 through 10 comprise the self-expression factor.

PII FOR ADVERTISING: PIIA
(Zaichkowsky 1990)

Construct: In measuring involvement toward advertising, a measure must be able to capture both personal rational relevance as well as personal emotional relevance of the ad. Furthermore, an involvement measure toward advertising should be able to discriminate between high and low involvement with advertising (Zaichkowsky 1990).

Description: The PIIA is a 10-item semantic differential scale. All items are scored on a 7-point basis. The items are summed to form an overall measure of advertising involvement. The scale is considered unidimensional.

Development: The PIIA was developed along recommended scaling procedures. After a review of the advertising involvement literature, 15 bi-polar adjective pairs were added to the original 20-item PII (Zaichkowsky 1985). These 35 items were judged for content validity, and then via item analysis and reliability estimates, the final 10-item PIIA was derived. The PIIA was checked again for content validity, as well construct validity and dimensionality.

Sample(s): Four samples and a panel of experts were used in developing the PIIA. The first sample of 54 students was used to assess the internal consistency of the 35 items across two products. Items with low reliability were deleted, resulting in 22 items retained. The second sample of 52 students rated the remaining 22 items on a number of ads and products (twice over a three week interval). Again, items with low reliability or redundant items were dropped, resulting in the final 10-item PIIA. Content validity and dimensionality were also assessed with the second sample. Two more student samples of 79 and 53 subjects were used to assess the validity of the scale (Zaichkowsky 1990).

Validity: A number of reliability and validity assessments were performed on the PIIA. With the second sample (n = 52), coefficient alpha for the final 10-item PIIA ranged from .91 to .96 across products and ads. For the latter two samples, reported alphas ranged from .68 to .95 across ads. Furthermore, factor analysis (n = 52) revealed a unidimensional structure for the PIIA.

The 10-item PIIA was correlated with a number of measures reflecting behavioral response of involvement with products (n = 52). The pattern of correlations suggests an adequate level of construct validity for the PIIA. For example, the correlations between the PIIA and a measure of interest in reading product information ranged from .15 to .40 across three product categories. The correlations between the PIIA and a measure of comparing product attributes across brands ranged from .21 to .50, and the correlations between the PIIA and a measure of having a most preferred brand ranged from .40 to .66 across the three product categories. Construct validity was also assessed in two studies across a number of ads. The pattern of means and statistical significance tests indicate that the PIIA possessed construct validity and was able to discriminate between groups that showed high and low involvement with ads.

Scores: A number of scores across various ads and treatment levels are reported by Zaichkowsky (1990, Table 3, p. 31). As indicated above, these scores showed that the PIIA was able to discriminate between high- and low-involved groups.

Source: Zaichkowsky, Judith Lynne, (1990), "The Personal Involvement Inventory: Reduction and Application to Advertising," *Unpublished Working Paper*, Burnaby, British Columbia: Simon Fraser University

Other evidence: N/A.

Other sources: N/A.

References: Zaichkowsky, Judith Lynne (1985), "Measuring the Involvement Construct," *Journal of Consumer Research*, 12 (December), 341-352.

PERSONAL II FOR ADVERTISING: PIIA
(Zaichkowsky 1990)

1) important - unimportant*
2) boring - interesting
3) relevant - irrelevant*
4) exciting - unexciting*
5) means nothing - means a lot to me
6) appealing - unappealing*
7) fascinating - mundane*
8) worthless - valuable
9) involving - uninvolving*
10) not needed - needed

NOTE: * denotes items that are reversed scored.

REVISED RPII: RRPII
(McQuarrie and Munson 1991)

Construct: McQuarrie and Munson (1991) propose a new version of their RPII that captures two facets of involvement: perceived importance and interest. The conceptual base of the RRPII is similar to the conceptual base of the RPII. However, the RRPII captures the two facets of involvement proposed by McQuarrie and Munson (1986), and shows improved criterion validity.

Description: The RRPII is a 10-item semantic differential measure where the items are evaluated on 7-point scales. The scale has two dimensions. Item scores can be summed within each dimension to form indices for each dimension, or can be summed over all 10 items for an overall involvement measure.

Development: The original PII (Zaichkowsky 1985) and 2 new items generated by the authors served as the initial item pool. Over twelve product categories and multiple buying situations, a large sample responded to the 22 items. Eight of the PII items and the two new items were chosen to represent the final scale. The RRPII was then assessed for reliability, factor structure, and various forms of validity.

Sample(s): A sample of 146 students and 103 nonstudents was used to derive the RRPII and assess its reliability, validity and dimensionality.

Validity: Internal consistency estimates were reported for the 2 subscales and the overall RRPII. Across products, the subscales of importance and perceived interest, as well as the overall RRPII, exhibited alphas in the low to mid .80 range or better. (Three-fourths of the time, alpha was .90 or better.) Test-retest reliability from a subsample of 60 students over three product categories and a three week interval ranged from .53 to .78.

In 8 of 15 factor analyses, two factors emerged (importance and interest). The correlation between the two factors was reported to be .66 overall.

Several estimates of validity were also performed. Both the subscales and the RRPII were correlated with measures of attitude, information search, and information processing for 3 products. Correlations of the importance and interest factors with the attitude measure were .74 and .65. These estimates were lower than the correlation between the PII and the attitude measure (.76) and were taken as evidence of discriminant validity. The RRPII also accounted for more variance in information search and processing (45%) than the PII (40%). The RRPII was also more highly correlated with a number of behavioral outcomes than the PII, and across nine of the products, predictive validity for the RRPII dimensions was found.

Scores: Mean scores for three products over two situations were reported for the 10-item RRPII. For "everyday use," mean scores ranged from 34 to 49, and for "special occasions," mean scores ranged from 51 to 56.

Source: McQuarrie, Edward F. and J. Michael Munson (1991), "A Revised Product Involvement Inventory: Improved Usability and Validity," in *Advances in Consumer Research*, Vol. 19, John F. Sherry and Brian Sternthal (eds.), Provo, UT: The Association for Consumer Research (forthcoming).

Other evidence: N/A.

Other sources: N/A.

References: McQuarrie, Edward F. and J. Michael Munson (1986), "The Zaichkowsky Personal Involvement Inventory: Modification and Extension," in *Advances in Consumer Research*, Vol. 14, Paul Anderson and Melanie Wallendorf (eds.), Provo, UT: Association for Consumer Research, 36-40.

Zaichkowsky, Judith Lynne (1985), "Measuring the Involvement Construct," *Journal of Consumer Research*, 12 (December), 341-352.

REVISED RPII: RRPII
(McQuarrie and Munson 1991)

1) important - unimportant*
2) irrelevant - relevant
3) means a lot to me - means nothing to me*
4) unexciting - exciting
5) dull - neat
6) matters to me - doesn't matter*
7) fun - not fun*
8) appealing - unappealing*
9) boring - interesting
10) of no concern - of concern to me

NOTE: * denotes items that are reversed scored.

Items 1 through 3, 6, and 10 comprise the importance factor. Items 4, 5, and 7 through 9 comprise the interest factor.

OTHER INVOLVEMENT MEASURES GENERAL TO SEVERAL PRODUCTS

ENDURING INVOLVEMENT INDEX
(Bloch, Sherrell, and Ridgeway 1986)

Construct: In a study investigating the antecedents and consequences of search, Bloch, Sherrell, and Ridgeway (1986, p. 120) viewed involvement as enduring in character, representing a continuing interest or enthusiasm rather than a temporary product interest resulting from purchase requirements.

Description: The Bloch et al. enduring involvement index is composed of five items. The first three items assess the importance of the product category to the individual's social life and career. These three items are measured on 7-point scales from "not important at all" to "extremely important." The fourth item is an interest item scored on a 4-point format from "not at all interested" to "very interested," and the fifth item is a frequency of thought item scored on a 5-point scale from "never or almost never" to "very frequently." Scores from the three-item importance facet can be summed to form an importance index or all five items can be summed to form an overall enduring involvement index.

Development: Little information as to the development of the index was offered. However, reliability and validity estimates were reported.

Sample(s): A sample of 679 (usable responses) consumers participated in the study. Subsamples based on interest in clothing and computers, the focal products of the study, were also derived.

Validity: Coefficient alpha estimates of internal consistency were reported for the three-item importance facet. These estimates were .83 and .77 for clothing and computers, respectively. Summed over all five items, the enduring involvement index showed correlations of .70 and .67 (for clothing and computers) for a measure of search, offering evidence of nomological validity.

Scores: Neither mean nor percentage scores were reported.

Source: Bloch, Peter H., Daniel L. Sherrell, and Nancy M. Ridgeway (1986), "Consumer Search: An Extended Framework," *Journal of Consumer Research*, 13 (June), 119-126.

Other evidence: N/A.

Other sources: N/A.

References: N/A.

ENDURING INVOLVEMENT INDEX
(Bloch, Sherrell, and Ridgeway 1986)

How important is knowledge of _____ to:

1) The quality of your social life?
2) Your present job or career?
3) Your future job or career plans?

4) How interested are you in the subject of _____ ?

      _____ Not at all interested
      _____ Slightly interested
      _____ Moderately interested
      _____ Very interested

5) How frequently do you find yourself thinking about _____ ?

Never or
almost never   ____:____:____:____:____   Very
frequently

NOTES: Items 1 through 3 are scored on a seven-point "not at all important" to "extremely important" format. The product category of interest is inserted where the _____ are.

FOOTE, CONE & BELDING INVOLVEMENT SUBSCALE: FCBI
(Ratchford 1987; Vaughn 1986)

Construct: The FCBI conceptualization views involvement as implying personal importance (i.e., relevance), and consequent attention to an object or product (cf. Ratchford 1987; Vaughn 1986). This view is similar to the S-O-R paradigm of Houston and Rothschild (1977) and Zaichkowsky's (1985) concept of involvement as well.

Description: The FCBI is a three-item semantic differential measure. Each item is scored on a seven-point scale and item scores are summed to form an overall score.

Development: Scale development procedures are described in Ratchford (1987) and generally adhere to prescribed psychometric scaling procedures. Fifty items were originally developed. This pool of items was reduced to 30. These thirty items were tested over five studies for internal consistency, ability to discriminate between products, and respondent understanding. These five studies resulted in the three-item FCBI (Ratchford 1987; Vaughn 1986).

Samples: Five samples were used in the derivation of the final FCBI (i.e., adult samples of 30, 50, 30, 249, and 50), and numerous products were examined (e.g., 75 products for the n = 249 sample). In addition, the final scale was administered to a sample of 1,792 adults over 254 possible products.

The first sample of 30 was used to trim the 30 items to 11 items. The decision was also made to trim this 11-item measure to 3 items for the remaining studies. The third, fourth and fifth studies, as well as the major study (n = 1,792), assessed the validity of the final three-item FCBI.

Validity: Internal consistency estimates for the FCBI in Studies Three through Five and the major study were .81, .74, .75, and .77, respectively. A measure of consistency for the product ratings across studies was also taken and indicated a very high level of consistency (correlations ranged from .84 to .96). Item-to-factor correlations are also reported by Vaughn (1986), and ranged from .90 to .97 for the three FCBI items on the overall FCBI measure.

Several assessments of validity were also taken. Correlations with ratings from Zaichkowsky's (1985) mean scores, and mean scores reported by Laurent and Kapferer (1985), indicated high correlations with the FCBI (.38 to .86), suggesting convergent validity (using the n = 1,792 data). Numerous estimates of discriminant and criterion validity also show support for the FCBI (n = 1,792 data).

Scores: Mean scores were reported based on a 100-point scoring system and are plotted for 60 products (see Ratchford 1987, p. 31).

Sources: Ratchford, Brian T. (1987), "New Insights About the FCB Grid," *Journal of Advertising Research*, 27 (August-September), 24-38.

Vaughn, Richard (1986), "How Advertising Works: A Planning Model Revisited," *Journal of Advertising Research*, 27 (February-March), 57-66.

Other evidence: N/A.

Other sources: N/A.

References: Houston, Michael J. and Michael Rothschild (1977), "A Paradigm for Research on Consumer Involvement," *Unpublished Working Paper*, Madison, WI: University of Wisconsin.

Laurent, Gilles and Jean-Noel Kapferer (1985), "Measuring Consumer Involvement Profiles," *Journal of Marketing Research*, 22 (February), 41-53.

Zaichkowsky, Judith Lynne (1985), "Measuring the Involvement Construct," *Journal of Consumer Research*, 12 (December), 341-352.

FOOTE, CONE & BELDING INVOLVEMENT SUBSCALE: FCBI
(Ratchford 1987; Vaughn 1986)

1) very important decision - very unimportant decision*
2) decision requires a lot of thought - decision requires little thought*
3) a lot to lose if you chose the wrong brand - little to lose of you choose the wrong brand*

NOTES: * denotes items that are reversed scored.

NEW INVOLVEMENT PROFILE: NIP
(Jain and Srinivasan 1990)

Construct: In an effort to compare a number of the scales designed to measure involvement, and assess whether involvement is a multi-faceted or unidimensional construct, Jain and Srinivasan (1990) developed the NIP. The NIP takes a multi-dimensional approach to measuring involvement that includes 5 facets: relevance, pleasure, sign, risk importance, and risk probability. These facets are consistent with Laurent and Kapferer's (1985) approach.

Description: The NIP is composed of 15 semantic differential items. The items are scored on a seven-point basis. There are five factors, each composed of three items (i.e., relevance, pleasure, sign, risk importance, and risk probability). Item scores can be summed within each factor to form indices of each factor.

Development: The NIP was developed with an original pool of 49 items from Zaichkowsky's (1985) PII, McQuarrie and Munson's (1986) RPII, Higie and Feick's (1988) EIS, Laurent and Kapferer's (1985) CIP, and the FCBI (Ratchford 1987; Vaughn 1986). All items were adjusted to a semantic differential format. These items were administered to 375 students across 10 products. Through factor structure comparisons, domain overlap testing, and reliability analysis, the 15-item, five-factor scale was derived.

Sample(s): A sample of 375 of mostly undergraduate students was used to derive the NIP.

Validity: The internal consistency reliability estimates for the relevance, pleasure, sign, risk importance, and risk probability factors of NIP were .80, .84, .84,. .80, and .56, respectively. Correlations among the factors ranged from -.02 to .58. It should be noted that the correlations among the first four factors were relatively strong (i.e., .33 to .58), whereas the correlations among the risk probability factor with the other four factors were low (i.e., -.02 to .23).

These five factors were also correlated with measures of the consequences of involvement (i.e., information search and brand preference). The pattern of correlations suggests that the five NIP factors possess predictive validity. For example, the NIP factors explained 35% of the variance in information search, and 13% of the variance in brand preference.

Scores: Mean scores across the 10 products studied are reported in Table 5 of Jain and Srinivasan (1990, p. 601) for the Zaichkowsky PII and for a recent version of Laurent and Kapferer's CIP. These mean scores are standardized on a 100-point basis. Mean scores for the NIP factors were not reported.

Source: Jain, Kapil and Narasimhan Srinivasan (1990), "An Empirical Assessment of Multiple Operationalizations of Involvement," in *Advances in Consumer Research*, Vol. 17, Marvin Goldberg, Gerald Gorn, and Richard Pollay (eds.), Provo, UT: The Association for Consumer Research, 594-602.

Other evidence: N/A.

Other sources: N/A.

References: Higie, Robin A. and Lawrence F. Feick (1988), "Enduring Involvement: Conceptual and Methodological Issues," in *Advances in Consumer Research*, Vol. 16, Thomas K. Srull (ed.), Provo, UT: Association for Consumer Research, 690-696.

Laurent, Gilles and Jean-Noel Kapferer (1985), "Measuring Consumer Involvement Profiles," *Journal of Marketing Research*, 22 (February), 41-53.

McQuarrie, Edward F. and J. Michael Munson (1986), "The Zaichkowsky Personal Involvement Inventory: Modification and Extension," in *Advances in Consumer Research*, Vol. 14, Paul Anderson and Melanie Wallendorf (eds.), Provo, UT: The Association for Consumer Research, 36-40.

Ratchford, Brian T. (1987), "New Insights About the FCB Grid," *Journal of Advertising Research*, 27 (August-September), 24-38.

Vaughn, Richard (1986), "How Advertising Works: A Planning Model Revisited," *Journal of Advertising Research*, 27 (February-March), 57-66.

Zaichkowsky, Judith Lynne (1985), "Measuring the Involvement Construct," *Journal of Consumer Research*, 12 (December), 341-352.

NEW INVOLVEMENT PROFILE: NIP
(Jain and Srinivasan 1990)

1) essential - non-essential*
2) beneficial - not beneficial*
3) not needed - needed
4) I do not find it pleasurable - I find it pleasurable
5) unexciting - exciting
6) fun - not fun*
7) tells others about me - doesn't tell others about me*
8) others use to judge me - others won't use to judge me*
9) does not portray an image of me to others - portrays an image of me to others
10) it is really annoying to make an unsuitable purchase - it is not annoying to make an unsuitable purchase*
11) a poor choice wouldn't be upsetting - a poor choice would be upsetting
12) little to lose by choosing poorly - a lot to lose by choosing poorly
13) in purchasing it, I am certain of my choice - in purchasing it, I am uncertain of my choice
14) I never know if I am making the right purchase - I know for sure that I am making the right purchase*
15) I feel a bit at a loss in choosing it - I don't feel at a loss in choosing it*

NOTES: * denotes items that are reversed scored.

Items 1 through 3 comprise the relevance factor; items 4 through 6 comprise the pleasure factor; items 7 through 9 comprise the sign factor; items 10 through 13 comprise the risk importance factor; and items 14 through 15 comprise the risk probability factor.

PURCHASING INVOLVEMENT

PURCHASING INVOLVEMENT: PI
(Slama and Tashchian 1985)

Construct: Purchasing involvement is defined as the self-relevance of purchasing activities to the individual (Slama and Tashchian 1985, p. 73). Purchasing involvement is expected to affect consumer decision processes from pre-search to post-search evaluation, as well as attitudes and behaviors toward purchasing.

Description: The PI is comprised of 33 six-point Likert items (strongly disagree to strongly agree). The items are summed to form an overall purchasing involvement score. Thus, scores on the scale can range from 33 to 198.

Development: Following the literature review and construct definition, 150 items were generated to tap the domain of the construct. This pool of items was trimmed to 75 by a panel familiar with the involvement literature. The remaining pool of items was administered to two samples and by using a number of reliability and validity checks, the final 33-item scale was derived.

Sample(s): Three samples were used in the scale development process. The first sample consisted of 30 marketing research students familiar with the involvement literature to trim the initial pool of items. Items on which at least 75% of these judges agreed upon as reflective of the construct were retained, resulting in 75 items. The second sample consisted of 365 adults from a small southern city. With this sample the 75 items were trimmed to the final 33-item scale using item-to-total correlations as a guide. Internal consistency and validity of the scale were also assessed with this sample. The third sample consisted of 76 students to assess test-retest reliability.

Validity: Coefficient alpha internal consistency for the PI was .93 (n = 356), and test-retest reliability over a two-week period was .86 (n = 76).

Convergent and discriminant validity of the scale was assessed via a multi-trait multi-method analysis. The correlations between the PI, measures of religious involvement, measures of automobile involvement, and other measures of purchasing involvement indicated that the PI had adequate levels of convergent and discriminant validity. For example, the PI exhibited convergent validity correlations .56 and .48 with other involvement measures. Furthermore, the scale was relatively free of social desirability bias (r = .06, ns, n = 365).

Scores: Mean scores were reported by various demographic characteristics, including family life cycle, education, income, gender, working status of wife, and race (Slama and Tashchian 1985, p. 78). The mean scores ranged from a low of 136 (for an advanced family life cycle group) to a high of 155.05 (for a married, but wife unemployed group).

The pattern of means and statistical significance tests also shows general support for hypothesized predictions pertaining to the validity of the PI. (See Table 6, p. 78.)

Source: Slama, Mark, E. and Armen Tashchian (1985), "Selected Socio-economic and Demographic Characteristics Associated with Purchasing Involvement," *Journal of Marketing*, 49 (Winter), 72-82.

Other evidence: N/A.

Other sources: N/A.

References: N/A.

PURCHASING INVOLVEMENT: PI
(Slama and Tashchian 1985)

1) On most purchase decisions the choice I make is of little consequence.*

2) Usually reading about products or asking people about them won't really help you make a decision.*

3) I have little or no interest in shopping.*

4) *Consumer Reports* is not very relevant to me.*

5) I am not interested in bargain seeking.*

6) I am not interested in sales.*

7) You can't save a lot of money by careful shopping.*

8) I often take advantage of coupon offers in the newspapers.

9) Because of my personal values, I feel that "smart purchasing" ought to be important to me.

10) I am usually not annoyed when I find out I could have bought something cheaper than I did.

11) Being a smart shopper is worth the extra time it takes.

12) Even with inexpensive products like shampoo, I will often evaluate a recent purchase and become annoyed because the product doesn't adequately meet my needs.

13) Sales don't excite me.*

14) I am not really committed to getting the most for my money.*

15) For expensive items I spend a lot of time and effort making my purchase decision, since it is important to get the best deal.

16) Consumerism issues are irrelevant to me.*

17) I view the purchasing of goods and services as a rather petty activity, not relevant to my main concerns in life.*

18) It is important to me to be aware of all the alternatives before buying an expensive item.

19) It is important to me to keep up with special deals being offered by the grocery stores in my area.

20) I am too absorbed in more personally relevant matters to worry about making smart purchases.*

21) It is part of my value system to shop around for the best buy.

22) The consumer and business sections of the newspaper are highly relevant to me.

23) If I were buying a major appliance it wouldn't make much difference which brand I chose.*

24) The brands of goods I buy make very little difference to me.*

25) It is not worth it to read *Consumer Reports* since most brands are about the same.*

26) You can save a lot of money by clipping coupons from the newspaper.

27) Thinking about what you are going to buy before going shopping won't make much difference in your long run expectations.*

28) It doesn't make much sense to get upset over a purchase decision since most brands are about the same.*

29) I am willing to spend extra time shopping in order to get the cheapest possible price on goods of like quality.

30) I pay attention to advertisements for products I am interested in.

31) Shopping wisely is rather a petty issue compared to thinking about how to make more money.*

32) I don't like worrying about getting the best deal when I go shopping; I like to spend money as I please.*

33) I don't like to waste a lot of time trying to get good deals on groceries.*

NOTES: * denotes items that are reversed scored.

PURCHASE DECISION INVOLVEMENT: PDI
(Mittal 1989)

Construct: Purchase decision involvement (PDI) is defined as the extent of interest and concern that a consumer brings to bear upon a purchase-decision task (Mittal 1989). PDI is felt to be analogous to the situational involvement of Houston and Rothschild (1977), has the purchase decision task as its goal object, and is considered a mindset - not a response behavior (Mittal 1989).

Description: The PDI scale is a 4-item measure on 7-point bi-polar phrases. The item scores are summed, and then divided by 4, to form an average score of PDI.

Development: Development of the PDI scale generally followed recommended scaling procedures. An initial pool of nine items was derived via a review of the literature, an open-ended question regarding purchase decision involvement (n = 20), and the author's definition of the construct. These items were then administered to 40 consumers over a variety of products. Inter-item correlations, factor analyses, and the author's judgment resulted in the final four items. Then, two more studies assessing the validity of the scale were conducted, as well as a study that assessed the test-retest reliability of the scale.

Sample(s): Overall, five samples were used in scale development and validation. One sample (n = 20) was used for generating items; one sample (n = 40) was used to arrive at the final four items; two samples (n = 256 nonstudents, and n = 138 students) were used for validation purposes; and one sample (n = 85 students) was used to look at test-retest reliability.

Validity: The first validation study looked at the convergent, discriminant, and criterion validity of the PDI scale (n = 256). The factor structure and correlations with product importance/ involvement demonstrated convergent and discriminant validity for the PDI scale. Correlations with a measure of consumer information search (.50 for beer and .67 for a camera) indicated criterion validity for the PDI scale.

The second validation study examined the mean responses to the PDI scale with respect to several product categories ranked with respect to financial and product importance. The pattern of means across the PDI measures suggests that the PDI scale is a valid measure of PDI (Mittal 1989, p. 157, Table 3). For example, the mean scores ranged from a high of 6.27 (sd = .58) for eyeglasses (i.e., a high involvement product) to 1.91 (sd = 1.32) for pencils (i.e., a low involvement product).

Test-retest reliability (n = 85) over a two-week period was .79 for the PDI scale. Though coefficient alpha was not offered, factor loadings for items on the scale ranged from .58 to .88 across three product categories.

Scores: As stated above, mean scores across 15 different products were reported. The mean scores ranged from a high of 6.27 (sd = .58) for eyeglasses to 1.91 (sd = 1.32) for pencils.

Source: Mittal, Banwari (1989), "Measuring Purchase-Decision Involvement," *Psychology & Marketing*, 6 (Summer), 147-162.

Other evidence: N/A.

Other sources: N/A.

References: Houston, Michael J. and M. L. Rothschild (1977), "A Paradigm for Research on Consumer Involvement," *Working Paper 11-77-46*, University of Wisconsin, Madison.

PURCHASE DECISION INVOLVEMENT: PDI
(Mittal 1989)

1) In selecting from many types and brands of this product available in the market, would you say that:

   I would not care at all   1 2 3 4 5 6 7   I would care a great deal
   as to which one I buy.   as to which one I buy.

2) Do you think that the various types and brands of this product available in the market are all very alike or are all very different?

   They are alike.   1 2 3 4 5 6 7   They are all different.

3) How important would it be to you to make a right choice of this product?

   Not at all important   1 2 3 4 5 6 7   Extremely important

4) In making your selection of this product, how concerned would you be about the outcome of your choice?

   Not at all concerned   1 2 3 4 5 6 7   Very much concerned.

INFORMATION PROCESSING

OPTIMAL STIMULATION MEASURES

Three measures have been used in the consumer behavior literature as operationalizations of optimal stimulation (see Wahlers and Etzel 1990 for a review). These measures are Mehrabian and Russell's (1974) Arousal Seeking Tendency (AST) scale, Zuckerman's (1979) Form V Sensation Seeking scale (SS), and Raju's (1980) Exploratory Tendencies in Consumer Behavior (ETCBS) scale.

AROUSAL SEEKING TENDENCY: AST
(Mehrabian and Russell 1974)

Construct: Optimal Stimulation Level (OSL) is viewed as a uniquely determined, homeostatic degree of stimulation with which an individual is comfortable with. If the environment is deficient at providing this level of stimulation, the individual will tend to seek complexity or novelty. If the environment provides more stimulation than the desired optimal level, the individual will engage in behavior to reduce stimulation (e.g., Raju 1980; Wahlers and Etzel 1990). OSL is considered to be predictive of a wide range of consumer-related behaviors.

Likewise, arousal seeking tendency is viewed as a characteristic which varies across individuals. An individual's preference for an environment is closely related to his/her preferred arousal level. Some people prefer calm settings, whereas others actively seek to increase their arousal by choosing novel, complex, or unpredictable settings (Mehrabian and Russell 1974). The AST is designed to measure this preference.

Description: The AST is a 40-item scale, where each item is evaluated on a nine-point Likert format (i.e., very strong disagreement [-4] to very strong agreement [+4]). The scale can be summed for an overall index assessing OSL, and can be broken down into five underlying factors by summing item scores within factors: arousal from change, arousal from unusual stimuli, arousal from sensuality, arousal from risk, and arousal from new environments.

Though Mehrabian and Russell report a five-factor structure that corresponds to their five sources of arousal, they do not state exactly which items compose the five factors. They provide example items only (p. 42) and go on to state that arousal from change is composed of 12 items, arousal from unusual stimuli is composed of 11 items, arousal from risk is composed of 9 items, arousal from sensuality is composed of 5 items, and arousal from new environments is composed of 3 items. They do, however, state that the overall 40 items can be used as a measure assessing a single trait.

Development: Drawing from a vast literature search and previous scales measuring various aspects of change seeking, sensation seeking, and stimulus seeking, 312 items were initially generated. In the first scale development study, items highly correlated with social desirability (.15 or greater) and low item-to-total correlations (less than .20) were eliminated. The remaining items were factor analyzed. Items with high factor loadings on a given factor, high item-to-total correlations (.25 and above), low social desirability bias, simple wording and low redundancy with other items were retained, resulting in 125 items. A second study was performed to cross-validate the 125 items, and a third study was performed to derive the final 40-item scale. Here, items with item-to-total correlations of .40 and above, and social desirability bias of .10 and below, were retained. A fourth study re-examined the final 40 items, and a fifth study assessed the factor structure of the scale (Mehrabian and Russell 1974).

Sample(s): Five samples were used in scale development. For studies one through five mentioned above, student samples of 203, 316, 214, 202, and 530, respectively, were used.

Validity: Mehrabian and Russell (1974) report a coefficient alpha of .87 for the 40-item AST from their third study (n = 214), and based on a subsample from their third study (n = 78), test-retest reliability over a four to seven week interval was .88. Though factor analysis indicated five factors (n = 530), no estimates of internal consistency on a factor-by-factor basis were provided. However, correlations among the five factors ranged from .27 to .65. Mehrabian and Russell also offer estimates of scale validity. Throughout their first three studies, the final 40 items comprising the AST were correlated with various personality trait measures (i.e., extroversion, anxiety, trait arousal, etc.). These correlations ranged from .05 to .70 (in absolute value). The pattern of correlations between the AST and these measures offers evidence of construct validity.

Scores: Mehrabian and Russell (1974) report a mean score of 39 (sd = 34) for their samples of 214 and 202.

Source: Mehrabian, Albert and James A. Russell (1974), *An Approach to Environmental Psychology*, Cambridge, MA: The MIT Press.

Other evidence: In consumer behavior related studies, the AST has also been examined. Raju (1980) examined the relationship of AST with a number of personality traits and behavioral response scales with two student samples of 185 and 109, and two homemaker samples of 197 and 336. Wahlers et al. (1986) used 69 students to examine the relation of the AST to other OSL measures. Wahlers and Etzel (1990) used a sample of 697 from a midwestern consumer panel to compare measures of OSL.

In the Raju (1980) study, reliability estimates for the AST were not reported. However, the AST was found to be significantly correlated with various personality traits and behavioral measures reflecting OSL tendencies, supporting the AST as a measure of OSL. For example, AST correlations with a measure of intolerance of ambiguity were -.60 and -.55 for two samples. AST correlations with a measure of rigidity were -.43 and -.45.

In the Wahlers et al. (1986) study, the internal consistency estimate for the 40-item AST was .88. (Reliability estimates for the 5 subscales were not reported.) The AST was also highly correlated with other measures of arousal seeking, and OSL in general (ranging from .17 to .96), suggesting convergent validity for the AST.

In the Wahlers and Etzel (1990) study, the internal consistency estimate for the 40-item AST was reported as .85. Though no direct estimate of subscale reliability was offered, it was stated that the subscales possessed adequate internal consistency. Furthermore, the correlation of the AST with another measure of OSL was extremely high (r = .95), indicating convergent validity.

Other sources: Raju, P. S. (1980), "Optimum Stimulation Level: Its Relationship to Personality, Demographics, and Exploratory Behavior," *Journal of Consumer Research*, 7 (December), 272-282.

Wahlers, Russell G. Mark G. Dunn and Michael J. Etzel (1986), "The Congruence of Alternative OSL Measures With Exploratory Behavior Tendencies," in *Advances in Consumer Research*, Vol. 13, Richard Lutz (ed.), Provo, UT: Association for Consumer Research, 398-402.

Wahlers, Russell G. and Michael J. Etzel (1990), "A Structural Examination of Two Optimal Stimulation Level Measurement Models," in *Advances in Consumer Research*, Vol. 17, Marvin Goldberg, Gerald Gorn and Richard Pollay (eds.), Provo, UT: Association for Consumer Research, 415-425.

References: N/A.

AROUSAL SEEKING TENDENCY: AST
(Mehrabian and Russell 1974)

1) I seldom change the pictures on my walls.*

2) I am not interested in poetry.*

3) It is unpleasant seeing people in strange weird clothes.*

4) I am continually seeking new ideas and experiences.

5) I much prefer familiar people and places.*

6) When things get boring, I like to find some new and unfamiliar experience.

7) I like to touch and feel a sculpture.

8) I don't enjoy doing daring foolhardy things just for fun.*

9) I prefer a routine way of life to an unpredictable one full of change.*

10) People view me as quite an unpredictable person.

11) I like to run through heaps of fallen leaves.

12) I sometimes like to do things that are a little frightening.

13) I prefer friends who are reliable and predictable to those who are excitingly unpredictable.*

14) I prefer an unpredictable life full of change to a more routine one.

15) I wouldn't like to try the new group therapy techniques involving strange body sensations.*

16) Sometimes I really stir up excitement.

17) I never notice textures.*

18) I like surprises.

19) My ideal home would be peaceful and quiet.*

20) I eat the same kind of food most of the time.*

21) As a child, I often imagined leaving home just to explore the world.

22) I like to experience novelty and change in my daily routine.

23) Shops with thousands of exotic herbs and fragrances fascinate me.

24) Designs and patterns should be bold and exciting.

25) I feel best when I am safe and secure.*

26) I would like the job of a foreign correspondent of a newspaper.

27) I don't pay much attention to my surroundings.*

28) I don't like the feeling of wind in my hair.*

29) I like to go somewhere different nearly every day.

30) I seldom change the decor and furniture arrangement at my place.*

31) I am interested in new and varied interpretations of different art forms.

32) I wouldn't enjoy dangerous sports such as mountain climbing, airplane flying, or sky diving.*

33) I don't like to have lots of activity around me.*

34) I am interested only in what I need to know.*

35) I like meeting people who give me new ideas.

36) I would be content to live in the same house the rest of my life.*

37) I like continually changing activities.

38) I like a job that offers change, variety, and travel even if it involves some danger.

39) I avoid busy, noisy places.*

40) I like to look at pictures that are puzzling in some way.

NOTES: * denotes items that are reversed scored.

Though Mehrabian and Russell report a five-factor structure that corresponds to their five sources of arousal, they do not state exactly which items compose the five factors. They provide example items only (p. 42) and go on to state that arousal from change is composed of 12 items, arousal from unusual stimuli is composed of 11 items, arousal from risk is composed of 9 items, arousal from sensuality is composed of 5 items, and arousal from new environments is composed of 3 items. They do, however, state that the overall 40 items can be used as a measure assessing a single trait.

FORM V SENSATION SEEKING SCALE: SS
(Zuckerman 1979)

Construct: Optimal Stimulation Level (OSL) is viewed as a uniquely determined, homeostatic degree of stimulation with which an individual is comfortable with. If the environment is deficient at providing this level of stimulation, the individual will tend to seek complexity or novelty. If the environment provides more stimulation than the desired optimal level, the individual will engage in behavior to reduce stimulation (e.g., Raju 1980; Wahlers and Etzel 1990). OSL is considered to be predictive of a wide range of consumer-related behaviors.

Likewise, sensation seeking is viewed as the need for varied, novel, and complex sensations and experiences, and the willingness to take physical and social risks for the sake of such experience (Zuckerman 1979).

Description: The Form V SS consists of 40 pairs of statements in a forced choice format (0,1 scoring). Form V is the fifth in a series of five SS scales that have been developed and refined from the early 1960s on (cf. Zuckerman 1979, pp. 95-121 for a review of the development of all forms of the SS). Four factors underlie the SS: thrill and adventure seeking (TAS), experience seeking (ES), boredom susceptibility (BS), and disinhibition (DIS) (Zuckerman 1979). Items can be summed within factors to form indices for each factor, or summed over the entire 40 items for an overall sensation seeking score.

Development: The Form V SS was refined from a previous 72-item Form IV version and a 113-item Form III version of the SS across two samples. The 71 items common to both versions III and IV were then factor analyzed. The goal was to choose 10 items for each of the four factors with the highest loading on the respective factors across samples. This resulted in the 40-item four-factor Form V SS. The SS was then extensively checked for reliability and validity (Zuckerman 1979).

Sample(s): Though numerous samples were used in the development of all versions of the SS, three main samples were used for Form V, a British sample of twins (n = 947), and at least two samples composed of American college students (n = 330 and n = 92).

Validity: Internal consistency estimates for the overall 40-item scale ranged from .82 to .86 across samples. The internal consistency estimates for each of the 10-item subscales ranged from .77 to .82 for the TAS subscale, .61 to .67 for ES, .74 to .78 for DIS, and .56 to .65 for BS. Correlations among the subscales ranged from .06 to .48. Reliabilities and correlations among subscales were also reported for male and female subsamples (Zuckerman 1979).

Zuckerman (1979) reports correlations of the Form V SS with a number of other constructs theoretically related to SS (i.e., extraversion, neuroticism, impulsivity, and tough-mindedness) across numerous samples (pp. 136-181). The pattern of correlations shows strong evidence of convergent, discriminant and criterion validity. Biological correlates of SS are also reported (pp. 314-354).

Scores: A variety of mean scores are also reported by Zuckerman (1979). Specifically, see Appendix Table 1 for Form V (p. 402) for mean scores for the four subscales (for samples of 377 males and 646 males).

Source: Zuckerman, Marvin (1979), *Sensation Seeking: Beyond the Optimal Level of Arousal*, Hillsdale, NJ: Lawrence Erlbaum Associates.

Other evidence: In consumer behavior related studies, the Form V SS has also been examined. Wahlers et al. (1986) used a student sample of 69 to examine the relation of the SS to other OSL measures. The internal consistency estimate for the 40-item SS was .80. (Reliability estimates for the 4 subscales were not reported.) The SS was also highly correlated with other measures of arousal seeking and OSL in general (ranging from .17 to .96), suggesting convergent validity of the SS.

Wahlers and Etzel (1990) used a sample of 697 from a midwestern consumer panel to also compare various measures of OSL. The internal consistency estimate for the 40-item SS was reported as .851. Though no direct estimates of subscale reliability were offered, it was stated that the subscales possessed adequate internal consistency. Furthermore, the correlation of the SS with another measure of OSL was extremely high (r = .95), indicating convergent validity.

Ridgeway and Russell (1980) also examined the psychometric properties of the SS with 336 student subjects (181 females and 155 males). In this study, the reliabilities for the total sample were .69, .54, .65, .48, and .75 for the TAS factor, ES factor, DIS factor, BS factor, and total scale, respectively. Intercorrelations among factors ranged from .02 to .40. Estimates of predictive validity were also offered, but were moderate, as the SS correlations with a variable reflecting emotional arousing stimuli were .19 and .28 for males and females, respectively.

Ridgeway and Russell (1980) also report mean scores of 20.75 (sd = 6.11) for males and 18.92 (sd = 4.81) for females for the 40-item SS.

Other sources:
Ridgeway, Doreen and James A. Russell (1980), "Reliability and Validity of the Sensation-Seeking Scale: Psychometric Problems in Form V," *Journal of Consulting and Clinical Psychology*, 48, 662-664.

Wahlers, Russell G., Mark G. Dunn and Michael J. Etzel (1986), "The Congruence of Alternative OSL Measures With Exploratory Behavior Tendencies," in *Advances in Consumer Research*, Vol. 13, Richard Lutz (ed.), Provo, UT: Association for Consumer Research, 398-402.

Wahlers, Russell G. and Michael J. Etzel (1990), "A Structural Examination of Two Optimal Stimulation Level Measurement Models," in *Advances in Consumer Research*, Vol. 17, Marvin Goldberg, Gerald Gorn and Richard Pollay (eds.), Provo, UT: Association for Consumer Research, 415-425.

References:
Raju, P. S. (1980), "Optimum Stimulation Level: Its Relationship to Personality, Demographics, and Exploratory Behavior," *Journal of Consumer Research*, 7 (December), 272-282.

FORM V SENSATION SEEKING SCALE: SS
(Zuckerman 1979)

The Form V SS Directions and Items

Directions. Each of the items below contains two choices, A and B. Please indicate which of the choices most describes *your likes or the way you feel*. In some cases you may find items in which both choices describes your likes or the way you feel. Please choose the one which better describes your likes and feeling. In some cases you may find items in which you do not like either choice. In these cases, mark the choice you dislike *the least*.

It is important you respond to *all items with only one choice*, A or B. We are interested only in your likes or feelings, not in how others feel about these things or how one is supposed to feel. There are no right or wrong answers as in other kinds of tests. Be frank and give your honest appraisal of yourself.

1) A. I like "wild" uninhibited parties.
    B. I prefer quiet parties with good conversation.

2) A. There are some movies I enjoy seeing a second or even a third time.
    B. I can't stand watching a movie that I've seen before.

3) A. I often wish I could be a mountain climber.
    B. I can't understand people who risk their necks climbing mountains.

4)   A. I dislike all body odors.
     B. I like some of the earthy body smells.

5)   A. I get bored seeing the same old faces.
     B. I like the comfortable familiarity of everyday friends.

6)   A. I like to explore a strange city or section of town by myself, even if it means getting lost.
     B. I prefer a guide when I am in a place I don't know well.

7)   A. I dislike people who do or say things just to shock or upset others.
     B. When you can predict almost everything a person will do and say he or she must be a bore.

8)   A. I usually don't enjoy a movie or a play where I can predict what will happen in advance.
     B. I don't mind watching a movie or a play where I can predict what will happen in advance.

9)   A. I have tried marijuana or would like to.
     B. I would never smoke marijuana.

10) A. I would not like to try any drug which might produce strange and dangerous effects on me.
     B. I would like to try some of the new drugs that produce hallucinations.

11) A. A sensible person avoids activities that are dangerous.
     B. I sometimes like to do things that are a little frightening.

12) A. I dislike "swingers."
     B. I enjoy the company of real "swingers."

13) A. I find that stimulants make me uncomfortable.
     B. I often like to get high (drinking liquor or smoking marijuana).

14) A. I like to try foods that I have never tasted before.
     B. I order the dishes with which I am familiar, so as to avoid disappointment or unpleasantness.

15) A. I enjoy looking at home movies or travel slides.
     B. Looking at someone's home movies or travel slides bores me tremendously.

16) A. I would like to take up the sport of water-skiing.
     B. I would not like to take up water-skiing.

17) A. I would like to try surf-board riding.
     B. I would not like to try surf-board riding.

18) A. I would like to take off on a trip with no pre-planned or definite routes or timetables.
     B. When I go on a trip I like to plan my route and timetable fairly carefully.

19) A. I prefer the "down-to-earth" kinds of people as friends.
     B. I would like to make friends in some of the "far out" groups like artists or "hippies."

20) A. I would not like to learn to fly an airplane.
     B. I would like to learn to fly an airplane.

21) A. I prefer the surface of the water to the depths.
     B. I would like to go scuba diving.

22) A. I would like to meet some persons who are homosexuals (men or women).
     B. I stay away from anyone I suspect of being "gay."

23) A. I would like to try parachute jumping.
     B. I would never want to try jumping out of a plane with or without a parachute.

24) A. I prefer friends who are excitingly unpredictable.
B. I prefer friends who are reliable and predictable.

25) A. I am not interested in experience for its own sake.
B. I like to have new and exciting experiences and sensations even if they are a little frightening, unconventional or illegal.

26) A. The essence of good art is in its clarity, symmetry of form and harmony of colors.
B. I often find beauty in the "clashing" colors and irregular forms of modern painting.

27) A. I enjoy spending time in the familiar surroundings of home.
B. I get very restless if I have to stay around home for any length of time.

28) A. I like to dive off the high board.
B. I don't like the feeling I get standing on the high board (or I don't go near it at all).

29) A. I like to date members of the opposite sex who are physically exciting.
B. I like to date members of the opposite sex who share my values.

30) A. Heavy drinking usually ruins a party because some people get loud and boisterous.
B. Keeping the drinks full is the key to a good party.

31) A. The worst social sin is to be rude.
B. The worst social sin is to be a bore.

32) A. A person should have considerable sexual experience before marriage.
B. It's better if two married persons begin their sexual experience with each other.

33) A. Even if I had the money I would not care to associate with flighty persons like those in the "jet set."
B. I could conceive of myself seeking pleasure around the world with the "jet set."

34) A. I like people who are sharp and witty even if they do sometimes insult others.
B. I dislike people who have their fun at the expense of hurting the feelings of others.

35) A. There is altogether too much portrayal of sex in movies.
B. I enjoy watching many of the "sexy" scenes in movies.

36) A. I feel best after taking a couple of drinks.
B. Something is wrong with people who need liquor to feel good.

37) A. People should dress according to some standards of taste, neatness, and style.
B. People should dress in individual ways even if the effects are sometimes strange.

38) A. Sailing long distances in small sailing crafts is foolhardy.
B. I would like to sail a long distance in a small but seaworthy sailing craft.

39) A. I have no patience with dull or boring persons.
B. I find something interesting in almost every person I talk with.

40) A. Skiing fast down a high mountain slope is a good way to end up on crutches.
B. I think I would enjoy the sensations of skiing very fast down a high mountain slope.

NOTES: The TAS factor and a high score on the TAS are derived from the following items and their respective answers: 3A, 11B, 16A, 17A, 20B, 21B, 23A, 28A, 38B, 40B.

The ES factor and a high score on the ES are derived from the following items and their respective answers: 4B, 6A, 9A, 10B, 14A, 18A, 19B, 22A, 26B, 37B.

The DIS factor and a high score on the DIS are derived from the following items and their respective answers: 1A, 12A, 13B, 25B, 29A, 30B, 32A, 33B, 35B, 36A.

The BS factor and a high score on the BS are derived from the following items and their respective answers: 2B, 5A, 7B, 8A, 15B, 24A, 27B, 31B, 34A, 39A.

All versions of the SS are proprietary. The potential user of the SS should write Professor Marvin Zuckerman, Department of Psychology, University of Delaware, Newark, DE 19716 for permission to use the scale. The book from which the SS is drawn is copyrighted under Professor Zuckerman's name.

EXPLORATORY TENDENCIES IN CONSUMER BEHAVIOR SCALES: ETCBS
(Raju 1980)

Construct: Exploratory tendency behavior is viewed as behavior aimed at modifying stimulation from the environment. In a consumer behavior context, these behaviors include (Raju, 1980, pp. 278-279):

Repetitive behavior proneness - the tendency to stick with the same response over time.

Innovativeness - eagerness to buy or know about new products and services.

Risk taking - a preference for taking risks or being adventurous.

Exploration through shopping - a preference for shopping and investigating.

Interpersonal communication - communicating with friends about purchases.

Brand switching - switching brands primarily for change and variety.

Information seeking - interest in knowing about various products and brands mainly out of curiosity.

Description: The ETCBS is composed of 39 items that measure the above seven exploratory tendency behaviors, all measured on seven-point agree-disagree scales. Items scores can be summed within each category to form an overall score for each category.

Development: An initial pool of 90 statements was developed to reflect the seven exploratory tendency behaviors. With two samples, this pool of items was trimmed to 60 by eliminating items with high social desirability bias and low item-to-total correlations. The remaining items common to both samples (i.e., 39 items) were used as the final measures for the seven exploratory tendency behaviors. The final 30 items possessed high face validity, low social desirability, and adequate reliability (Raju 1980).

Sample(s): Two samples were used in the development of the ETCBS: a sample of 105 students and 336 homemakers.

Validity: The Spearman-Brown reliability coefficient for the repetitive behavior proneness measure, innovativeness measure, risk taking measure, exploration through shopping measure, interpersonal communication measure, brand switching measure, and information seeking measures were .697 and .700, .804 and .845, .808 and .831, .759 and .866, .725 and .738, .784 and .832, and .761 and .842 for the homemaker and student samples, respectively. In addition, average item-to-total correlations across all measures (both samples) ranged from .458 to .696 (Raju 1980, p. 279).

Correlations of the seven exploratory tendency behavior measures with a measure of optimal stimulation level ranged from .218 to .622 across the two samples, offering evidence for the validity of the ETCBS.

Scores: Mean and/or percentage scores for the ETCBS were not reported.

Source: Raju, P. S. (1980), "Optimum Stimulation Level: Its Relationship to Personality, Demographics, and Exploratory Behavior," *Journal of Consumer Research*, 7 (December), 272-282.

Other evidence: In another study, Wahlers et al. (1986) used a convenience sample of 69 students to examine the dimensionality of the ETCBS and correlated it with measures of optimal stimulation level. In this study, reliability coefficients for the repetitive behavior proneness measure, innovativeness measure, risk taking measure, exploration through shopping measure, interpersonal communication measure, brand switching measure and information seeking measures were reported to be .591, .745, .761, .803, .561, .677, and .669, respectively.

Wahlers et al. (1986) also report significant correlations of the ETCBS factors with various measures of optimum stimulation level ranging from -.35 to .47 (Table 5, p. 401).

Other sources: Wahlers, Russell G., Mark G. Dunn and Michael J. Etzel (1986), "The Congruence of Alternative OSL Measures With Exploratory Behavior Tendencies," in *Advances in Consumer Research*, Vol. 13, Richard Lutz (ed.), Provo, UT: Association for Consumer Research, 398-402.

References: N/A.

EXPLORATORY TENDENCIES IN CONSUMER BEHAVIOR SCALES: ETCBS
(Raju 1980)

1) Even though certain food products are available in a number of different flavors, I always tend to buy the same flavor.

2) I have little interest in fads and fashion.

3) When I eat out, I like to try the most unusual items the restaurant serves, even if I am not sure I would like them.

4) I like to shop around and look at displays.

5) I get very bored listening to others talk about their purchases.

6) I like to browse through mail order catalogs even when I don't plan to buy anything.

7) When I see a new or different brand on the shelf, I often pick it up just to see what it is like.

8) I often read the information on the packages of products just out of curiosity.

9) I am the kind of person who would try any new product once.

10) I shop around a lot for my clothes just to find out more about the latest styles.

11) A new store or restaurant is not something I would be eager to find out about.

12) When I go to a restaurant, I feel it is safer to order dishes I am familiar with.

13) I am very cautious in trying new/different products.

14) Even for an important date or dinner, I wouldn't be wary of trying a new or unfamiliar restaurant.

15) I generally read even my junk mail just to know what it is about.

16) I don't like to talk to my friends about my purchases.

17) I enjoy sampling different brands of commonplace products for the sake of comparison.

18) I like introducing new brands and products to my friends.

19) I would rather stick with a brand I usually buy than try something I am not very sure of.

20) I usually throw away mail advertisements without reading them.

21) If I like a brand, I rarely switch from it just to try something different.

22) I don't care to find out what types or brand names of appliances and gadgets my friends have.

23) I hate window shopping.

24) I often read advertisements just out of curiosity.

25) I would rather wait for others to try a new store or restaurant than try it myself.

26) I get bored with buying the same brands even if they are good.

27) When I see a new brand somewhat different from the usual, I investigate it.

28) I never buy something I don't know about at the risk of making a mistake.

29) I would get tired of flying the same airline every time.

30) If I buy appliances, I will buy only well established brands.

31) Investigating new brands of grocery and other similar products is generally a waste of time.

32) My friends and neighbors often come to me for advice.

33) I rarely read advertisements that just seem to contain a lot of information.

34) When I hear about a new store or restaurant, I take advantage of the first opportunity to find out more about it.

35) I would prefer to keep using old appliances and gadgets even if it means having to get them fixed, rather than buying new ones every few years.

36) A lot of the time I feel the urge to buy something really different from the brands I usually buy.

37) I enjoy taking chances in buying unfamiliar brands just to get some variety in my purchases.

38) If I did a lot of flying, I would probably like to try all the different airlines, instead of flying just one most of the time.

39) I enjoy exploring several different alternatives or brands while shopping.

NOTES: Though not indicated by Raju (1980), items that require reverse scoring seem to include items 1, 2, 5, 11 through 14, 16, 19 through 23, 25, 18, 30, 31, 33, and 35.

Several items cross-load on the seven ETCBS measures. Items 1, 21, 26, 29, 35, 36, and 38 measure repetitive behavior proneness. Items 7, 9, 11, 13, 14, 25, 27, 31, 34, and 37 measure innovativeness. Items 3, 9, 12, 13, 14, 19, 28, 30, and 37 measure risk taking. Items 2, 4, 6, 10, 23, 27, and 39 measure exploration through shopping. Items 16, 18, and 32 measure interpersonal communication. Items 17, 19, 21, 26, 36, 38, and 39 measure brand switching. Items 5, 6, 8, 10, 11, 15, 17, 20, 24, 33, and 34 measure information seeking.

OTHER INFORMATION PROCESSING MEASURES

DIMENSIONS OF EMOTIONS: PAD
(Mehrabian and Russell 1974)

Construct: Emotional reactions to one's environment can be characterized by the three response dimensions of pleasure, arousal, and dominance. These dimensions are conceptualized to be relatively independent from one another (Mehrabian and Russell 1974, pp. 18-20):

Pleasure - refers to a positive affective state that is felt to be distinguishable from preference, liking, positive reinforcement, and approach avoidance.

Arousal - is a feeling state that varies along a single dimension from sleep to frantic excitement.

Dominance - is based on the extent to which one feels unrestricted or free to act in a variety of ways.

Description: The PAD is composed of 18 semantic differential items scored on a +4 to -4 basis. There are six items representing each of the dimensions described above. Item scores are summed within dimensions to form indices for each dimension.

Development: Initially, 28 adjective pairs were generated by the authors. Then, based on 40 different hypothetical situations, 134 students responded to the 28 items. The responses were factor analyzed and the six items in each dimension with the highest factor loadings were retained. In a second study, five additional items for dominance were generated, and the resulting 23 items were presented to another sample, and then factor analyzed. Based on the eigenvalue greater than one rule, and again choosing the 6 items in each dimension with the highest loadings on their respective factors, a three-factor, 18-item version was retained (i.e., the final version of the PAD). The scale was then assessed for reliability and validity in another study.

Samples: Three student samples of 134, 163, and 214 were used in the initial scale development and validation.

Validity: From the third study (n = 214) estimates of internal consistency and test-retest reliability were performed. Internal consistency reliability was .81 for pleasure, .50 for arousal, and .77 for dominance. Test-retest (over four to seven weeks) was .72, .69, and .77 for pleasure, arousal, and dominance, respectfively.

As originally conceptualized, the PAD dimensions were considered independent of one another. Factor analysis results across the three studies revealed low and mostly nonsignificant correlations among the three factors, ranging from -.07 to .26, providing evidence that the dimensions are distinct. The PAD factors were also used as independent variables to predict a number of emotional states and traits (i.e., anxiety, neuroticism, sensitivity to rejection). The results suggest predictive validity for the three PAD dimensions (Mehrabian and Russell 1974, Table 3.4, p. 47). For example, multiple Rs for the three PAD dimensions as predictor variables ranged from .24 to .73.

Scores: Appendix A (Mehrabian and Russell 1974, pp. 206-215) offers normalized scores for the PAD dimensions across 65 scenarios.

Source: Mehrabian, Albert and James Russell (1974), *An Approach to Environmental Psychology*, Cambridge, MA: The MIT Press.

Other evidence: Though used numerous times in social psychology applications, only evidence from consumer behavior studies is reviewed here. Holbrook et al. (1984), in a study of how emotions affect enjoyment of games, used a seven-point format for the PAD dimensions and found coefficient alpha estimates of .89, .89, and .88 for pleasure, arousal, and dominance, respectively.

Holbrook et al. (1984) also reported that the PAD dimensions were related to complexity and performance.

Havlena and Holbrook (1986) looked at how the PAD dimensions related to various consumption experiences by comparing PAD to another index of emotional response (i.e., Plutchik 1980). A reduced set of 12 PAD items was used. On a sample of 10 MBAs, coefficient alpha for each PAD dimension exceeded .90. Intrajudge reliability among the 10 respondents ranged from .79 to .95 for the PAD dimensions. (Seven-point scales were used for the PAD items.)

The correlations between the PAD dimensions and the other emotional index showed evidence of convergent validity. For example, average correlations between the PAD dimensions and the other index were .81 and .71 (based on vector spaces derived through discriminant and canonical analyses). Furthermore, the PAD was judged to be a better method for assessing emotions toward consumption experiences than the other index.

Other sources: Havlena, William J. and Morris Holbrook (1986), "The Varieties of Consumption Experience: Comparing Two Typologies of Emotions in Consumer Behavior," *Journal of Consumer Research*, 13 (December), 394-404.

Holbrook, Morris B., Robert W. Chestnut, Terence A. Oliva, and Eric A. Greenleaf (1984), "Play as Consumption Experience: The Roles of Emotions, Performance, and Personality in the Enjoyment of Games," *Journal of Consumer Research*, 11 (September), 728-739.

References: Plutchik, Robert (1980), *Emotions: A Psychoevolutionary Synthesis*, New York: Harper & Row.

DIMENSIONS OF EMOTIONS: PAD
(Mehrabian and Russell 1974)

Each pair of words below describes a feeling dimension. Some of the pairs might seem unusual, but you may generally feel more one way than the other. So, for each pair, put a check mark (Example: __ : x : __) to show how you feel about _____. Please take your time so as to arrive at a real characteristic description of your feelings.

Pleasure

1) happy - unhappy
2) pleased - annoyed
3) satisfied - unsatisfied
4) contented - melancholic
5) hopeful - despairing
6) relaxed - bored

Arousal

7) stimulated - relaxed
8) excited - calm
9) frenzied - sluggish
10) jittery - dull
11) wide awake - sleepy
12) aroused - unaroused

Dominance

13) controlling - controlled
14) influential - influenced
15) in control - cared for
16) important - awed
17) dominant - submissive
18) autonomous - guided

NOTES: All items must be recoded to reflect higher levels of the traits. The reduced set of items used by Havlena and Holbrook (1986) are items 1 through 4 for pleasure, items 7, 8, 9, and 12 for arousal, and items 13, 14, 17, and 18 for dominance.

CONSUMER IMAGE OF RETAIL STORES: CIRS
(Dickson and Albaum 1977)

Construct: Though no formal definition was offered, consumer image of retail stores was felt to encompass attitudes toward retail prices, products, store layout and facilities, service and personnel, promotion, and "others" (Dickson and Albaum 1977).

Description: The CIRS is composed of 29 seven-point semantic differential items designed to measure the aforementioned attitudes. The item scores are summed to form an overall CIRS index.

Development: Adjective pairs were generated via depth interviews with 27 consumers. A total of 31 pairs was generated. Another sample of students was then used to trim this pool of items to the final 29-item form. Another study was then performed to assess scale reliability and factor structure.

Samples: Three samples were used throughout scale development: a sample of 27 consumers for item generation, a sample of 59 students to trim the item pool, and a sample of 82 (composed of students and their spouses) to check reliability and the factor structure.

Validity: Test-retest reliability (based on a subsample of 30 from the sample of 82) over a two week period was .91. The Spearman rank-order reliability coefficient (split-halves) was .88. Factor analysis of the 29 items extracted 5 factors accounting for over 50% of the variance in examining supermarket/discount stores, and six factors accounting for over 50% of the variance in examining department/shoe stores.

Scores: Neither mean nor percentage scores were offered.

Source: Dickson, John and Gerald Albaum (1977), "A Method for Developing Tailormade Semantic Differentials for Specific Marketing Content Areas," *Journal of Marketing Research*, 14 (February), 87-91.

**Other
evidence:**   N/A.

**Other
sources:**   N/A.

References: N/A.

CONSUMER IMAGE OF RETAIL STORES: CIRS
(Dickson and Albaum 1977)

1) crammed merchandise - well spaced merchandise
2) bright store - dull store*
3) ads frequently seen by you - ads infrequently seen by you*
4) low quality products - high quality products
5) well organized layout - unorganized layout*
6) low prices - high prices*
7) bad sales on products - good sales on products
8) unpleasant store to shop in - pleasant store to shop in
9) good store - bad store*
10) inconvenient location - convenient location
11) low pressure salesman - high pressure salesman*
12) big store - small store*
13) bad buys on products - good buys on products
14) unattractive store - attractive store
15) unhelpful salesman - helpful salesman

16) good service - bad service*
17) too few clerks - too many clerks
18) friendly personnel - unfriendly personnel*
19) easy to return purchases - hard to return purchases*
20) unlimited selection of products - limited selection of products*
21) unreasonable prices for value - reasonable prices for the value
22) messy - neat
23) spacious shopping - crowded shopping*
24) attracts upper class customers - attracts lower class customers*
25) dirty - clean
26) fast checkout - slow checkout*
27) good displays - bad displays*
28) hard to find items you want - easy to find items you want
29) bad specials - good specials

NOTES: * denotes items that are reversed scores. Also Dickson and Albaum note that items 1, 2, 5, 8, 14, 22, 23, 25, 27, and 28 could be used as a "shopping environment" factor, and that items 6, 7, 13, 21, and 29 used as a "product promotion-price" factor.

ROLE OVERLOAD OF THE WIFE
(Reilly 1982)

Construct: Role overload for a housewife is defined as the conflict that occurs when the sheer volume of behavior demanded of the wife exceeds her available time and energy (Reilly 1982). This definition is consistent with the organizational behavior literature view of role overload (House and Rizzo 1972; Rizzo, House, and Lirtzman 1970).

Description: The role overload scale is composed of 13 Likert items scored on a five-point basis from strongly disagree to strongly agree. Item scores are summed to form an overall index of role overload.

Development: The author and several doctoral students wrote a number of items to reflect the construct. These items were administered to a sample of housewives, and items with low item-to-total correlations were eliminated, resulting in the final 13-item scale. Reliability and validity estimates were also obtained.

Samples: A sample of 106 married women responded to the scale.

Validity: Coefficient alpha for the scale was .88, and item-to-total correlations ranged from .50 to .80. Correlations with other constructs showed some evidence of validity. For example, correlations of the scale with women's work attitude and work status were .15 and .17, respectively.

Scores: Neither mean nor percentage scores were provided.

Source: Reilly, Michael D. (1982), "Working Wives and Convenience Consumption," *Journal of Consumer Research*, 8 (March), 407-417.

Other evidence: In a study of time use (Kaufman, Lane, and Lindquist 1991), the role overload scale had a coefficient alpha of .86, and was negatively correlated with a measure of time use (-.146), offering further evidence of the scale's reliability and validity.

Other sources: Kaufman, Carol Felker, Paul M. Lane, and Jay D. Lindquist (1991), "Exploring More than 24 Hours a Day: A Preliminary Investigation of Polychronic Time Use," *Journal of Consumer Research*, 18 (December), 392-401.

References: House, Robert L. and John R. Rizzo (1972), "Role Conflict and Ambiguity as Critical Variables in a Model of Organizational Behavior," *Organizational Behavior and Human Performance*, 7, 467-505.

Rizzo, John R., Robert J. House, and Sidney Lirtzman (1970), "Role Conflict and Ambiguity in Complex Organizations," *Administrative Science Quarterly*, 15, 150-163.

ROLE OVERLOAD OF THE WIFE
(Reilly 1982)

1)   I have to do things which I don't really have the time and energy for.

2)   There are too many demands on my time.

3)   I need more hours in the day to do all the things which are expected of me.

4)   I can't ever seem to get caught up.

5)   I don't ever seem to have any time for myself.

6)   There are times when I cannot meet everyone's expectations.

7) Sometimes I feel as if there are not enough hours in the day.

8) Many times I have to cancel my commitments.

9) I seem to have to overextend myself in order to be able to finish everything I have to do.

10) I seem to have more commitments to overcome than some of the other wives I know.

11) I find myself having to prepare priority lists (lists which tell me which things I should do first) to get done all the things I have to do. Otherwise, I forget because I have so much to do.

12) I feel I have to do things hastily and maybe less carefully in order to get everything done.

13) I just can't find the energy in me to do all the things expected of me.

MOOD SHORT FORM: MSF
(Peterson and Sauber 1983)

Construct: The term "mood" or "mood state" has a wide range of usage and definitions (cf., Peterson and Sauber 1983 and Gardner 1985 for critical reviews). However, most definitions of mood agree that "mood" has a state of emotional or affective arousal that is varying and transient. The transient and varying nature of mood is emphasized in MSF (Peterson and Sauber 1983).

Description: The MSF is a four-item scale composed of Likert statements scored on five-point formats (strongly disagree - strongly agree). Item scores are summed to form a unidimensional MSF index.

Development: A large pool of items was generated to reflect the content domain of mood. Some items were drawn from Mehrabian's (1972) nonverbal communication scale and the Mood Adjective Check List (Nowlis 1965), as well other items generated by the authors. This pool of items was then administered to a sample and factor analyzed, resulting in 6 items retained. After further item analysis and reliability checks, the four-item MSF was derived.

Sample(s): A sample of 323 undergraduate business students was used for scale development purposes. A subset of this sample (n = 177) was also used for test-retest reliability purposes. Four more samples were used to investigate other psychometric properties of the MSF: n = 1,434, n = 713, n = 248, and n = 114 (all non-students).

Validity: Coefficient alpha for the scale was reported to be .78, .74, and .77 for the samples of 1,343, 713, and 248, respectively. Test-retest reliability over a 30-day period (n = 177) was .18, indicating that mood does vary over time. Validity checks revealed that the MSF was marginally correlated with measures of satisfaction with the future (a beta weight of .22) and confidence in the American economic system (a beta weight of .24).

Scores: Mean scores were reported for the samples of 1,434, 713, and 248 and were 8.2, 7.8, and 8.1, respectively. (Scores could range from a low of 4 to a high of 20).

Source: Peterson, Robert A. and Matthew Sauber (1983), "A Mood Scale for Survey Research," in *American Marketing Association Educators Proceedings*, Patrick Murphy et al. (eds.), Chicago: The American Marketing Association, 409-414.

Other evidence: N/A.

Other sources: N/A.

References: Gardner, Meryl P. (1985), "Mood States and Consumer Behavior: A Critical Review," *Journal of Consumer Research*, 12 (December), 281-300.

Mehrabian, Albert (1972), *Nonverbal Communications*, Chicago: Aldine-Altherton.

Nowlis, V. (1965), "Research With the Mood Adjective Check List," in *Affect, Cognition, and Personality*, S.S. Tomkins and C.E. Izard (eds.), New York: Springer.

MOOD SHORT FORM: MSF
(Peterson and Sauber 1983)

1) Currently, I am in a good mood.

2) As I answer these questions I feel cheerful.

3) For some reason I am not very comfortable right now.*

4) At this moment I feel edgy or irritable.*

NOTE: * denotes items that are reversed scored.

SPOUSAL CONFLICT AROUSAL SCALE: SCAS
(Seymour and Lessne 1984)

Construct: Conflict arousal in a spousal decision-making setting can be defined as the level of dyadic discordance resulting from the initiation of a joint purchase decision between husband and wife (Seymour and Lessne 1984). Four components underlie conflict arousal in consumer decision-making:

Interpersonal need - the level of strength of bonds in establishing and maintaining the desire to interact with another individual (i.e., the dyad members of husband and wife).

Power - the ability to influence others and resist being subject to their wills (i.e., the dyad members of husband and wife).

Involvement - the degree to which an individual is willing to engage in complex combinations of decision alternatives.

Utility - the level of motivation to acquire a product derived from the product's ability to satisfy individual wants.

Description: The SCAS is a 20-item scale where all the items are scored on 7-point Likert formats (strongly disagree - strongly agree). The scale is further broken down into the four components above, with each component being represented by 5 items. Item scores can be summed within components to form component scores. However, a recommended overall scoring procedure is offered by Seymour and Lessne (1984). (See Appendix.)

Development: A pool of 44 items was generated to tap the four components. (The items were generated for a car purchase scenario.) A sample of 132 married subjects then responded to the 44 items, and items with less than a .50 item-to-total correlation on the respective components were eliminated, resulting in 33 items. Factor analysis was then used to assess dimensionality and further reduce the number of items resulting in the final 20-item SCAS. Two other samples of married subjects were also used to further assess reliability and validity (Seymour and Lessne 1984).

Sample(s): Three samples of married subjects were used by Seymour and Lessne (1984). A sample of 132 was used for initial scale reduction, dimensionality, and reliability. (A subsample from this group [n =121] was also used to assess various forms of reliability.) A sample of 90 married people was used to assess discriminant and convergent validity, as well as reliability. Lastly, a sample of 46 husbands and wives was used to assess predictive validity.

Validity: A number of reliability estimates were reported. Coefficient alpha for the four SCAS components ranged from .79 to .89, and item-to-total correlations (within each component) ranged from .64 to .86 (n = 121). Test-rest reliability was .81 over a three-week period for the entire 20 items. In addition, the hypothesized factor structure was shown to be stable over time. Concurrent validity estimates were also high, ranging from .40 to .81 across the four components (n = 121).

In the n = 90 sample, a multitrait-multimethod matrix involving the SCAS component measures and other measures assessing aspects of spousal conflict indicated strong convergent validity for the utility, involvement and power components and marginal support for the interpersonal need component. In addition, discriminant validity was not found between the utility and involvement components.

The sample of 46 husbands and wives was used to assess predictive validity by correlating the SCAS with a behavioral measure of conflict arousal. A correlation of .40 was found between the two measures, supporting the predictive validity of SCAS.

Scores: Direct mean scores were not reported. The SCAS uses a linear transformation procedure to derive an overall score of conflict arousal that ranges from 0 to 1. (See Appendix.)

Source:	Seymour, Daniel and Greg Lessne (1984), "Spousal Conflict Arousal: Scale Development," *Journal of Consumer Research*, 11 (December), 810-821.
Other evidence:	N/A.
Other sources:	N/A.
References:	N/A.

SPOUSAL CONFLICT AROUSAL SCALE: SCAS
(Seymour and Lessne 1984)

The following survey is an attempt to understand your opinions in your roles as a consumer and family member. Each spouse should fill out a *separate survey*. Please *do not* discuss your responses before or during the time you are responding to the survey. All information contained herein is for research purposes only and will be treated anonymously.

1) An automobile, like many other products, is an expression of social image.

2) In making a decision as to which automobile to buy, it is important to get as much information as possible regardless of the time or cost involved.

3) A great deal of personal satisfaction can be gotten from buying an automobile.

4) The type of automobile one buys often represents their level of personal achievement.

5) Because buying an automobile can be a fairly complex decision, a "satisfactory" solution is better than taking a great deal of energy to try and find the "best" solution.*

6) The greater the number of automobiles considered when buying an automobile, the better the results.

7) If information could be seen in terms of dollars, it is reasonable to spend a great deal of money for information before making an automobile purchase.

8) The function that an automobile performs is *not* very important to me.*

9) With the exception of price, there is not much difference between one automobile and another.

10) I get a great deal of enjoyment out of using an automobile.

11) In general, I do *not* have a large amount of experience in the "ways of the world."*

12) I think my (husband/wife) trusts my ability to make a choice which affects our family.

13) I believe that criticism of my (husband/wife's) actions is a natural part of any close relationship.

14) If I were lonely, my first thought would be to seek my (husband/wife's) companionship.*

15) When I know something is important to my (husband/wife), I always try to satisfy (his/her) wishes.*

16) In general, I derive a great deal of satisfaction out of researching a difficult problem and making a decision.

17) I consider myself to be a fairly attractive individual.

18) I would forgive my (husband/wife) for practically anything.*

19) I do need a partner who will listen to my problems.*

20) It would be hard for me to get along without my (husband/wife).*

NOTES: * denotes items that are reversed scored.

Items 13, 15, 16, 19, and 20 comprise the interpersonal need component. Items 1, 3, 4, 8, and 10 comprise the utility component. Items 2, 5, 6, 7, and 9 comprise the involvement component, and items 11, 12, 14, 17, and 18 comprise the power component.

Though automobile is used as the focal product in several of the above items, it is felt that other "high ticket" purchases can be used inter-changeably in the statements (Seymour and Lessne 1984, p. 812).

Appendix

Derivation of conflict arousal score

conflict arousal score = TCI - 1.33(DCI)/280

A linear transformation is needed to derive the above equation where:

TCI = total conditional influence which is equal to the sum of the husband's and wife's score on the 20 item SCAS.

DCI = the difference in conditional influence which is equal to the husband's score minus the wife's score on the 20 item SCAS.

the values 1.33 and 280 are constants such that the conflict arousal score ranges from 0 to 1, higher scores reflecting a higher level of conflict.

Thus, the following should hold true:

1) As DCI increases, conflict arousal decreases.
2) As TCI increases, conflict arousal increases.
3) When TCI is at a maximum of 280 (i.e., 20 items x 7-point scales across both husband and wife), and DCI is at a minimum (i.e., husband's SCAS score minus wife's SCAS score equals 0), the conflict arousal score should be 1.
4) When DCI is at a minimum of 120 (i.e., the max of any spouse's SCAS is 140 minus the minimum of any spouse's SCAS is 20), and TCI equals 160, the conflict arousal score should be 0.
5) The maximum conflict arousal score is 1 and the minimum is 0.

ATTENTION TO SOCIAL COMPARISON INFORMATION: ATSCI
(Lennox and Wolfe 1984)

Construct: Attention to social comparison assesses the extent to which one is aware of the reactions of others to one's behavior and is concerned about or sensitive to the nature of those reactions. These individuals care what other people think about them and look for clues as to the nature of others' reactions toward them (Lennox and Wolfe 1984).

Description: ATSCI is a 13-item scale where the items are scored from 0 (always false) to 5 (always true). Scores on the items are summed to form on overall index (Lennox and Wolfe 1984).

Development: Three studies were performed to arrive at the final 13-item ATSCI. Each study contained Snyder's (1974) self-monitoring scale, from which the ATSCI is derived. (The items were adjusted to six-point formats as Snyder's scale was originally scored in a dichotomous format.) Also included in the studies were several other items and measures hypothesized to be related to various aspects of ATSCI and self-monitoring. Via factor analysis, reliability, and validity checks, the final form of the ATSCI was derived (Lennox and Wolfe 1984).

Sample(s): Three student samples (n = 128, 224, 201) were used to develop the ATSCI across the three studies. Some of these samples were also used to check for reliability and validity.

Validity: For the third study reported by Lennox and Wolfe (n = 224), the ATSCI had an alpha of .83 and was correlated with other measures reflecting concern for the opinions of others (i.e., ability to modify self-presentation [r = .40], fear of negative evaluation [r = .64], and cross-situational variability[(r = .42]). These correlations offer evidence of validity for the ATSCI.

Scores: Mean scores per item are reported by Lennox and Wolfe (1984, p. 1,362) for their n = 224 sample.

Source: Lennox, Richard D. and Raymond N. Wolfe (1984), "Revision of the Self-Monitoring Scale," *Journal of Personality and Social Psychology*, 46, 1349-1364.

Other evidence: In a consumer behavior context, the ATSCI was examined using student samples of 62, 99, 63, and 85 in four studies (Bearden and Rose 1990).

Bearden and Rose (1990) report alpha estimates for the ATSCI of .85, .83, .88, and .89 across their four studies. Furthermore, correlations of the ATSCI with a number of variables reflecting concern for the opinion of others (e.g., public self-consciousness,[(r = .60, .40 and .46] fear of negative evaluation [r = .50], and consumer behavior measures) show strong support for the validity of the ATSCI.

Other sources: Bearden, William O. and Randall L. Rose (1990), "Attention to Social Comparison Information: An Individual Difference Factor Affecting Consumer Conformity," *Journal of Consumer Research*, 16 (March), 461-471.

References: Snyder, Mark (1974), "The Self-Monitoring of Expressive Behavior," *Journal of Personality and Social Psychology*, 30, 526-537.

ATTENTION TO SOCIAL COMPARISON INFORMATION: ATSCI
(Lennox and Wolfe 1984)

1) It is my feeling that if everyone else in a group is behaving in a certain manner, this must be the proper way to behave.

2) I actively avoid wearing clothes that are not in style.

3) At parties I usually try to behave in a manner that makes me fit in.

4) When I am uncertain how to act in a social situation, I look to the behavior of others for clues.

5) I try to pay attention to the reactions of others to my behavior in order to avoid being out of place.

6) I find that I tend to pick up slang expressions from others and use them as a part of my own vocabulary.

7) I tend to pay attention to what others are wearing.

8) The slightest look of disapproval in the eyes of a person with whom I am interacting is enough to make me change my approach.

9) It's important to me to fit into the group I'm with.

10) My behavior often depends on how I feel others wish me to behave.

11) If I am the least bit uncertain as to how to act in a social situation, I look to the behavior of others for cues.

12) I usually keep up with clothing style changes by watching what others wear.

13) When in a social situation, I tend not to follow the crowd, but instead to behave in a manner that suits my particular mood at the time.*

NOTE: * denotes items that are reversed scored.

THE STYLE OF PROCESSING SCALE: SOP
(Childers, Houston, and Heckler 1985)

Construct: Childers, Houston, and Heckler (1985) conceptualize processing style as a preference and propensity to engage in a verbal and/or visual modality of processing information about one's environment.

Description: The SOP is a 22-item scale, where the items are scored from 1 (always true) to 4 (always false). Eleven items reflect a visual processing style, and eleven items reflect a verbal processing style. The scale can be broken down into two components by summing item scores within components, or used to compute a summed overall score of SOP representing a point on a continuum reflecting a preference for one of the two processing styles (Childers et al. 1985)

Development: After defining the construct and reviewing the literature, items from existing measures of processing style and newly generated items were used as an initial pool. Six items from Richardson's (1977) VVQ and 36 new items were generated. These 42 items were then administered to a sample and trimmed to 22 items based on item-to-total correlations. The reliability, validity, and structure of the 22-item SOP were examined in later samples.

Sample(s): A sample of 35 undergraduate students was used to trim the initial pool of items from 42 to 22. A sample of 106 undergraduate students was used to examine the reliability, validity, and structure of the SOP (Childers et al. 1985).

Validity: The 11-item verbal component and the 11-item visual component of the SOP had alphas of .81 and .86, respectively. The alpha of the overall 22-item SOP was .88. Furthermore, factor analysis revealed that the SOP was best represented by a two-factor structure (i.e., 11 items for the verbal and 11 items for the visual components).

Correlations of the SOP with other measures of processing style demonstrated discriminant validity for the SOP, and correlations of the SOP with measures of ad recall ($r = -.34$) and recognition ($r = -.31$) showed evidence of criterion validity for the SOP.

Scores: No mean and/or percentage scores were reported.

Source: Childers, Terry L., Michael J. Houston, and Susan Heckler (1985), "Measurement of Individual Differences in Visual Versus Verbal Information Processing," *Journal of Consumer Research*, 12 (September), 125-134.

Other evidence: N/A.

Other sources: N/A.

References: Richardson, Alan (1977), "Verbalizer-Visualizer: A Cognitive Style Dimension," *Journal of Mental Imagery*, 1, 109-126.

THE STYLE OF PROCESSING SCALE: SOP
(Childers, Houston, and Heckler 1985)

The aim of this exercise is to determine the style or manner you use when carrying out different mental tasks. Your answers to the questions should reflect the manner in which you typically engage in each of the tasks mentioned. There are no right or wrong answers, we only ask that you provide honest and accurate answers. Please answer each question by circling one of the four possible responses. For example, if I provided the statement "I seldom read books," and this was your *typical* behavior, even though you might read one book a year, you would circle the ALWAYS TRUE response.

1)   I enjoy doing work that requires the use of words.

2)   There are some special times in my life that I like to relive by mentally "picturing" just how everything looked.*

3)   I can never seem to find the right word when I need it.*

4)   I do a lot of reading.

5)   When I'm trying to learn something new, I'd rather watch a demonstration than read how to do it.*

6)   I think I often use words in the wrong way.*

7)   I enjoy learning new words.

8)   I like to picture how I could fix up my apartment or a room if I could buy anything I wanted.*

9)   I often make written notes to myself.

10) I like to daydream.*

11) I generally prefer to use a diagram rather than a written set of instructions.*

12) I like to "doodle."*

13) I find it helps to think in terms of mental pictures when doing many things.*

14) After I meet someone for the first time, I can usually remember what they look like, but not much about them.*

15) I like to think of synonyms for words.

16) When I have forgotten something I frequently try to form a mental "picture" to remember it.*

17) I like learning new words.

18) I prefer to read instructions about how to do something rather than have someone show me.

19) I prefer activities that don't require a lot of reading.*

20) I seldom daydream.

21) I spend very little time trying to increase my vocabulary.*

22) My thinking often consists of mental "pictures" or images.*

NOTES: * denotes items that are reversed scored.

Items 1, 3, 4, 6, 7, 9, 15, 17, 18, 19, and 21 comprise the verbal component. Items 2, 5, 8, 10 through 14, 16, 20, and 22 comprise the visual component.

POLYCHRONIC ATTITUDE INDEX: PAI
(Kaufman, Lane, and Lindquist 1991)

Construct: Polychronic time use is defined in terms of combining activities such that several goals can be attained at the same time. Thus, two or more activities are performed in the same time block at the same time. Conceptually, it is proposed that polychronic time use is a strategic process whereby individuals enrich their time budgets producing the output of more than 24 hours of single, monochronic time use (Kaufman, Lane, and Lindquist 1991, p. 394). The PAI was designed to measure attitudes toward polychronic time use.

Description: The PAI is composed of four items measured on 5-point strongly agree - strongly disagree Likert scales. The item scores are summed to form an overall PAI and the PAI is considered unidimensional.

Development: Based on the conceptual description and a literature review, 15 statements were initially generated to tap the domain of the construct. With two student sample pretests, item-to-total correlations were used to delete eleven items, resulting in the final 4-item version of the PAI. Dimensionality, reliability, and validity checks were also performed on a later sample.

Sample(s): As stated above, the PAI items were initially pretested on two student samples (n not specified). The final version of the scale was administered to a sample of 310 (42% male and 58% female) in the Philadelphia metropolitan area.

Validity: Factor analysis revealed that the PAI was unidimensional and had a coefficient alpha of .68. The PAI was negatively correlated with a measure of role overload (-.15), and the pattern of correlations of the PAI with activity statements reflecting polychronic time use showed modest evidence of validity (range of .02 to .13 in absolute value). The PAI was also found to be positively correlated with education, employment, and club membership.

Scores: Neither mean nor percentage scores were reported.

Source: Kaufman, Carol Felker, Paul M. Lane, and Jay D. Lindquist (1991), "Exploring More than 24 Hours a Day: A Preliminary Investigation of Polychronic Time Use," *Journal of Consumer Research*, 18 (December), 392-401.

Other evidence: N/A

Other sources: N/A

POLYCHRONIC ATTITUDE INDEX: PAI
(Kaufman, Lane, and Lindquist 1991)

1) I do not like to juggle several activities at the same time.

2) People should try not to do too many things at once.

3) When I sit down at my desk, I work on one project at a time.

4) I am comfortable doing several things at the same time.

NOTES: Items 1, 2, and 3 require reverse scoring.

SOURCES FOR CHAPTER FOUR

Bloch, Peter H. (1981), "An Exploration Into the Scaling of Consumers' Involvement With a Product Class," in *Advances in Consumer Research*, Vol. 8, Kent B. Monroe (ed.), Provo, UT: Association for Consumer Research, 61-65; Table 1, p. 63.

Bloch, Peter H., Daniel L. Sherrell, and Nancy M. Ridgeway (1986), "Consumer Search: An Extended Framework," *Journal of Consumer Research*, 13 (June), 119-126; p. 123.

Childers, Terry L., Michael J. Houston and Susan Heckler (1985), "Measurement of Individual Differences in Visual Versus Verbal Information Processing," *Journal of Consumer Research*, 12 (September), 125-134; Exhibit, p. 129.

Dickson, John and Gerald Albaum (1977), "A Method for Developing Tailormade Semantic Differentials for Specific Marketing Content Areas," *Journal of Marketing Research*, 14 (February), 87-91; Table 2, p. 89.

Higie, Robin A. and Lawrence F. Feick (1988), "Enduring Involvement: Conceptual and Methodological Issues," in *Advances in Consumer Research*, Vol. 16, Thomas Srull (ed.), Provo, UT: Association for Consumer Research, 690-696; Exhibit, p. 693.

Jain, Kapil and Narasimhan Srinivasan (1990), "An Empirical Assessment of Multiple Operationalizations of Involvement," in *Advances in Consumer Research*, Vol. 17, M. Goldberg, G.Gorn, and R. Pollay (eds.), Provo, UT: Association for Consumer Research, 594-602; Table 2, 597-598.

Kaufman, Carol Felker, Paul M. Lane, and Jay D. Lindquist (1991), "Exploring More than 24 Hours a Day: A Preliminary Investigation of Polychronic Time Use," *Journal of Consumer Research*, 18 (December), 392-401; Appendix A, p. 400.

Lastovicka, John L. and David M. Gardner (1979), "Components of Involvement," in *Attitude Research Plays for High Stakes*, J. C. Maloney and B. Silverman (eds.), Chicago: American Marketing Association, 53-73; Table 1, pp. 62-63.

Laurent, Gilles and Jean-Noel Kapferer (1985), "Measuring Consumer Involvement Profiles," *Journal of Marketing Research*, 22 (February), 41-53; Table 1, p. 44.

Lennox, Richard D. and Raymond N. Wolfe (1984), "Revision of the Self-Monitoring Scale," *Journal of Personality and Social Psychology*, 46, 1349-1464; Table 9, p. 1316.

McQuarrie, Edward F. and J. Michael Munson (1986), "The Zaichkowsky Personal Involvement Inventory: Modification and Extension," in *Advances in Consumer Research*, Vol. 14, Paul Anderson and Melanie Wallendorf (eds.), Provo, UT: Association for Consumer Research, 36-40; Exhibit, p. 38.

McQuarrie, Edward F. and J. Michael Munson (1991), "A Revised Product Involvement Inventory: Improved Usability and Validity," Unpublished Working Paper, Santa Clara, CA: Santa Clara University; Exhibit, p. 19.

Mehrabian, Albert and James Russell (1974), *An Approach to Environmental Psychology*, Cambridge, MA: The MIT Press; Appendix B and C, pp. 216, 218-219.

Mittal, Banwari (1989), "Measuring Purchase-Decision Involvement," *Psychology & Marketing*, 6 (Summer), 147-162; Figure 1, p. 152.

Peterson, Robert A. and Matthew Sauber (1983), "A Mood Scale for Survey Research," in *American Marketing Association Educators' Proceedings*, Patrick Murphy et al. (eds.), Chicago: American Marketing Association, 409-414; Table 1, p. 411.

Raju, P. S. (1980), "Optimum Stimulation Level: Its Relationship to Personality, Demographics, and Exploratory Behavior," *Journal of Consumer Research*, 7 (December), 272-282; Table 3, p. 278.

Ratchford, Brian T. (1987), "New Insights About the FCB Grid," *Journal of Advertising Research*, 27 (4) (August-September), 24-38; Table 1, p. 28.

Reilly, Michael D. (1982), "Working Wives and Convenience Consumption," *Journal of Consumer Research*, 8 (March),407-417; Appendix A, p. 417.

Seymour, Daniel and Greg Lessne (1984), "Spousal Conflict Arousal: Scale Development," *Journal of Consumer Research*, 11 (December), 810-821; Exhibit 1, pp. 815-816.

Slama, Mark E. and Armen Tashchian (1985), "Selected Socioeconomic and Demographic Characteristics Associated with Purchasing Involvement," *Journal of Marketing*, 49 (Winter), 72-82; Appendix, 79-80.

Tigert, Douglas J., Lawrence R. Ring, and Charles W. King (1976), "Fashion Involvement and Buying Behavior: A Methodological Study," in *Advances in Consumer Research*, Vol. 3, Beverly B. Anderson (ed.), Provo, UT: Association for Consumer Research, 46-52; p. 47 and Table 1, p. 49.

Traylor, Mark B. and W. Benoy Joseph (1984), "Measuring Consumer Involvement with Products: Developing a General Scale," *Psychology & Marketing*, 1 (Summer), 65-77; Table 1, p. 69.

Zaichkowsky, Judith Lynne, (1990), "The Personal Involvement Inventory: Reduction and Application to Advertising," *Unpublished Working Paper*, Burnaby, British Columbia: Simon Fraser University; Appendix A, p. 35.

Zaichkowsky, Judith Lynne, (1985), "Measuring the Involvement Construct," *Journal of Consumer Research*, 12 (December), 341-352; Appendix A, p. 350.

Zuckerman, Marvin (1979), *Sensation Seeking: Beyond the Optimal Level of Arousal*, Hillsdale, NJ: Lawrence Erlbaum Associates; Appendix G, pp 397-400.

5

Reactions to Advertising Stimuli

MEASURES RELATING TO AD EMOTIONS AND AD CONTENT

EMOTIONAL QUOTIENT SCALE (EQ) AND REACTION PROFILE
(Wells 1964a)

Construct: An important dimension of ad recall is emotional appeal. Wells (1964a) developed two scales that assess emotional reaction to ads. The first is the Emotional Quotient Scale (EQ) which measures a "global" emotional reaction toward ads, and the second is the Reaction Profile which assesses three specific emotional reactions toward ads:

Attractiveness - the physical appeal of the ad.

Meaningfulness - the degree to which the ad delivers a message the respondent understands, will accept, and finds personally significant.

Vitality - the vividness of the ad.

Both scales were originally designed to test emotional reactions to print advertisements.

Description: The EQ is composed of 12 Likert-type statements (6 favorably worded and 6 unfavorably worded). A scale score is derived by summing the number of agreements with the favorable items and the number of disagreements with the unfavorable items, then dividing by 12 and multiplying by 100. Thus, an individual's score can range from 0 to 100.

The Wells' Reaction Profile is a 25-item scale operationalized as a series of semantic differential scales, 12 for attractiveness, 9 for meaningfulness, and 5 for vitality (one item overlapped on the attractiveness and vitality dimensions). All items are scored on 8-point scales, and item scores can be summed within dimensions, and then averaged by the number of items in each dimension, to form scores for each dimension.

Development: For the EQ, items were generated such that they would discriminate between high appeal and low appeal ads. Then, 100 consumers rated the items with respect to 18 to 24 print ads designed to differ in emotional appeal over three progressive refinement procedures. Item analysis was performed over the three procedures and the 12-item EQ was derived.

The Reaction Profile was created from a pool of 26 semantic differential scales. Twenty of these scales were originally titled "Son of EQ" and were designed to measure emotional dimensions not tapped by EQ. The remaining six items were generated to reflect other words and phrases respondents might think of when reacting to ads. A large sample of housewives responded to the 26 items after viewing 48 full page print advertisements (i.e., 50 respondents rated each ad). Through a series of tests (via ANOVA and factor analysis), items were eliminated that failed to distinguish between persons who differ in the quality being measured and that failed to measure the same quality as other items within the same dimensions. This resulted in the final 25-item Reaction Profile. Then, using two large samples, the predictive validity of the Reaction Profile was examined.

Sample(s): For the EQ, a sample of 100 consumers was used to develop the scale. For the Reaction Profile, a sample of 100 housewives responded to the "Son of EQ" items, and a sample of 600 housewives responded to the total Reaction Profile for scale development and refinement. Two more samples of 190 housewives and 950 consumers responded to the Reaction Profile for assessing predictive validity (Wells 1964a).

Validity: Little evidence of validity was offered for the EQ, and the validity evidence for the Reaction profile was restricted to factor analysis and predictive validity. Factor analysis of the Reaction Profile supported the three-factor structure of attractiveness, meaningfulness, and vitality. With ad recall as the dependent variable, the predictive validity of the reaction profile dimensions was examined. The multiple correlation between the three dimensions of the reaction profile and ad recall was .94 (using cluster scores as predictors). For the n = 950 sample, the multiple correlations between the Reaction Profile dimensions and recall was .94 across 10 black and white ads, and .75 across 19 color ads (Wells 1964a).

Scores: Neither mean nor percentage scores were offered by Wells (1964a).

Source: Wells, William D. (1964a), "EQ, Son of EQ, and the Reaction Profile," *Journal of Marketing*, 28 (October), 45-52.

Other evidence: An abbreviated version of the Reaction Profile was employed to predict recall and recognition scores (Wells 1964b). These versions were three-item subscales from the "attractiveness" and "meaningfulness" factors. (The items were scored on 7-point scales.) The correlations between the attractiveness subscale and recognition and recall measures across 20 ads were .55 and .31, respectively. The correlations between the meaningfulness subscale and recognition and recall measures were .40 and .52, offering evidence of nomological validity.

Zinkhan and Fornell (1985) compared the Wells Profile to a version of Leavitt's (1970) profile. For the Wells profile, 20 different print ads were used. Four hundred subjects were recruited by an advertising agency and prescreened to confirm they were members of the target audience of the particular ad. For each individual ad, 20 subjects were exposed to a print ad along with other material which might appear in a national magazine. Each subject was exposed to only one ad. After exposure, the subjects completed a version of the reaction profile in which scale items were randomly rotated. In general, the dimensional structure was confirmed for Wells' profile as the coefficient of congruence (which measures the fit between the hypothesized structure and the rotated solutions) was very high (CC=.94). Furthermore, the attractiveness and meaningfulness factors had significant beta weights for the prediction of attitude-toward-the-brand (i.e., .55 and .14), and attractiveness had a significant beta weight for the prediction of purchase intention (.29), offering evidence of predictive validity.

Other sources: Wells, William D. (1964b), "Recognition, Recall, and Rating Scales," *Journal of Advertising Research*, 4, 2-8.

Zinkhan, George M. and Claes Fornell (1985), "A Test of Two Consumer Response Scales in Advertising," *Journal of Marketing Research*, 22 (November), 447-52.

References: Leavitt, Clark (1970), "A Multidimensional Set of Rating Scales for Television Commercials," *Journal of Applied Psychology*, 54, 427-9.

EMOTIONAL QUOTIENT SCALE (EQ) AND REACTION PROFILE
(Wells 1964a)

EMOTIONAL QUOTIENT SCALE (EQ)

1) This ad is very appealing to me.
2) I would probably skip this ad if I saw it in a magazine.
3) This is a heart-warming ad.
4) This ad makes me want to buy the brand it features.
5) This ad has little interest for me.
6) I dislike this ad.
7) This ad makes me feel good.
8) This is a wonderful ad.
9) This is the kind of ad you forget easily.
10) This is a fascinating ad.
11) I'm tired of this kind of advertising.
12) This ad leaves me cold.

NOTES: Items 1, 3, 4, 7, 8, and 10 represent the favorably worded items, and the remaining items represent the unfavorably worded items.

REACTION PROFILE

1) Beautiful/ugly
2) Pleasant/unpleasant
3) Gentle/harsh
4) Appealing/unappealing
5) Attractive/unattractive
6) In good taste/in poor taste
7) Exciting/unexciting
8) Interesting/uninteresting
9) Worth looking at/not worth looking at
10) Comforting/frightening
11) Colorful/colorless
12) Fascinating/boring
13) Meaningful/meaningless
14) Convincing/unconvincing
15) Important to me/unimportant to me
16) Strong/weak
17) Honest/dishonest
18) Easy to remember/hard to remember
19) Easy to understand/hard to understand
20) Worth remembering/not worth remembering
21) Simple/complicated
22) New/ordinary
23) Fresh/stale
24) Lively/lifeless
25) Sharp/washed out

NOTES: Items 1 through 12 represent the "attractiveness" factor. Items 13 through 21 represent the "meaningfulness" factor, and items 22 through 25 and item 11 represent the "vitality" factor (Wells 1964a). All items require reverse coding to reflect higher scores.

Items 1, 2, and 5 were the items used by Wells (1964b) to represent "attractiveness," while items 13, 15, and 20 were used to operationalize "meaningfulness."

LEAVITT'S REACTION PROFILE
(Leavitt 1970)

Construct: The likability or emotional reaction to ads is what Leavitt (1970) attempts to measure. Specifically, Leavitt set out to assess the dimensions on which viewers affectively rate TV commercials.

Description: The original Leavitt profile consisted of 45 single word or phrase descriptors designed to capture reactions to television commercials. These 45 descriptors formed eight factors reflecting different dimensions of emotional reactions to ads. All items were scored on a five-point basis from "does not fit" to "fits extremely well." Though not specified, it seems that item scores can be summed within dimensions to form indices of each dimension.

Development: An original pool of 525 words and phrases was generated to reflect possible affective reactions toward TV ads. Four filtering procedures were then employed to trim the items to the final 45 descriptors. First, over 11 commercials, 30 respondents evaluated a third of the original pool. Words checked by 20% or more of the sample were retained. Then, on a five-point scale, 110 respondents rated the remaining items over 11 commercials. Via ANOVA, those items that significantly discriminated among commercials were retained, resulting in 206 items. These 206 were then factor analyzed. Redundant words and descriptors with loadings of less than .50 were eliminated, resulting in 73 items. The 73 items were refactored and 45 items with loadings of .50 or greater were retained. Although another sample was used to rate 250 more items (over 11 new commercials), the 45-item scale was retained.

Sample(s): Samples of 30, 110, and 110 were used to develop and factor analyze Leavitt's profile.

Validity: Little evidence of reliability or validity was offered. Of the eight factors extracted, the energetic factor accounted for 55% of the total variance, personal relevance accounted for 22%, sensuality accounted for 9%, familiarity 5%, and novelty, authoritative, and disliked accounted for 3%, 2%, and 2%, respectively.

Scores: Neither mean nor percentage scores were reported by Leavitt (1970).

Source: Leavitt, Clark (1970), "A Multidimensional Set of Rating Scales for Television Commercials," *Journal of Applied Psychology*, 54, 427-9.

Other evidence: Wells, Leavitt and McConville (1971) derived a modified 30-item version of the Leavitt profile encompassing six factors: humor, vigor, sensuousness, uniqueness, personal relevance, and irritation (five items per factor). Over 10 anti-smoking commercials, the personal relevance factor had a correlation of .80 with a measure of "personal product response," and an overall measure of recall had a correlation of -.64 with the sensuousness factor. Furthermore, rating scores across factors for 3 different commercials supported the validity of the reduced profile.

With a sample of 155, Sullivan and O'Connor (1983) examined an abridged version of Leavitt's profile over four public service announcements (PSAs). Five factors were extracted: stimulating, monotonous, relevant, irritating, and likable accounting for 27.3%, 16.75%, 26.1%, 17.5%, and 12.4% of the variance, respectively. However, none of the factors exhibited significant beta weights for the prediction of behavioral intentions toward the messages from the PSAs.

Zinkhan and Fornell (1985) looked at a 27-item reduced version of Leavitt's profile using 400 subjects and 20 different ads. The coefficient of congruence (which measures the fit between the hypothesized structure and the rotated solution) was moderate (CC=.58) for four factors examined (i.e., energetic/amusing, personal relevance, familiarity, and sensuousness). The validity of the four factors for predicting attitude-toward-the-brand and purchase intention was also examined. The beta coefficients for all four factors were significant for predicting A-brand (i.e., .37, .13, -.23, and .31 for energetic/amusing, relevance, familiarity, and sensuous, respectively). The beta coefficients for predicting purchase intention were significant for energetic/amusing (.11) and personal relevance (.11).

Other Sources: Sullivan, Gary L. and P. J. O'Connor (1983), "Search for a Relationship Between Viewer Responses to the Creative Aspects of Televised Messages and Behavioral Intention," in *Advances in Consumer Research*, Vol. 10, Richard P. Bagozzi and Alice M. Tybout (eds), Ann Arbor, MI: Association for Consumer Research, 32-5.

Wells, William D., Clark Leavitt, and Maureen McConville (1971), "A Reaction Profile for TV Commercials," *Journal of Advertising Research*, 11 (December), 11-17.

Zinkhan, George M. and Claes Fornell (1985), "A Test of Two Consumer Response Scales in Advertising," *Journal of Marketing Research*, 22 (November), 447-52.

References: N/A

LEAVITT'S REACTION PROFILE
(Leavitt 1970)

Energetic factor
1) Lively
2) Exhilarated
3) Vigorous
4) Enthusiastic
5) Energetic
6) Excited

Amusing factor
7) Merry
8) Jolly
9) Playful
10) Joyful
11) Amusing
12) Humorous

Personal relevance factor
13) Important to me
14) Helpful
15) Valuable
16) Meaningful for me
17) Worth remembering
18) Convincing

Authoritative factor
19) Confident
20) Business-like
21) Consistent-in-style
22) Responsible
23) Frank
24) Dependable

Sensual
25) Lovely
26) Beautiful
27) Gentle
28) Serene
29) Tender
30) Sensitive

Familiarity
31) Familiar
32) Well-known
33) Saw before

Novel
34) Original
35) Unique
36) Imaginative
37) Novel
38) Ingenious
39) Creative

Disliked
40) Phony
41) Terrible
42) Stupid
43) Irritating
44) Unimportant to me
45) Ridiculous

NOTES: Items 2 through 6 comprise the "vigor" factor of Wells et al. (1971). Items 7 through 9, 11 and 12 comprise their "humor" factor. Items 12, 15, 16, 17, and an added item (i.e., "for me") comprise their "personal relevance" factor. Items 25, 27, 28, 29 and an added item (i.e., "soothing") comprise their "sensuousness" factor. Items 34 through 38 comprise their "uniqueness" factor, and items 40 through 43 and 45 comprise their "irritation" factor. Wells et al. suggest a scoring procedure of fits "extremely well" (5) to fits "not well at all" (1).

Items 1, 6, 11, 35, 36, and 39 and two other items ("clever" and "new") represent Sullivan and O'Connor's "stimulating" factor. All new items for their "monotonous" factor were generated and were "dull," "sluggish," "old," and "repetitious." Items 14, 16, 17, 18, and 23, and four new items (i.e., "believable," "natural," "realistic," and "informative") represent their "relevant" factor. Their "irritating" factor is comprised of item 42 and four new items (i.e., "in poor taste," "silly," "confusing," and "unclear"). Lastly, item 31 and three new items (i.e., "attractive," "agreeable," and "soothing") comprise their "likable" factor (Sullivan and O'Connor 1983).

Items 1 through 12 reflect the "energetic/amusing" factor of Zinkhan and Fornell (1985). Their "personal relevance," "sensuousness," and "familiarity" items were identical to those of the original Leavitt profile reported above.

VIEWER RESPONSE PROFILE: VRP
(Schlinger 1979)

Construct: The Viewer Response Profile gauges affective reactions to advertisements. It focuses on the emotional component of communication effects and indicates how people feel after seeing a commercial rather than what they know (Schlinger 1979, p. 37). The VRP assesses seven facets relating to how people feel about an advertisement:

Entertainment - the degree to which a commercial is pleasurable, enjoyable, and fun to watch.

Confusion - the degree to which the viewer feels that the commercial is difficult to follow.

Relevant news - the degree to which viewers feel that the commercial has told them something important and interesting about a brand, or some useful information.

Brand reinforcement - the degree to which the ad reinforces existing positive attitudes toward the brand.

Empathy - the degree to which viewers participate vicariously in events, feelings, and behaviors that are shown in the ad. This empathy can be positive or negative.

Familiarity - the degree to which viewers see commercials as unusual and different either from advertising in general or from current campaigns for the product category or brand.

Alienation - the degree to which the ad is felt to be irrelevant or irritating (i.e., negative judgments about the message or the execution of the message).

Description: The VRP is composed of 32 Likert items on seven-point scales from strongly disagree to strongly agree. There are 7 items for entertainment, 4 for confusion, 5 for relevant news, 2 for brand reinforcement, 5 for empathy, 3 for familiarity, and 6 for alienation. Item scores are summed within the facets, and then divided by the number of items in each facet, to form indices for each facet.

Development: A number of procedures, samples, and analyses were used in scale development. Six-hundred statements were initially generated based on the open-ended responses of 400 viewers to 14 commercials and storyboards. This pool of items was trimmed to 139 items (both positively and negatively worded) via subjective judgment. Then, two samples, one of 500 women for 25 different commercials (20 women per commercial), and one of 500 for 10 commercials (50 per commercials), responded to the items. Via factor analyses, these two studies retained 70 items that had loadings of .50 or greater on a given factor and discriminated among commercials. Two more large samples were used to further trim the pool of items over a total of 82 commercials and 377 story boards. Across several factor analyses, the final 32-item, seven-factor scale was derived. A number of reliability and validity checks using new samples were also performed.

Sample(s): As stated above, several samples were used in scale development and validation. Samples of n = 400 in item generation, two samples of n = 500 women in item purification, and two more samples of n = 1,504 and n = 1,871 men and women were used in item purification. Also, at least five more samples ranging from 12 to 50 were used to assess the reliability and validity of the VRP. (As stated by Schlinger [1979, p. 46], over 5,000 individual interviews were conducted in development and validation of the VRP over a 5-year period.)

Validity: Test-retest reliability ranged from .62 for familiarity to .96 for brand reinforcement. Though coefficient alpha was not reported, item-factor loadings ranged from .33 to .88 over the first four samples (i.e., 500, 500, 1,504, and 1,871) discussed above.

A number of mean differences provided support for the validity of the scale. In addition, the VRP factors were used as independent variables to predict ad awareness. The VRP facets explained 52% of the variance in ad awareness, offering evidence of predictive validity.

Furthermore, the VRP was strongly correlated with the Wells et al. (1971) reaction measure, offering evidence of convergent validity (i.e., together, the VRP and Wells et al. measure accounted for 78% of the variance when jointly factor analyzed).

Scores: A number of mean scores are presented in Tables 3, 4, and 5 of Schlinger (1979, pp. 43-44). These scores range from 3.8 to 5.3 for entertainment, 2.1 to 2.6 for confusion, 2.8 to 4.9 for relevant news, 3.8 to 5.6 for brand reinforcement, 2.5 to 3.9 for empathy, 2.1 to 3.5 for familiarity, and 2.6 to 3.6 for alienation.

Source: Schlinger, Mary (1979), "A Profile of Responses to Commercials," *Journal of Advertising Research*, 19 (April), 37-46.

Other evidence: N/A.

Other sources: N/A.

References: Wells, William, Clark Leavitt, and Maureen McConville (1971), "A Reaction Profile for TV Commercials," *Journal of Advertising Research*, 11 (December), 11-17.

VIEWER RESPONSE PROFILE: VRP
(Schlinger 1979)

Entertainment

1) The commercial was lots of fun to watch and listen to.

2) I thought it was clever and entertaining.

3) The enthusiasm of the commercial is catching - it picks you up.

4) The ad wasn't just selling the product - it was entertaining me and I appreciate that.

5) The characters (or persons) in the commercial capture your attention.

6) It's the kind of commercial that keeps running through your mind after you've seen it.

7) I just laughed at it - I thought it was very funny and good.

Confusion

8) It was distracting - trying to watch the screen and listen to the words at the same time.

9) It required a lot of effort to follow the commercial.

10) It was too complex. I wasn't sure of what was going on.

11) I was so busy watching the screen, I didn't listen to the talk.

Relevant news

12) The commercial gave me a new idea.

13) The commercial reminded me that I'm dissatisfied with what I'm using now and I'm looking for something better.

14) I learned something from the commercial that I didn't know before.

15) The commercial told about a new product I think I'd like to try.

16) During the commercial I thought how that product might be useful to me.

Brand reinforcement

17) That's a good brand and I wouldn't hesitate recommending it to others.

18) I know that the advertised brand is a dependable, reliable one.

Empathy

19) The commercial was very realistic - that is, true to life.

20) I felt that the commercial was acting out what I feel at times.

21) I felt as though I was right there in the commercial experiencing the same thing.

22) That's my idea - the kind of life that commercial showed.

23) I liked the commercial because it was personal and intimate.

Familiarity

24) This kind of commercial has been done many times. . . it's the same old thing.

25) I've seen this commercial so many times - I'm tired of it.

26) I think this is an unusual commercial. I'm not sure I've seen another like it.*

Alienation

27) What they showed didn't demonstrate the claims they were making about the product.

28) The ad didn't have anything to do with me or my needs.

29) The commercial did not show me anything that would make me want to use their products.

30) The commercial made exaggerated claims. The product would not live up to what they said or implied.

31) It was an unrealistic ad - very far fetched.

32) The commercial irritated me - it was annoying.

NOTES: * denotes items that are reverse scored.

RELEVANCE, CONFUSION, AND ENTERTAINMENT
(Lastovicka 1983)

Construct: Three copy-testing concepts were examined by Lastovicka (1983) with respect to convergent and discriminant validity. These concepts were (Lastovicka 1983, p. 16):

Relevance - questioning the meaningfulness of the ad and its product with respect to the viewer's need.

Confusion - the degree to which the commercial is perceived as being misunderstood.

Entertainment - an overall positive evaluation or feeling, as opposed to irritation with respect to a commercial's execution.

Description: Sixteen structured questions were administered using a Likert-type format with a scale range from 1 (Strongly Disagree) to 6 (Strongly Agree). Item scores are summed within each factor to form indices of relevance, confusion, and entertainment. Thus, the scale is multidimensional.

Development: With respect to the three concepts of relevance, confusion, and entertainment, two measurement methods were applied: 1) structured questioning using Likert-type "disagree - agree" multiple scales, many of which were culled from Schlinger's (1979) VRP; and 2) open questioning in which viewers were asked to retrospectively list their thoughts while viewing the commercials. Each student answered the open-ended question and then answered a battery of sixteen structured questions. Checks on product relevance (i.e., beer, blue jeans, soft drinks, and automobiles) showed that 83 percent of the respondents had used or purchased some brand from each of the four different product classes represented in the six test ads during the month preceding the study. The open-ended question read as follows: "What were your thoughts while you viewed the television commercial?" The sixteen structured items were selected from Leo Burnett Storyboard Test research. These selected items loaded highly on empirically derived factors measuring the dimension of interest. Again, each item was used with a 1-6 (Strongly Disagree to Strongly Agree) scale. Confirmatory factor analysis (via LISREL) of the 16 items empirically supported the battery of items into the three subscales of relevance, confusion, and entertainment. Scale reliability was also assessed, as well as validity.

Sample(s): The sample consisted of 634 undergraduates from a university business school. Each subject was exposed to one of six different 60-second television commercials in a classroom setting. Each student answered the open-ended question and the sixteen structured questions.

Validity: Some of the major results of the Lastovicka (1983) study are summarized as follows. Modest support for the convergent and discriminant validity of the standardized versions of the relevance, confusion, and entertainment dimensions was found as a three-factor model of relevance, confusion, and entertainment provided a strong fit to the data (chi-square = 11.91, df = 7, p = .11). Scale reliabilities were reported for each dimension: relevance (.85), confusion (.73), and entertainment (.87). The intercorrelations among the three subscales were .68 for relevance-entertainment, -.68 for relevance-confusion, and -.59 for confusion-entertainment.

Scores: Mean scores were not offered by Lastovicka (1983).

Source: Lastovicka, John L. (1983), "Convergent and Discriminant Validity of Television Commercial Rating Scales," *Journal of Advertising*, 12 (2) 14-23.

Other evidence: N/A

Other sources: N/A

References: Schlinger, Mary (1979), "A Profile of Responses to Commercials," *Journal of Advertising Research*, 19 (April), 37-46.

RELEVANCE, CONFUSION, AND ENTERTAINMENT
(Lastovicka 1983)

Relevance

1) During the commercial I thought how the product might be useful for me.

2) I felt as though I was right there in the commercial experiencing the same thing.

3) The commercial was meaningful to me.

4) The ad did not have anything to do with me or my needs.*

5) The commercial gave me a good idea.

6) As I watched I thought of reasons why I would buy or not buy the product.

Confusion

7) I clearly understood the commercial.*

8) The commercial was too complex. I was not sure what was going on.

9) I was not sure what was going on in the commercial.

10) I was so busy watching the screen, I did not listen to the talk.

11) The commercial went by so quickly that it just did not make an impression on me.

Entertainment

12) The commercial was lots of fun to watch and listen to.

13) I have seen this commercial before.*

14) I have seen this commercial so many times that I am tired of it.*

15) I thought the commercial was clever and quite entertaining.

16) The ad was not just selling - it was entertaining me. I appreciated that.

NOTES: * denotes items that are reverse scored.

INFORMATIONAL AND TRANSFORMATIONAL AD CONTENT
(Puto and Wells 1984)

Construct: An informational advertisement was defined as an ad which provides consumers with factual, relevant brand data in a clear and logical manner such that they have greater confidence in their ability to assess the merits of buying the brand after having seen the advertisement. An important aspect of the definition is that the ad becomes informational if consumers perceive it as such. For an ad to be judged informational, it must reflect the following characteristics: 1) present factual, relevant information about the brand; 2) present information which is immediately and obviously important to the potential consumer; and 3) present data which the consumer accepts as being verifiable. A transformational advertisement is one which associates the experience of using (consuming) the advertised brand with a unique set of psychological characteristics which would not typically be associated with the brand experience to the same degree without exposure to the advertisement. Specifically, the advertisement itself links the brand with the capacity to provide the consumer with an experience that is different from the consumption experience which would normally be expected to occur without ad exposure. For an ad to be judged transformational, it must reflect the following characteristics: 1) the experience of using the product must be made richer, warmer, more exciting and/or more enjoyable, than that obtained solely from an objective ad description; and 2) the experience of the advertisement and the experience of using the brand must be so tightly connected that the consumers cannot remember the brand without recalling the experience generated by the advertisement. The transformation occurs when the descriptors are explicitly related by consumers to the experience of owning or consuming the advertised brand. Advertisements can be classified as belonging to one of four basic categories: 1) high transformational / low information, 2) low transformational / high information, 3) high transformational / high information, and 4) low transformational / low information (Puto and Wells 1984, p. 638).

Description: Puto and Wells' measures include twenty-three items scored on six-point "strongly agree" and "strongly disagree" scales. Fifteen of the items tap the transformation construct, while the eight remaining relate to the information construct. The responses are averaged across the items within each subscale to form indices of each subscale.

Development: Scale items which were considered candidates for inclusion on the informational scales were derived from items used in prior research on the informational content of advertisements (e.g., Aaker and Norris 1982). Additionally, a set of items was generated from the definition of informational advertisements. Though research with respect to the emotional and experiential aspects of transformation was also examined, the majority of this research was concerned with measuring empathetic tendencies of individuals. Since the research objectives of this study were concerned with products, it was necessary to develop original items for this aspect of the transformational scale. Personal relevance aspects of the transformation scale were derived from the viewer response profile measures (Schlinger 1979). In sum, a total of 23 items were retained to represent the transformational and informational measures.

To test these items, approximately 400 television commercials were reviewed and 20 were selected for the initial study. The two basic criteria for commercial selection were 1) either they were mainly informational or mainly transformational, and 2) they promoted products of interest to the test audience. From these 20 commercials, five were kept as informational and eight as transformational ads (i.e., 13 in all).

Subjects were then exposed to the 13 commercials and immediately after seeing each commercial, they reported their prior exposure to the commercial and their overall opinion of each ad. Lastly, subjects responded to the 23 transformational and informational items with respect to the commercials. Reliability and validity checks were then assessed.

Sample(s): Two judges, knowledgeable of the definitions of informational and transformational ads, but blind to prior classifications of the ads, independently judged the commercials with respect to the information and transformation constructs. The subjects were 130 undergraduate psychology students.

Validity:	Reliability coefficients were computed separately for each commercial and then averaged across the 13 test commercials. The average internal consistency reliability estimates across advertisements were 0.73 and 0.88 for the information and transformation scales, respectively. The mean scale values for the information and transformation scales for each commercial differed at the $p < .01$ level (one tailed t-test). These differences reflect the author's a priori assessment of an ad either being primarily informational or primarily transformational, and offer evidence for the validity of the scales. (Those commercials below the 3.5 mid-point were classified as being "low" on the specific dimension while those above it were classified as being "high.")
Scores:	Means and standard deviations for each commercial were presented in Table 4 on page 642 of the Puto and Wells' (1984) study. As an example, the mean information and transformation scores for the first advertisement (i.e., an informational toothbrush advertisement) were 4.00 (sd = .69) and 3.08 (sd = .70), respectively.
Source:	Puto, Christopher P. and William D. Wells (1984), "Informational and Transformational Advertising: The Differential Effects of Time," in Thomas C. Kinnear (ed.), *Advances in Consumer Research*, Vol. 11, Provo, Utah: Association for Consumer Research, 638-643.
Other evidence:	N/A
Other sources:	N/A
References:	Aaker, David, A. and Donald Norris (1982), "Characteristics of TV Commercials Perceived as Informative," *Journal of Advertising Research*, 22, 61-70.
	Schlinger, Mary (1979), "A Profile of Responses to Commercials," *Journal of Advertising Research*, 19, 37-46.

INFORMATIONAL AND TRANSFORMATIONAL AD CONTENT
(Puto and Wells 1984)

1. I learned something from this commercial that I didn't know before about (this brand).

2. I would like to have an expertise like the one shown in the commercial.

3. The commercial did not seem to be speaking directly to me.

4. There is nothing special about (this brand) that makes it different from the others.

5. While I watched this commercial, I thought how (this brand) might be useful to me.

6. The commercial did not teach me what to look for when buying (this product).

7. This commercial was meaningful to me.

8. This commercial was very uninformative.

9. (This brand) fits my lifestyle very well.

10. I could really relate to this commercial.

11. Using (this brand) makes me feel good about myself.

12. If they had to, the company could provide evidence to support the claims made in this commercial.

13. It's hard to give a specific reason, but somehow (this brand) is not really for me.

14. This commercial did not really hold my attention.

15. This commercial reminded me of some important facts about (this brand) which I already knew.

16. If I could change my lifestyle, I would make it less like the people who use (this brand).

17. When I think of (this brand), I think of this commercial.

18. I felt as though I were right there in the commercial, experiencing the same thing.

19. I can now accurately compare (this brand) with other competing brands on matters that are important to me.

20. This commercial did not remind me of any experiences or feelings I've had in my own life.

21. I would have less confidence in using (this brand) now than before I saw this commercial.

22. It is the kind of commercial that keeps running through your head after you've seen it.

23. It's hard to put into words, but this commercial leaves me with a good feeling about using (this brand).

NOTES: ( ) denotes brand name of the advertised product is substituted here.

                Items 1, 4, 6, 8, 12, 15, 19, and 21 comprise the informational content measure. The remaining items comprise the transformational content scale.

                Though not specified by the authors, it seems that items 3, 6, 8, 12, 14, and 20 use reverse coding to reflect higher transformational and informational scores.

FEELINGS TOWARD ADS
(Edell and Burke 1987)

Construct: Feelings toward the ad are felt to be composed of both positive affective feelings toward a given ad and negative affective feelings toward a given ad. Furthermore, positive affective feelings are composed of "warm" and "upbeat" feelings toward the ad. These feelings affect both attitude-toward-the-ad and attitude-toward-the-brand (Edell and Burke 1987).

Description: The feelings toward the ad scales were originally composed of 65 items comprising three subdimensions: upbeat feelings (32 items), warm feelings (13 items), and negative feelings (20 items). A 52-item version of the scale was also used in Edell and Burke's Study Two where 26, 14, and 12 items were used to measure upbeat, warm, and negative feelings, respectively. All items are measured on five-point scales, and scores on items within each subdimension are summed to form indices of each subdimension.

Development: A pool of 169 feelings (items) gleaned from previous research served as the initial pool of items (Wells 1964; Wells et al. 1971). Sixty subjects viewed 16 TV ads in a theatre setting. The 16 ads were selected to represent a variety of products and executional styles. After viewing the ads, the subjects were given the list of feelings and asked to indicate which feelings they experienced while viewing the ads. Sixty items checked by at least 50% of the sample were retained. Also, nine more items that were mentioned via an open-ended task (but not on the checklist) were added, resulting in 69 items. Two studies then examined the dimensionality and reliability of the items. From the first study, 65 items were retained for the original scale. Four items were dropped that did not load highly on any factor (i.e., less than .50). In the second study, the shorter 52-item version was derived by eliminating items with item-to-total correlations greater than .90 (i.e., redundant items).

Sample(s): In the first study, a sample of 29 people was used, and in the second study, a sample of 32 people was used. Both samples were obtained via announcements on a university campus.

Validity: In the first study, factor analysis retained 65 of the 69 items. Three factors were retained from the factor analysis. Coefficient alpha estimates for the three factors were .98, .96, and .93 for the upbeat, negative, and warm feelings factors, respectively. For the reduced versions of the scales (i.e., Study Two), corresponding alpha estimates were .95, .89, and .90. In both studies the three dimensions of feelings toward the ad were related to measures of Aad and Abrand, providing evidence of predictive validity. For example, in Study One, standardized regression coefficients for the prediction of Aad and Abrand ranged from -.02 to .32 for upbeat feelings, -.09 to -.55 for negative feelings, and -.02 to .18 for warm feelings. Also, R-square estimates for the prediction of transformational and informational ads for the three subscales as predictors ranged from .63 to .78 across high/low conditions of transformational/informational ad content.

Scores: Mean or percentage scores were not reported.

Source: Edell, Julie A. and Marian Chapman Burke (1987), "The Power of Feelings in Understanding Advertising Effects," *Journal of Consumer Research*, 14 (December), 421-433.

Other evidence: Burke and Edell (1989) looked at the predictive power of the feelings scales (slightly modified versions) with a sample of 191 people recruited via announcements and newspaper ads on a university campus. Coefficient alpha estimates were .95, .89, and .88. for the upbeat, warm, and negative scale dimensions. All three dimensions were found to be related to several affective based measures of Aad and Abrand. For example, across six Aad/Abrand type dependent variables, standardized predictive coefficients ranged from -.02 to .80 for upbeat feelings, -.19 to .72 for warm feelings, and -.02 to .48 for negative feelings.

Other sources: Burke, Marian Chapman and Julie Edell (1989), "The Impact of Feelings on Ad-Based Affect and Cognition," *Journal of Marketing Research*, 26 (February), 69-83.

References: Wells, William D. (1964), "EQ, Son of EQ, and the Reaction Profile," *Journal of Marketing*, 28 (October), 45-52.

Wells, William D., Clark Leavitt, and Maureen McConville (1971), "A Reaction Profile for TV Commercials," *Journal of Advertising Research*, 22 (December), 11-17.

FEELINGS TOWARD ADS
(Edell and Burke 1987)

Instructions

We would like you to tell us how the ad you just saw made you *feel*. We are interested in *your reactions* to the ad, *not* how you would describe it. Please tell us how much you felt each of these feelings while you were watching this commercial. If you felt the feeling very strongly . . . put a "5"; strongly . . . put a "4"; somewhat strongly . . . put a "3"; not very strongly . . . put a "2"; not at all . . . put a "1."

Column 1	Column 2	Column 3
1) active	angry	affectionate
2) adventurous	annoyed	calm
3) alive	bad	concerned
4) amused	bored	contemplative
5) attentive	critical	emotional
6) attractive	defiant	hopeful
7) carefree	depressed	kind
8) cheerful	disgusted	moved
9) confident	disinterested	peaceful
10) creative	dubious	pensive
11) delighted	dull	sentimental
12) elated	fed-up	touched
13) energetic	insulted	warm-hearted
14) enthusiastic	irritated	
15) excited	lonely	
16) exhilarated	offended	
17) good	regretful	
18) happy	sad	
19) humorous	skeptical	
20) independent	suspicious	
21) industrious		
22) inspired		
23) interested		
24) joyous		
25) lighthearted		
26) lively		
27) playful		
28) pleased		
29) proud		
30) satisfied		
31) stimulated		
32) strong		

NOTES: Column one represents the "upbeat" factor; column two represents the "negative" factor; and column three represents the "warm" factor.

Item numbers 1, 3 through 13, 18 through 25, and 27 through 32 of the first column comprise the reduced version of the upbeat factor used in Study Two of Edell and Burke (1987). Items 4 through 11, and 15 through 20 of the second column comprise the reduced version of the negative factor in

Study Two of Burke and Edell (1987). Items 1 through 11, and 13 of column three comprise the reduced version of the warm factor in Study Two of Edell and Burke (1987).

In the Burke and Edell (1989) study, items 1, 3 through 13, 18 through 25, 27 through 32 of column one comprise the warm factor. An additional item, "silly," was also used as an item for this factor. Items 4 through 11, and 15 through 20 of column two comprise the negative factor items used in the Burke and Edell (1989) study. Items 1 through 11, and 13 of column three comprise the warm factor in the Burke and Edell (1989) study.

STANDARDIZED EMOTIONAL PROFILE: SEP
(Holbrook and Batra 1987a)

Construct: The purpose of designing the Standardized Emotional Profile (SEP) was to create a parsimonious scale of multi-item indices that can be used to assess emotional responses to print ads or television ads. This set of scales is especially useful in exploring the effects attributable to the nonverbal components of advertising (cf. Holbrook and Batra 1987a). The dimensions of the SEP, as well as subdimensions, were defined as follows:

Pleasure - refers intuitively to such feelings as joy, affection, gratitude, and pride. Subdimensions were labeled as faith, affection, and gratitude.

Arousal - reflects interest, activation, surprise, and involvement. Subdimensions were labeled as interest, activation, and surgency.

Domination - involves a sense of helplessness, sadness, fear, and distrust. Subdimensions were labeled as sadness, fear, and skepticism.

Note that these dimensions coincide with the Mehrabian and Russell PAD measures referred to in Chapter 4 of this volume.

Description: The final SEP consists of 27 items. An example of the seven-point format for responding to each item is as follows:

Very   Not at
                                  all

I felt. . .BORED___ : ___: ___ : ___ : ___ : ___ : ___

Subdimension scores are based on the sum of the items in each dimension, and though not specified, dimension scores can be derived by summing the subdimension scores within dimensions.

Development: Holbrook and Batra (1987a) derived a large set of items based on a review and synthesis of literature (Wells 1964; Wells et al. 1971; Mehrabian and Russell 1974; Schlinger 1979). Through author judgement, 109 items reflecting 29 emotions were used as the initial item pool. In a purification study, they reduced the items to a more compact battery of scales accounting for the most variance in emotional responses to advertising content. Specifically, the authors used the 109 items in response to 72 TV commercials in order (1) to assess the reliability of emotions toward advertising, (2) to isolate the key underlying dimensions of emotional response to TV commercials, and (3) to select a more parsimonious battery of scales for the purpose of constructing the SEP (cf. Holbrook and Batra 1987a, pp. 101-102). Twelve judges rated the seventy-two commercials on the 109 items using the seven-point format described above. Across items, Holbrook and Batra (1987a, p. 103) viewed judges as items in constructing a 12-item multi-judge index for assessing reliability across the 72 commercials. The overall mean of this interjudge reliability was .52. Next, each of the 29 emotions was formed by combining three or four items (based on the scores of the twelve judges). The multi-item reliabilities for these emotions range from 0.47 to 0.96, with a mean of 0.81. Then, in a principal components analysis, a three dimensional solution (pleasure, arousal, and domination) with eigenvalues of 13.6, 4.9, and 2.8 which accounted for 73.3 percent of the variance in the data was retained. Though this effort did not result in the final form of the SEP, estimates of concurrent validity were then assessed. The three dimensions were further reduced to form the final 27-item SEP via the following four procedures:

1) The elimination of items whose average multi-judge reliability was less than .50.

2) Eliminate any subdimension whose multi-item reliability falls below .80.

3) Retain the three subdimensions that loaded most strongly on each dimension.

4) For those subdimensions with four rather than three items, eliminate the item with the lowest multi-judge reliability.

Sample: The SEP ratings were provided by 12 adult females recruited from the community (but not associated with the business school). As stated above, 72 commercials were chosen to provide a judgmental representation of a range of emotions likely to be found in television advertisements.

Validity: Specific estimates of reliability and validity were only offered for preliminary versions of the SEP. However, the four procedures used to derive the final form of the SEP suggest internal consistency estimates of .80 or above. Furthermore, concurrent validity for a preliminary version of the SEP showed that the three dimensions had significant beta weights for predicting the five ad criteria of ad approval, agreement, disagreement, favorable predisposition, and unfavorable predisposition. Multiple Rs for these dependent variables were .92, .83, .84, .90, and .85, respectively.

Score: Mean scores for the scales were not reported in the Holbrook and Batra (1987a) article.

Source: Holbrook, Morris B. and Rajeev Batra (1987a), "Toward a Standardized Emotional Profile (SEP) Useful in Measuring Responses to the Nonverbal Components of Advertising," in *Nonverbal Communications in Advertising*, Sidney Hecker and David W. Stewart (eds.), Lexington, MA: D.C. Heath, 95-109.

Other evidence: Portions of the above analyses are also reported in Holbrook and Batra (1987b). Further evidence of the nomological validity of the SEP is also offered by Holbrook and Batra (1987b). Their Table 6 (p. 417) reveals that the ad content factors of emotional, threatening, mundane, sexy, cerebral, and personal explained 72% of the variance in pleasure, 69% of the variance in arousal, and 16% of the variance in dominance. Furthermore, when the SEP was used as a predictor of Aad and Abrand, significant beta weights for the three SEP dimensions were found (i.e., .29, .63, and - .23 in predicting Aad for pleasure, arousal, and dominance, respectively).

Other sources: Holbrook, Morris B. and Rajeev Batra (1987b), "Assessing the Role of Consumer Responses to Advertising," *Journal of Consumer Research*, 14 (December), 404-419.

References: Mehrabian, Albert and James A. Russell (1974), *An Approach to Environmental Psychology*, Cambridge, MA: The MIT Press.

Schlinger, Mary (1979), "A Profile of Responses to Commercials," *Journal of Advertising Research*, 19, 37-46.

Wells, William D. (1964), "EQ, Son of EQ, and the Reaction Profile," *Journal of Marketing*, 28 (October), 45-52.

Wells, William D., Clark Leavitt, and Maureen McConville (1971), "A Reaction Profile for TV Commercials," *Journal of Advertising Research*, 22 (December), 11-17.

STANDARDIZED EMOTIONAL PROFILE: SEP
(Holbrook and Batra 1987a)

Dimension	Subdimension	Items
Pleasure	Faith	Reverent Worshipful Spiritual
	Affection	Loving Affectionate Friendly
	Gratitude	Grateful Thankful Appreciative
Arousal	Interest	Attentive Curious Interested[a]
	Activation	Aroused Active Excited
	Surgency	Playful Entertained Lighthearted
Domination	Sadness	Sad Distressed Sorrowful
	Fear	Fearful Afraid Anxious
	Skepticism	Skeptical Suspicious Distrustful

NOTES: "a" denotes this item was added to complete the Interest subdimension.

Reprinted with the permission of Lexington Books, an imprint of MacMillan, Inc., from **Nonverbal Communication in Advertising** *by Sidney Hecker and David W. Stewart. Copyright 1988 by D. C. Heath and Company .*

VASE SCALES: SEXUAL EMBEDS IN ADVERTISING
(Widing, Hoverstad, Coulter, and Brown 1991)

Construct: These measures are designed to asses several attitudinal aspects or viewpoints regarding the use of sexual embeds in print advertisements. Six dimensions with the following definitions were derived (Widing et al. 1991, p. 4):

Moral - refers to whether the subjects feel the use of sexual embeds in ads is morally harmful to the viewer.

Objectionable - is a measure of general reaction and refers to whether subjects personally object to the use of sexual embeds in advertising.

Manipulative - refers to whether subjects find the use of sexual embeds to be manipulative of viewers' attitudes.

Controlled - refers to whether subjects find the use of sexual embeds requires tighter control.

Widespread - refers to the subject's perception about how frequently sexual embeds are used in advertising.

Tool - the subject's perception of the economic benefits of using sexual embeds in ads.

Description: The 6 dimensions are each operationalized using nine-point bipolar semantic differential formats. Three separate phrases are used to reflect each of the six factors. Subjects are requested to respond to each of the randomly dispersed 18 items following the introductory statement: "I feel the use of sex in advertising that the viewer is not intended to be consciously aware of is..." Item scores are summed within each dimension to form indices for each dimension. Thus, VASE is considered multidimensional.

Development: The specific procedures for developing the initial item pool or overall scale were not described. However, a number of reliability and validity tests were performed.

Sample(s): One hundred and seven undergraduate student subjects were used in the evaluation of the measures. Fifty-one of the sample were female.

Validity: The reliability of the six three-item dimensions was reported. Following exposure and discussion regarding several ads including sexual embeds, coefficient alpha estimates of internal consistency reliability were as follows: 0.87 (Moral), 0.84 (Objectionable), 0.79 (Manipulative), 0.89 (Controlled), 0.82 (Tool), and 0.90 (Widespread).

Some modest evidence of validity was provided by a series of correlations with measures of attitudes toward three advertisements varying in their inclusion of overt sex or sexual embeds. For example, the Objectionable scale was positively correlated with attitudes toward an "Edge" ad ($r=0.29$, $p<.05$) and a "Calvin" ad ($r=0.05$, $p< 0.05$) as expected. (See Table 11 in Widing et al 1991, p. 7.) In addition, the correlations were generally significantly different from correlations obtained between the four scales and attitudes toward an ad not containing overt sex or sexual embeds. Evidence of validity for the fifth and sixth scales (i.e., Tool and Widespread) was not provided.

Scores: Mean scores for the measures were not presented.

Source: Widing, Robert E., II, Ronald Hoverstad, Ronald Coulter, and Gene Brown (1991), "The VASE Scales: Measures of Viewpoints About Sexual Embeds in Advertising," *Journal of Business Research*, 22, 3-10.

VASE SCALES: SEXUAL EMBEDS IN ADVERTISING
(Widing, Hoverstad, Coulter, and Brown 1991)

I feel the use of sex in advertising that the viewer is not intended to be consciously aware of is...

Moral

1. Morally harmful-not at all morally harmful.
2. A cause of lower moral values-not at all a cause of lower moral values.
3. A contributor to lower sexual standards-not at all a contributor to lower sexual standards.

Objectionable

4. Very objectionable-not at all objectionable.
5. Not at all offensive-very offensive.
6. Very unethical-not at all unethical.

Manipulative

7. Very manipulative of viewers-not at all manipulative of viewers.
8. A very unfair method of persuasion-not at all an unfair method of persuasion.
9. Not at all exploitative of viewers-very exploitative of viewers.

Controlled

10. Controlled well enough-not at all controlled well enough.
11. Too loosely regulated-not at all too loosely regulated.
12. Restricted well enough-not restricted well enough.

Widespread

13. Very widespread-not at all widespread.
14. Used very frequently-used very infrequently.
15. Very common in advertising-not at all common in advertising.

Tool

16. A very effective selling tool-a very ineffective selling tool.
17. Not at all profitable-very profitable.
18. A method to increase sales-a method to decrease sales.

NOTES: Items 5, 9, 11, and 17 require reverse coding.

Reprinted with permission of the publisher from Widing, Robert E., II, Ronald Hoverstad, Ronald Coulter, and Gene Brown (1991), "The VASE Scales: Measures of Viewpoints About Sexual Embeds in Advertising," **Journal of Business Research**, *22, 3-10. Copyright 1992 by Elsevier Science Publishing Co., Inc.*

MEASURES RELATED TO AD BELIEVABILITY

TV ADVERTISING BELIEVABILITY SCALE
(Beltramini 1982)

Construct: Ad believability is viewed as the extent to which an ad is capable of evoking sufficient confidence in its truthfulness to render it acceptable to consumers (Beltramini 1982).

Description: The believability scale consists of 10 semantic differentials each operationalized using a five-place scale response format. The scale is considered applicable to ad claims across various types of products. Scores are derived by averaging over the ten items, such that higher scores reflect greater believability.

Development: A large pool of items was originally generated and then reduced to the final 10-item scale through a pretest. A large group of students (n = 584) then responded to the items for three print ads (i.e., one for tires, one for cars, and one for cigarettes). The scale was then tested for reliability and convergent validity (Beltramini 1982). (Beltramini and Evans [1985] also describe this process.)

Sample(s): A sample of 584 students was used in the development of the scale.

Validity: Coefficient alpha estimates across the three products were .94, .95, and .95 for tires, cars, and cigarettes, respectively. The high average inter-item correlations across the three products (.61, .69, and .69) offer evidence of convergent validity. Some evidence of discriminant validity was also offered by correlating the scale with a five-item distractor measure. These correlations were .43, .42, and .47 across the three products.

Scores: Mean scores for the scale across the three ads were 4.55 (sd = 1.78), 5.61 (sd = 2.08), and 6.28 (sd = 1.93) for the tires, cars, and cigarette ads, respectively.

Source: Beltramini, Richard (1982), "Advertising Perceived Believability Scale," *Proceedings of the Southwestern Marketing Association*, D. R. Corrigan, F. B. Kraft, and R. H. Ross (eds.), Southwestern Marketing Association, Wichita State University, Wichita, KS: 1-3.

Other evidence: Beltramini (1988) also used the scale to measure the variability and intensity of attitudes toward cigarette warning labels. Questionnaire booklets were administered to business students at a major American university. A total of 727 usable surveys were returned. Cronbach's alpha across four measurements (ads) ranged from .78 to .94, with an average of .90. Furthermore, those who held more firmly that smoking is harmful were found to perceive the ad claim information as significantly more believable than those who held less firmly that smoking is harmful, offering evidence of predictive validity. Mean scores and standard deviations were calculated for the four ads. These means and (standard deviations) ranged from 3.54 (1.01) to 4.30 (0.60).

Other source: Beltramini, Richard F. (1988), "Perceived Believability of Warning Label Information Presented in Cigarette Advertising," *Journal of Advertising*, 17 (1), 26-32.

References: Beltramini, Richard F. and Kenneth R. Evans (1985), "Perceived Believability of Research Results Information in Advertising, *Journal of Advertising*, 14, 18-24, 31.

TV ADVERTISING BELIEVABILITY SCALE
(Beltramini 1982)

Advertising Believability Scale

1) Unbelievable / Believable
2) Untrustworthy / Trustworthy
3) Not convincing / Convincing
4) Not credible / Credible
5) Unreasonable / Reasonable
6) Dishonest / Honest
7) Questionable / Unquestionable
8) Inconclusive / Conclusive
9) Not authentic / Authentic
10) Unlikely / Likely

EXPERTISE, TRUSTWORTHINESS, AND ATTRACTIVENESS OF CELEBRITY ENDORSERS
(Ohanian 1990)

Construct: The celebrity endorser's source credibility is posited to be characterized by three dimensions: the source's expertise, trustworthiness, and attractiveness (Ohanian 1990). In the persuasive communications literature, these three dimensions have been shown to be effective in attitude change studies. Each of the dimensions is briefly defined below:

Expertise - consistent with the work of Hovland, Janis, and Kelley (1953), Ohanian views expertise as the extent to which the communicator is perceived to be a source of valid assertions about the object/message. This includes the source's competence, expertness, and qualifications with regard to the object/message.

Trustworthiness - Also consistent with Hovland et al., trustworthiness is viewed as the degree of confidence in the communicator's intent to communicate the assertions s/he considers most valid. This includes both trust and acceptance of speaker and message.

Attractiveness - In this context, attractiveness is referred to as physical attractiveness of the source to the listener and, to a lesser extent, the emotional attractiveness of the source. This includes elements of physical beauty, sexiness, chicness, and elegance.

Description: Each dimension of source credibility is composed of five semantic differential items scored on seven-point scales. Thus, the measure is multidimensional and scores on each dimension are derived by summing the responses per items within each dimension.

Development: Development of the scale closely adhered to recommended scaling procedures. Based on definitions of the construct dimensions, 182 adjective pairs were initially generated. Based on author judgment, and a sample of 38 student judges, this initial pool was trimmed to 104 items. Then, 52 students were supplied with the definitions of the source components and eliminated those items they felt did not represent the definitions, resulting in 72 adjective pairs. Using three celebrity spokespeople and several product categories (derived from a pretest of n = 40), two samples responded to the 72 items. Via exploratory factor analysis using stringent a priori decision rules and coefficient alpha statistics, five items within each dimension with the highest item-to-total correlations were retained. The final five-item scales were then subjected to confirmatory factor analysis and MTMM analysis using another sample. Reliability and validity checks were also gathered.

Sample(s): Several samples were used throughout the scale development process. Three samples of 38, 52, and 40 students were used to judge the initial pool of items or generate celebrity names and products required for scale development. Two more samples of 250 and 240 students were used in the exploratory factor analyses to derive the final five-item scales. For the confirmatory factor analyses, two more samples of 138 and 127 nonstudents were used to examine the factor structure and further validate the scales.

Validity: Construct reliability from confirmatory factor analysis (via LISREL) showed strong internal consistency for the three subscales. These estimates were .904 and .893 for attractiveness, .895 and .896 for trustworthiness, and .885 and .892 for expertise across the samples of 138 and 127, respectively. The correlations among the factors across these two samples ranged from .319 to .621, and the hypothesized three-factor model offered the best fit to the data. In sum, the reliability and dimensionality of the scales were supported.

Numerous assessments of convergent, discriminant, and nomological validity are offered by Ohanian (1990, Table 5, p. 48). The correlations across measures used in this analysis range from .145 to .661, and offer support for the scale's validity. Also, MTMM analysis also supports the discriminant and convergent validity for the measures.

Scores: Mean or percentage scores were not reported.

Source:	Ohanian, Roobina (1990), "Construction and Validation of a Scale to Measure Celebrity Endorsers' Perceived Expertise, Trustworthiness, and Attractiveness," *Journal of Advertising*, 19, 39-52.
Other evidence:	N/A.
Other sources:	N/A.
References:	Hovland, Carl I., Irving K. Janis, and Harold H. Kelley (1963), *Communication and Persuasion*, New Haven, CT: Yale University Press.

EXPERTISE, TRUSTWORTHINESS, AND ATTRACTIVENESS OF CELEBRITY ENDORSERS
(Ohanian 1990)

Attractiveness:

1) unattractive - attractive
2) not classy - classy
3) ugly - beautiful
4) plain - elegant
5) not sexy - sexy

Trustworthiness:

6) undependable - dependable
7) dishonest - honest
8) unreliable - reliable
9) insincere - sincere
10) untrustworthy - trustworthy

Expertise:

11) not an expert - expert
12) inexperienced - experienced
13) unknowledgeable - knowledgeable
14) unqualified - qualified
15) unskilled - skilled

MEASURES RELATED TO CHILDREN'S ADVERTISING

CHILDREN'S ATTITUDES TOWARD TV COMMERCIALS
(Rossiter 1977)

Construct: The scale developed by Rossiter (1977) was designed for the purpose of providing a short, standardized test of children's attitudes toward television commercials. A range of cognitions and affective reactions toward television commercials is reflected in the scale, including (Rossiter 1977, p. 180):

(1) perceived truthfulness,
(2) potential annoying qualities,
(3) objectivity in describing advertised products,
(4) overall likability,
(5) perceived persuasive power,
(6) believability of characters, and
(7) trustworthiness as guides to product purchase.

Description: After an initial explanation of the rating system by the tester, the finalized version of the instrument is designed for self-administration. The survey consists of 7 items which represented the seven components listed above. A four-point agreement scale is used for each item because the pretest revealed this to be the maximal level of discrimination for most third graders. Since each item is scored 1 to 4, the range of the total scale is 7 to 28. Three of the items are negatively worded. The brevity of the test is commendable given that its intent is for children (i.e., it can be administered in about 5 to 10 minutes, depending on the ages of the children involved).

Development: The test of children's attitudes toward television commercials began with the generation of an initial pool of 12 attitude items which were pretested with a group of 20 third grade children. Seven items were retained for the final instrument. The items reflected the range of cognitive and affective reactions toward television commercials described above. The retained items were administered in a class setting to 208 children comprising groups of 25 to 30 children at a time. Several reliability tests were performed.

Sample(s): Following a pretest with a group of 20 third grade children, the revised attitude test was administered to a sample of 208 children, covering grades 4, 5, and 6 (ages 9 through 12) of a predominately middle class, suburban Philadelphia primary school. Approximately equal numbers of boys and girls were tested (Rossiter 1977, pp. 180-181).

Validity: Pearson's r was used to assess item intercorrelations. All but 2 were in the range between .10 and .60 and all were positive. The item-to-total correlations range from .49 to .67, indicating an even set of item-test contributions. The coefficient alpha estimate of internal consistency reliability was .69. Two correlational results for the one-month retest of the instrument were reported, using both Pearson's r and Kendall's tau. These estimates for the scale as a whole were tau = .66 and r = .67.

Scores: Mean scores were not reported in the Rossiter (1977) article.

Source: Rossiter, John R. (1977), "Reliability of a Short Test Measuring Children's Attitudes toward TV Commercials," *Journal of Consumer Research*, 3 (March), 179-184.

Other evidence: In a validation study, Bearden, Teel, and Wright (1979) used two samples drawn from separate elementary schools (grades 4 through 6). One sample was of medium to high income children (n = 76) and the other was of low income children (n = 62). Based on the replication sample (i.e., the medium-to-high income group), an alpha of 0.75 supported the internal consistency of the scale. The corrected item-test correlations ranged from 0.53 to 0.70 for the replication study, which was comparable to Rossiter's (1977) study. However, the alpha coefficient for the low income group was 0.57, which suggested that the test may have greater internal consistency for middle-income children than for lower-income children. Although the item-test correlations based on the children from the low-income school were within the range of 0.30 to 0.80, they were generally lower and more dispersed than those for the moderate-to-high income students. The test-retest Pearson correlation coefficient of 0.80 for the replication supports the test's overall reliability for medium-to-high income children.

In another study, Lindquist and Belonax (1979) used a sample of approximately 500 children selected from grades 3 through 6 to evaluate the internal consistency and test-retest reliability of the seven-item scale. Four different media were used including television, children's magazines, radio, and comic books. Minor modifications were made to the scale when gathering data on magazines, radio, and comic books. The alpha (i.e., 0.53) for the television instrument was a bit low for a standard measuring device. The alphas for the magazine and radio commercials were 0.64 and 0.66, respectively, while the comic book based alpha was 0.70. Test-retest reliability ranged from .44 to .63 across the four media.

Riecken and Samli (1981) also examined the reliability of the scale. A sample of 152 children, with ages ranging from 8 to 12, from a variety of socioeconomic backgrounds served as subjects. Also, the scale was extended to three specific product categories. In all cases, satisfactory internal consistency and moderate test-retest estimates were found. For example, Cronbach's alpha ranged from .69 to .76, and test retest ranged from .59 to .63 across three product categories.

Other sources: Bearden, William O., Jesse E. Teel and Robert R. Wright (1979), "Family Income Effects on Measurement of Children's Attitudes Toward Television Commercials," *Journal of Consumer Research*, 6 (December), 308-311.

Lindquist, Jay D. and Joseph J. Belonax, Jr. (1979), "A Reliability Evaluation of a Short Test Designed to Measure Children's Attitudes Toward Advertising in Audio-Visual and Print Media" , *Advances in Consumer Research,*, Vol. 7, Jerry C. Olson (ed.), Provo, Utah: Association for Consumer Research, 676-679.

Riecken, Glen and A. Coskun Samli (1981), "Measuring Children's Attitudes Toward Television Commercials: Extension and Replication," *Journal of Consumer Research*, 8 (June), 57-61.

References: N/A

CHILDREN'S ATTITUDES TOWARD TV COMMERCIALS
(Rossiter 1977)

INSTRUCTIONS:

PRINT YOUR NAME, SCHOOL AND GRADE HERE BEFORE YOU BEGIN.

NAME(First name) _____ (Last name) _____
SCHOOL _____ GRADE _____

WHAT DO YOU THINK OF THE COMMERCIALS ON TV? READ EACH QUESTION CAREFULLY, THEN PUT AN X ON THE LINE FOR YOUR ANSWER.

THE BOXES MEAN: YES - I agree very much
                         yes - I agree
                         no - I disagree
                         NO - I disagree very much

1. Television commercials tell the truth. (Truth)

____ YES   ____ yes   ____ no   ____ NO

2. Most TV commercials are in poor taste and very annoying. (Annoy)*

____ YES   ____ yes   ____ no   ____ NO

3. Television commercials tell only the good things about a product - they don't tell you the bad things. (Good Only)*

____ YES   ____ yes   ____ no   ____ NO

4. I like most television commercials. (Like)

____ YES   ____ yes   ____ no   ____ NO

5. Television commercials try to make people buy things they don't really need. (Persuade)*

____ YES   ____ yes   ____ no   ____ NO

6. You can always believe what the people in commercials say or do. (Believe)

____ YES   ____ yes   ____ no   ____ NO

7. The products advertised the most on TV are always the best products to buy. (Best Buy)

____ YES   ____ yes   ____ no   ____ NO

MAKE SURE YOU HAVE ANSWERED EVERY QUESTION AND THAT YOUR NAME, SCHOOL AND GRADE ARE PRINTED AT THE TOP OF THE PAGE.

NOTES: * denotes that items 2, 3, and 5 are reversed scored. The cognition measured is in parenthesis.

PRESCHOOL NONVERBAL (BRAND) ATTITUDE SCALE: PAS
(Macklin and Machleit 1990)

Construct: Based on the need for a multi-item scale for preschool children, a five-item standardized attitude scale was developed. This "Preschool Attitude Scale" (PAS) was specifically designed for measuring 3- to 5-year-old children's affective attitudes toward products with careful efforts to ensure the scale's age appropriateness. The PAS appears to achieve age-appropriateness, and indicates that young students can respond to it in a reliable and valid manner (Macklin and Machleit 1990).

Description: The final version of the scale contains five items (2 of which have male and female versions) operationalized by placing five visual scale points per item on 14" X 5 1/2" poster boards. In addition, descriptors were used with each pictorial scale item. Items scores can be summed to form an overall index and the scale is considered unidimensional. Overall, the PAS presents visual items, requires nonverbal (pointing) responses, and is child-friendly due to its game-like procedure.

Development: This investigation was divided into four phases. Phase 1 (n=91) was a feasibility study. Phase 2 (n=38) and Phase 3 (n=61) were directed at refinements of the measure and of the procedures for administration, and Phase 4 (n=61) confirmed the results with respect to scale usefulness. In the scale development process, the authors incorporated items similar to the ones that are commonly used in industry (Harrigan and Benzinger 1988) and created several of their own. Originally, seven scale items were developed by placing five visual scale points per item on 14" by 5 1/2" poster boards. Additionally, oral descriptors which were within a child's vocabulary were used with each pictorial scale item. In the first phase of the study, the feasibility of using the measures was assessed. Specifically, the reliability and factor structure of the scale were evaluated. Furthermore, the physical appearance of the scale (horizontal versus vertical scale presentation) was considered (Macklin and Machleit 1990, p. 254). Phase 2 was designed to repeat the Phase 1 study. Also, the scale's ability to stand up to more difficult tasks was assessed. Two of the original seven items (i.e., the reversed scored items) were eliminated in this phase. The purpose of Phase 3 was three-fold. First, the dimensionality of the scale without using reverse coded items was assessed. Second, a training session was included in the administration procedure in an effort to help children understand the more subtle distinctions among the points on the scale. Third, three brands within a different product category were evaluated. The purpose of Phase 4 was to address the question, "Does the scale-item basis versus 'product basis' administration procedure make a difference in reliability and predictive validity?" Five scale items were retained in the final version of PAS. As stated above, numerous reliability, dimensionality and validity checks were performed across the phases.

Sample(s): A total of 251 children (ages 3 to 5 years with a relatively equal breakdown across gender) were individually interviewed during the multi-phase project (n = 91, 61, 61, and 38 for Phases 1 though 4, respectively).

Validity: Though reliability and validity estimates were reported throughout all four phases, we will concentrate on the final 2 phases (i.e., the final form of the scale). In Phases 3 and 4, the scale consistently exhibited a unidimensional factor structure. In Phase 3, coefficient alpha values were high for each of the three brands of candy rated by the children (0.94, 0.91, and 0.92). In Phase 4, coefficient alphas ranged from 0.96 to 0.97 across three candy bars rated. Also in Phases 3 and 4, mean differences via MANOVA showed evidence of predictive validity for the scale. Specifically, mean scores were significantly different among candy bars rated as the children's 1st, 2nd, and 3rd choices.

Scores: Mean attitude scores are reported in Table 2 of the Macklin and Machleit (1990, p. 263) article for both the multi-item PAS and the univariate scale items to facilitate comparison. The overall mean scores for the first, second, and third choice of candies in Phase 3 were 23.60, 20.77, and 16.73, respectively. Mean scores for the first, second, and third choice of candies in Phase 4 were 24.48, 21.88, and 20.10, respectively.

Source: Macklin, M. Carole and Karen A. Machleit (1990), "Measuring Preschool Children's Attitude," *Marketing Letters*, 1 (3), 253-265.

Other evidence: N/A

Other sources: N/A

References: Harrigan, Judy and Peter Benzinger (1988), "Children's Research: Where It's Been, Where It Is Going," *Transcript Proceedings Second Bi-Annual ARF Workshop on Childrens Research*, New York: Advertising Research Foundation, 5-21.

PRESCHOOL NONVERBAL (BRAND) ATTITUDE SCALE: PAS
(Macklin and Machleit 1990)

Oral Descriptors:

	5	4	3	2	1
Happy Faces	real happy	somewhat happy	not happy nor sad	a little bit sad	real sad
Big Star	like a whole lot	like somewhat	like a little bit	don't like a little	don't like at all
Multiple Stars	great	a little bit great	so-so	a little bit terrible	terrible
Smiley	like a lot	like some	like a little	don't like much	don't like at all
Jump	very exciting	somewhat exciting	a little exciting	not very exciting	not at all exciting

NOTES: Pictorial scale items were mounted on 14" by 5 1/2" poster boards. Scale points are articulated orally by the scale's administrator. Training instructions are available on page 264 of the Macklin and Machleit (1990) article. For "smiley faces" and "jump," both male and female pictorial versions are required.

THE PICTORIAL SCALES ARE NOT REPRODUCED HERE. THE PROSPECTIVE USER SHOULD CONSULT THE SOURCE FOR THESE SCALES (cf., Macklin and Machleit 1990, p. 264).

SOURCES FOR CHAPTER 5

Beltramini, R.F. (1982), "Advertising Perceived Believability Scale," *Proceedings of the Southwestern Marketing Association*, D. R. Corrigan, F. B. Kraft, and R. H. Ross (eds.), Southwestern Marketing Association, Wichita State University, Wichita, KS: 1-3; Figure 1, p. 1.

Edell, Julie A. and Marian Chapman Burke (1987), "The Power of Feelings in Understanding Advertising Effects," *Journal of Consumer Research*, 14 (December), 421-433; Table 1, p. 424.

Holbrook, Morris B and Rajeev Batra (1987), "Toward a Standardized Emotional Profile (SEP) Useful in Measuring Responses to the Nonverbal Components of Advertising," in *Nonverbal Communications in Advertising*, Sidney Hecker and David W. Stewart (eds), Lexington, MA: D. C. Heath, 95-109; Table 7-6, p. 108.

Lastovicka, John L. (1983), "Convergent and Discriminant Validity of Television Commercial Rating Scales," *Journal of Advertising*, 12 (2), 14-23; Table 2, p. 17.

Leavitt, C. (1970), "A Multidimensional Set of Rating Scales for Television Commercials," *Journal of Applied Psychology*, 54, 427-9; Table 1, p. 428.

Macklin, M. Carole and Karen A. Machleit (1990), "Measuring Preschool Children's Attitude," *Marketing Letters*, 1 (3), 253-265; Appendix, p. 264.

Ohanian, Roobina (1990), "Construction and Validation of a Scale to Measure Celebrity Endorsers' Perceived Expertise, Trustworthiness, and Attractiveness," *Journal of Advertising*, 19, 39-52; Appendix, p. 50.

Puto, Christopher P. and William D. Wells (1984), "Informational and Transformational Advertising: The Differential Effects of Time," in *Advances in Consumer Research*, Vol. 11, Thomas C. Kinnear (ed.), Provo, UT: Association for Consumer Research, 638-643; Table 1, p. 641.

Rossiter, John R. (1977), "Reliability of a Short Test Measuring Children's Attitudes toward TV Commercials," *Journal of Consumer Research*, 3 (March), 179-184; Appendix, p. 183.

Schlinger, Mary J. (1979), "A Profile of Responses to Commercials," *Journal of Advertising Research*, 19 (April), 37-46; Table 1, p. 40.

Wells, William D. (1964), "EQ, Son of EQ, and the Reaction Profile," *Journal of Marketing*, 28 (October), 45-52; Table 1, p. 46, Table 3, p. 48, Table 5, p. 49, and Table 6, p. 50.

Widing, Robert E., II, Ronald Hoverstad, Ronald Coulter, and Gene Brown (1991), "The VASE Scales: Measures of Viewpoints About Sexual Embeds in Advertising," *Journal of Business Research*, 22, 3-10, p. 4.

6

Attitudes About the Performance of Business Firms, Social Agencies, and the Marketplace

CONSUMER ATTITUDES TOWARD BUSINESS PRACTICES

SOCIAL RESPONSIBILITY SCALE FOR MARKETING PERSONNEL
(Peters 1972)

Construct: A marketing decision-maker scoring high in social responsibility is hypothesized to possess four characteristics: (1) concern for his/her firm's practice on the end user; (2) honesty; (3) consistency in social responsibility in all areas of life; and, (4) concern for social responsibility beyond the need for immediate return to his or her company. This conceptual definition centers upon the inner orientation of the individual in terms of business ethics and altruism (i.e., concern for the protection and welfare of the customer) (Peters 1972, p. 225).

Description: The scale consists of 26 statements each operationalized using five-place bipolar scales labeled "strongly disagree" to "strongly agree." (There is some indication that the items might have been seven-place scales.) Approximately half of the statements require reverse coding. The dimensions were described as related, and, thus, items scores are summed to represent a total social responsibility score.

Development: An initial pool of 100 items was reduced to a set of 38 items based upon an analysis of the content validity of the items by two expert judges. The 38 items were reduced to the final scale of 26 items "based upon Beta values for high intensity" (Peters 1972, p. 226).

Sample(s):   The results from two samples were described by Peters (1972). These samples included 77 business administration graduate students from the University of Wisconsin and 21 staff members of a corporate marketing department.

Validity: The author described this research as a pilot test. Hence, extensive evidence of validity was not provided. The scale did discriminate, however, between individuals scoring high and low in social responsibility as judged by their peers (i.e., other student team members and/or other executives). An initial reliability estimate of 0.73 was reported for the 38 items.

231

Scores:	The mean score for the 77 students was 104.6 (range 80-128, standard deviation = 11.0) compared to a mean of 104.5 (range 79-121, standard deviation = 10.3) for the 21 marketing executives (Peters 1972, p. 228).
Source:	Peters, William H. (1972), "Social Responsibility in Marketing Personnel: Meaning and Measurement," in Helmut Becker (ed.), *Proceedings of American Marketing Association Educators' Conference*, Chicago: American Marketing Association, 224-229.
Other evidence:	N/A.
Other sources:	N/A.
References:	N/A.

SOCIAL RESPONSIBILITY SCALE FOR MARKETING PERSONNEL
(Peters 1972)

1. To maximize profits should be the single most important goal of business. (Disagree)

2. The federal regulations concerning packaging of consumer products are anti-business and nothing like them should have been passed by Congress. (Disagree)

3. I would probably quit a company that I felt was unethical in the way they promoted their product. (Agree)

4. We have a long way to go before most companies routinely take the consumer's welfare into consideration when making marketing decisions. (Agree)

5. I am not concerned about the decisions my company makes when I know that I can do nothing to change them.* (Disagree)

6. Business is an institution of society and therefore the problems of society should also be important problems for business to help solve even if there is no immediate monetary reward for the efforts. (Agree)

7. Program content of T.V. should be mostly under the control of the advertiser. (Disagree)

8. One should not be unduly critical of one's company. After all, everybody tries his best in his own way. (Disagree)

9. There is no real reason to worry about the effects on the public of what is known as "legitimate puffery" in advertising and sales promotion materials. (Disagree)

10. It is the proper role of government to make regulations involving the quality and the promotion of products developed and sold by private industry. (Agree)

11. I often wonder if we are giving the consumer the kind of product they should have.* (Agree)

12. I do not understand people like Ralph Nader, who are always out to make trouble for us. They should leave us alone. After all, business usually does the right thing by the consumer. (Disagree)

13. It is probably best for our society in the long run, if consumer organizations are established and do represent the interests of the consumer before the government and the courts. (Agree)

14. There is basically nothing wrong with using the "buyer beware" concept as a guiding philosophy in one's product development program in industry. (Disagree)

15. I do not think it is basically wrong for a bank to advertise, without qualification, that it is in the best interests of the people to put their money in one of the bank's savings accounts that pays 4 1/2 percent annual interest rate when the rate of inflation in the country is 6 percent. (Disagree)

16. I think it is wrong for a company to encourage the consumer to use more of its product than is needed. (Disagree)

17. There is nothing wrong in a student occasionally cheating on an examination. (Disagree)

18. It is all right if an advertisement implies that your company's product is better than it actually is as long as the ad's copy does not lie outright or break the law. (Disagree)

19. It is not proper to distort evidence about a product's usefulness by quoting the information out of context. (Agree)

20. Generally speaking, I think that students who protest and demonstrate on campus should be expelled from school. (Disagree)

21. I feel that a man's only major responsibility to his family is to provide well for them. (Disagree)

22. I do not feel that a married woman's place has to be in the home. (Agree)

23. Generally speaking, I do not favor the type of fellow who compromises easily so that things will go smoothly. (Agree)

24. The only reason I care what the consumer thinks and wants is because that it is the way to please him and get a bigger share of the market. (Disagree)

25. A good dictator is one who is on our side. (Disagree)

26. The main reason a company should actively take care about the effects of its marketing strategy decisions upon the public's welfare is because this makes for good public relations which in turn makes for more sales. (Disagree)

NOTES: The items are related to the four dimensions or characteristics as follows: concern for the firm's practices 1-13; honesty 14-19; consistency in social responsibility 20-21; and concern for social responsibility beyond need 23-26.

            * denotes items that were slightly modified to be appropriate for a student sample. Items agreed with (Agree) denote a higher level of social responsibility. Items with (Disagree) at the end require recoding

PUBLIC ATTITUDES REGARDING WELFARE PROGRAMS: THE ACCEPTANCE OF WELFARE SCALE
(Ahmed and Jackson 1979)

Construct: Acceptance of welfare is defined as a higher order construct consisting of five facets (Ahmed and Jackson 1979, p. 232):

Independence from government—a desire to be free from government interference in personal, social, and economic activity versus a belief in the value and importance of government responsibilities for health, welfare, and economic well-being.

Morality of welfare—a general sentiment that government participation in welfare is morally justified and beneficial versus the sentiment that welfare is ethically wrong both for the recipient and government.

Nurturance—a personality trait and value relating to the importance of helping the needy, deprived and unfortunate.

Work ethic—a belief in the morality of work as an end in itself.

Altruism—the acceptance of generalized responsibility to help, to share, and to be generous toward one's fellow human beings.

Description: The total scale consists of 40 items each operationalized using five-place agree-disagree response formats. Eight items (each reflecting four positive and four negatively worded statements) are representative of each of the five factors. The analyses suggest that both the total acceptance of welfare scale and the individual factors (e.g., independence from government) are appropriate for use. Item scores can be summed overall or within factors.

Development: An initial pool of approximately 400 items was developed (i.e., taken and adapted if necessary) to reflect the various issues involved. Items were taken from previous surveys, attitude scales, and personality measures. Item selection for inclusion in the final scale included relevance to scale definition, judged ability to elicit both "anti-" and "pro-" responses, judged freedom from acquiescence bias, and perceived applicability to all age, cultural, and socioeconomic groups (Ahmed and Jackson 1979, p. 233). The final scale was double translated from French to English and vice-versa.

Sample(s):   The scale presentation and subsequent tests was based upon the responses of a national sample of 931 Canadian residents surveyed in 1975. Four hundred and twenty-four of the participants were male; 194 of the sample were interviewed in French. The average family income was $11,600.

Validity: The estimate of internal consistency reliability for the total scale was 0.85. Similar reliability estimates for the individual factor scales were as follows: (1) independence from government, 0.72; (2) morality of welfare, 0.62; (3) nurturance, 0.66; (4) work ethic, 0.51; and altruism, 0.68. Correlations among the factors revealed considerable common variance among the factors. Low correlations with a measure of response bias revealed that "response bias was not a problem with these measures" (Ahmed and Jackson 1979, 235). Correlations among the five factors and a general measure of acceptance of welfare ranged from .48 (work ethic) to .83 (independence from government), offering evidence of convergent validity. Some group differences were also observed. For example, individuals residing in the Western provinces were less favorable toward programs than their Eastern resident counterparts. Attitudes toward welfare were found independent of marital status, gender, age, education and income. The five factor subscales were also correlated with opinions regarding a series of welfare issues obtained earlier through another survey of the same respondents. These results (while not described in detail) were said to be supportive of the validity of the measures. For example, the altruism scale was most strongly correlated with willingness to accept a tax increase while nurturance was most strongly correlated with willingness to provide welfare assistance. In general, the strongest relationships were said to be associated with the government scale.

Scores:	Only individual item mean scores were reported by Ahmed and Jackson (1979). See Table 2 (pp. 243-235).
Source:	Ahmed, Sadrudin A. and Douglas N. Jackson (1979), "Psychographics for Social Policy Decisions: Welfare Assistance," *Journal of Consumer Research*, 5 (March), 229-239.
Other evidence:	N/A.
Other sources:	N/A.
References:	N/A.

PUBLIC ATTITUDES REGARDING WELFARE PROGRAMS: THE ACCEPTANCE OF WELFARE SCALE
(Ahmed and Jackson 1979)

Independence from Government

1) People should solve their own problems and not have to depend on government help.

2) People should not need the government to help them.

3) The government should not spend money on medical and dental care for low-income groups.

4) Government welfare programs should be cut back because they restrict people's freedom.

5) Retraining unemployed people is an important responsibility of the government.

6) People like deserted wives and children deserve increased support from government.

7) The government should see that every Canadian enjoys the basic necessities of life.

8) The government should speed up its plan to take care of the needy.

Morality of Welfare

1) People who accept welfare for a long time become unable to hold a job.

2) Receiving welfare makes people feel worthless.

3) It is wrong to give people payments when they haven't worked for them.

4) Only a person with no self-respect would accept public assistance.

5) One of the most important government services is to provide public assistance.

6) Welfare is necessary for those who cannot work, like the handicapped.

7) Government spending on welfare is money well spent.

8) Public assistance helps make the poor more productive members of our society.

Nurturance

1) Helping troubled people cope with their problems is very important to me.

2) People in need deserve our sympathy and support.

3) Someone who is disabled will get my attention and aid.

4) People can always count on me for help.

5) If someone is in trouble, it is best not to get involved.

6) It is a waste of time feeling sorry for the poor.

7) Giving sympathy and comfort to people serves no useful purpose.

8) Trying to help the needy often does more harm than good

Work Ethic

1) If a person is willing to work hard, there is no reason why he should not succeed.

2) I have no sympathy for people who are able to work but choose not to work.

3) A job of any kind, even if the pay is poor, is better than having to be supported.

4) A person deserves to get only things he has worked for.

5) I can understand why a person would choose to live on welfare rather than work.

6) I think that people put too much emphasis on the value of work.

7) I often think that a job keeps a person from getting the most out of life.

8) Hard work is no longer essential for the well-being of society.

Altruism

1) People should pay taxes gladly, because the money goes for good causes.

2) People who have enough for themselves have a responsibility to provide for the needy.

3) Everyone should contribute generously to help those less fortunate.

4) I believe in giving generously to needy organizations.

5) Most charitable organizations are dishonest.

6) Money spent on welfare would be better used to lower taxes.

7) Most of the money given to the poor is wasted.

8) I don't believe in giving anything away for nothing.

NOTES: To reflect a greater acceptance of welfare, items 1-4 of the "independence from government" factor, items 1-4 of the morality of welfare" factor, and items 1-4 of the "work ethic" factor require reverse coding. Items 5-8 of the "nurturance" and "altruism" factors also require reverse coding to reflect a greater acceptance of welfare.

ATTITUDES OF CONSUMERS AND BUSINESS PEOPLE TOWARD CONSUMERISM
(Klein 1982)

Construct: The following measures are designed to assess general attitudes of both business people and consumers toward consumerism issues. The scales were designed to be applicable for research on both U.S. and Swedish subjects, including both business executives and consumers. The initial consumerism issues around which items were first constructed included the following: environmental issues; advertising and promotion; product testing; consumer education; control and regulation; warranty and service; and public responsibility (Klein 1982, p. 124). Some caution is urged prior to the unquestioned use of the measures described here. Little evidence of reliability and external validation was provided.

Description: The final instrument consists of 20 items reflecting six factors. The factor labels along with the number of statements comprising each factor are as follows: 1) most businesses are concerned about and responsive to consumers—5; 2) consumers need protection and education to compete effectively with business—4; 3) generally the quality of products has been decreasing—3; 4) our business system is more efficient than that of most other countries—3; 5) packaging today is essentially honest—2; and 6) business is primarily self-serving in nature—3. Six-point, Likert-type rating scales (without a neutral position) were used to operationalize each statement. Respondents are required to indicate their degree of agreement or disagreement with each statement using "strongly disagree" — "strongly agree" bipolar adjective sets. Though not specified, it seems summing overall items to obtain an overall score, and summing items within factors, is appropriate.

Development: The initial pool of items was developed from a review of related measures and a brainstorming session. The questionnaire used in the preliminary stages of development included 113 items. Student interviewers from California State University, Long Beach, were used to collect pretest data from samples of 213 and 50 consumers and business persons, respectively. The items were factor analyzed using orthogonal, varimax rotation. Items were retained based upon common meaning (within each factor) and loadings above 0.50 (Klein 1982). A final version to be used in eventual scale development consisted of 42 items. (See the Appendix [Klein 1982].) These 42 items were selected from the pretest results, item-to-total correlations, and consultation with Swedish researchers involved in the project. Data were collected for the 42-item version from 204 Swedish residents and 243 Long Beach residents in 1979. In addition, data were obtained from business samples of 55 and 75 Swedish and American firms, respectively. Uppsala, Sweden, was selected based upon its demographic and geographic similarity to Long Beach, California. Factor analysis of these data was used as the primary means of constructing the final 20-item instrument. Only those items loading similarly in both cultures were included in the final scale(s) (Klein 1982, p. 130).

Sample(s): The first administration (i.e., the pretest) (of the 113 items) obtained responses from 213 consumers across varying social classes (i.e., upper, middle, and working classes) and census tract divisions in both the U.S. and Swedish data collections. In all cases, an attempt was made to collect data from an equal number of male and female consumers. An additional 50 responses were obtained from local business executives. Data were obtained also from 204 Uppsala residents and 243 Long Beach residents in 1979. For the Swedish sample, fifty-seven percent were female, forty percent had no college education, and fifty-eight percent were below 35 years of age. For the American respondents, fifty-percent were female, forty-eight percent had no college work, and thirty-three percent were under 35 years of age. Comparable data from 55 Swedish and 75 U.S. business persons were obtained as well.

Validity: No evidence beyond the face validity of the items and the stated consistency of factor analysis results between cultures was provided for the scale.

Scores: Neither total scale, factor, nor item mean scores were provided.

Source: Klein, Gary D. (1982), "Development of a Cross-Cultural Instrument to Measure the Attitudes of Consumers and Business People toward Consumerism," *Journal of Marketing and Public Policy*, 1, 123-137.

**Other
evidence:** N/A.

**Other
sources:** N/A.

References: N/A.

ATTITUDES OF CONSUMERS AND BUSINESS PEOPLE TOWARD CONSUMERISM
(Klein 1982)

Most business is concerned about and responsive to consumers.

(3)   Most business firms make a sincere effort to help displeased customers.

(12) Most manufacturers really want to fulfill warranty obligations.

(22) In general, business firms usually accept responsibility for their products and guarantees.

(35) When consumers have problems with products they have purchased, it is usually easy to get them corrected.

(38) Most companies' complaint departments back up their products and effectively handle consumer problems.

Consumers need protection and education to compete effectively with business.

(2)   The government should set minimum standards of quality for all products sold to the consumer.

(6)   More frequent health and safety warnings on packages are necessary to adequately inform the consumer of possible dangers.

(7)   Business should be legally liable for the pollution it or its products cause.

(8)   Consumer education should be a required portion of a manufacturer's advertising budget.

Generally, the quality of products has been decreasing.

(21) Products that last a long time are a thing of the past.

(29) In general, the quality of repairs and maintenance service provided by manufacturers is getting worse.

(40) In general, I am dissatisfied with the quality of most products today.

Our business system is more efficient than that of most other countries.

(4)   Consumers in the (U.S./Sweden) are much more protected by government regulation than in most other countries.

(13) (American/Swedish)-made products are less dangerous than those of most other countries.

(33) The (American/Swedish) business system operates more efficiently than that of most other countries.

Packaging today is essentially honest.

(16) What is seen on the outside of a package is often not what you get on the inside.

(26) Package sizes show in a correct way the amount of product contained inside.

Business is primarily self-serving in nature.

(5)   All business really wants to do is make the most money it can.

(25) The main reason a company is socially responsible is to make more sales.

(34) Companies try to influence the government to better their own standing.

NOTE: Item numbers are as they appeared in the original article. To reflect a more positive view toward consumerism, items 21, 29, 40, and 16 require reverse coding.

ATTITUDES TOWARD THE SOCIAL ROLE OF CORPORATIONS
(Williams 1982)

Construct: An individual's attitude toward the social role of corporations was defined as a three dimensional construct involving opinions: (1) about the corporation as a public institution versus beliefs that corporations have predominantly individual rights; (2) regarding whether or not the actions of the corporation should be guided by personal conscience (intuition) or social responsibility (rationality); and (3) about the legitimacy of outside policymakers to influence the policies and goals of corporations.

Description: The scale consists of 23 items each operationalized using five-place scales ranging from "strongly disagree" to "strongly agree." Items scores can be summed for an overall index, or summed within factors for factor indices.

Development: A total of 45 statements was included in the original battery of items. A random ordering of the statements was administered to a sample of 145 business students. Within-dimension item-to-total correlations employing a 0.40 cutoff were used to delete items. In addition, several items with low factor loadings following the item-to-total tests were also deleted. However, the resulting subscales did not correspond to the conceptual dimensionality of 3 factors. In fact, 7 factors were retained. Estimates of test-retest reliability and predictive validity were also obtained.

Sample(s): The initial development of the scale was conducted using 145 business students. Sixty-one students participated in a subsequent study involving the evaluation of social data. Forty-seven students were involved in a test-retest administration.

Validity: Test-retest estimates for the original set of 45 items ranged from 0.60 to 0.75 (most items were from 0.3 to 0.7). Similar estimates for the subscales ranged from 0.40 to 0.79. Little additional information was provided. Twenty-eight percent of the variation in perceptions of the relevance of social data was explained by a regression equation using the seven subscales as independent predictors, offering evidence for the scale's predictive validity.

Scores: Mean scores were not provided for either individual factors or the total scale.

Source: Williams, Paul F. (1982), "Attitudes toward the Corporation and the Evaluation of Social Data," *Journal of Business Research*, 10, 119-131.

Other evidence: N/A.

Other sources: N/A.

References: N/A.

ATTITUDES TOWARD THE SOCIAL ROLE OF CORPORATIONS
(Williams 1982)

1. A large corporation is like a university because both have as their central purpose serving the public interest.

2. The role of the president of a firm like Eastman-Kodak is that of a public servant.

3. The management of a corporation is responsible to many definable interests in society.

4. There exist higher laws, not related to human legislation, which may be discovered by intuition.

5. The internal conduct of business affairs is not a matter for public involvement.

6. Corporations should have as much right to engage in political activity as any other private citizen.

7. The purpose of the corporation can be quite simply summarized as service to society.

8. Representatives of the public, as well as management, should have significant roles in determining the conduct of business affairs.

9. The management of a corporation should do more than the law requires in its concerns with the social impacts of its actions.

10. Right and wrong conduct for business corporations can be meaningfully defined only by the law.

11. A law should be disobeyed when it conflicts with the dictates of one's conscience.

12. Standards for corporate performance must be left to the determination of management.

13. Concern for the welfare of others should be the principle that guides an individual's conduct.

14. Standards for corporate performance come legitimately from the public.

15. The large business corporation should be considered to have the same freedom as do individuals.

16. In doing business, the management of a corporation should do no more than is required by law.

17. Management should be the sole determinant of a corporation's objectives.

18. In all situations, one must accept the authority of the law.

19. It is not appropriate that representatives for the public interest be included on the boards of directors of large corporations.

20. Conscience is a better guide to a manager's actions than whatever the law might say.

21. Since most people are dependent on private industry for employment, corporations should be willing to sacrifice some efficiency in order to provide jobs.

22. Empathy, the ability to walk a mile in the other guy's shoes, is what assures a just society.

23.. A business corporation is just like any other corporation.

NOTES: The items are distributed across the dimensions as follows: public - 1, 2, 3, 7; private - 6, 15, 23; intuitive - 4, 9, 11, 20; rational - 10, 16, 18; management - 5, 12, 17, 19; outsiders - 8, 14; compassion - 13, 21, 22.

Information about statements requiring recoding was not provided. However, Williams (1982, p. 122) states that only items with positive loadings were included.

Reprinted by permission of the publisher from Williams, Paul F. (1982), "Attitudes toward the Corporation and the Evaluation of Social Data," Journal of Business Research, 10, 119-131. Copyright 1992 by Elsevier Science Publishing Co., Inc.

CONSUMER SATISFACTION WITH SOCIAL SERVICES
(Reid and Gundlach 1984)

Construct: This research attempts to develop a scale for the measurement of consumer satisfaction with social services, i.e., the development of a consumer satisfaction scale of general utility. The measure purports to reflect the elements of social service provisions that influence consumer satisfaction. Overall, the items reflect provisions related to satisfaction judgments derived from three attributes:

Relevance - the extent to which a service corresponds to the individual's perception of his or her problem needs.

Impact - the extent to which the service reduces the problem experienced by the client.

Gratification - the extent to which the service enhances the individual's self-esteem and sense of integrity.

Description: The final scale is comprised of 34 items reflecting three related subfactors. The dimensions and the corresponding number of items are as follows: (1) relevance, 11 items; (2) impact, 10 items; and (3) gratitude, 13 items. Item wording is varied to inhibit acquiescence bias. Each item is scored from 1 to 5. Total and individual factor scores reflect averages across the number of items involved in each subscale or the total scale. Consequently, the total scale and each subscale range from 1 to 5. A disagree-agree response format was used to operationalize the individual items.

Development: Based upon the experience of the authors and questions suggested in related research, a pool of thirty-five items (see Table 1) (Reid and Gundlach 1984, pp. 44-46) was developed. Again, these items were designed to reflect the three attributes of service provision described above. Coefficient alpha estimates of reliability were used to examine the total scale and each of the three subscales. One item (i.e., #19) was dropped based upon the reliability analyses.

Sample(s): The initial study involved the responses of 166 heads of households of families involved with a Head Start program in Jackson, Michigan. The respondents were predominantly female (81.3 percent). In addition, most of the respondents reported little education and low family incomes. Utilization data revealed that the subjects were heavy users of various social services.

Validity: The pairwise correlations among the three subscales ranged from 0.75 to 0.84. Guttman lambda estimates of reliability for the total scale and the three subscales of relevance, impact, and gratification were .96, .88, .82, and .86, respectively.

Some evidence of validity (other than the content of the items themselves) was provided by differences in scores across sample subgroups and analysis of relationships with certain program related variables. These results are summarized in Tables 3 and 4 of Reid and Gundlach (1983). For example, higher satisfaction scores were obtained for white respondents, while lower scores were found for single and/or divorced respondents. Lower scores were generally observed for the unemployed. Interestingly, satisfaction seemed to have an inverse relationship to program importance with lower than mean scores being associated with the Department of Social Services and Medicaid, i.e., the two services ranked most highly in terms of importance.

Scores: The total scale had a mean and standard deviation of 3.22 and 0.54, respectively. The relevance and impact factors had means of 3.35 and 3.20. The mean for the gratitude factor was 3.14.

Source: Reid, P. Nelson and James H. Gundlach (1984), "A Scale for the Measurement of Consumer Satisfaction with Social Services," *Journal of Social Service Research*, 7 (1), 37-54.

Other evidence: N/A.

Other sources: N/A.

References: N/A.

CONSUMER SATISFACTION WITH SOCIAL SERVICES
(Reid and Gundlach 1984)

Relevance Items

1. The social worker took my problems very seriously. (+)

2. If I had been the social worker, I would have dealt with my problems in just the same way. (+)

3. The worker I had could never understand anyone like me. (-)

4. Overall, the agency has been very helpful to me. (+)

5. If a friend of mine had similar problems, I would tell them to go to the agency. (+)

6. The social worker asks a lot of embarrassing questions. (-)

7. I can always count on the worker to help if I'm in trouble. (+)

8. The social agency will help me as much as they can. (+)

9. I don't think the agency has the power to really help me. (-)

10. The social worker tries hard but usually isn't too helpful. (-)

11. The problem the agency tried to help me with is one of the most important in my life. (+)

Impact Items

12. Things have gotten better since I have been going to the agency. (+)

13. Since I've been using the agency my life is more messed up than ever. (-)

14. The agency is always available when I need it. (+)

15. I got from the agency exactly what I wanted. (+)

16. The social worker loves to talk but won't really do anything for me. (-)

17. Sometimes I just tell the social worker what I think she wants to hear. (-)

18. The social worker is usually in a hurry when I see her. (-)

19. I went to the agency with one problem but they ended up helping me on another. (-)

20. No one should have any trouble getting some help from this agency. (+)

21. The worker sometimes says things I don't understand. (-)

22. The social workers are always explaining things carefully. (+)

Gratitude Items

23. I never looked forward to my visits to the social agency. (-)

24. I hope I'll never have to go back to the agency for help. (-)

25. Every time I talk to my worker I feel relieved. (+)

26. I can tell the social worker the truth without worrying. (+)

27. I usually feel nervous when I talk to my worker. (-)

28. The social worker is always looking for lies in what I tell her. (-)

29. It takes a lot of courage to go to the agency. (-)

30. When I enter the agency, I feel very small and insignificant. (-)

31. The agency is very demanding. (-)

32. The social worker will sometimes lie to me. (-)

33. Generally, the social worker is an honest person. (+)

34. I have the feeling that the worker talks to other people about me. (-)

35. I always feel well treated when I leave the social agency. (+)

NOTES: (-) denotes items that are negatively coded; (+) denotes items that are positively coded.

THE INDEX OF CONSUMER SENTIMENT TOWARD MARKETING
(Gaski and Etzel 1986)

Construct: This measure represents an index of consumer sentiment toward marketing practices. The measure is designed to provide a continuing "barometer of how marketing is doing in the eyes of the consumer public" (Gaski and Etzel 1986, p. 72). The index is offered for several reasons: (1) it may sensitize marketers to consumers' perceptions; (2) it would serve to identify the nature of public relations tasks facing marketing; (3) it should assist in gauging whatever progress is or is not being made; and (4) it may demonstrate marketer concern for public opinion. The measure is designed to reflect composite opinion about *four* aspects of marketing corresponding roughly to the four elements of the marketing mix: (1) product quality; (2) the prices of products; (3) advertising; and (4) retailing or selling.

Description: Each of the four factors is represented by five Likert agree-disagree items which range from -2 to +2. The scale positions are labeled as follows: (1) agree strongly, (2) agree somewhat (3) neither agree nor disagree, (4) disagree somewhat, and (5) disagree strongly. After recoding the items such that higher scores reflect more positive opinions, items from each factor are summed and then weighted from 1 (not at all important) to 5 (extremely important). The range of the index is -200 to +200. The index is computed as: sum[w(j) sumx(ij)] where j represents one of the four categories and w(j) represents the weight for that category. Thus, though multidimensional, an overall index is derived.

Development: An initial pool of items was developed by the authors in consultation with Market Facts, Inc. personnel. Two items from each factor with low item-to-total correlations were deleted. Data from 50 pretest subjects were used in these purification efforts. The scale was further tested via factor analysis, coefficient alpha, and validity. (Pretest versions of the scale are reported in Gaski and Etzel [1985].)

Sample(s): The original pool of items (see Gaski and Etzel [1986]) was purified using a pretest sample of 50 subjects from the Consumer Mail Panel of Market Facts, Inc. Data is now being collected annually from a sample of 2,000 members of the Market Facts Panel (n=200,000). The first survey reported in Gaski and Etzel (1986) involved responses from 1,428 individuals to the initial mailing. The panel is designed to reflect U.S. Census data in terms of geographic region, annual income, population density, age, sex, and family size.

Validity: A series of tests was performed in efforts to examine the validity of the Index using the responses to the first panel mailing (n=1,428). Estimates of internal consistency reliability ranged from 0.76 to 0.82. All within factor item-to-total correlations exceeded 0.48. Evidence of discriminant validity was provided by comparisons of the reliability estimates with the factor correlations. The results from principal axis factor analysis with oblique rotation revealed a factor structure consistent with the item content for each of the four factors. Significant evidence of convergent validation was provided by a series of correlations of the Consumer Sentiment Index with overall global impressions (r=0.63), satisfaction (r=0.73), and problems (r=0.63). (These items are also shown in the Appendix in Gaski and Etzel [1986].)

Scores: The mean consumer sentiment score for the first national sample was -14.85 (i.e., slightly in the unfavorable range). The mean attitude score was -12.36 for women and -17.71 for men (t=2.08, p<.05).

Source: Gaski, John F. and Michael J. Etzel (1986), "The Index of Consumer Sentiment Toward Marketing," *Journal of Marketing*, 50 (July), 71-81.

Other evidence: N/A.

Other sources: N/A.

References: Gaski, John F. and Michael J. Etzel (1985), "A Proposal for a Global, Longitudinal Measure of National Consumer Sentiment Toward Marketing Practice," in *Advances in Consumer Research, Vol. 12*, Elizabeth C. Hirschman and Morris B. Holbrook (eds.), Provo, UT: Association for Consumer Research, 65-70.

THE INDEX OF CONSUMER SENTIMENT TOWARD MARKETING
(Gaski and Etzel 1986)

Product Scale

1. I am satisfied with most of the products I buy.
2. Most products I buy wear out too quickly.*
3. Too many of the products I buy are defective in some way.*
4. The companies that make products I buy don't care enough about how well they perform.*
5. The quality of products I buy has consistently improved over the years.

Advertising Scale

1. Most advertising is very annoying.*
2. Most advertising makes false claims.*
3. If most advertising were eliminated, consumers would be better off.*
4. I enjoy most ads.
5. Most advertising is intended to deceive rather than inform.*

Price Scale

1. Most products I buy are overpriced.*
2. Businesses could charge lower prices and still be profitable.*
3. Most prices are reasonable given the high cost of doing business.
4. Most prices are fair.
5. In general, I am satisfied with the prices I pay.

Retailing/Selling Scale

1. Most retail stores serve their customers well.
2. Because of the way retailers treat me, most of my shopping is unpleasant.*
3. I find most retail salespeople to be very helpful.
4. When I need assistance in a store, I am usually <u>not</u> able to get it.*
5. Most retailers provide adequate service.

NOTES: * denotes items that require reverse coding to reflect a more favorable sentiment toward marketing practices.

SERVICE QUALITY: SERVQUAL
(Parasuraman, Zeithaml, and Berry 1986, 1988)

Construct: The construct of quality as measured by this scale involves perceived quality (as opposed to objective quality). Perceived quality is the consumer's judgment of an entity's overall excellence or superiority, similar to an overall attitude. Perceived service quality is defined as the degree and direction of discrepancy between consumers' perceptions and expectations (Parasuraman, Zeithaml, and Berry 1986, 1988). Quality is distinguished from satisfaction in that the latter is assumed to involve specific transactions. As part of the conceptualization, expectations are viewed as desires or wants of consumers (not predictions of what will be provided).

Description: The scale is comprised of two matched sets of 22 items, each describing expectations for a particular service category and then perceptions of a particular service provider. Both sets of items are operationalized using seven-place bipolar scales labeled "Strongly Agree" (7) to "Strongly Disagree" (1). Approximately half the items are worded negatively as marked +/- below. Scores for the total scale and each factor range from -6 to +6 where positive scores reflect perceptions exceeding expectations. Difference scores for the 1 to 7 scales are computed and then averaged over the number of items in either the total scale or for each subscale. Furthermore, five factors comprise the two subscales: tangibility, reliability, responsiveness, assurance, and empathy.

The ensuing scale was developed to contain items appropriate for the multiple service categories used in the construction of the present scale. "Therefore, while SERVQUAL can be used in its present form to assess and compare quality across a wide variety of firms, appropriate adaptation of the instrument may be desirable when only a single service is investigated" (Parasuraman et al. 1988, pp. 27-28).

Development: Ninety-seven items were originally developed to represent 10 dimensions of service quality. Each was cast as an expectation and a perception statement. Responses (n=200) were pooled across five service categories; difference scores were then used as input into "within-dimension" coefficient alpha analyses. These tests resulted in a reduced set of 54 items after deleting those statements with low corrected item-to-total correlations. Oblique factor analysis resulted in further reductions in the number of items and a revision in the dimensionality of the anticipated scale (i.e., 34 items reflecting 7 dimensions). Analysis of this initial data then revealed a seven-factor measure comprised of 34 items.

Data from the second developmental sample were used to reevaluate the dimensionality and reliability of the 34-item measure. Analysis of the factor loadings (both the pattern and the loading values) in addition to examination of corrected item-to-total correlations resulted in further revisions to the scale. Specifically, two pairs of factors were combined and several additional items were deleted. These analyses resulted then in the final 22-item (actually pairs of items), five-factor scale as described above. Estimates of internal consistency and validity were gathered.

Sample(s): Initial purification was based upon the responses of a quota sample of 200 adults surveyed by a market research firm in a large Southwestern metropolitan mall. Respondents were all above 25 years of age and were equally divided among males and females. Forty recent users (i.e., within three months) of five service categories were surveyed. The reduced set of 34 items was reexamined using the responses of 200 recent users of four service providers (n=800).

Validity: The estimates of internal consistency reliability for both the factors and the total scale for the four service companies in the second study were consistently high. The total scale estimates of internal consistency reliability for a linear combination ranged from 0.87 to 0.90. Factor analysis of the second phase data and reanalysis of the first wave data supported the dimensionality and expected item loadings for both data sets. Additional evidence of the validity of the scale was provided by mean difference tests across subject groups formed by overall quality ratings (collected in phase 2) for the individual firms. As expected, higher average SERVQUAL scores were obtained for subjects providing more positive responses to the overall rating. Relationships with questions about "recommendations to friends" and "reports of problems" also provided some evidence of the scale's validity. Further supportive evidence was provided by the ability of the subscales to predict overall quality judgments (i.e., R-Square estimates ranged from 0.27 to 0.52).

Scores: A series of mean scores are provided in Table 5 of Parasuraman et al. (1988) for the second sample. Across the four categories of services considered, the means are generally slightly negative, suggesting that service expectations generally exceed consumer perceptions. As an example, for the combined scale and across three categories of banking firms (i.e., excellent, good, and fair/poor), the corresponding mean scores were -0.22, -0.92, and -1.61, respectively.

Source(s):   Parasuraman, A., Valarie Zeithaml, and Leonard L. Berry (1986), "SERVQUAL: A Multiple-Item Scale for Measuring Customer Perceptions of Service Quality," *Report No. 86-108*, *Marketing Science Institute*, Cambridge, Massachusetts.

Parasuraman, A., Valarie A. Zeithaml, and Leonard L. Berry (1988), "SERVQUAL: A Multiple-Item Scale for Measuring Consumer Perceptions of Service Quality," *Journal of Retailing*, 64 (Spring), 12-40.

Other evidence: Carmen (1990) tested SERVQUAL in four different service settings, including a business school placement center, a tire store, a dental school patient clinic, and an acute care hospital. The results provide corroborating evidence for the reliability of the scale. Some evidence regarding the need to vary item wording across settings and several questions regarding the uniqueness or structure of the original 10 dimensions were raised.

The overall fit statistics from a confirmatory factor analysis study by Finn and Lamb (1991) using the responses from a telephone survey involving retail shopping experiences did not provide support for the multidimensional (i.e., five correlated factors) measurement model implied by the SERVQUAL scale. However, individual factor reliabilities ranged from 0.59 to 0.83.

Other sources: Carmen, James M. (1990), "Consumer Perceptions of Service Quality: An Assessment of the SERVQUAL Dimensions," *Journal of Retailing*, 66 (Spring), 33-55.

Finn, David W. and Charles W. Lamb (1991), "An Evaluation of the SERVQUAL Scales in a Retail Setting," in *Advances in Consumer Research*, Vol 18, Rebecca H. Holman and Michael R. Solomon (eds.), Provo,UT: Association for Consumer Research, 483-490.

References: N/A.

SERVICE QUALITY: SERVQUAL
(Parasuraman, Zeithaml, and Berry 1986, 1988)

EXPECTATIONS

Directions: This survey deals with your opinions of _____ services. Please show the extent to which you think firms offering _____services should possess the features described by each statement. Do this by picking one of the seven numbers next to each statement. If you strongly agree that these firms should possess a feature, circle the number 7. If you strongly disagree that these firms should possess a feature, circle 1. If your feelings are not strong, circle one of the numbers in the middle. There are no right or wrong answers. All we are interested in is a number that best shows your expectations about firms offering _____ services.

E1.   They should have up-to-date equipment.

E2.   Their physical facilities should be visually appealing.

E3.   Their employees should be well dressed and appear neat.

E4.   The appearance of the physical facilities of these firms should be in keeping with the type of services provided.

E5.   When these firms promise to do something by a certain time, they should do so.

E6.   When customers have problems, these firms should be sympathetic and reassuring.

E7.   These firms should be dependable.

E8.   They should provide their services at the time they promise to do so.

E9.   They should keep their records accurately.

E10. They shouldn't be expected to tell customers exactly when services will be performed. (-)

E11. It is not realistic for customers to expect prompt service from employees of these firms. (-)

E12. Their employees don't always have to be willing to help customers. (-)

E13. It is okay if they are too busy to respond to customer requests promptly. (-)

E14. Customers should be able to trust employees of these firms.

E15. Customers should be able to feel safe in their transactions with these firms' employees.

E16. Their employees should be polite.

E17. Their employees should get adequate support from these firms to do their jobs well.

E18. These firms should not be expected to give customers individual attention. (-)

E19. Employees of these firms cannot be expected to give customers personal attention. (-)

E20. It is unrealistic to expect employees to know what the needs of their customers are. (-)

E21. It is unrealistic to expect these firms to have their customers' best interests at heart. (-)

E22. They shouldn't be expected to have operating hours convenient to all their customers. (-)

NOTES: The items are distributed among the five dimensions of Tangibility (items E1 to E4), Reliability (E5 to E9), Responsiveness (items, E10 to E13), Assurance (E14 to E17), and Empathy (items E18 to E22).

(-) denotes reverse coded items.

PERCEPTIONS

Directions: The following set of statements relate to your feelings about XYZ. For each statement, please show the extent to which you believe XYZ has the feature described by the statement. Once again, circling a 7 means that you strongly agree that XYZ has that feature, and circling a 1 means that you strongly disagree. You may circle any of the numbers in the middle that show how strong your feelings are. There are no right or wrong answers. All we are interested in is a number that best shows your perceptions about XYZ.

P1.   XYZ has up-to-date equipment.

P2.   XYZ's physical facilities are visually appealing.

P3.   XYZ's employees are well dressed and appear neat.

P4.   The appearance of the physical facilities of XYZ is in keeping with the type of services provided.

P5.   When XYZ promises to do something by a certain time, it does so.

P6.   When you have problems, XYZ is sympathetic and reassuring.

P7.   XYZ is dependable.

P8.   XYZ provides its services at the time it promises to do so.

P9.   XYZ keeps its records accurately.

P10. XYZ does not tell customers exactly when services will be performed. (-)

P11. You do not receive prompt service from XYZ's employees. (-)

P12. Employees of XYZ are not always willing to help customers. (-)

P13. Employees of XYZ are too busy to respond to customer requests promptly. (-)

P14. You can trust the employees of XYZ.

P15. You feel safe in your transactions with XYZ's employees.

P16. Employees of XYZ are polite.

P17. Employees get adequate support from XYZ to do their jobs well.

P18. XYZ does not give you individual attention. (-)

P19. Employees of XYZ do not give you personal attention. (-)

P20. Employees of XYZ do not know what your needs are. (-)

P21. XYZ does not have your best interests at heart. (-)

P22. XYZ does not have operating hours convenient to all its customers. (-)

NOTES: The items are distributed among the five dimensions of Tangibility (items P1 to P4), Reliability (P5 to P9), Responsiveness (items P10 to P13), Assurance (P14 to P17), and Empathy (items P18 to P22).

(-) denotes reverse coded items.

BUSINESS ETHICS

A SCALE TO MEASURE ETHICAL BEHAVIOR IN RESEARCH ORGANIZATIONS
(Ferrell and Skinner 1988)

Construct: Though ethics has been defined as "inquiry into the nature and grounds of morality" (Taylor 1975), Ferrell and Skinner (1988) argue that ethics warrants a special analysis in marketing research organizations. In the case of research organizations, this focus is on honesty in reporting results to clients, including all aspects of a research project.

Description: The ethics scale is composed of six Likert statements scored on six-point scales (definitely disagree [6] - definitely agree [1]). Item scores are summed and the scale is unidimensional.

Development: A pool of 70 items was generated via prestudy interviews with marketing researchers from three organizations. These items were then judged by 11 more researchers and items were eliminated that lacked face validity. The remaining items were factor analyzed and items with loadings less than .30 were eliminated. This resulted in the final 6-item scale. Reliability and validity estimates were also gathered.

Sample(s): A sample of 550 marketing researchers from an AMA mailing list was used in the study to develop and validate the scale. This sample was broken down into subsamples of subcontractors (30%), research firms (45%), and corporate research departments (25%).

Validity: Construct reliability for the six-item scale (via LISREL) was .71. Standardized loadings across the items ranged from .43 to .66. In terms of predictive validity, the scale was used as the dependent variable with predictor variables of formalization, centralization, and controls. Across the three subsamples, the ethics scale was positively related to formalization (betas ranged from .18 to .27). Mixed results were found for the other two independent variables.

Scores: No mean or percentage scores were reported.

Source: Ferrell, O. C. and Steven J. Skinner (1988), "Ethical Behavior and Bureaucratic Structure in Marketing Research Organizations," *Journal of Marketing Research*, 25 (February), 103-109.

Other evidence: N/A.

Other sources: N/A.

References: Taylor, Paul W. (1975), *Principles of Ethics: An Introduction*, Encino, CA: Dickensen Publishing Company, Inc.

A SCALE TO MEASURE ETHICAL BEHAVIOR IN RESEARCH ORGANIZATIONS
(Ferrell and Skinner 1988)

1) Sometimes I compromise the reliability of a study to complete the project.

2) Sometimes I only report part of the data because I know my client may not like the results.

3) I sometimes have to cover up nonresponse and sampling error to please my clients.

4) I have continued a research project after knowing I made errors early.

5) Sometimes I have to alter the sampling design in order to obtain enough respondents.

6) Sometimes I claim to use the latest research techniques as a selling tool, even though I don't use the techniques.

A CORPORATE ETHICS SCALE: CEP
(Hunt, Wood, and Chonko 1989)

Construct: As conceptualized by Hunt, Wood, and Chonko (1989), corporate ethics reflects three broad based perceptions: 1) the extent to which employees perceive that managers are acting ethically in their organizations; 2) the extent to which employees perceive that managers are concerned about the issues of ethics in their organization; and 3) the extent to which employees perceive that ethical (unethical) behavior is rewarded (punished) in their organization.

Description: The CEP is a five-item scale that is summed, and then divided by five, to form an overall index of corporate ethics. All items are scored on 7-point strongly disagree - strongly agree scales. Thus, scores on the scale can range from 1 to 7. The scale is considered unidimensional.

Development: From two studies (Hunt, Chonko, and Wilcox 1984; Hunt et al. 1989), five items from a larger pool of items were chosen for the CEP. Factor analysis and coefficient alpha were used to assess the dimensionality and reliability of the scale.

Sample(s): A total of 1,246 respondents (499 marketing managers, 417 marketing researchers, and 330 advertising agency managers) were used as the sample in deriving the scale.

Validity: Coefficient alpha for the scale was .78 and factor analysis revealed a unidimensional structure. Furthermore, the CEP was found to be a significant predictor of organizational commitment, (i.e., numerous regression coefficients are offered on p. 86) providing evidence of criterion validity for the scale. For example, beta coefficients for the scale ranged from .17 to .58 across four subsamples of the data.

Scores: Mean scores for the three sub-sample groups were 5.3 (sd = 1.12), 5.08 (sd = 1.17), and 5.88 (sd = 1.22) for the marketing managers, marketing researchers, and ad agency managers, respectively.

Source: Hunt, Shelby D., Van R. Wood, and Lawrence B. Chonko (1989), "Corporate Ethical Values and Organizational Commitment in Marketing," *Journal of Marketing*, 53 (July), 79-90.

Other evidence: N/A.

Other sources: N/A.

References: Hunt, Shelby D., Lawrence B. Chonko, and James B Wilcox (1984), "Ethical Problems of Marketing Researchers," *Journal of Marketing Research*, 21 (August), 309-324.

A CORPORATE ETHICS SCALE: CEP
(Hunt, Wood, and Chonko 1989)

1) Managers in my company often engage in behaviors that I consider to be unethical.*

2) In order to succeed in my company, it is often necessary to compromise one's ethics.*

3) Top management in my company has let it be known in no uncertain terms that unethical behaviors will not be tolerated.

4) If a manger in my company is discovered to have engaged in unethical behavior that results primarily in *personal gain* (rather than corporate gain), he or she will be promptly reprimanded.

5) If a manger in my company is discovered to have engaged in unethical behavior that results primarily in *corporate gain* (rather than personal gain), he or she will be promptly reprimanded.

NOTE: * items that are reversed scored.

A SCALE FOR IMPROVING EVALUATIONS OF BUSINESS ETHICS
(Reidenbach and Robin 1990)

Construct: Business ethics is defined as "individual ethical judgment in business decision contexts" (Reidenbach and Robin 1990). The five major moral philosophies said to underlie the generation of items are: justice, relativism, utilitarianism, egoism, and deontology.

Description: The scale is comprised of eight semantic differential items distributed across three factors as follows: (1) Moral Equity, 4 items; (2) Relativistic, 2 items; and (3) Contractualism, 2 items. Each item is operationalized using seven-place bipolar scales. Item scores can be summed within factors to form factor indices, or overall for an overall measure of ethics.

Development: An initial set of 33 items was developed to reflect the five normative philosophies. The categorization was verified using a panel of three expert "ethics literature" judges. Three scenarios (with varying behaviors of questionable ethics) along with the 33 items were administered to a sample of 218 business students (i.e., the item responses reflected opinions about the behaviors in the scenarios). Four scale items were deleted at this stage (with the deletion procedures not specified). Stage two involved tests of the factor structure employing both Likert and bipolar formats. (No differences across formats were observed.) Examination of the pattern of factor loadings, the size of the loadings, and item-to-total correlations were used to reduce the number of items to 14. From this stage, three factors emerged. In the last phase, 105 small business operators evaluated the three scenarios. Using the same factor analysis and item reduction criteria, the number of items was reduced to 8. Reliability and validity estimates were also obtained.

Sample(s): A sample of 218 business students was surveyed in the first stage. A sample of 108 retail managers and owners participated in the second phase. 105 small business operators were the participants in the last phase in which the number of items was reduced to eight (i.e., the number included in the final scale). A final study involving mail survey responses from 152 business managers was used to evaluate the validity of the scale.

Validity: Factor analysis of the final survey of business managers replicated the anticipated factor structure. In addition, the three-factor solution explained an average of 79% of the variance across the three scenarios. Based on the responses from reaction to three scenarios, a multitrait-multicontext analysis provided some correlational evidence of convergent and discriminant validity. These analyses revealed that the intercorrelations among factors were generally within the 0.20 to 0.40 range. The subscale reliabilities ranged from 0.71 to 0.92. The subscales were also correlated with single-item measures of overall perceptions of the ethical nature of the behavior and a measure of behavioral intentions. For the former, the subscales explained an average of 72% of the variance, and for the latter, the subscales explained an average 34% of the variance. The multiple-item scales were also found to be better predictors of intentions than the single-item, overall measure. Thus, evidence of predictive validity was found.

Scores: Means scores for the total scale, the subscales or the individual items were not presented.

Source: Reidenbach, R. Eric and Donald P. Robin (1990), "Toward the Development of a Multidimensional Scale for Improving Evaluations of Business Ethics," *Journal of Business Ethics*, 9 (August), 639-653.

Other evidence: A series of follow-up studies was conducted in an effort to further evaluate the scale (Reidenbach, Robin, and Dawson 1991). Across four studies and 15 trials employing different contexts (i.e., 8 scenarios), the factor structure and reliability of the scale was replicated. For example, across the 15 trials, the three-factor solution explained between 57.5% and 82.8% of the variance in the data, with an average of 75%. As predictors of a univariate ethics measure and a measure of ethics intention, the three factors explained between 25% and 83% of the variance in these criterion variables

Other sources: Reidenbach, R. Eric, Donald P. Robin and Lyndon Dawson (1991), "An Application and Extension of a Multidimensional Ethics Scale to Selected Marketing Practices and Marketing Groups," *Journal of the Academy of Marketing Science*, 19 (Spring), 115-122.

References: N/A.

A SCALE FOR IMPROVING EVALUATIONS OF BUSINESS ETHICS
(Reidenbach and Robin 1990)

MORAL EQUITY DIMENSION

1. Fair/unfair

2. Just/unjust

3. Acceptable to my family/unacceptable to my family

4. Morally right/not morally right

RELATIVISTIC DIMENSION

5. Traditionally acceptable/traditionally unacceptable

6. Culturally acceptable/culturally unacceptable

CONTRACTUALISM DIMENSION

7. Violates/does not violate an unspoken promise

8. Violates/does not violate an unwritten contract

NOTES: Items 1 through 6 require recoding to reflect a higher level of morality.

BUSINESS ATTITUDES TOWARD THE MARKETPLACE

MANAGEMENT CONSERVATISM
(Sturdivant, Ginter, and Sawyer 1985)

Construct: This measure is designed to assess "the conservatism of managers' *personal* values" (Sturdivant, Ginter, and Sawyer 1985, p.17). The assumption underlying the research is that the collective personal values of senior management in a firm will have substantial impact on corporate goals. The scale is designed to focus on the social and political issues that are of special concern to executives.

Description: The scale consists of thirty items designed to reflect two factors: (1) government/business and the general welfare (16 items) and (2) human rights and responsibilities (14 items). Each statement is operationalized using a six-place response format: (1) agree very much, (2) agree on the whole, (3) agree a little, (4) disagree a little, (5) disagree on the whole, and (6) disagree very much. The wording of the items (i.e., positive vs. negative) is varied to inhibit response bias. Summed across the two factors (which were reportedly uncorrelated), the scores for the scale could range from 30 to 180 with higher scores reflecting greater conservatism. Summing item scores within factors is also possible to derive factor indices.

Development: The scale was developed from an initial pool of 65 items. The two factors were developed from a series of factor analysis procedures including both oblique and orthogonal rotations and split sample replications (n=580). The two factors were selected based upon explained variance considerations and were named after examination of the item content loading on each factor. The factor analyses were also replicated on a subsequent sample of executives (n=377). Several estimates of reliability and validity were obtained.

Sample(s): Seven different samples (labeled A through G) were used in the development and evaluation of the scale. Most subjects were executives participating in executive development seminars. Two of the samples included MBA student groups (n=38 and n=24). The executive sample sizes were: 580, 377, 173, 69, 235, and 28.

Validity: Considerable evidence of reliability and validity is provided in the text of the article and in the Appendix to the article. Only some of those results are summarized here. (In addition, the analysis of a series of relationships between conservatism and firm financial performance provided additional evidence regarding the usefulness of the scale.) Estimates of internal consistency reliability for the 16-item factor and the 14-item factor (for Sample A) were 0.84 and 0.78, respectively. The linear composite estimate of reliability for the entire scale was 0.85. For Sample B, the corresponding estimates of reliability were 0.85, 0.81, and 0.86. Based on a two-week test-retest administration to 24 Executive MBA students, the test-retest correlations for Factors 1 and 2 and the total scale were 0.87, 0.87, and 0.92, respectively. Some evidence of discriminant validity was provided from a series of low correlations with measures of a variety of constructs including social desirability, dogmatism, Machiavellianism, and internal-external locus of control. Neither the total scale nor either factor was correlated with social desirability. One measure of authoritarianism was correlated with the total scale (r=0.58) and dogmatism was correlated with factor 1 (r=0.30). Evidence of convergent validity was also provided by correlations with two general conservatism scales.

Scores: Mean scores for 48 companies that were said to vary in terms of social performance were provided. See Figure 1 (Sturdivant et al. 1986, p. 27). The grand mean for the overall scale across groups was 96.3. The subgroup means based on social performance were: social activists, 66.4; best, 103.6; honorable mention, 103.9; and worst, 113.8.

Source: Sturdivant, Frederick D., James L. Ginter, and Alan G. Sawyer (1985), "Managers' Conservatism and Corporate Performance," *Strategic Management Journal*, 6, 17-38.

Other evidence:	N/A.

Other sources:	N/A.

References:	N/A.

MANAGEMENT CONSERVATISM
(Sturdivant, Ginter, and Sawyer 1985)

Government/Business and the General Welfare

1. Corporations have too much influence on the outcome of the presidential elections.

2. Current tax laws allow wealthy individuals to pay less than their fair share.

3. The disadvantaged in our society suffer because of the economic power exerted by large corporations.

4. Tax laws should be changed to close loopholes that allow wealthy individuals to pay proportionately less taxes than low-income individuals.

5. Product quality standards should be set by regulatory agencies to protect consumers.

6. One of the principal purposes of government should be to protect the citizen from the economic power generated by large corporations.

7. Advertising is often a devious method used by companies to lure customers into purchasing their products.

8. To ensure adequate care of the sick, we need to change the present system of privately owned and controlled medical care.

9. Executives of toy producing companies should be subject to jail sentences for failure to inform parents that their products may be hazardous.

10. All individuals, regardless of ability to pay, should be given the same medical care.

11. Business should be required to fund schools that will be used to train and educate handicapped children.

12. Funds for school construction should come from state and federal government loans at no interest or very low interest.

13. Companies should not have business dealings with other companies which ignore their responsibility to protect the environment.

14. The quickened pace of business and competition has taken a heavy toll on the quality of life.

15. Regulatory agencies must be given the power to set and enforce standards for the purpose of guarding against environmental deterioration.

16. Business should give environmental protection groups access to the information they need to properly inform the public

Human Rights and Responsibilities

1. Government programs to aid the poor usually support those people too lazy to work.

2. The children that are born as a result of racially mixed marriages are detriments to society.

3. Protesters and radicals are good for society even though they may cause a change in normally accepted standards.

4. We would not have so many juvenile delinquents if parents were stricter with their children.

5. There are too many professors in our colleges and universities who are radical in their social and political beliefs.

6. A business should not hire a person if they suspect him of being homosexual.

7. Labor unions should not have the right to strike when the survival of the business is threatened.

8. Inherited racial characteristics play more of a part in the achievement of individuals and groups than is generally known.

9. Police should be able to forcefully enter a person's home if they suspect him of unlawful activity.

10. Many blacks would be executives of major corporations today if they had not been discriminated against in the past.

11. Employers should be able to require their employees to have their hair cut to a specified length.

12. Parents deserve more respect from their children than they receive.

13. Even though the resulting cost may mean a reduction in profits, businesses should set and attempt to meet minority hiring quotas.

14. If experts determine that marijuana has no harmful effects, it should be legalized.

NOTES: Items 1, 2, 4-9, 11, 12 of the "human rights and responsibilities" factors require recoding to reflect a higher level of management conservatism.

Reprinted by permission of the publisher from Sturdivant, Frederick D., James L. Ginter, and Alan G. Sawyer (1985), "Managers' Conservatism and Corporate Performance," Strategic Management Journal, *6, 17-38. Copyright 1992 by John Wiley & Sons, Ltd.*

A SCALE TO MEASURE EXCELLENCE IN BUSINESS: EXCEL
(Sharma, Netemeyer, and Mahajan 1990)

Construct: Corporate excellence is viewed as those managerial practices and principles that lead to sustained performance (Sharma, Netemeyer, and Mahajan 1990). These principles are posited to be a necessary but not sufficient condition for superior corporate performance. Furthermore, these principles are based on the eight attributes of excellence espoused by Peters and Waterman (1990). These attributes are: 1) a bias for action, 2) being close to customers, 3) autonomy and entrepreneurship, 4) being productive through people, 5) an active shared value system among all levels, 6) a simple and lean staff, 7) simultaneous loose-tight properties (i.e., certain core values are centralized while others are decentralized), and 8) "sticking to the knitting" (i.e., a resistance to conglomeracy and a focus on what is known or done best).

Description: The EXCEL scale is a 16-item scale designed to measure the eight attributes of excellence espoused by Peters and Waterman. All items are scored on Likert scales from strongly disagree to strongly agree. Though originally hypothesized to be an eight factor measure based on the eight attributes, factor analysis revealed a single higher-order factor structure composed of eight secondary factors that reflect the eight attributes of excellence. Thus, the items are summed to form an overall score of excellence, where scores can range from 16 to 112 (Sharma et al. 1990).

Development: The EXCEL scale was developed using recommended scaling procedures. Using the conceptual base of Peters and Waterman (1982), the book was content analyzed by three independent researchers to generate an initial pool of items. Twenty-five items were generated for each attribute (i.e., 200 items). Two expert panels were then used to delete redundant and ambiguous items, trimming the initial pool to 32 items. Both panels were asked to indicate the attribute that each statement reflected. Items were retained that met a stringent a priori decision rule (i.e., for the first panel, 7 of 8 judges had to agree that the item reflected a given attribute, and for the second panel, 70 percent agreement was the decision rule for item retention). Two samples were gathered to purify and finalize the scale via a variety of item analyses and reliability and validity tests (Sharma et al. 1990).

Sample(s): The first expert panel consisted of six business strategy professors and 2 Ph.D. students in public policy. The second expert panel consisted of 10 additional business strategy professors from 4 different universities. The first purification sample consisted of 678 business policy/strategy professors drawn from the Academy of Management membership listing. This sample indicated their level of agreement that the statement measured the respective attribute. In addition, 12 firms were rated by 7 industry analysts.

Validity: The purification samples produced the final 16-item EXCEL scale. Though eight factors were hypothesized, factor analysis on Sample One data (n=678) revealed that a single higher-order factor structure composed of eight secondary factors best fit the data. Coefficient alpha for this version of the scale was 0.89. Alpha for the industry analyst sample was 0.90.

The validity of the scale was examined by correlating scores on the scale with financial ratios, measures of stock market performance, and rankings from *Fortune* magazine. These correlations showed strong support for the nomological validity of the EXCEL scale across both samples. For example, the correlation between the Treynor financial index and the EXCEL score was 0.62 (p=.05). The coefficient of concordance between the EXCEL rankings and a set of *Fortune* rankings was 0.92 (p=0.08). A coefficient of concordance also indicated a high degree of agreement among the industry analysts (W=0.77).

Scores: Mean scores for a computer industry sample are provided in Table 2 of Sharma et al.(1990, p. 326). These scores ranged from a low of 46.80 (for the least excellent firm in the sample) to 95.00 (for the highest evaluated firm).

Source: Sharma, Subhash, Richard G. Netemeyer, and Vijay Mahajan (1990), "In Search of Excellence Revisited: An Empirical Evaluation of Peters and Waterman's Attributes of Excellence," in

Enhancing Knowledge Development in Marketing, Vol. 1, William O. Bearden and A. Parasuraman (eds.), Chicago: American Marketing Association, 322-328.

Other evidence: N/A.

Other sources: N/A.

References: Peters, Thomas J. and Robert H. Waterman (1982), *In Search of Excellence: Lessons from America's Best Run Companies*, New York: Harper and Row.

A SCALE TO MEASURE EXCELLENCE IN BUSINESS: EXCEL
(Sharma, Netemeyer, and Mahajan 1990)

1. The firm encourages employees to develop new ideas.

2. The firm has a small staff that delegates authority efficiently.

3. The firm's top level management believes that its people are of the utmost importance to the company.

4. The firm instills a value system in all its employees.

5. The firm provides personalized attention to all its customers.

6. The firm's top management creates an atmosphere that encourages creativity and innovativeness.

7. The company's values are the driving force behind its operation.

8. The firm is flexible and quick to respond to problems.

9. The company concentrates in product areas where it has a high level of skill and expertise.

10. The firm has a small, but efficient management team.

11. The company develops products that are natural extensions of its product line.

12. The firm truly believes in its people.

13. The firm considers after-the-sale service just as important as making the sale itself.

14. The firm believes in experimenting with new products and ideas.

15. The company believes that listening to what consumers have to say is a good skill to have.

16. The firm is flexible with employees but administers discipline when necessary.

NOTE: The eight attributes and the corresponding items designed to reflect each are as follows: a bias for action, 8; close to the customer, 5, 13, 15; autonomy and entrepreneurship, 1, 6, 14; productivity through people, 3, 12; hands on value driven, 4, 7; stick to the knitting, 9, 11; simple form and lean staff, 2, 10; loose-tight properties, 16.

MARKET ORIENTATION
(Narver and Slater 1990)

Construct: Market orientation is the organizational culture that most effectively and efficiently creates the necessary behaviors for the creation of superior value for buyers and, thus, continuous superior performance for the business (Narver and Slater 1990, p. 21). Furthermore, market orientation consists of three behavioral components (i.e., customer orientation, competitor orientation, and interfunctional coordination), and two decision criteria (i.e., long term focus and profitability). Each of these is described below:

Customer orientation - is the sufficient understanding of one's target buyers to be able to create superior value for them continuously. It requires that the seller know the buyer's entire value chain.

Competitor orientation - means that a seller understands the short-term strengths and weaknesses and long term capabilities and strategies of both the key current and the key potential competitors.

Interfunctional coordination - is the coordinated utilization of company resources in creating superior value for target customers at any and all points in the buyer's value chain.

Long-term focus - in relation to profits and in implementing each of the three behavioral components is required to be market oriented.

Profitability - the creation of economic wealth is an overriding objective in market orientation.

Description: The authors describe their scale as a one-dimensional construct but develop multiple-item measures for each of the above facets. The final scale is composed of 15 Likert items scored on 7-point scales ranging from "the business unit does not engage in the practice at all" (1) to "the business unit engages in the practice to a very great extent" (7). Indices for the first three components are derived by summing the item scores within components and dividing by the number of items in the component. An overall market orientation index is derived by averaging the items scores across all the items of the three behavioral components. The other two components (i.e., long-term focus and profitability) were not included in calculating the market orientation index because of their low levels or reliability.

Development: Based on a literature review, several items were generated by the authors to tap the domain of the construct. Two expert panels reviewed and judged the items for face validity and several items were deleted. The remaining items were further examined by six SBU managers, and based on their evaluation, items were refined that reflect the final instrument. In a separate study, a number of reliability and validity checks were performed.

Samples: As stated above, two panels of academicians (3 in each group) and 6 SBU managers were used in item generation and face validity analysis. A sample of 371 managers from various SBUs responded to the final form of the scale.

Validity: Coefficient alpha estimates for the 6-item customer orientation facet were .85 and .87 (the sample of 371 was split into two groups of 190 and 175). Corresponding estimates for the 4-item competitor orientation and 5-item interfunctional coordination facets were .72 and .73, and .71 and .73, respectively. For the overall sample, the correlations among these three components ranged from .66 to .73, and alpha for the 15-item scale (i.e., items from the three components as one overall scale) was .88. Thus, these three components exhibited satisfactory levels of internal consistency.

The 3-item long-term focus and 3-item profit emphasis components exhibited low levels of internal consistency (i.e., .47 and .48 for the former, and .14 and .00 for the latter). Subsequently, they were excluded from further analyses.

Discriminant and concurrent validity of the scale were also assessed. Discriminant validity was examined by correlating the 15-item market orientation measure with a measure of human resource management policy. The correlations between the three components of market orientation and the human resource measure ranged from .45 to .53, and were significantly less than the correlations among the three components of market orientation. This was taken as evidence of discriminant validity. The correlations of the overall scale and the three components with measures for return on assets (ROA), low cost advantage, and the use of a differentiation strategy were used to assess concurrent validity. For ROA, correlations with the overall scale and its three components ranged from .23 to .39. For low cost advantage, corresponding correlations ranged from .18 to .23, and for differentiation strategy, the correlations ranged from .33 to .45. This supports the marketing orientation scale's concurrent validity.

Scores: Mean scores were reported for the overall scale and its components across four different business typologies. For the overall scale, grand mean scores (Narver and Slater 1990, Table 5, p. 28) ranged from 4.28 to 4.77. The grand mean ranges for the customer orientation, competitor orientation, and interfunctional coordination components ranged from 4.53 to 5.05, 4.06 to 5.71, and 4.25 to 4.53, respectively.

Source: Narver, John C. and Stanley F. Slater (1990), "The Effect of Market Orientation on Business Profitability," *Journal of Marketing*, 54 (October), 20-35.

Other evidence: N/A.

Other sources: N/A.

References: N/A.

MARKET ORIENTATION
(Narver and Slater 1990)

To what extent does your business firm engage in the following practices?

1) customer commitment
2) create customer value
3) understand customer needs
4) customer satisfaction objectives
5) measure customer satisfaction
6) after-sales service
7) salespeople share competitor information
8) respond rapidly to competitor's actions
9) top managers discuss competitor's strategies
10) target opportunities for competitive advantage
11) interfunctional customer calls
12) information shared among functions
13) functional integration in strategy
14) all functions contribute to customer value
15) share resources with other business units
16) quarterly profits are primary objective
17) require rapid payback
18) positive margin in long-term
19) profit performance measured market by market
20) top managers emphasize market performance
21) all products must be profitable

NOTES: Only the first 15 items comprise the overall market orientation scale. Items 1 through 6 comprise the "customer orientation" component. Items 7 through 10 comprise the "competitor orientation" component, and items 11 through 15 comprise the "interfunctional coordination" component. Items 16 through 18, and items 19 through 21 comprise the "long term horizon" and "profit emphasis" components, respectively. The latter two sets of items were not included in the final scale.

SOURCES FOR CHAPTER 6

Ahmed, Sadrudin A. and Douglas N. Jackson (1979), "Psychographics for Social Policy Decisions: Welfare Assistance," *Journal of Consumer Research*, 5 (March), 229-239; Table 2, pp. 234-235.

Ferrell, O. C. and Steven J. Skinner (1988), "Ethical Behavior and Bureaucratic Structure in Marketing Research Organizations," *Journal of Marketing Research*, 25 (February), 103-109; Appendix, pp. 107-108.

Gaski, John F. and Michael J. Etzel (1986), "The Index of Consumer Sentiment Toward Marketing," *Journal of Marketing*, 50 (July), 71-81; Appendix, pp. 78-79.

Hunt, Shelby D., Van R. Wood, and Lawrence B. Chonko (1989), "Corporate Ethical Values and Organizational Commitment in Marketing," *Journal of Marketing*, 53 (July), 79-90; Tables 6 and 7, p. 317.

Klein, Gary D. (1982), "Development of a Cross-Cultural Instrument to Measure the Attitude of Consumers and Business People Toward Consumerism," *Journal of Marketing and Public Policy*, 1, 123-137; Table 4, p. 132.

Narver, John C. and Stanley F. Slater (1990), "The Effect of Market Orientation on Business Profitability," *Journal of Marketing*, 54 (October), 20-35; Tables 1 and 2, pp 24-25.

Parasuraman, A., Valarie Zeithaml, and Leonard L. Berry (1986), "SERVQUAL: A Multiple-Item Scale for Measuring Customer Perceptions of Service Quality," *Report No. 86-108, Marketing Science Institute*, Cambridge, Massachusetts; Appendix, pp. 31-34.

Peters, William H. (1972), "Social Responsibility in Marketing Personnel: Meaning and Measurement," in *Proceedings of American Marketing Association Educators' Conference*, Helmut Becker (ed.), Chicago: American Marketing Association, 224-229; Table 1, pp. 226-227.

Reid, P. Nelson and James H. Gundlach (1984), "A Scale for the Measurement of Consumer Satisfaction with Social Services," *Journal of Social Service Research*, 7 (1), 37-54; Table 1, pp. 44-46.

Reidenbach, R. Eric and Donald P. Robin (1990), "Toward the Development of a Multidimensional Scale for Improving Evaluations of Business Ethics," *Journal of Business Ethics*, 9 (August), 639-653; Table VI, p. 649.

Sharma, Subhash, Richard G. Netemeyer, and Vijay Mahajan (1990), "In Search of Excellence Revisited: An Empirical Evaluation of Peters and Waterman's Attributes of Excellence," in *Enhancing Knowledge Development in Marketing*, Vol. 1, William O. Bearden and A. Parasuraman (eds.), Chicago: American Marketing Association, 322-328; Figure 1, p. 326.

Sturdivant, Frederick D., James L. Ginter, and Alan G. Sawyer (1985), "Managers' Conservatism and Corporate Performance," *Strategic Management Journal*, 6, 17-38; Table 3, pp. 25-26.

Williams, Paul F. (1982), "Attitudes toward the Corporation and the Evaluation of Social Data," *Journal of Business Research*, 10, 119-131; Appendix, pp. 128-130.

7

Sales, Sales Management, and Inter-Intrafirm Issues

SALES AND SALES MANAGEMENT ISSUES

JOB SATISFACTION

INDUSTRIAL SALESPERSON JOB SATISFACTION: INDSALES
(Churchill, Ford, and Walker 1974)

Construct: This scale was designed to measure the job satisfaction construct as it applies to the industrial salesperson. Differences in occupational requirements and work settings make generalizations about satisfaction quite tenuous and the unique character of the industrial salesperson's role provided the rationale for the development of this scale. Though the construct's domain was originally defined on 8 dimensions, seven determinants of job satisfaction were retained: (1) the job itself, (2) fellow workers (3) supervisors, (4) company policy and support, (5) pay, (6) promotion and advancement, and (7) customers.

Description: The final version of the instrument consisted of 95 items which represent the seven components listed above. A 5-point Likert scale format ranging from "strongly disagree" to "strongly agree" was used for each item. Numerical scores for negatively stated items were reversed so that a higher numerical value on any item always indicated more satisfaction. Item scores can be summed within each dimension to form indices for each dimension, or overall to form an overall INDSALES score.

Development: Initially, the construct's domain was defined as consisting of eight determinants of job satisfaction. Through an extensive literature review and open-ended questions with salesmen and a work psychologist, items were generated for each determinant. The initial pool consisted of 185 items. The first purification study reduced the pool to 117 items through several item analytic procedures (n = 183). Via factor and reliability analysis of the data from the second purification study (n = 265), 95 items that consistently demonstrated satisfactory reliability were retained for the final scale. Furthermore, though the a priori specification of the component structure posited eight dimensions, seven dimensions for the 95 items were retained in the final version. Several other reliability and validity checks were also reported.

Sample(s): Following open-ended interviews with salespersons in a variety of industries and an experienced psychologist who had worked with industrial salespersons, two purification studies were conducted to develop the final form of the scale. In the first study, the respondents consisted of 183 salespersons randomly selected from the commercial division of a large manufacturer of heating and cooling equipment. In the second study, a more heterogeneous sample consisting of 265 salespersons was drawn from 10 firms in 7 different industries ranging from machine tools and computers to cleaning supplies.

266

Validity: Alpha estimates of internal consistency reliability for the overall scale and each of its components ranged from .82 to .96. Also, split half correlations for the total scale were above the .80 level for 5 of the 7 components. Only the fellow worker and the customer component had split-half correlations below .80. An assessment of construct validity was made by examining whether the measure behaves as expected with respect to other related constructs. Specifically, there is a substantial amount of empirical support to suggest that dissatisfied employees tend to quit their jobs more frequently than satisfied employees. The measures obtained were related to turnover in the sample of respondents. Approximately five months after the instrument was administered, all names of the salespersons of the participating firms who had subsequently quit their jobs were contacted. Twelve salespersons had completed both forms of the instrument. The total mean INDSALES score for these salespersons was 47.35, as compared to an average of 50.13 for all other respondents from the same firms. While the difference in test scores was not statistically significant, it was in the predicted direction ($z = 1.10$, $p < .28$).

Scores: The distribution of raw scores obtained in the final administration of the job satisfaction scale was normalized employing the method of "base-line units of unequal size." The normalized scores were then standardized so as to have a mean of 50 and a standard deviation of 10. Table 4 on page 260 presented a sample of the normalized scores for each component as well as the total scale.

Source: Churchill, Gilbert, Neil M. Ford and Orville C. Walker, Jr. (1974), "Measuring the Job Satisfaction of Industrial Salesmen," *Journal of Marketing Research*, 11 (August), 254-60.

Other evidence: The satisfaction scales for work, coworkers, supervision, pay, and promotion of the INDSALES and the JDI (Smith et al. 1969) were compared from a national sample of 209 salesmen in the health care industry (Futrell 1979). The seven satisfaction scales in INDSALES showed high internal reliability ranging from .85 to .96. The five satisfaction scales common to INDSALES and the JDI showed evidence of convergent and discriminant validity for INDSALES as correlations ranged from .36 to .75 across the corresponding INDSALES and JDI facets.

Childers, Churchill, Ford, and Walker (1980) designed a study to replicate and refine the INDSALES instrument. A mail survey of 113 industrial salespeople was used in the study. A systematic purification process was used to reduce the length of the scale to 61 items with respect to the seven components of job satisfaction. Results showed that the scale reduction was accomplished without compromising its desirable reliability and validity properties. The reliability of the overall scale was .97. The coefficient alphas for the seven facets ranged from .80 to .94. This revised INDSALES measure was also correlated with measures of role conflict and ambiguity. These correlations were -.25 and -.32 for the overall INDSALES score and role ambiguity and conflict, respectively. These correlations offer evidence of nomological validity.

Comer, Machleit, and Lagace (1989) conducted a psychometric assessment of the reduced version of INDSALES (Childers et al. 1982). With the use of a split sample of 295 sales reps qualitative techniques were coupled with factor, item, and reliability analyses (via LISREL) to further reduce INDSALES to a balanced 28-item scale with respect to the seven determinants of job satisfaction. The reliabilities of the reduced scale dimensions ranged from .77 to .87, and correlations among the seven facets ranged from .07 to .68, offering evidence of discriminant validity among the facets. Nomological validity was also confirmed. For example, the total score on the 28-item scale was correlated with role ambiguity (-.38), with reward power (.59), with closeness of supervision (.37), and with propensity to leave (-.38). These correlations offer evidence of nomological validity.

Other sources: Childers, Terry L., Gilbert A. Churchill, Neil M. Ford, and Orville C. Walker (1980) "Towards a More Parsimonious Measurement of Job Satisfaction for the Industrial Salesforce," *AMA Educator's Conference Proceedings*, Richard P. Bagozzi et al. (eds.), 344-349.

Comer, James M., Karen A. Machleit, and Rosemary R. Lagace (1989), "Psychometric Assessment of a Reduced Version of INDSALES," *Journal of Business Research*, 18, 291-302.

Futrell, Charles M. (1979), "Measurement of Salespeople's Job Satisfaction: Convergent and Discriminant Validity of Corresponding INDSALES and Job Description Index Scales," *Journal of Marketing Research*, 16 (November), 594-597.

References: Smith, Patricia C., Loring M. Kendall, and Charles L. Hulin (1969), *The Measurement of Satisfaction in Work and Retirement: A Strategy for the Study of Attitudes*, Chicago: Rand McNally & Company.

INDUSTRIAL SALESPERSON JOB SATISFACTION: INDSALES
(Churchill, Ford, and Walker 1974)

The job

1) My work is creative.
2) My work is valuable.
3) I have plenty of freedom on my job to use my own judgment.
4) My job is exciting.
5) My work is satisfying.
6) I'm really doing something worthwhile in my job.
7) I am unproductive in my work.*
8) My work is useless.*
9) My job is interesting.
10) My work is challenging.
11) My job is often dull and monotonous.*
12) My work gives me a sense of accomplishment.

Fellow workers

1) My fellow workers are stimulating.
2) The people I work with help each other out when someone falls behind or gets in a tight spot.
3) My fellow workers are boring.*
4) My fellow workers are sociable.
5) My fellow workers are pleasant.
6) My fellow workers are obstructive.*
7) The people I work with are very friendly.
8) My fellow workers are loyal.
9) The people I work with get along well together.
10) My fellow workers are selfish.*
11) My fellow workers are intelligent.
12) My fellow workers are responsible.

Supervision

1) My supervisor is up-to-date.
2) My boss has taught me a lot about sales.
3) My sales manager has the work well organized.
4) My boss does a good job of helping sales representatives develop their own potential.
5) My sales manager has always been fair in his dealings with me.
6) My boss really takes the lead in stimulating sales efforts.
7) My supervisor is intelligent.
8) My sales manager is too interested in his own success to care about the needs of employees.*
9) My sales manager gives credit and praise for work well done.
10) My sales manager lives up to his promises.
11) My sales manager knows very little about his job.*
12) My sales manager is tactful.
13) My sales manager really tries to get our ideas about things.
14) My sales manager doesn't seem to try too hard to get our problems across to management.*
15) My sales manager sees that we have the things we need to do our jobs.
16) My sales manager gets the sales personnel to work together as a team.

Company policy and support

1) Compared with other companies, employee benefits here are good.
2) Sometimes when I learn of management's plans I wonder if they know the territory situation at all.*
3) The company's sales training is not carried out in a well-planned program.*
4) I feel that the company is highly aggressive in its sales promotion efforts.
5) Management is progressive.
6) Management keeps us in the dark about things we ought to know.*
7) Management is progressive.
8) Our sales goals are set by the higher-ups without considering market conditions.*
9) Management really knows its job.
10) This company operates efficiently and smoothly.
11) Our home office isn't always cooperative in servicing our customers.*
12) I'm satisfied with the way employee benefits are handled around here.
13) We have a real competitive advantage in selling because of the quality of our products.
14) Management is weak.*
15) I have confidence in the fairness and honesty of management.
16) Management here is really interested in the welfare of employees.
17) The company has satisfactory profit sharing.
18) Sales representatives in this company receive good support from the home office.
19) Management here sees to it that there is cooperation between departments.
20) There isn't enough training for sales representatives who have been on the job for a while.*
21) Management fails to give clear cut orders and instructions.*

Pay

1) My pay is high in comparison with what others get for similar work in other companies.
2) My pay doesn't give me much incentive to increase my sales.*
3) My selling ability largely determines my earnings in this company.
4) My income provides for luxuries.
5) My pay is low in comparison with what others get for similar work in other companies.*
6) In my opinion the pay here is lower than in other companies.*
7) I'm paid fairly compared with other employees in this company.
8) I am very much underpaid for the work that I do.*
9) My income is adequate for normal expenses.
10) I can barely live on my income.*
11) I am highly paid.

Promotion and advancement

1) My opportunities for advancement are limited.*
2) Promotion here is based on ability.
3) I have a good chance for promotion.
4) Regular promotions are the rule in this company.
5) The company has an unfair promotion policy.*
6) There are plenty of good jobs here for those who want to get ahead.
7) This is a dead-end job.*
8) My opportunities for advancement are reasonable.

Customers

1) My customers are fair.
2) My customers blame me for problems that I have no control over.*
3) My customers respect my judgment.
4) I seldom know who really makes the purchase decisions in the companies I call upon.*
5) My customers are unreasonable.*
6) My customers are friendly.
7) My customers are loyal.
8) My customers are understanding.
9) My customers are inaccessible.*
10) My customers are well organized.
11) My customers expect too much from me.*

12) My customers are trustworthy.
13) My customers are intelligent.
14) My customers are interested in what I have to say.
15) My customers live up to their promises.

NOTES: In their original paper, Churchill et al. (1974) offered a sample of items. A complete enumeration of items for each INDSALES facet is offered above. "*" denotes items that require reverse scoring.

The Childers et al. (1980) 61-item version as well as the Comer et al. (1989) 28-item version of INDSALES are offered below.

The job

1)   My work is challenging.
2)   My job is often dull and monotonous.*
3)   My work gives me a sense of accomplishment.
4)   My job is exciting.
5)   My job does not provide me with a sense of worthwhile accomplishment.*
6)   My work is satisfying.
7)   I'm really doing something worthwhile in my job.
8)   My job is routine.*
9)   My job is interesting.

Fellow Workers

10) My fellow workers are selfish.*
11) My fellow workers are intelligent.
12) My fellow workers are responsible.
13) The people I work with are very friendly.
14) My fellow workers are loyal.
15) My fellow workers are stimulating.
16) The people I work with help each other out when someone falls behind or gets in a tight spot.
17) My fellow workers are obstructive.*
18) My fellow workers are pleasant.

Supervision

19) My regional sales manager is tactful.
20) My regional sales manager really tries to get our ideas about things.
21) My regional sales manager is up-to-date.
22) My regional sales manager does a good job of helping salespersons develop their own potential.
23) My regional sales manager has always been fair in dealings with me.
24) My regional sales manager is intelligent.
25) My regional sales manager gets the salesforce to work together as a team.
26) My regional sales manager gives us credit and praise for work well done.
27) My regional sales manager lives up to his/her promises.
28) My regional sales manager knows very little about his/her job.*

Company policy and support

29) Management is progressive.
30) Top management really knows its job.
31) This company operates efficiently and smoothly.
32) The formal recognition programs in this company don't give me much incentive to work harder.*
33) I am satisfied with the way our formal recognition programs are administered.
34) Salespersons in my company receive good support form the home office.
35) Management ignores our suggestions and complaints.*
36) Formal recognition programs in our company compare favorably with those of other companies.
37) I do not get enough formal recognition for the work I do.*

38) Recognition awards are based on ability.
39) I have confidence in the fairness and honesty of management.

Pay

40) My pay is high in comparison with what others get for similar work in other companies.
41) My income provides for luxuries.
42) My pay is low in comparison with what others get for similar work in other companies.*
43) In my opinion, the pay here is lower than in other companies.*
44) I am highly paid.
45) I'm paid fairly compared with other employees in this company.
46) My income is adequate for normal expenses.
47) I'm very much underpaid for the work I do.*

Promotion

48) My opportunities for advancement are limited.*
49) Promotion here is based on ability.
50) I have a good chance for promotion.
51) The company has an unfair promotion policy.*
52) There are plenty of good jobs here for those who want to get ahead.
53) This is a dead-end job.*
54) My opportunities for advancement are reasonable.

Customers

55) My customers are fair.
56) My customers are intelligent.
57) My customers are interested in what I have to say.
58) My customers live up to their promises.
59) My customers are trustworthy.
60) My customers are loyal.
61) My customers are understanding.

NOTES: Items 3, 4, 6, 7 comprise Comer et al.'s job factor; items 10, 13, 16, and 18 comprise their fellow workers factor; items 20, 23, 26, and 27 comprise their supervision factor; items 29, 30, 31, and 34, comprise their policy factor; items 42 through 46 comprise their pay factor; items 48, 50, 51, and 52 comprise their promotion factor; and items 58 through 61 comprise their customer factor. "*" denotes items requiring reverse scoring.

JOB CHARACTERISTIC INVENTORY: JCI
(Sims, Szilagyi, and Keller 1979)

Construct: The Job Characteristic Inventory (JCI) measures characteristics of job satisfaction and performance for six areas of the job. These areas, originally described by Turner and Lawrence (1965) are as as follows (Sims et al. 1979):

Variety - The degree to which a job requires employees to perform a wide range of operations in their work and/or the degree to which employees must use a variety of equipment and procedures in their work.

Autonomy - The extent to which employees have a major say in scheduling their work, selecting the equipment they will use, and deciding on procedures to be followed.

Task identity - The extent to which employees do an entire or whole piece of work and can clearly identify the results of their efforts.

Feedback - The degree to which employees receive information as they are working which reveals how well they are performing on the job.

Dealing with others - The degree to which a job requires employees to deal with other people to complete the work.

Friendship opportunities - The degree to which a job allows employees to talk with one another on the job and to establish informal relationships with other employees at work.

Description: Thirty items comprise the final JCI (Sims et al. 1979, p. 200). Responses for each question were made on a five-point Likert scale, some with scale points ranging from "very little" = 1, "a moderate amount" = 3, to "very much" = 5, and others with scale points ranging from a "minimum amount" = 1, "a moderate amount" = 3, and "a maximum amount" = 5. Scores are averaged across items within each subscale to form subscale indices.

Development: After a review of the literature, a questionnaire was administered to a medical center sample that contained 23 items. Many of the items were taken from the Hackman-Lawler (1971) research which investigated employee reactions to job characteristics. In order to improve reliability, other questions which appeared to have face validity were added to item pool. Based on the results of the validity and reliability analysis of this sample, certain items were deleted from the scale and 14 new items were developed and administered to the manufacturing firm. This resulted in 37 items retained. These 37 items were administered to subjects in a manufacturing firm sample, and based on factor and reliability analyses, the final 30-item JCI was derived. Several estimates of validity were reported.

Sample(s): The JCI was administered to two highly dissimilar samples. The first sample consisted of 1,161 medical center personnel (containing several subsamples), and the second sample was 192 managers and supervisors employed by a manufacturing organization.

Validity: The range of reliability coefficients for the final scale (after a subsequent item analysis) was .72 to .86 across subscales. Factor analysis results confirmed the a priori dimensionality of the JCI across samples, and the scale's validity was also assessed. Multiple discriminant analysis showed that the JCI successfully discriminated among satisfied and dissatisfied employees, offering evidence of predictive validity. Furthermore, correlations of the JCI subscales with measures of task complexity, role ambiguity, adequacy of authority, and warmth showed evidence of discriminant validity in a MTMM format. For example, correlations between the JCI subscales and task complexity ranged from .11 to .53, and the JCI subscales and role ambiguity ranged from -.10 to -.41.

Scores: Mean scores and standard deviations for each subdimension are reported for the two sample groups in Tables 2 and 7 (Sims et al. 1979, pp. 203, 207). For example, the mean scores for the manufacturing sample with respect to the five factors were as follows: variety 3.46, autonomy 3.76, feedback 3.33, task identity 3.66, dealing with others 3.68, and friendship 3.77.

Source:	Sims, Henry P. Jr., Andrew D. Szilagyi, and Robert T. Keller (1979), "The Measurement of Job Characteristics," *Academy of Management Journal*, 19 (June), 195-212.
Other evidence:	In a marketing application, Hunt, Chonko, and Wood (1985) used a version of the JCI for 4 a priori job dimensions of variety, autonomy, identity, and feedback. The sample used was 916 marketing management personnel and marketing researchers. A confirmatory factor analysis was performed. The results indicated a high degree of reliability for all four job dimensions with reliabilities ranging from .79 to .89, and average variance explained ranging from .48 to .69.
Other sources:	Hunt, Shelby D., Lawrence B. Chonko, and Van R. Wood (1985), "Organizational Commitment and Marketing," *Journal of Marketing*, 49 (Winter), 112-126.
References:	Hackman, J.R. and E.E. Lawler (1971), "Employee Reactions to Job Characteristics," *Journal of Applied Psychology*, 55, 259-286.
	Turner, A.N. and P.R. Lawrence (1965), *Industrial Jobs and the Worker*, Boston: Harvard University Graduate School of Business Administration.

JOB CHARACTERISTIC INVENTORY: JCI
(Sims, Szilagyi, and Keller 1979)

1. To what extent do you start work that is finished by another employee?

2. How much variety is there in your job?

3. How much are you left on your own to do your own work?

4. How often do you see projects or jobs through to completion?

5. To what extent do you find out how well you are doing on the job as you are working?

6. How much opportunity is there to meet individuals whom you would like to develop friendships with?

7. How much of your job depends upon your ability to work with others?

8. How repetitious are your duties?

9. To what extent are you able to act independently of your supervisor in performing your job function?

10. To what extent do you complete work that has been started by another employee?

11. To what extent do you receive information from your superior on your job performance?

12. To what extent do you have the opportunity to talk informally with other employees while at work?

13. To what extent is dealing with other people a part of your job?

14. How similar are the tasks you perform in a typical work day?

15. To what extent are you able to do your job independently of others?

16. To what extent is your job equivalent to being one small cog in a big machine?

17. To what extent are the results of your work clearly evident?

18. The feedback from my supervisor on how well I'm doing.

19. Friendship from my co-workers.

20. The opportunity to talk to others on my job.

21. The opportunity to do a number of different things.

22. The freedom to do pretty much what I want on my job.

23. The degree to which the work I'm involved with is handled from beginning to end by myself.

24. The opportunity to find out how well I am doing on my job.

25. The opportunity in my job to get to know other people.

26. Working pretty much by myself.

27. The amount of variety in my job.

28. The opportunity for independent thought and action.

29. The opportunity to complete work I start.

30. The feeling that I know whether I am performing my job well or poorly.

31. The opportunity to develop close friendships in my job.

32. Meeting with others in my work.

33. The control I have over the pace of my work.

34. The opportunity to do a job from the beginning to end (i.e., the chance to do a whole job).

35. The extent of feedback you receive from individuals other than your supervisor.

36. To what extent do you do a "whole" piece of work (as opposed to doing part of a job which is finished by some other employee)?

37. The opportunity, in my job, to give help to other people.

NOTES: All 37 items examined are listed above. The final version of the scale is comprised of items 2 through 9, 11 through 15, 18 through 25 and 26 through 35.

The item numbers comprising each factor are as follows: variety - 2, 8, 14, 21, 27; autonomy - 3, 9, 15, 22, 28, 33; feedback - 5, 11, 18, 24, 30; dealing with others - 7, 13, 35; task identity - 4, 23, 29, 34; friendship - 6, 12, 19, 20, 25, 31, 32.

Items 1 through 17 and 36 are scored on the "very little" to "very much" format, and the remaining items are scored on the "minimum amount" to "maximum amount" format.

JOB SATISFACTION
(Wood, Chonko, and Hunt 1986)

Construct: Wood, Chonko, and Hunt (1986) characterize job satisfaction as multidimensional. The dimensions of satisfaction were as follows:

(1) satisfaction with information
(2) satisfaction with variety and freedom
(3) satisfaction with the ability to complete tasks
(4) satisfaction with pay and security

Description: The job satisfaction measure consists of 14 items scored on a Likert format (with 1=Strongly Disagree and 7=Strongly Agree). Item scores are summed within dimensions to form dimension scores, or scores on the 14 items can be summed to form an overall index of satisfaction.

Development: Seven of the job satisfaction items were developed by Wood, Chonko, and Hunt (1986) from pretested responses, and they focused on various elements of the respondents' jobs. Additionally, seven items were selected from the Job Characteristic Inventory (Sims et al. 1976). These 14 items served both as the initial pool and final versions of the scale. Factor analysis and coefficient alpha were used to judge the scales dimensionality and reliability.

Sample(s): A self-administered questionnaire was sent to 4,282 marketing practitioners. The subjects were chosen based on a systematic sample of one out of every four marketing practitioners in the American Marketing Association directory. Educators and students were excluded from the sample. A total of 1,076 usable questionnaires were returned.

Validity: An alpha coefficient of .89 was obtained for the total 14-item satisfaction scale. Alpha coefficients for each of the factors were .93 for information, .88 for variety and freedom, .80 for completion of tasks, and .56 for pay and security. The fourteen satisfaction items were factor analyzed, and the four-factor solution of (1) satisfaction with information, (2) satisfaction with variety and freedom, (3) satisfaction with ability to complete tasks, and (4) satisfaction with pay and security was retained. Factor loadings ranged from .51 to .91 on the respective factors, and the four-factor solution accounted for 81% of the variance in the data. Furthermore, correlations of the satisfaction dimensions with income ranged from .08 to .23, providing some evidence of nomological validity.

Scores: Mean scores indicated that the average respondent had a high perceived satisfaction score with respect to job variety, job closure, the job in general, and a marketing career. The overall mean for the 14-item job satisfaction scale was 40.95 with a standard deviation of 2.47. The means and standard deviations for each factor are as follows: satisfaction with information 13.69 (6.40), satisfaction with variety 12.91 (6.23), satisfaction with closure 4.65 (2.37), and satisfaction with pay 6.78 (3.06).

Source: Wood, Van R., Lawrence B. Chonko, Shelby Hunt (1986), "Social Responsibility and Personal Success: Are They Incompatible?" *Journal of Business Research*, 14, 193-212.

Other evidence: N/A

Other sources: N/A

References: Sims, Henry P., Jr., Andrew D. Szilagyi, and Robert T. Keller (1976), "The Measurement of Job Characteristics," *Academy of Management Journal*, 19 (June), 195-212.

JOB SATISFACTION
(Wood, Chonko, and Hunt 1986)

Satisfaction with Information

1. I am satisfied with the information I receive from my superior about my job performance.

2. I receive enough information from my supervisor about my job performance.

3. I receive enough feedback from my supervisor on how well I'm doing.

4. There is enough opportunity in my job to find out how I am doing.

Satisfaction with Variety

5. I am satisfied with the variety of activities my job offers.

6. I am satisfied with the freedom I have to do what I want on my job.

7. I am satisfied with the opportunities my job provides me to interact with others.

8. There is enough variety in my job.

9. I have enough freedom to do what I want in my job.

10. My job has enough opportunity for independent thought and action.

Satisfaction with Closure

11. I am satisfied with the opportunities my job gives me to complete tasks from beginning to end.

12. My job has enough opportunity to complete the work I start.

Satisfaction with Pay

13. I am satisfied with the pay I receive for my job.

14. I am satisfied with the security my job provides me.

NOTES: *Reprinted by permission of the publisher from Wood, Van R., Lawrence B. Chonko, Shelby Hunt (1986), "Social Responsibility and Personal Success: Are They Incompatible?"* **Journal of Business Research**, *14, 193-212. Copyright 1992 by Elsevier Science Publishing Co., Inc.*

JOB IN GENERAL SCALE: JIG
(Ironson, Smith, Brannick, Gibson, and Paul 1989)

Construct: The JIG was designed to assess overall feelings about one's job. As such, it is considered a global measure of job satisfaction (Ironson, Smith, Brannick, Gibson, and Paul 1989).

Description: The JIG is composed of 18 adjective or short phrase evaluative items concerning feelings about one's job. The format and scoring of the items are the same as those for the JDI (Smith et al. 1969). That is, a respondent is asked to write "Y" (for Yes) if an item applies to his work, "N" (for No) if an item does not apply, and "?" if the respondent is undecided. A score of 3 is given to a "Y" answer for a positive item and "N" for a negative item. A score of 2 is given for a "?," and a score of 1 is given to a "Y" for a negative item and "N" for a positive item. The JIG is considered a unidimensional measure of global job satisfaction. Thus, it appears that item scores can be summed to form an overall JIG score.

Development: A pool of 42 adjective and short phrases from an extensive literature review served as the initial pool of items. Twenty-two of these items were negatively worded. These items were administered to a combined sample (n = 1,149). Via item-to-total correlations, principal components, and an index of favorableness, the pool of items was trimmed down to a smaller number. Then, with another large sample (4,490) from archival data, the index of favorableness was used to reduce the JIG to its final 18-item form. Numerous estimates of reliability and validity were assessed.

Sample(s): The combined sample of 1,149 was composed of employees from an urban county in Florida. The archival sample of 4,490 was from the Bowling Green Data Archives and was composed of employees of a wide range of job descriptions (i.e., blue collar, white collar, professional, etc.). Another large sample of 648 nuclear power plant workers was also collected. (See Ironson et al. [1989, pp. 194-195]) for a description of the samples and subsamples.)

Validity: Principal components analysis of the 18-item JIG showed that the first general factor accounted for 87% of the variance in the data, supporting the scale's unidimensionality. Coefficient alpha for the scale ranged from .91 to .95 across the samples and subsets of the samples. Correlations of the JIG with other measures of job satisfaction ranged from .67 to .80, providing evidence of convergent validity for the scale. Discriminant validity was also demonstrated as the JIG showed significantly greater validity than the JDI scales in predicting work related variables. Also, with the nuclear power plant sample, the JIG showed strong evidence of nomological validity. For example, correlations of the JIG with intention to leave, trust in management, and job definition were -.54, .51, and .50, respectively.

Scores: Percentages of those respondents responding favorably to each item are offered in Table 1 of Ironson et al. (1989). These scores range from .23 to .88.

Source: Ironson, G.H., P.C. Smith, M.T. Brannick, W.M. Gibson, and K.B. Paul (1989), "Construction of a Job in General Scale: A Comparison of Global, Composite, and Specific Measures," *Journal of Applied Psychology*, 74 (2), 193-200.

References: Smith, Patricia C., Loring M. Kendall, and Charles L. Hulin (1969), *The Measurement of Satisfaction in Work and Retirement: A Strategy for the Study of Attitudes*, Chicago: Rand McNally & Company.

JOB IN GENERAL SCALE: JIG
(Ironson, Smith, Brannick, Gibson, and Paul 1989)

JIG items

1) pleasant
2) bad*
3) ideal
4) waste of time*
5) good
6) undesirable*
7) worthwhile
8) worse than most*
9) acceptable
10) superior
11) better than most
12) disagreeable*
13) makes me content
14) inadequate*
15) excellent
16) rotten*
17) enjoyable
18) poor*

NOTES: * denotes items that are reverse coded. See the JDI for instructions.

APPENDIX TO JOB SATISFACTION
Probably the most commonly used measure of job satisfaction in both the organizational behavior and sales
management literature is the JDI - the Job Descriptive Index (Smith, Kendall, and Hulin 1969). The JDI is a
copyrighted proprietary measure, and therefore, the JDI items are not reproduced here. The potential user of the
JDI should contact Prof. Patricia Smith, Department of Psychology, Bowling Green State University, Bowling
Green OH 43403. Below, we offer a summary of the JDI.

JOB DESCRIPTION INDEX: JDI
(Smith, Kendall, and Hulin 1969)

Construct: The Job Description Index (JDI) measures employee satisfaction with five dimensions of a job: the type of work, the pay, the opportunities for promotion, the supervision and the co-workers on the job (Smith, Kendall, and Hulin 1969, p. 69).

Description: For each of the five job-related categories stated above, there is a corresponding list of adjectives or short phrases. The respondent is instructed to indicate whether each word or phrase is descriptive with respect to the particular facet of his/her job. The respondent is asked to write "Y" (for Yes) if the word applies to a facet of his work, "N" (for No) if the word does not apply, and "?" if the respondent is undecided. A score of 3 is given to a "Y" answer for a positive item and "N" for a negative item. A score of 2 is given for a "?," and a score of 1 is given to a "Y" for a negative item and "N" for a positive item. An alternative scoring system is also tenable where a score of 0 is given for a "Y" to a negative item and "N" for a positive item. (It is this alternative scoring system that is more widely used.) Thirty-seven of the items were positively worded and thirty-five were negatively worded. Thus, the final version of the JDI included a total of 72 scale items. Eighteen items were written for each of the following three job-related areas: work, supervision, and co-workers. Nine scale items were associated with both the pay and promotion categories. Item scores are summed within categories to form indices for each facet, and can be summed overall to derive an overall satisfaction score.

Recently, a revised version of the JDI has been proposed (cf., Smith et al. 1985, 1987).

Development: The original item pool was developed by selecting items from other job-satisfaction indices and from available lists of adjectives and short phrases which the authors felt tapped various aspects of job satisfaction. This original search generated from 30 to 40 items per category. Initial item analysis discarded items that failed to show significant differences in response frequency between best and worst jobs. After further item analysis and several purification studies, the final 72-item JDI was derived. A number of reliability and validity checks were performed over several samples.

Sample(s): Using subjects from a wide range of occupational and educational groups, preliminary JDI scales were administered to 17 janitors, 25 secretaries, and 16 cafeteria workers at Cornell University. The first large-scale study used a convenience sample of 317 Cornell University students and Ithaca residents. Based on the results from the group, the scale was revised and administered to 81 randomly selected employees of a New York Farmers' Cooperative. The next sample of subjects included 163 men and 73 women randomly chosen from three companies. In the final item-development study, the JDI was administered to 192 male employees randomly selected from two plants of an electronics firm. Various tests were performed on the scale after the final item-development study. These studies tested a large sample of approximately 2,600 subjects with varying backgrounds.

Validity: Numerous studies were conducted to assess the discriminant and convergent validity of several aspects of job satisfaction. Specifically, preliminary studies with small groups of janitors, secretaries, and cafeteria workers showed that the JDI score correlated significantly with supervisory ratings and rankings of job satisfaction. The second study was a more extensive attempt to compare two JDI scoring methods and more direct measures of satisfaction involving global ratings and ratings focused on critical incidents. The study also evaluated effects of item selection on validity. A third study was developed to evaluate the validity and soundness of these final JDI scales and the "Faces" rating scale. This study served as the crucial field test of the measures finally selected. A fourth study was performed which not only showed that the discriminability obtained for the several areas applies to total scores cumulated for each area, but that adequate discriminability exists at the level of specific items which make up the content of total scales. In sum, the original scale development procedures showed evidence of validity for the JDI. For a more extensive review of validation procedures, the interested reader is referred to the original Smith, Kendall, and Hulin (1969) book.

A variety of data was provided by Smith et al. (1969) on scale reliability. For example, they report random split-half estimates of reliability ranging from .67 to .78 across subscales, and Spearman-Brown reliabilities between .80 and .88 for the n = 80 sample. In addition, factor intercorrelations ranged from .28 to .42 for the sample of 980 males, and .16 to .52 for 627 females.

Scores: Mean scores for the 5 JDI scales are based on a sample of nearly 2,000 male and over 600 female workers. The samples were obtained by pooling employees across a total of 21 plants, which represented 19 different companies and 16 different standard Metropolitan Statistical Areas. For the male sample, means and (standard deviations) were 36.57 (10.54), 29.90 (14.53), 22.06 (15.77), 41.10 (10.58), and 43.49 (10.02) for work, pay, promotion, supervisor, and co-workers, respectively. Corresponding means for the female sample were 35.74 (9.88), 27.90 (13.65), 17.77 (13.28), 41.13 (10.05), and 42.09 (10.51). A more comprehensive presentation of means and standard deviations can be found in Smith et al. (1969, p. 80).

Source: Smith, Patricia C., Loring M. Kendall, and Charles L. Hulin (1969), *The Measurement of Satisfaction in Work and Retirement: A Strategy for the Study of Attitudes*, Chicago: Rand McNally & Company.

Smith, Patricia C., Loring M. Kendall, and Charles L. Hulin (1985), *The Job Descriptive Index* (Revised Ed.), Bowling Green, OH: Department of Psychology, Bowling Green State University.

Smith, Patricia C., Loring M. Kendall, and Charles L. Hulin (1987), "The Revised JDI: A Facelift for an Old Friend," *Industrial Organizational Psychologist*, 24 (4), 31-33.

Other evidence: The JDI has been extensively used in the work and organizational behavior literature. For an excellent critical review of the JDI see Kinicki, Carson, and Schriesheim (1990). There have been several applications of the JDI in the marketing literature as well. Two of these are briefly discussed here.

The satisfaction scales for work, co-workers, supervision, pay, and promotion of the INDSALES (Churchill, Ford, and Walker 1974) and the JDI were compared on a national sample of 209 salesmen in the health care industry (Futrell 1979). Alpha estimates for the JDI facets of work, co-workers, supervisor, pay, and promotion were .85, .93, .91, .67, and .88. Correlations among facets ranged from .19 to .62. Furthermore, the five satisfaction scales common to INDSALES and the JDI show both convergent and discriminant validity as correlations for the corresponding JDI and INDSALES dimensions ranged from .36 to .75. Mean scores (standard deviations) for the JDI facets of work, co-workers, supervisor, pay, and promotion were 38.80 (10.54), 45.27 (11.68), 40.72 (13.54), 16.99 (5.70), and 12.86 (8.61).

Over two time periods, Johnston et al. (1990) reported construct reliabilities for the overall JDI of .85 and .92. In addition, correlations of the JDI with measures of role conflict, role ambiguity, organizational commitment, propensity to leave an organization, and turnover were -.55, -.36, .58, -.59, and -.33, respectively, offering evidence of nomological validity.

Other sources: Futrell, Charles M. (1979), "Measurement of Salespeople's Job Satisfaction: Convergent and Discriminant Validity of Corresponding INDSALES and Job Description Index Scales," *Journal of Marketing Research*, 16 (November), 594-597.

Johnston, Mark W., A. Parasuraman, Charles M. Futrell, and William C. Black (1990), "A Longitudinal Assessment of the Impact of Selected Organizational Influences on Salespeople's Organizational Commitment During Early Employment," *Journal of Marketing Research*, 27 (August), 333-344.

References: Churchill, Gilbert, Neil M. Ford and Orville C. Walker, Jr. (1974), "Measuring the Job Satisfaction of Industrial Salesmen," *Journal of Marketing Research*, 11 (August), 254-60.

Kinicki, Angelo, Kenneth A. Carson, and Chester Schriesheim (1990), "The Construct Validity of the Job Descriptive Index (JDI): Review, Critique, and Analysis," *Working Paper*, Arizona State University, 1-103.

Another job related measure is the Job Diagnostic Survey - the JDS (Hackman and Oldham 1975). Given its length (over 10 pages), and that it has seen only limited application in the marketing literature, the JDS items and measures were not included in this volume. However, we do offer a summary of the JDS below. The entire JDS and scoring procedures can be found in Hackman and Oldham (1980, Appendix A, pp. 275-294).

JOB DIAGNOSTIC SURVEY: JDS
(Hackman and Oldham 1975, 1980)

Construct: The JDS is intended to a) diagnose existing jobs to determine if (and how) they might be redesigned to improve employee motivation and productivity, and b) to evaluate the effects of job changes on employees. The JDS is based on a theory of how job design affects work motivation, and provides measures of a) objective job dimensions, b) individual psychological states resulting from these dimensions, c) affective reactions of employees to the job and work setting, and d) individual growth need strength (i.e., the readiness of individuals to respond to "enriched" jobs [Hackman and Oldham 1975, p. 159]).

Description: The JDS is a multi-faceted, multidimensional measure. Within the four facets alluded to above, there are numerous subdimensions. The "objective job dimensions" facet is composed of seven subscales: skill variety, task identity, task significance, autonomy, feedback from the job, feedback from agents, and dealing with others. All of these subscales are composed of three items each. The "psychological states" facet is composed of three subdimensions: experienced meaningfulness of the work (4 items), experienced responsibility for the work (6 items), and knowledge of results (4 items). The "affective reactions" facet is composed of seven subdimensions: general satisfaction (5 items), internal work motivation (6 items), satisfaction with job security (2 items), satisfaction with pay (2 items), social satisfaction (3 items), satisfaction with supervision (3 items), and satisfaction with growth (4 items). The "growth need strength" facet is composed of two subdimensions: would like format (6 items), and job choice format (12 items). Across facets and dimensions, item scoring varies from 5 to 7 to 10-point scales. Item scores can be summed and then divided by the number of items within a subdimension to form subdimension scores. Also, a motivating potential score (MPS) can be calculated by combining, in a multiplicative fashion, subdimensions of the job dimensions facet. The JDS also contains questions pertaining to biographical characteristics.

Development: The JDS has its developmental origins in previous methodologies (e.g., Hackman and Lawler 1971). In fact, the JDS reported in Hackman and Oldham (1980) represents a revision of the JDS over an extensive period of time. In essence, the JDS has been revised to maximize the substantive richness of the measures, while maintaining high levels of reliability and validity. The JDS measures have undergone extensive structure, reliability, and validity analyses over numerous samples.

Sample(s):   The sample on which the "validity" results presented below was based on 658 employees representing 62 different jobs in 7 organizations. These jobs included blue collar, white collar, and professionals from various parts of the country in both industrial and service organizations.

Validity: Spearman-Brown internal consistency estimates ranged from .59 to .78 for the subscales of the "job dimensions" facet. Correlations among the subscales ranged from .02 to .51. Spearman-Brown internal consistency estimates ranged from .72 to .76 for the subscales of the "psychological states" facet. Correlations among the subscales ranged from .32 to .64. Spearman-Brown internal consistency estimates ranged from .56 to .84 for the subscales of the "affective responses" facet. Correlations among the subscales ranged from .31 to .67, and Spearman-Brown internal consistency estimates were .88 and .71 for the "would like" and "job choice" format of the "growth need" facet. The correlation between these two subscales was .50.

Various estimates of validity were also offered including correlations among facet scores and mean differences via ANOVA. For example, the MPS showed a median correlation of -.25 with absenteeism and .24 with performance effectiveness. Correlations among all subdimensions of the JDS ranged from -.01 to .67. Mean differences (Table 3, p. 163) are also reported that support the validity of the JDS. (See also Hackman and Oldham 1980.)

Scores: Mean scores for each subdimension are reported in Table 3, p.165 of Hackman and Oldham (1975).

Source(s): Hackman, J. Richard and Greg Oldham (1975), "Development of the Job Diagnostic Survey," *Journal of Applied Psychology*, 60, 159-170.

Hackman, J. Richard and Greg Oldham (1980), *Work Redesign*, Reading, MA: Addison-Wesley Publishing Co.

Other evidence: The JDS has seen extensive use in the organizational behavior literature (cf., Hackman and Oldham 1980). Our discussion of other evidence will be limited to one marketing application of the JDS. Using a sample of 211 industrial salespeople, Becherer et al. (1982) reported numerous correlations and regression coefficients pertaining to the subdimensions of the JDS. For example, five of the subdimensions of the objective job dimensions facet (i.e., skill variety, task identity, task significance, autonomy, and feedback) showed correlations ranging from .23 to .36 with internal motivation, .14 to .33 with general satisfaction, and .28 to .48 with growth satisfaction. Similar results were reported for the subdimensions of the psychological states facet. For example, meaningfulness of work showed correlations of .52, .69, and .69 with internal motivation, general satisfaction, and growth satisfaction, respectively.

Other sources: Becherer, Richard C., Fred W. Morgan and Lawrence M. Richard (1982), "The Job Characteristics of Industrial Salespeople: Relationships to Motivation and Satisfaction," *Journal of Marketing*, 46 (Fall), 125-135.

References: Hackman, J. Richard and E.E. Lawler, III (1971), "Employee Reactions to Job Characteristics," *Journal of Applied Psychology Monograph*, 55, 259-286.

ROLE PERCEPTIONS AND JOB TENSION

ROLE CONFLICT AND AMBIGUITY
(Rizzo, House, and Lirtzman 1970)

Construct: Both role conflict (RC) and ambiguity (RA) are important intervening variables that mediate the effects of various organizational practices on individual and organizational outcomes. Role conflict was defined in terms of dimensions of congruency-incongruency or compatibility-incompatibility in the requirements of the role, where congruency or compatibility is judged relative to a set of standards or conditions which impinge upon role performance. The role conflict components were stated as follows:

1) Conflict between the focal person's internal standards or values and the defined role behavior.

2) Conflict between the time, resources, or capabilities of the focal person and defined role behavior.

3) Conflict between several roles for the same person which require different or incompatible behaviors, or changes in behavior as a function of the situation; i.e., role overload.

4) Conflicting expectations and organizational demands in the form of incompatible policies, conflicting requests from others, and incompatible standards of evaluation.

Role ambiguity is defined in terms of (1) the predictability of the outcome or responses to one's behavior, and (2) the existence or clarity of behavioral requirements, often in terms of input from the environment, which would serve to guide behavior and provide knowledge that the behavior is appropriate (Rizzo, House, and Lirtzman 1970).

Description: The original RC/RA questionnaire consisted of 30 items, 15 for RA (even numbers) and 15 for RC (odd numbers). However, it is the reduced 6-item RA and 8-item RC measures that are commonly employed for research purposes. Subjects are requested to respond to the items by indicating the degree to which the condition the item describes existed for him/her on a seven-point scale ranging from very false to very true. Items scores are summed within RC and RA scales and then divided by the number of items in each scale to form RC and RA scores.

Development: Approximately 350 items were contained in the original pool of items. Based on the results of factor and item analysis, 30 items reflecting role conflict and role ambiguity emerged as separate dimensions, accounting for 56 percent of the variance in the data. Factor 1 was named role conflict. Of the 15 role conflict items, 9 with loadings greater than or equal to .30 were retained. Factor 2, role ambiguity, also retained 9 items with loadings greater than or equal to .30. Examination of the items revealed that the two factors strongly parallel the theoretical concepts of role conflict and role ambiguity. Reliability analysis was then used to derive the final 6 and 8-item RA and RC scales. A number of validity checks followed.

Sample(s): The questionnaire was administered to a 35 percent random sample of the employees in central offices and main plant of a firm and to 100 percent sample of the research and engineering division. The total number of respondents was treated as two separate samples. There were 199 respondents in the first sample and 91 respondents in the second sample. The instrument was administered to groups ranging from 10 to 50. Anonymity was assured and participation was voluntary.

Validity: Coefficient alpha estimates of internal consistency for the 8-item RC scale were .82 and .82 for samples one and two. Corresponding estimates for the 6-item RA scale were .78 and .81. The correlations between the two scales were .25 and .01 for the two samples, offering evidence of discriminant validity between RC and RA. Nomological validity was assessed by correlating RC and RA with 41 different work-related attitudes and outcomes. The overall pattern of these correlations showed evidence of nomological validity for RC and RA. For example, the correlations between RA and personal recognition were -.43 and -.56 for the two studies. For RC, corresponding correlations were -.22 and -.11. Correlations between RA and job induced tension were .12 and .22, and the correlations between RC and tension were .20 and .12. RC and RA were also positively correlated with a measure of propensity to leave the organization.

Scores: The composite means and (standard deviations) for role conflict were 4.19 (1.21) and 3.86 (1.21) for the two samples. With respect to role ambiguity the means and (standard deviations) were 3.79 (1.08) and 4.03 (1.15) for the two samples.

Source: Rizzo, John R., Robert J. House and Sidney I. Lirtzman (1970), "Role Conflict and Ambiguity in Complex Organizations," *Administrative Science Quarterly*, 15 (June), 150-164.

Other evidence: The RC and RA scales have been extensively used and examined in the organizational behavior literature. For two meta-analytic reviews of role conflict and role ambiguity, see Fisher and Gitelson (1983) and Jackson and Schuler (1985). The scales have also seen wide application in the sales literature. Two of these applications are briefly reviewed here.

In a study of industrial salespeople's job satisfaction, Teas (1983) reported alpha estimates of .88 and .82 for RC and RA. Furthermore, correlations of RC with job satisfaction, employee feedback, and leadership consideration were -.51, -.31, and -.44, respectively. Corresponding correlations of these variables with RA were -.42, -.40, and -.48.

In another study, Johnston et al. (1990) reported internal consistency estimates via LISREL of .807 and .846 for the 8-item role conflict measure, and .807 and .815 for the 6-item role ambiguity measure. Furthermore, these scales were found related to a number of organizational variables including satisfactory commitment and leadership, offering support for the scales' nomological validity. For example, the correlation of RC with job satisfaction, commitment, and propensity-to-leave the organization were -.53, -.49, and .45. Corresponding correlations of these variables with RA were -.36, -.45, and .47.

Other Sources: Johnston, Mark, A. Parasuraman, Charles M. Futrell and William C. Black (1990), "A Longitudinal Assessment of the Impact of Selected Organizational Influences on Salespeople's Organizational Commitment During Early Employment," *Journal of Marketing Research*, 27 (August), 333-344.

Teas, R. Kenneth (1983), "Supervisory Behavior, Role Stress, and the Job Satisfaction of Industrial Salespeople," *Journal of Marketing Research*, 20 (February), 84-93.

References: Fisher, C.D. and R. Gitelson (1983), "A Meta-Analysis and Conceptual Critique of Role Conflict and Ambiguity," *Journal of Applied Psychology*, 68, 320-333.

Jackson, S.E. and R.S. Schuler (1985), "A Meta- Analysis and Conceptual Critique of Role Ambiguity and Role Conflict in Work Settings," *Organizational Behavior and Human Decision Processes*, 36, 16-78.

ROLE CONFLICT AND AMBIGUITY
(Rizzo, House, and Lirtzman 1970)

1. I have enough time to complete my work.
2. I feel certain about how much authority I have.
3. I perform tasks that are too easy or boring.
4. Clear, planned goals and objectives for my job.
5. I have to do things that should be done differently.
6. Lack of policies and guidelines to help me.
7. I am able to act the same regardless of the group I am with.

8. I am corrected or rewarded when I really don't expect it.
9. I work under incompatible policies and guidelines.
10. I know that I have divided my time properly.
11. I receive an assignment without the manpower to complete it.
12. I know what my responsibilities are.
13. I have to buck a rule or policy in order to carry out an assignment.
14. I have to "feel my way" in performing my duties.
15. I receive assignments that are within my training and capability.
16. I feel certain how I will be evaluated for a raise or promotion.
17. I have just the right amount of work to do.
18. I know that I have divided my time properly.
19. I work with two or more groups who operate quite differently.
20. I know exactly what is expected of me.
21. I receive incompatible requests from two or more people.
22. I am uncertain as to how my job is linked.
23. I do things that are apt to be accepted by one person and not accepted by other.
24. I am told how well I am doing my job.
25. I receive an assignment without adequate resources and materials to execute it.
26. Explanation is clear of what has to be done.
27. I work on unnecessary things.
28. I have to work under vague directives or orders.
29. I perform work that suits my values.
30. I do not know if my work will be acceptable to my boss.

NOTE: All of the original 30 items are listed above. Items 2, 4, 10, 12, 20, and 26 comprise the 6-item RA scale, and items 5, 11, 13, 19, 21, 23, 25, and 27 comprise the 8-item RC scale. Items 2, 4, 10, 12, 20, and 26 require reverse coding to reflect higher levels of RC and RA.

ROLE CONFLICT AND AMBIGUITY SCALES FOR INDUSTRIAL SALESPEOPLE
(Ford, Walker, and Churchill 1975)

Construct: Ford, Walker, and Churchill (1975) define role conflict (RC) and ambiguity (RA) as follows. RC is the belief that two or more individuals or groups are making incompatible demands about how a job should be performed. Examples of these individuals or groups include sales manager and customer, sales manager and family, and sales manager and members of other departments. RA is defined as feelings of uncertainty about the kinds of behaviors expected in relation to various role partners. These partners include top management (company policy), sales manager, customer, and family.

Description: The final version of the RC scale consisted of 30 possible activity/expectation items across four role-partner groups: company, sales manager, customers, and family. Because all the items were not relevant to all four role partner groups, the number of expectation differences that are possible to calculate for each dyad of role partners is as follows: company-sales manager = 14; company-customers = 14; customer-family = 17; sales manager-customers = 22; and sales manager-family = 11. The total number of expectation differences used to calculate a total perceived conflict score was 68. A five-point Likert scale was used for each RC item, with 1=strongly disagree and 5=strongly agree. The amount of RC was measured by calculating the absolute differences in the respondent's scale scores for the two role partners on each item. A perceived conflict score for each dyad of role partners was calculated across all common items. A total perceived conflict score for the respondent was then calculated by summing the conflict scores for all possible role-partner dyads.

With respect to RA, the instrument was constructed to measure the respondent's perceived ambiguity with respect to the (1) company's policies and procedures concerning how job activities should be performed, evaluation criteria concerning job performance and ways performance is rewarded; (2) sales manager's expectations concerning performance of job activities and the evaluation criteria used; (3) customers' expectations concerning job performance and their evaluation criteria; and (4) expectations of the family concerning job performance. The final version of the RA scale consisted of 41 items, 21 related to company policies and evaluation criteria, 7 items related to sales managers' expectations, 7 items dealt with customer expectation, and 6 items were relevant to expectation of family members. Six-point Likert scales ranging from "absolutely certain" to "absolutely uncertain" were used for the items. Ambiguity scores for each of the four dimensions were calculated by summing the scores on all items within each component. A total ambiguity score can be calculated by summing the four component scores.

Development: The procedures for scale development included item purification, estimates of reliability and validity, and derivation of scores on the scales. An extensive review of the literature, open-ended interviews with salespersons, and a psychologist who had a number of salespersons as patients were used to define the constructs' domain and generate the initial item pool. The initial RC instrument consisted of 34 items across 84 dyadic expectation comparisons. Forty-six items were selected for the initial RA pool. A purification study, based on responses from 249 salespersons, was performed for each construct. Based on inter-item correlations of the RC items, the total number of dyadic expectation comparisons was reduced from 84 to 68. The final number of RC items was then reduced to a possible of 30 for each group (i.e., company, sales manager, customers, family). A similar procedure was used to reduce the number of items on the RA instrument from 46 to 41. Estimates of reliability and validity followed.

Sample(s): To test and refine the initial instrument, a sample of 249 salesmen was randomly drawn from the commercial division of a large heating and cooling equipment manufacturer. Completed questionnaires were received from 74 percent (183) of the salesmen. The revised instrument was tested on a sample of 479 industrial salesmen drawn from 10 firms in seven different industries. A total of 265 salesmen completed the instrument.

Validity: The final 30- and 41-item versions of the role conflict and role ambiguity scales yielded alpha estimates of .85 and .91, respectively. The conflict and ambiguity scales were further evaluated by using a split-half procedure. The resulting corrected correlation coefficient for the split-halves of the conflict scale was .67, while the coefficient for the ambiguity scale was .82. The construct validity of each scale was examined by the construction of a multitrait-multimethod matrix. Convergent validity correlations ranged from .40 to .46. Correlations of RC and RA with a measure of job satisfaction were -.24 and -.36, respectively, offering evidence of nomological validity.

Scores: The scores obtained in the final test of the conflict and ambiguity scales were both normalized and standardized. The distributions of raw scores were normalized employing the method of "base-line units of unequal size." The normalized scores were standardized with a mean of 50 and a standard deviation of 10. For RC, the normalized mean score was 35, and for RA it was 101.

Source: Ford, Neil M., Orville C. Walker, Jr., and Gilbert A. Churchill, Jr. (1975), "Expectation-Specific Measures of the Intersender Conflict and Role Ambiguity Experienced by Industrial Salesmen," *Journal of Business Research*, 3 (April), 95-112.

Other evidence: N/A

Other sources: N/A

References: N/A

ROLE CONFLICT AND AMBIGUITY SCALES FOR INDUSTRIAL SALESPEOPLE
(Ford, Walker, and Churchill 1975)

Role-Partner

Role-Conflict Scale

My company expects me:

1) to expedite orders for my customers.
2) to follow the "hard sell" approach.
3) to do systems-design work for my customers.
4) to show customers how our products can be coordinated with those of our competitors.
5) to supervise the installation of equipment for my customers.
6) to "stretch the truth" to make a sale.
7) to "hold firm" on our normal deliver dates.
8) to be a technical "trouble-shooter."
9) to train customers in the use of our equipment.
10) to be completely honest with my customers.
11) to handle back charges and adjustments for my customers.
12) to tailor deliver schedules to my customer's needs.
13) to negotiate on price.
14) to do product design work for my customers.
15) to tailor credit terms to fit the needs of customers.
16) to perform field tests on newly installed equipment.

My sales manager expects me:

1) to expedite orders for my customers.
2) to perform engineering services for my customers.
3) to do systems-design work for my customers.
4) to show customers how our products can be coordinated with those of our competitors.
5) to supervise the installation of equipment for my customers.
6) to "stretch the truth" to make a sale.

7) to "hold firm" on our normal deliver dates.
8) to be a technical "trouble-shooter."
9) to train customers in the use of our equipment.
10) to be completely honest with my customers.
11) to call on customers even if they are unlikely to place an order.
12) to tailor deliver schedules to my customer's needs.
13) to negotiate on price.
14) to do product design work for my customers.
15) to tailor credit terms to fit the needs of customers.
16) to perform field tests on newly installed equipment.
17) to be available to my customers at all times.
18) to be gone overnight much of the time.
19) to spend little or no time socializing with my customers.
20) to work on weekends.
21) to be a company salesman 24 hours a day.
22) to work in the evenings.
23) to leave my job behind when I go home from work.
24) to include my wife when entertaining my customers.
25) to be available for customer telephone calls at any hour of the night or day.
26) to drink with my customers.
27) to be liberal with my expense account in entertaining customers.
28) to develop close personal relationships with my customers.

My "average" customer expects me:

1) to expedite orders for him.
2) to perform engineering services for him.
3) to do systems-design work for him.
4) to show him how our products can be coordinated with those of our competitors.
5) to supervise the installation of equipment for him.
6) to "stretch the truth" to make a sale.
7) to "hold firm" on our normal deliver dates.
8) to follow the "hard sell" approach
9) to train him in the use of our equipment.
10) to be completely honest with him.
11) to call upon him even if he is unlikely to place an order.
12) to tailor delivery schedules to him.
13) to negotiate on price.
14) to handle back charges and adjustments for them.
15) to tailor credit terms to fit his needs.
16) to perform field tests on newly installed equipment.
17) to be available to him at all times.
18) to spend little or no time socializing with him.
19) to work on weekends.
20) to work in the evenings.
21) to be available for customer telephone calls at any hour of the night or day.
22) to drink with him.
23) to be liberal with my expense account in entertaining him.
24) to develop close personal relationships with him.

My family expects me:

1) to be available to my customers at all times.
2) to be gone overnight much of the time.
3) to spend little or no time socializing with my customers.
4) to work on weekends.
5) to be a company salesman 24 hours a day.
6) to work in the evenings.
7) to leave my job behind when I go home from work.
8) to include them when entertaining my customers.

9) to be available for customer telephone calls at any hour of the night or day.
10) to drink with my customers.
11) to be liberal with my expense account in entertaining customers.
12) to develop close personal relationships with my customers.

Role-ambiguity Scale

I AM

| absolutely certain | very certain | moderately certain | moderately uncertain | very uncertain | absolutely uncertain |

Company policies and evaluations:

1) about the limits of my authority.
2) to what extent I can negotiate on price.
3) about the frequency with which I should call upon my customers.
4) to what extent I can modify normal delivery schedules.
5) to what extent I can extend more liberal credit than normal.
6) to what extent I should be a technical trouble-shooter.
7) what is the best way to close a sale.
8) about how much time I should spend socializing with my customers.
9) about our company rules and regulations.
10) about how to handle back charges and adjustments for my customers.
11) to what extent I should do product design work for my customers.
12) about what is the best way to sell.
13) about how to develop close personal relationships with my customers.
14) about how I should perform my job in order to satisfy my customers.
15) about where to go to get assistance to do my job.
16) about what activities in my job are least important to my sales manager.
17) about how I can best use my expense account in entertaining customers.
18) about how to handle unusual problems or situations.
19) to what extent I should supervise the installation of equipment for my customers.
20) to what extent I should do systems work for my customers.
21) about what kind of engineering services I can offer my customers.

Sales manager's expectations and evaluations:

1) how my sales manager expects me to allocate my time among accounts.
2) how satisfied my sales manager is with my performance on the job.
3) about what activities in my job are most important to my sales manager.
4) about how much time my sales manager feels I should spend on the job.
5) about what my sales manager expects of me in performing my job.
6) about how I should perform my job in order to satisfy my sales manager.
7) about how my sales manager feels I should allocate my time on the job.

Customers' expectations and evaluations:

1) about what my customers expect of me in performing my job.
2) about how frequently my customers expect me to call on them.
3) about how satisfied my customers are with my performance on the job.
4) about what activities in my job are least important to my customers.
5) to what extent I should train customers in the use of our equipment.
6) about what activities in my job are most important to my customers.
7) about the rules and procedures my customers expect me to follow in dealing with them.

Family's expectations and evaluations:

1) about how much time my family feels I should spend on the job.
2) about what my family expects of me in performing my job.

3)   about what activities in my job are most important to my family.
4)   about what activities in my job are least important to my family.
5)   about how satisfied my family is with my job performance.
6)   about how I should perform my job in order to satisfy my family.

NOTES: Ford et al. (1974) offered a sample of items. Above is a complete enumeration of their RC and RA items. Note that there are 30 possible RC items. Some were applicable to certain groups and others were not. Also, the authors did not totally specify which RA items belong to which RA facet. The above assignment reflects our best estimate of items to facets.

Reprinted by permission of the publisher from Ford, Neil M., Orville C. Walker, Jr., and Gilbert A. Churchill, Jr. (1975), "Expectation-Specific Measures of the Intersender Conflict and Role Ambiguity Experienced by Industrial Salesmen," **Journal of Business Research**, *3 (April), 95-112. Copyright 1992 by Elsevier Science Publishing Co., Inc.*

ROLE CONFLICT AND AMBIGUITY SCALES FOR SALESPEOPLE
(Chonko, Howell, and Bellenger 1986)

Construct: Chonko et al. (1986) view role conflict (RC) as conflict generated by a combination of role expectations and the role expectations of the salespeople. In this sense, their view of RC is analogous to the view of Kahn et al. (1964), where RC was defined as "incompatibility between the expectations of the salesperson and the expectations otherwise associated with the salesperson's position." Sources of RC include one's family, supervisors, customers, personal principles, and the job itself. Role ambiguity (RA) is viewed as the degree to which a sales rep is uncertain about others' expectations with respect to the job, the best way to fulfill known expectations, and the consequences of role performance. Sources of RA include the job, family, supervisors, customers, and the sales organization.

Description: The RC and RA scales are multi-item, multi-dimensional measures. The RC items are all scored on a 5-point basis ranging from "complete agreement" to "no agreement." Each source of conflict can be considered a separate dimension of RC. Scores on items are summed within dimension, and then divided by the number of items in each dimension, to form dimension scores. The RA items are scored on a 5-point basis ranging from "completely certain" to "not certain at all." Each source of ambiguity can be considered a separate dimension of RA, and scores on items are summed within dimension, and then divided by the number of items in each dimension, to form dimension scores.

Development: Construction of the RC and RA measures started with personal interviews of salespeople to obtain a more clear understanding of their responsibilities. Open-ended questioning of more salespeople was then performed to elicit possible sources of RC and RA. From these two procedures, a large pool of items was generated. Using a sample of 121 salespeople, the RC and RA measures were refined via item-to-total correlations and factor analysis. Estimates of validity were also assessed.

Sample(s): A sample of 121 salespeople from an industrial products firm responded to the RC and RA measures.

Validity: Coefficient alpha estimates for the five sources of ambiguity ranged from .63 to .88. Corresponding estimates for the five sources of conflict ranged from .85 to .92. Correlations between the RC and RA and congruence of performance evaluation indicated some evidence of nomological validity. For RA, family, job, company, supervisors, and customer showed correlations of .16, -.15, .18, .10, and -.12, respectively, with congruence of performance evaluation. For RC, family, job, supervisor, customer, and self principles showed correlations of -.21, -.14, -.17, -.20, and -.02 with congruence of performance evaluation.

Scores: Mean scores for each dimension (i.e., source) of RC and RA are reported in Table 2, p. 41 of Chonko et al. (1986). Mean scores (standard deviations) for the RA sources ranged from 2.26 (.60) to 2.60 (.77). Corresponding estimates for the RC sources ranged from 2.27 (.76) to 3.29 (1.39).

Source: Chonko, Lawrence B., Roy D. Howell, and Danny Bellenger (1986), "Congruence in Sales Force Evaluations: Relation to Sales Force Perceptions of Conflict and Ambiguity," *Journal of Personal Selling & Sales Management*, 6 (May), 35-48.

Other evidence: N/A.

Other sources: N/A.

References: Kahn, R.L., D.M Wolfe, R.P. Quinn, J.D. Snoek and R. A. Rosenthal (1964), *Organizational Stress Studies in Role Conflict and Ambiguity*, New York: John Wiley & Sons.

ROLE CONFLICT AND AMBIGUITY SCALES FOR SALESPEOPLE
(Chonko, Howell, and Bellenger 1986)

Role-Conflict Measures

Instructions: As an industrial sales representative, you often must satisfy a number of people in the performance of your job. Your sales supervisor, your family, your customers, and you, yourself, have expectations about the activities you should perform in your job, and how you should perform these activities. Please circle the number code that best expresses your feeling about the degree of agreement between you and various people with whom you must work. Please use the following scale.

1=complete agreement	2=very much agreement	3=moderate agreement	4=some agreement	5=no agreement

Family:

How much agreement would you say there is between you and your family on. . .

1) the time you spend working.
2) the time you spend socializing with other salespeople.
3) the time you spend socializing with customers.
4) how much you travel on your job.

Job:

How much agreement would you say there is between. . .

1) the amount of sales territory I expected to cover and the territory I actually cover.
2) the number of customers I am expected to have and the number of customers I actually have.
3) the nonselling tasks I am expected to perform and nonselling tasks I actually perform.
4) the amount of leisure time I am expected to have and leisure time I actually have.

Supervisor:

How much agreement would you say there is between you and your supervisor on. .

1) your role in setting sales goals.
2) how often you should report to your supervisor.
3) how much customer research I should provide.
4) how much troubleshooting I should do for my customers.
5) how far I should stretch the truth to make a sale.
6) how much maintenance service you should provide for your customers.
7) how much authority you should have regarding delivery adjustments for your customers.
8) what "acceptable" performance is to you.
9) how you can best help to achieve the organization's objectives.
10) how much authority you should have regarding price negotiations with customers.
11) how much training you should provide your customers.

Customers:

How much agreement would you say there is between you and your customers on. .

1) your performance of field tests for customers.
2) how much training you should provide customers.
3) the extent to which you should develop personal relations with your customers.
4) how you should handle competition in your sales presentation.
5) how you should present the benefits of your firm's product to your customers.
6) how much maintenance service you should provide for your customers.

Self:

How much agreement would you say there is between your personal principles and

1) how often your customers offer you favors to bend the rules of your company.
2) how often your customers offer you favors to bend government laws or regulations.
3) how often you try to sell a product to a customer even if you feel that the product has little or no value to the customer.
4) how often you feel pressure to stretch the truth in order to make a sale.
5) how often you feel pressure to apply the "hard sell" in order to make a sale.

Role-ambiguity Measures

Instructions: In your role as an industrial sales representative, you may not always be clear as to what your supervisor, your customers, and your family expect of you. In general, sales reps tend to be more clear on some things than others. Very few representatives are equally certain about all aspects of their job. Please indicate your degree of certainty regarding the following statements by placing a circle around the appropriate number code.

I AM

1=completely certain	2=very certain	3=moderately certain	4=somewhat certain	5=not at all certain

Family:

1) about how much time my family feels I should spend on my job.
2) about how much nonwork time I should spend with my customers.
3) how my family feels about my job.

Job:

1) how to best close a sale.
2) about how much time I should spend on various aspects of my job.
3) how to handle customer objections.
4) how to file my sales report.
5) how to plan and organize my sales presentations.
6) how to handle unusual problems or situations.
7) when to call on my customers.
8) which of my mannerisms my customers do not like.
9) how I should speak to my customers.
10) of the type of sales personality I should have.
11) where to get assistance in doing my job.
12) how often to call on my customers.

Company:

1) about the extent to which I can extend more liberal credit to my customers.
2) how to handle my expense account.
3) to what extent I should be a troubleshooter.
4) to what extent I should provide maintenance service for my customers.
5) about the limits of my authority.
6) to what extent I should train my customers to use our equipment.
7) of my company's rules and regulations.

Manager:

1) of the method my supervisor will use to evaluate my performance.
2) how satisfied my supervisor is with my performance.
3) how my sale goals are set.
4) of those aspects of my job that are most important to my supervisor.

5) how my sales commission rates are set.

6) that my performance is a critical factor in the determination of my promotion and advancement.

7) how my supervisor expects me to allocate my time among my accounts.

Customers:

1) of the role played by each person I must see in order to make a sale to a customer.

2) who I must see in my customers' organizations in order to make a sale.

3) how satisfied my customers are with my performance.

4) when to call on my customers.

5) what my customers expect of me in performing my job.

6) what aspects of my job are most important to my customers.

7) how much time my customers expect me to socialize with them.

MULTI-FACETED, MULTI-DIMENSIONAL ROLE AMBIGUITY: MULTIRAM
(Singh and Rhoads 1991)

Construct: Singh and Rhoads (1991a, pp. 330-331) define role ambiguity as the following: "Perceived role ambiguity is a multidimensional, multifaceted evaluation about the lack of salient information needed to perform a role effectively. Specifically, this evaluation may include ambiguity about role definition, expectations, responsibilities, tasks, and behaviors in one or more facets of the task environment. These facets, in turn, reflect one or more members of the boundary spanner's role set (e.g., customer, boss) and/or activities required to perform a role (e.g, ethical conduct). Finally, each facet may be viewed as a multidimensional evaluation of the ambiguity about that facet." Thus, role ambiguity reflects the salient uncertainties faced by boundary spanners in performing their roles and embraces the entire domain of ambiguity as defined in the literature (e.g., Kahn, Wolfe, Quinn, and Snoek 1964; King and King 1990).

Description: MULTIRAM contains 45 items, scored on 5-point scales from very certain to very uncertain, reflecting 7 facets of role ambiguity. The seven facets are company, boss, customer, ethical, other managers, coworkers, and family. Furthermore, the first 4 facets listed are considered multidimensional, and thus, MULTIRAM can be estimated as a second-order factor model. Item scores can be summed within facets and within facet dimensions to form indices of each facet or indices of each dimension within the facets.

Development: A number of procedures were used in scale development and validation. From an extensive literature review and six focus groups from an office equipment and supply firm, the definition and domain of the construct were established. From this, 55 items were developed to reflect the construct's domain. Fifty of these items were retained based on responses from a two-group sample of salespeople and service representatives. These 50 items were administered to a large sample and both first-and second-order factor analysis (using stringent retainment rules) produced the final form of the seven facet, 13-dimension MULTIRAM. (Estimates of reliability and factor structure were also performed.) The final version of the scale was then administered to another large sample and the MULTIRAM's factor structure, reliability, and validity was further assessed.

Sample(s): Several samples were used in scale construction and validation. First, six focus groups consisting of six to eight people (i.e., salespeople and customer representatives) were used to refine the construct and help generate items. Two more samples (n unspecified) were used in item trimming. A sample of 472 from the Association of Sales and Marketing Executives was used in the derivation of the final scale, and a sample of 216 of U.S. based *FORTUNE 500* industrial manufacturer personnel was used in the validation study.

Validity: With the two large samples (n = 472, 216), a number of reliability estimates were gathered. The discussion here though will focus on the second sample. First, the results of the factor analyses with the first sample were largely replicated by the second sample in that the seven facet, 13-dimension second-order factor structure was validated, offering support for MULTIRAM's dimensionality and structure. Second, internal consistency and variance extracted estimates were high across dimensions and facets. Composite reliability for the "company" facet was .77 with a variance extracted estimate of .53. The "flexibility," "work," and "promotion" dimensions of the company facet had coefficient alphas of .70, .84, and .75, respectively. The "boss" facet had a composite reliability of .87 and a variance extracted estimate of .57. Its dimensions of "support" and "demands" both had alphas of .86. The "customer" facet had a composite reliability estimate of .81 and a variance extracted estimate of .59. The dimensions of "interaction," "objection," and "presentation" had alphas of .78, .81, and .81. The "ethical" facet had a composite reliability estimate of .86 with a variance extracted estimate of .55. The "external" and "internal" dimensions of this facet had alphas of .90 and .83. The "other managers," "coworkers," and "family" facets had composite reliability estimates of .83, .85, and .86, and variance extracted estimates of .71, .74, and .75, respectively. Corresponding coefficient alphas estimates for these facets were .88, .87, and .88.

Convergent and discriminant validity checks were also obtained by correlating the MULTIRAM's facets with the Rizzo, House, and Lirtzman (1970) measure of role conflict and ambiguity (n = 472). The correlations of the MULTIRAM facets were consistently higher with role ambiguity (ranging from .18 to .69) than role conflict (ranging from .10 to .50), offering evidence of convergent and discriminant validity. (These results were also replicated with the sample of 216.)

Finally, the MULTIRAM facets were also correlated with a number of job related variables. The pattern of these correlations suggests nomological validity. For example, the MULTIRAM facets range of correlations with "job satisfaction" was -.23 to -.64; with "job performance" -.21 to -.43; "job tension" .19 to .51; and "turnover intentions" .10 to .52. Other correlational estimates also supported MULTIRAM's nomological validity.

Scores: For the two large samples, means were reported for each facet. These mean values were computed by obtaining an equally weighted composite of the dimensions corresponding to the individual facets. For the first large sample, the means (standard deviations) were 2.28 (.72) for company, 2.42 (.85) for boss, 1.71 (.54) for customers, 1.98 (.78) for ethical, 2.32 (.79) for other managers, 2.96 (.68) for coworkers, and 1.98 (.73) for family. For the second large sample, the means (standard deviations) were 2.55 (.66) for company, 2.46 (.86) for boss, 1.92 (.60) for customers, 2.17 (.76) for ethical, 2.93 (.87) for other managers, 2.22 (.638) for coworkers, and 1.97 (.68) for family (Singh and Rhoads 1991b).

Source: Singh, Jagdip and Gary K. Rhoads (1991a), "Boundary Role Ambiguity in Marketing-Oriented Positions: A Multidimensional, Multifaceted Operationalization," *Journal of Marketing Research*, 28 (August), 328-338.

Singh, Jagdip and Gary K. Rhoads (1991b), "Boundary Role Ambiguity in Marketing Positions: Scale Development and Validation," *Marketing Science Institute Technical Working Paper*, Report # 91-115 (June), 1-69.

Other evidence: N/A.

Other sources: N/A.

References: Kahn, R. L., D. M. Wolfe, R. P. Quinn, and J. D. Snoek (1964), *Organizational Stress: Studies in Role Conflict and Ambiguity*, New York: John Wiley & Sons, Inc.

King, L. A. and D. W. King (1990), "Role Conflict and Role Ambiguity: A Critical Assessment of Construct Validity," *Psychological Bulletin*, 107, 48-64.

Rizzo, J. R., R. J. House, and S. I. Lirtzman (1970), "Role Conflict and Ambiguity in Complex Organizations," *Administrative Science Quarterly*, 15, 150-163.

MULTI-FACETED, MULTI-DIMENSIONAL ROLE AMBIGUITY (MULTIRAM)
(Singh and Rhoads 1991)

Company

1) How much freedom of action I am expected to have.

2) How I am expected to handle nonroutine activities on the job.

3) The sheer amount of work I am expected to do.

4) Which tasks I should give priority.

5) How much work I am expected to do.

6) How I should I handle my free time on the job.

7)   What I can do to get promoted.

8)   How vulnerable to job termination I am.

9)   What is the critical factor in getting promoted.

Boss

10) To what extent my boss is open to hearing my point of view.

11) How satisfied my boss is with me.

12) How far my boss will go to back me up.

13) The method my boss will use to evaluate my performance.

14) How my boss expects me to allocate my time among different aspects of my job.

15) How to meet the demands of my boss.

16) How I should respond to my boss's criticism.

17) What aspects of my job are most important to my boss.

18) The level of professionalism my boss expects of me.

Customer

19) How I am expected to interact with my customers.

20) How much service I should provide my customers.

21) How I should behave (with customers) while on the job.

22) How I am expected to handle my customer's objections.

23) How I am expected to handle unusual problems and situations.

24) How I am expected to deal with customer's criticism.

25) Which specific company strengths I should present to customers.

26) Which specific product benefits I am expected to highlight for customers.

Ethical

27) If I am expected to lie a little to win customer confidence.

28) If I am expected to hide my company's foul-ups from my customers.

29) How I should handle ethical issues in my job.

30) How top management expects to handle ethical situations in my job.

31) What I am expected to do if I find others are behaving unethically.

32) The ethical conduct my boss expects of me.

Other managers

33) How managers in other departments expect me to interact with them.

34) What managers in other departments think about the job I perform.

35) How I should respond to questions/criticisms of managers from other departments.

36) How much information I should provide managers from other departments.

Coworkers

37) How my coworkers expect me to behave on the job.

38) How much information my coworkers expect me to convey to my boss.

39) What my coworkers expect me to do for them.

40) The extent to which my coworkers expect me to share my job-related information with them.

41) The kind of attitude my coworkers expect me to have toward the company.

Family

42) About how much time my family feels I should spend on the job.

43) To what extent my family expects me to share my job-related problems.

44) How my family feels about my job.

45) What my family thinks about the ambiguity (e.g., nonroutine job, no fixed hours of work) in my job.

NOTES: Items are scored from "1" = very certain, "2" = certain, "3" = neutral, "4" = uncertain, and "5" = very uncertain. Items 1 and 2 reflect the "flexibility" dimension of the company facet; items 3, 4, 5, and 6 reflect the "work" dimension of the company facet; and items 7, 8, and 9, reflect the "promotion" dimension of the company facet. Items 10 through 13 reflect the "support" dimension of the boss facet; and items 14 through 18 reflect the "demands" dimension of the boss facet. Items 19 through 21 reflect the "interaction" dimension of the customer facet; items 22 through 24 reflect the "objection" dimension of the customer facet; and items 25 and 26 reflect the "presentation" dimension of the customer facet. Items 27 and 28 reflect the "external" dimension of the ethical facet and items 29 through 32 reflect the "internal" dimension of the ethical facet. The other three facets (i.e., other managers, coworkers, and family) are single dimensions.

JOB INDUCED TENSION
(House and Rizzo 1972)

Construct: Job induced tension is viewed as "the existence of tension and pressures growing out of job requirements, including possible outcomes in terms of feelings or physical symptoms (e.g., tiredness, stiffness, weakness, irritation, digestive problems)" (House and Rizzo 1972, pp. 481-482). The corresponding job induced tension measure has been used extensively in organizational behavior and sales research.

Description: The job induced tension scale is composed of seven items originally scored on a true = 2, false = 1 format. Scores on items are summed, and then divided by seven to form an overall index. The scale is considered unidimensional.

Development: From the description provided by House and Rizzo (1972), 26 items were generated to tap the domain of the construct. Through image covariance factor analysis, item analysis, and Kuder Richardson reliability analysis, the final 7-item job induced tension scale was derived with a sample of 200 respondents. Numerous estimates of nomological validity were also reported.

Sample(s):   The questionnaire that contained the scale was administered to a sample of the staff, research, development, and engineering personnel at an undisclosed firm. The total sample size was 200 respondents.

Validity: The scale had a KR-20 estimate of internal consistency of .825. The scale also showed evidence of nomological validity. For example, the correlations between the job induced tension scale and measures of role conflict and role ambiguity were .20 and .12, respectively.

Scores: A mean score of 1.24 (sd = .28) was reported for the scale (House and Rizzo 1972, p. 484).

Source: House, Robert, J. and John R. Rizzo (1972), "Role Conflict and Ambiguity as Critical Variables in a Model of Organizational Behavior," *Organizational Behavior and Human Performance*, 7, 467-505.

Other evidence: Though used on numerous occasions in the organizational behavior literature with evidence of reliability and validity, our discussion of other evidence will be limited to a few marketing applications.

Using a sample of 216 pharmaceutical salespeople, Fry et al. (1986) reported an internal consistency estimate of .88 for the job induced tension scale. Evidence of nomological validity was also offered. For example, as an independent variable for the prediction of satisfaction with company support and satisfaction with customers, the job induced tension scale showed path coefficients of -.14 and -.18 (p < .05), respectively. As a dependent variable, role conflict showed a path coefficient of .39 (p < .01) for predicting job induced tension.

In another application using a sample of 183 salespeople, Netemeyer et al. (1990) reported a composite reliability estimate of .82 for the job induced tension scale (using 5-point items). Furthermore, the scale was significantly correlated with role conflict (.43), role ambiguity (.28), job satisfaction (-.42), and propensity to leave an organization (.30).

Other sources: Fry, Louis W., Charles M. Futrell, A. Parasuraman, and Margaret A. Chmielewski (1986), "An Analysis of Alternative Causal Models of Salesperson Role Perceptions and Work-Related Attitudes," *Journal of Marketing Research*, 23 (May), 153-163.

Netemeyer, Richard G., Mark W. Johnston, and Scot Burton (1990), "Analysis of Role Conflict and Role Ambiguity in a Structural Equations Framework," *Journal of Applied Psychology*, 75, 148-157.

References: N/A.

JOB INDUCED TENSION
(House and Rizzo 1972)

1) I feel fidgety or nervous because of my job.

2) Problems associated with work have kept me awake at night.

3) My job tends to directly affect my health.

4) If I had a different job, my health would probably improve.

5) I often "take my job home with me" in the sense that I think about it when doing other things.

6) I feel nervous before attending meetings in the organization.

7) I sometimes feel weak all over.

NOTE: These items reflect wording used in marketing applications of the scale.

PERFORMANCE

SALES PERFORMANCE SCALE
(Behrman and Perreault 1982)

Construct: This scale was designed to measure the job performance construct as it relates to the industrial salesperson. Differences in such variables as sales territories, product lines, customer accounts, and long selling cycles can make generalizations about performance quite tenuous. Since quantitative sales data may be deceptive performance indicators due to factors beyond the control of the individual, a performance evaluation based on self-report was constructed as one possible measurement of performance. The construct's domain was defined as consisting of the following five categories: 1) sales presentation, 2) providing information, 3) technical knowledge, 4) sales objective, and 5) controlling expenses.

Description: The finalized version of the instrument consisted of 31 items which represent the five components listed above. A 7-cue rating scale format was used with possible responses ranging from "outstanding" to "needs improvement." Item scores are summed within factors to form factor indices, or can be summed overall items to form an overall performance measure.

Development: A review of the literature and an analysis of the job of industrial salespersons served as stimuli in developing the initial set of statements, resulting in 7 categories of items. A panel of judges reviewed the statements, and 65 items remained for the seven performance areas. Data were collected from the salespersons and their sales managers using self-administered questionnaires. The purification study which used item and factor analysis reduced the set of items to 31 which represented five aspects of industrial sales performance. Reliability and validity estimates followed.

Sample(s): Five noncompeting industrial companies were selected to participate in the study. Across these five firms, 219 salespersons and 43 managers were invited to participate. Of these subjects, 200 (91 percent) salespersons and 42 (98 percent) managers returned completed questionnaires.

Validity: Alpha coefficients ranged from .81 to .90 across the facets and was .93 for the overall scale. Test-retest estimates across the facets ranged from .54 to .77, and was .70 for the overall scale. The scale was significantly correlated with manager's evaluation (.26 for the total sample), profitability data (.21), and a need for achievement measure (.25). Individually, these relationships were not strong but in combination they suggest that the self-report captured some common variance with other surrogate indicators of sales performance. The 31 items were also factor analyzed with a hold-out sample, and the five extracted factors were consistent with the expected structure.

Scores: The means and (standard deviations) for the subcomponents were as follows: sales presentation 33.46 (4.69), providing information 26.52 (4.48), technical knowledge 32.41 (5.52), sales objectives 38.15 (5.82), and controlling expenses 39.96 (5.05). The overall scale mean and standard deviation were 170.51 and 19.46, respectively.

Source: Behrman, Douglas and William D. Perreault, Jr. (1982), "Measuring the Performance of Industrial Salespersons," *Journal of Business Research*, 10, 355-370.

Other evidence: N/A

Other sources: N/A

References: N/A

SALES PERFORMANCE SCALE
(Behrman and Perreault 1982)

1. Producing a high market share for your company in your territory

2. Making sales of those products with the highest profit margins

3. Generating a high level of dollar sales

4. Quickly generating sales of new company products

5. Identifying and selling major accounts in your territory

6. Producing sales or blanket contracts with long-term profitability

7. Exceeding all sales targets and objectives for your territory during the year

8. Knowing the design and specifications of company products

9. Knowing the applications and functions of company products

10. Being able to detect causes of operating failure of company products

11. Acting as a special resource to other departments that need your assistance

12. Keeping abreast of your company's production and technological developments

13. When possible, troubleshooting system problems and conducting minor field service to correct product misapplications and/or product failures

14. Carrying out company policies, procedures, and programs for providing information

15. Providing accurate and complete paperwork related to order, expenses, and other routine reports

16. Recommending on your own initiative how company operations and procedures can be improved

17. Submitting required reports on time

18. Maintaining company specified records that are accurate, complete, and up to date

19. Operating within the budgets set by the company

20. Using expense accounts with integrity

21. Using business gift and promotional allowances responsibly

22. Spending travel and lodging money carefully

23. Arranging sales call patterns and frequency to cover your territory economically

24. Entertaining only when it is clearly in the best interest of the company to do so

25. Controlling costs in other areas of the company (order processing and preparation, delivery, etc.) when taking sales orders

26. Listening attentively to identify and understand the real concerns of your customer

27. Convincing customers that you understand their unique problems and concerns

28. Using established contacts to develop new customers

29. Communicating your sales presentation clearly and concisely

30. Making effective use of audiovisual aids (charts, tables, and the like) to improve your sales presentation

31. Working out solutions to a customer's questions or objections

NOTES: The factors and item numbers are as follows: 1) sales objectives 1-7, 2) technical knowledge 8-13, 3) providing information 14-18, 4) controlling expenses 19-25, and 5) sales presentations 26-31.

*Reprinted by permission of the publisher from Behrman, Douglas and William D. Perreault, Jr. (1982), "Measuring the Performance of Industrial Salespersons," **Journal of Business Research**, 10, 355-370. Copyright 1992 by Elsevier Science Publishing Co., Inc.*

RETAIL SALESPERSON PERFORMANCE
(Bush, Bush, Ortinau, and Hair 1990)

Construct: Job performance of retail salespersons was evaluated by operationally defining the various behavioral dimensions of relevant selling activities. This approach differed from the traditional approach of evaluating outcomes to measure sales performance. The behavioral approach focused on what salespersons actually do on the job and how these activities relate to job performance. The construct's domain was defined as consisting of five behavior-based factors: (1) knowledge of merchandise procedures, (2) customer service ability, (3) sales ability, (4) product-merchandise knowledge, and (5) knowledge of store policy.

Description: The finalized version of the instrument, designed for self-administration, consisted of 22 items which represent the five dimensions stated above. All items are scored on a five-point, Likert-type format where 5 = very good, 4 = good, 3 = average, 2 = poor, 1 = very poor. Item scores can be summed within each dimension to form dimension scores, or overall to form an overall performance score. Since the purpose of the scale was based on management's evaluation of individual salesperson performance, each manager was instructed to appraise the salespeople directly under his/her control.

Development: Through an extensive literature review and 80 hours of focus group interviews with store managers, department sales managers, and industrial retail salespersons, Bush et al. (1990) identified work- related activities of retail salespersons that influence job performance. Items were then generated, screened, categorized or deleted by the principal investigators and a panel of retailing experts. Forty-one scale items were included in the initial retail performance measure. Based on data from 144 salespersons, factor and item analyses were performed on the 41 items to determine a set of underlying dimensions that make up the multidimensional construct of retail sales performance. Six factors of retail job satisfaction were identified and 32 items of the job performance scale were retained. The scale was subjected to confirmatory factor analysis (via LISREL) for data provided by 321 salespeople. After this procedure, 22 items representing five factors remained. Several reliability and validity checks followed.

Sample(s): A total sample of 144 salespeople evaluations was obtained from 43 department sales managers. These salespersons were employed in soft goods departments such as fashion apparel, accessories, fragrances, etc. The data were analyzed with respect to item purification in the pretesting phase of the study. In a further scale refinement effort, 48 additional retail sales department managers with instructions to evaluate employees yielded a sample of 321 salespeople. The final version of the 22-item job performance scale was sent to 57 retail sales department managers. A total of 285 retail salespeople were appraised.

Validity: For the sample of 285, alpha coefficients ranged from .84 to .88 across dimensions and was .86. for the total 22-item scale. Test-retest reliability was assessed based on a systematic sampling of 98 salespersons from the original sample. Test-retest correlations ranged from .61 to .70 across dimensions and was .67 for the total scale. Predictive validity was assessed by correlating contribution to gross margins of 192 salespersons with each of the five scale dimensions (all significant at $p < .05$ with a range from .24 to .36) and a correlation of .39 ($p < .05$) with the total scale of job performance. Concurrent validity was assessed by correlating the need for achievement of 285 salespeople with the five scale dimensions of retail sales performance. These correlations ranged from .19 to .39 across the five dimensions, and was .38 for the total scale, suggesting concurrent validity.

Scores: Mean scores and standard deviations were not reported in the Bush et al. (1990) article.

Source: Bush, Robert P., Alan J. Bush, David J. Ortinau, and Joseph F. Hair (1990), "Developing a Behavior-Based Scale to Assess Retail Salesperson Performance," *Journal of Retailing*, 66 (Spring), 119-129.

Other evidence: N/A

**Other
sources:**   N/A

References: N/A

RETAIL SALESPERSON PERFORMANCE
(Bush, Bush, Ortinau, and Hair 1990)

Merchandise Procedure

1. Employee accuracy in counting and inventorying merchandise.

2. Prevents merchandise shrinkage due to mishandling of merchandise.

3. Keeps merchandise in a neat and orderly manner on sales floor.

4. Gets merchandise on sales floor (shelves, racks, displays) quickly after merchandise arrival.

5. Knows the design and specifications of warranties and guarantees of the merchandise groups.

Customer Service Ability

1. Provides courteous service to customers.

2. Handles customers' complaints and/or service problems as indicated by store procedure.

3. Follows proper procedures concerning merchandise returns and lay-a-ways when conducted through credit transactions.

4. Suggests add-on or complimentary merchandise to customers.

Sales Ability

1. Has strong ability to close the sale.

2. Promotes sales of merchandise items having profit margins.

3. Acts as a resource to other departments or other salespeople needing assistance.

4. Works well with fellow workers in primary merchandise department.

Product-Merchandise Knowledge

1. Knowledge of design, style, and construction of merchandise group.

2. Knowledge of special promotions and/or advertised sale items.

3. Knowledge of material (fabric), color coordination, and complimentary accessories related to merchandise group.

4. Provides accurate and complete paperwork related to work schedules.

Knowledge of Store Policy

1. Provides accurate and complete paperwork related to work schedules.

2. Provides accurate and complete paperwork for cash and credit transactions.

3. Shows up on time for work, sales meetings, and training sessions.

4. Accurately follows day-to-day instructions of immediate supervisor.

5. Employee's overall job-related attitude.

NOTES: Item 4 of the "product-merchandise knowledge" factor is also part of the "knowledge of store policy" factor (item 1).

LEADERSHIP

PERCEIVED LEADERSHIP BEHAVIOR SCALES
(House and Dessler 1974)

Construct: The perceived leadership construct has its conceptual base in the path-goal theory of leadership (House 1971; House and Dessler 1974). Leader behavior is conceived as an explanatory variable that directly affects the psychological states and performance of subordinates. Furthermore, this leadership focuses on subordinate *perceptions* of their leader with respect to three aspects of leadership (House and Dessler 1974, pp.40-43):

Instrumental leadership - leader behavior directed at clarifying expectations, assigning specific tasks, and specifying procedures to be followed. (Also referred to as initiating structure.)

Supportive leadership - the degree to which leader behavior can be characterized as friendly and approachable, and considerate of the needs of subordinates. (Also referred to as leadership consideration.)

Participative leadership - a nondirective form of role clarifying behavior analogous to the more directive instrumental leadership. It considers the degree to which leaders allow subordinates to influence decisions by asking subordinates for input and suggestions. (Also referred to as leadership participation.)

Description: The perceived leadership behavior scale is a three-factor scale comprising the 3 aspects of perceived leadership described above. Across factors, items have been scored on a 5-point format ranging from "always" = 5, "often" = 4, "occasionally" = 3, "seldom" = 2, and "never" = 1. Item scores can be summed within each factor to form indices for each of the three aspects of leadership. Thus, the scale is considered multi-dimensional.

Development: Based on path-goal theory and an extensive literature review, a pool of 35 items was generated to reflect the aspects of perceived leadership. Several of these items were taken from earlier research on leadership theory (Fleishman 1957; Stogdill 1963). Via factor and reliability analyses over two samples, the number of items was trimmed and the final scales were derived. Numerous tests of validity were also assessed.

Samples: Two samples of 206 and 96 were used in scale development and validation. These samples were employees from two electronics firms and consisted of managers, professionals, foremen, blue collar workers, technicians, etc.

Validity: Principal components factor analysis revealed three factors corresponding to the three aspects of perceived leadership. Estimates of internal consistency reliability for subsets of the two samples were reported to be .72 and .76 for instrumental leadership (also referred to as initiating structure), .81 and .79 for supportive leadership (also referred to as leader consideration), and .67 and .68 for participative leadership (also referred to as leadership participation). These three factors were significantly intercorrelated (the actual correlations were not specified). Thus, partial correlations were used to examine the nomological validity of the leadership factors. To examine validity, the two samples were split into high, medium, and low task structure groups. Then, partial correlations of the three factors with a number of dependent variables were reported that offered evidence for the validity of the perceived leadership scales. For example, correlations of instrumental leadership with a measure of intrinsic job satisfaction for the low task structure group were .26 and .40 for the two samples. Correlations of supportive leadership with intrinsic job satisfaction for the high task structure group were .52 and .36 for the two samples. Numerous other estimates of validity were offered.

Scores: Neither mean nor percentage scores were reported by House and Dessler (1974).

Source:	House, Robert J. and Gary Dessler (1974), "The Path-Goal Theory of Leadership: Some Post Hoc and A Priori Tests," in *Contingency Approaches to Leadership*, James G. Hunt and Lars L. Larson (eds.), Carbondale, IL: Southern Illinois University Press.
Other evidence:	Though used on many occasions in the organizational behavior literature, our discussion of other evidence will be restricted to marketing applications of the perceived leadership behavior scales. Teas (1981), with a sample of 171 industrial salespeople, examined the relationship of the leadership behavior scales (modified versions) with various job related attitudes and outcomes. He reported coefficient alpha estimates of .84, .51, and .82 for supportive leadership (i.e., leadership consideration), instrumental leadership (i.e., initiation of structure), and participative leadership (i.e., participation), respectively. For these three scales as dependent variables, R-square estimates ranged from .24 to .44 with predictor variables that included job self-esteem, experience, and company feedback among others. Thus, some evidence for the nomological validity of the perceived leadership measures was found.
	In another marketing application of 114 salespeople, Kohli (1989) used the modified initiation structure and leadership consideration measures of Teas (1981). Reliability estimates were reported to between .64 and .84 (across all measures in the study). The initiation of structure and leadership consideration scales were used as independent variables across high and low group splits of several moderator variables. With job satisfaction and role clarity as dependent variables, regression coefficients ranged from .51 to 1.08 for initiation of structure, and .30 to .79 for leadership consideration, offering evidence of predictive validity.
Other sources:	Teas, R. Kenneth (1981), "An Empirical Test of Models of Salespersons' Job Expectancy and Instrumentality Perceptions," *Journal of Marketing Research*, 18 (May), 209-226.
	Kohli, Ajay (1989), "Effects of Supervisory Behavior: The Role of Individual Differences Among Salespeople," *Journal of Marketing*, 53 (October), 40-50.
References:	Fleishman, E.A. (1957), "A Leader Behavior Description for Industry," in *Leader Behavior: Its Description and Measurement*, R.M. Stogdill and A.E. Coons (eds.), Columbus, OH: The Ohio State University Bureau of Business Research.
	House, Robert J. (1971), "A Path-Goal Theory of Leader Effectiveness," *Administrative Science Quarterly*, 16 (September), 321-338.
	Stogdill, R.M. (1963), *Manual for Leadership Behavior Description Questionnaire Form XII*, Columbus, OH: The Ohio State University Bureau of Business Research.

PERCEIVED LEADERSHIP BEHAVIOR SCALES
(House and Dessler 1974)

Instrumental leadership (Initiating Structure.)

1) He lets group members know what is expected of them.
2) He decides what shall be done and how it shall be done.
3) He makes sure that his part in the group is understood.
4) He schedules the work to be done.
5) He maintains definite standards of performance.
6) He asks that the group members follow standard rules and regulations.
7) He explains the way any task should be carried out.

Supportive leadership (Leadership Consideration.)

1) He is friendly and polite.
2) He does little things to make it pleasant to be a member of the group.
3) He puts suggestions made by the group into operation.

4)   He treats all group members as his equals.
5)   He gives advance notice of changes.
6)   He keeps to himself.
7)   He looks out for the personal welfare of group members.
8)   He is willing to make changes.
9)   He helps me overcome problems which stop me from carrying out my task.
10) He helps me make working on my tasks more pleasant.

Participative leadership (Leadership Participation.)

1)   When faced with a problem, he consults with his subordinates.
2)   Before making decisions, he gives serious consideration to what his subordinates have to say.
3)   He asks subordinates for their suggestions concerning how to carry out assignments.
4)   Before taking action he consults with his subordinates.
5)   He asks subordinates for suggestions on what assignments should be made.

NOTES: Though not specified by the authors, it seems that item 6 of the supportive leadership factor requires reverse scoring.

Items 2, 4, 5, 6, and 7 comprise Teas's (1981) version of instrumental leadership. Items 1, 2, 4, 5, 7, and 10 comprise Teas's supportive leadership items. Teas used the entire leadership participation scale. Also, the Teas items used a slightly modified wording format to better fit the industrial salespeople sample, and used a "very true" (5) to "very false" (1) scoring format.

LEADERSHIP ROLE CLARITY AND CONSIDERATION
(Schriesheim 1978)

Constructs: Similar to House and Dessler's (1974) path-goal theory leadership concepts, Schriesheim (1978) offers leadership role clarity and leadership consideration constructs. Leadership role clarity refers to the extent to which a supervisor is perceived by subordinates as clearly establishing the tasks and performance level required of a job. Leadership consideration refers to the extent to which a supervisor is perceived by subordinates as providing coaching, guidance, support, and rewards necessary for high job satisfaction and performance.

Description: Leadership role clarity and consideration are measured using 5- and 11-item scales, respectively. The items can be scored on 5-point scales ranging from "very true" (5) to "very false" (1). Item scores are summed within each scale to form indices of leadership role clarity and consideration. Thus, they are considered separate dimensions of perceived leadership.

Development: Since the leadership role clarity and leadership scales were developed as part of the author's doctoral thesis, extensive information on the development of the scales was not available. However, other sources suggest that stringent psychometric procedures were used in scale development and numerous estimates of validity exist (e.g., Fry et al. 1986; Johnston et al. 1990).

Sample(s): N/A.

Scores: N/A.

Source: Schriesheim, Chester A. (1978), "Development, Validation, and Application of New Leadership Behavior and Expectancy Research Instruments," *Doctoral Dissertation*, College of Administrative Science, Ohio State University.

Other evidence: Two applications in marketing are discussed as other evidence. Fry et al. (1986) reported coefficient alpha internal consistency estimates of .93 and .84 for the role clarity and consideration leadership scales, respectively. Standardized path coefficients showed that for the prediction of role conflict, role ambiguity, job stress, and job and supervisor satisfaction, the two leadership scales exhibited predictive validity. For example, coefficients of -.36, -.57, .11, .32, and .41 were found for the prediction of role conflict, role ambiguity, job stress, job satisfaction, and satisfaction with supervisor, respectively, with leadership role clarity as the predictor. Corresponding coefficients with leadership consideration as the predictor were -.21, -.11, -.10, .22, and .55. Fry et al.'s sample was composed of 216 salespeople.

In another study, Johnston et al. (1990), based upon a longitudinal sample of 102 salespeople, reported composite reliabilities of .81 and .90 for leadership consideration, and .92 and .85 for leadership role clarity. Correlations of leadership consideration with role conflict, role ambiguity, job satisfaction, and organizational commitment were -.50, -.28, .43, and .43, respectively. Correlations of role clarity leadership with role conflict, role ambiguity, job satisfaction, and organizational commitment were -.27, -.30, .39, and .36. These results offer evidence for the nomological validity of the leadership scales.

Other sources: Fry, Louis W., Charles M. Futrell, A. Parasuraman, and Margaret A. Chmielewski (1986), "An Analysis of Alternative Causal Models of Salesperson Role Perceptions and Work-Related Attitudes," *Journal of Marketing Research*, 23 (May), 153-163.

Johnston, Mark W., A. Parasuraman, Charles M. Futrell, and William C. Black (1990), "A Longitudinal Assessment of the Impact of Selected Organizational Influences on Salespeople's Organizational Commitment During Early Employment," *Journal of Marketing Research*, 27 (August), 333-344.

References: House, Robert J. and Gary Dessler (1974), "The Path-Goal Theory of Leadership: Some Post Hoc and A Priori Tests," in *Contingency Approaches to Leadership*, James G. Hunt and Lars L. Larson (eds.), Carbondale, IL: Southern Illinois University Press.

LEADERSHIP ROLE CLARITY AND CONSIDERATION
(Schriesheim 1978)

Role Clarity

My supervisor. . .

1) Gives me vague explanations of what is expected of me on my job.*
2) Gives me unclear goals to reach on my job.*
3) Explains the level of performance that is expected of me.
4) Explains the quality of work that is expected of me.
5) Explains what is expected of me on my job.

Leadership Consideration

My supervisor. . .

1) Helps make working on my job more pleasant.
2) Says things to hurt my personal feelings.*
3) Considers my personal feelings before acting.
4) Maintains a friendly working relationship with me.
5) Behaves in a manner which is thoughtful of my personal needs.
6) Looks out for my personal welfare.
7) Acts rudely toward me.*
8) Does things to make my job less pleasant.*
9) Treats me without considering my feelings.*
10) Shows respect for my personal feelings.
11) Acts without considering my feelings.*

NOTES: "*" denotes items requiring reverse scoring. Also, these items reflect the wording used in the marketing applications of the measures.

COMMITMENT

ORGANIZATIONAL COMMITMENT: OCQ
(Mowday, Steers, and Porter 1979)

Construct: Organizational commitment (OC) is defined as the relative strength of an individual's identification with and involvement in a particular organization. OC can be characterized by three related factors: 1) a strong belief in and acceptance of the organization's goals and values, 2) a willingness to exert considerable effort on behalf of the organization, and 3) a strong desire to maintain membership in the organization (Mowday, Steers, and Porter 1979, p. 226). For an expanded discussion of OC see Mowday, Porter, and Steers (1982).

Description: The OCQ is composed of 15 Likert items scored on scales from strongly disagree (1) to strongly agree (7). Though the scale was originally designed to tap the aforementioned three factors, item scores are summed and divided by 15 to form an overall OC index. A reduced, nine-item version of the scale is also possible when only the positive item scores are summed and divided by nine to form a reduced OC index.

Development: The approach to developing the scale was to identify 15 items that tapped the three factors of commitment. Thus, 15 items were generated by the authors and then checked for factor structure, reliability, and validity over numerous samples.

Samples: Nine samples totaling 2,563 subjects were used to examine the reliability and validity of the OCQ. These samples were 569 public employees, 243 university employees, 382 hospital employees, 411 bank employees, 119 scientists and engineers, 115 auto company managers, 60 psychiatric technicians, 59 retail management trainees, and 605 telephone company employees.

Validity: Coefficient alpha across the samples ranged from .88 to .90 for the 15-item version and .82 to .93 for the nine-item version. Item-to-total correlations ranged from .36 to .72 across samples. Factor analyses generally supported a single dimension as the general factor (first factor) explained from 83.2% to 92.6% of the variance in the data. Test-retest reliabilities for the psychiatric technician sample were .53, .63, and .75 over periods of 2, 3, and 4 months, respectively. Test-retest reliabilities for the retail management employees were .72 and .62 over 2 and 3 month periods.

Convergent validity with a measure of organizational attachment ranged from .63 to .74 (for six of the samples). OCQ also had a correlation of .60 with an independent commitment rating measure for the retail trainees sample. Evidence of discriminant validity was found by correlations ranging from .30 to .56 (for four of the samples) between OCQ and job involvement, and correlations ranging from .01 to .68 (over five of the samples) between OCQ and the JDI. OCQ was also correlated with a measure of career satisfaction for two of the samples.

Predictive validity of the OCQ was also supported. Across nine data points, OCQ was significantly correlated with turnover eight times. The significant correlations ranged from -.17 to -.43. Similar correlations were found between OCQ and measures of tenure (.23 and .26), absenteeism (.08 to -.28), and performance (.05 to .36).

Scores: Mean scores and (standard deviations) were reported for each sample. The mean scores ranged from 4.2 (sd = .90) to 5.3 (sd = 1.05) for eight of the samples. For the psychiatric technician sample, mean scores were reported for "stayers" and "leavers" across four time periods. For "stayers," the mean score across the four time periods ranged from 4.0 (sd = 3.0) to 4.3 (sd = 3.5). For "leavers," corresponding scores ranged from 3.0 (sd = .98) to 3.5 (sd = 1.00).

Source: Mowday, Richard T., Richard M. Steers, and Lyman W. Porter (1979), "The Measurement of Organizational Commitment," *Journal of Vocational Behavior*, 14, 224-227.

Other
evidence: In the organizational behavior literature, the OCQ has been used and examined numerous times. For an excellent review, see Mathieu and Zajac (1990). And, though OCQ has been used several times in the marketing literature, our discussion here will be limited to just three marketing applications of the OCQ.

Michaels et al. (1988) reported an alpha of .90 for the 15-item OCQ. They also reported correlations of .32, -.47, -.48, and -.53 between OCQ and measures of organizational formalization, role ambiguity, role conflict, and work alienation (retail sales setting where n = 330).

Good et al. (1988), using a sample of 595 department store employees, reported an alpha of .91 for the 15-item OCQ. Correlations of -.59, -.60, -.41, -.77, and -.81 were reported between OCQ and measures of role ambiguity, role conflict, work-family conflict, job satisfaction, and intention to leave, respectively.

Johnston et al. (1990) using a sample of 102 retail salespeople reported composite reliability estimates (via LISREL) of .88 and .93 for the 15-item OCQ over two time periods. OCQ correlations with role conflict, role ambiguity, job satisfaction, propensity to leave, and turnover were -.49, -.45, .58, -.73, and -.33, respectively. In sum, these three marketing studies provided evidence for the reliability and nomological validity of OCQ.

Other
sources: Good, Linda K., Grovalynn F. Sisler, and James W. Gentry (1988), "Antecedents of Turnover Intentions Among Retail Management Personnel," *Journal of Retailing*, 64 (Fall), 295-314.

Johnston, Mark W., A. Parasuraman, Charles M. Futrell, and William C. Black (1990), "A Longitudinal Assessment of the Impact of Selected Organizational Influences on Salespeople's Organizational Commitment During Early Employment," *Journal of Marketing Research*, 27 (August), 333-344.

Michaels, Ronald E., William L. Cron, Alan J. Dubinsky, and Erich A. Joachimsthaler (1988), "The Influence of Formalization on the Organizational Commitment and Work Alienation of Salespeople and Industrial Buyers," *Journal of Marketing Research*, 25 (November), 376-383.

References: Mathieu, John E. and Dennis M. Zajac (1990), "A Review and Meta-Analysis of the Antecedents, Correlates, and Consequences of Organizational Commitment," *Psychological Bulletin*, 108, 171-194.

Mowday, Richard T., Lyman W. Porter and Richard M. Steers (1982), *Employee-Organizational Linkages: The Psychology of Commitment, Absenteeism, and Turnover*, New York: Academic Press.

ORGANIZATIONAL COMMITMENT: OCQ
(Mowday, Steers, and Porter 1979)

1) I am willing to put in a great deal of effort beyond that normally expected in order to help this organization be successful.

2) I talk up this organization to my friends as a great organization to work for.

3) I feel very little loyalty to this organization.*

4) I would accept almost any type of job assignment in order to keep working for this organization.

5) I find that my values and the organization's values are very similar.

6) I am proud to tell others that I am part of this organization.

7) I could just as well be working for a different organization as long as the type of work was similar.*

8)   This organization really inspires the very best in me in the way of job performance.

9)   It would take very little change in my present circumstances to cause me to leave this organization.*

10) I am extremely glad that I chose this organization to work for over others I was considering at the time I joined.

11) There's not too much to be gained by sticking with this organization indefinitely.*

12) Often, I find it difficult to agree with this organization's policies on important matters relating to its employees.*

13) I really care about the fate of this organization.

14) For me, this is the best of all possible organizations for which to work.

15) Deciding to work for this organization was a definite mistake on my part.*

NOTES: * denotes items that are reversed scored. The nine-item version of the OCQ is composed of those items that *are not* reverse scored.

ORGANIZATIONAL COMMITMENT
(Hunt, Chonko, and Wood 1985)

Construct: Organizational commitment was defined as a strong desire to remain a member of a particular organization, given opportunities to change jobs (Hunt, Chonko, and Wood 1985). The actual scale was developed to measure the degree of loyalty marketers would have to an organization, given attractive incentives to change companies. These incentives to change include higher pay, more creative freedom, more job status, and a friendlier environment.

Description: A four-item scale was designed to measure the degree of loyalty marketers would have to an organization, given attractive incentives for change companies. These incentives included higher pay, more freedom, more job status, and friendlier work environment. All items are rated using seven Likert response categories ranging from (1)=strongly agree to (7)=strongly disagree, and item scores are summed to form an overall commitment score.

Development: Little detail as to scale development procedures were provided by Hunt et al. (1985) as the purpose of the study was to develop a model of the relationships among organizational commitment and various other job characteristics. Factor analysis was used to assess the scale's dimensionality and coefficient alpha was used to assess its reliability. Checks for validity were performed by positing that commitment in marketing is a positive function of the personal attributes of income and age and a negative function of education; a positive function of the job characteristics of variety, autonomy, identity, and feedback; and that satisfaction is a positive function of commitment.

Sample(s): A self-administered questionnaire was mailed to 4,282 marketing professionals who were members of the American Marketing Association. A total of 1,706 usable questionnaires were received, providing a response rate of 25.1 percent.

Validity: Results of factor analysis indicated a unidimensional factor structure accounting for 69% of the variance and a having a high degree of internal consistency. The reported coefficient alpha was .85. An overall finding of this study was that while relationships among personal characteristics, job characteristics, and satisfaction exist, commitment is also a consistent predictor of satisfaction. Marketers who reported a high level of commitment tended to be more satisfied with their pay, job security, jobs in general, and choice of careers in marketing. This provided evidence for the validity of the scales. Furthermore, with commitment as the dependent variable, and a number of demographic (i.e., age, education, income) and work-related variables (i.e., variety, autonomy, feedback) as predictors, R-square estimates ranged from .02 to .17 over various splits of the 1,706 sample.

Scores: Table 4 on page 118 of Hunt, Chonko, and Wood (1985) presented an ANOVA analysis of the Commitment and Job Characteristic Inventory. Means and standard deviations were reported for the total sample, and for the classification of job types. The total sample mean and standard deviation for the commitment scale were 4.17 and 1.44, respectively.

Source: Hunt, Shelby D., Lawrence B. Chonko, and Van R. Wood (1985), "Organizational Commitment and Marketing," *Journal of Marketing*, 49 (Winter), 112-126.

Other evidence: N/A

Other sources: N/A

References: N/A

ORGANIZATIONAL COMMITMENT
(Hunt, Chonko, and Wood 1985)

1) I would be willing to change companies if the new job offered a 25% pay increase.

2) I would be willing to change companies if the new job offered more creative freedom.

3) I would be willing to change companies if the new job offered more status.

4) I would be willing to change companies if the new job was with people who were more friendly.

SALES APPROACHES

CUSTOMER ORIENTATION OF SALESPEOPLE: SOCO
(Saxe and Weitz 1982)

Construct: The SOCO scale (Sales Orientation-Customer Orientation) was designed to measure the degree to which a salesperson engages in customer-oriented selling (i.e., the degree to which salespeople practice the marketing concept by trying to help their customers make purchase decisions that will satisfy customer needs). Highly customer-oriented salespeople avoid actions that might result in customer dissatisfaction. Specifically, the SOCO scale measures six components:

1) A desire to help customers make good purchase decisions.

2) Helping customers assess their needs.

3) Offering products that will satisfy those needs.

4) Describing products accurately.

5) Avoiding deceptive or manipulative influence tactics.

6) Avoiding the use of high pressure.

Description: The SOCO scale consists of 24 items related to specific actions a salesperson might take when interacting with buyers. The items are scored on 9-point scales ranging from "True for none of my customers - NEVER" and "True for all my customers - ALWAYS." The negatively stated items were reversed-scored and a total score can be derived by summing the item scores.

Development: Initially, the construct's domain was characterized as consisting of seven components that described attitudes and behaviors that distinguish high and low customer-oriented salespeople. Items were generated for each component and the initial pool contained 104 scale items. Then, an assessment of the content validity of these items was made by surveying expert judges. After this assessment, 70 items were retained and distributed to salespersons. Based on an analysis of corrected item-to-total correlations, the 12 positively stated and 12 negatively stated items with the highest corrected-item-to-total correlations were chosen for the second instrument. The 24-item scale was then distributed to the second sample, and the original conception of the components underlying customer orientation was largely supported by the data with only one exception (i.e., matching sales presentation to customer interests was not revealed as a distinct component). A second group of salespeople was used to assess scale properties and hypotheses related to validity.

Sample(s): Following a survey of the literature, the concept of customer orientation was investigated and scale items were generated by interviewing 25 salespeople and sales managers. Then, 11 sales managers and 13 faculty were used as expert judges to assess content validity of these items. Salespersons from 48 firms returned a total of 119 usable responses. The scale was revised for a second study and was distributed to four uniquely different sales forces, resulting in 95 usable responses. After six weeks, 46 salespeople in the second sample were retested to assess test-retest reliability.

Validity: The administration of the 24-item SOCO scale to the second sample resulted in a coefficient alpha estimate of .83. The scale was readministered to part of the second sample to assess test-retest reliability. A correlation of .67 (p <. 01, one-tailed) indicated a reasonable degree of stability. A series of tests of nomological validity indicated that the SOCO scale was related to the ability of salespeople to help their customers and the quality of customer-salesperson satisfaction. For example, the correlation of SOCO with a measure of long vs. short term orientation was .56, and correlations of the SOCO scale with machiavellianism and social desirability were -.47 and .00. (Correlations of SOCO with 18 other variables are in Table 3, p. 349.) Known group validity was examined by comparing SOCO mean score across seven different sales positions. The pattern of means ranged from 159 to 187, providing evidence of known group validity.

Scores: For the nine-point items used in the final instrument, the mean score and standard deviation for the first sample were 183 and 24, respectively. The mean score for the second sample was 186 and the standard deviation was 18. (Table 2, p. 347 presents means across seven sales positions.)

Source: Saxe, Robert and Barton A. Weitz, (1982), "The SOCO Scale: A Measure of the Customer Orientation of Salespeople," *Journal of Marketing Research*, 19 (August), 343-51.

Other evidence: Michaels and Day (1985) used a national sample of purchasing professionals to replicate the SOCO scale with buyers assessing the customer orientation of salespeople who made calls on them. A total of 1,005 responses was usable. The factor structure and reliability results were almost identical to those obtained when salespeople assessed their own degree of customer orientation. The internal consistency reliability for the scale was .90 and a unidimensional factor structure was found. The mean score and standard deviation for the salespeople were 138 and 22.

Other sources: Michaels, Ronald E. and Ralph L. Day (1985), "Measuring Customer Orientation of Salespeople: A Replication With Industrial Buyers," *Journal of Marketing Research*, 22 (November), 443-446.

References: N/A

CUSTOMER ORIENTATION OF SALESPEOPLE: SOCO
(Saxe and Weitz 1982)

INSTRUCTIONS:
The statements below describe various ways a salesperson might act with a customer or prospect (for convenience, the word "customer" is used to refer to both customers and prospects). For each statement please indicate the proportion of your customers with whom you act as described in the statement. Do this by circling one of the numbers from 1 to 9. The meaning of the numbers are:

    1-True for NONE of your customers-NEVER
    2-True for ALMOST NONE
    3-True for A FEW
    4-True for SOMEWHAT LESS THAN HALF
    5-True for ABOUT HALF
    6-True for SOMEWHAT MORE THAN HALF
    7-True for a LARGE MAJORITY
    8-True for ALMOST ALL
    9-True for ALL of your customers-ALWAYS

For example, if you circled 6 below, you would indicate that you ask *somewhat more than half* of your customers a lot of questions.

	NEVER							ALWAYS
I ask customers a lot of questions. 1	2	3	4	5	6	7	8	9

Item
number

Stem-positively stated items

8. I try to help customers achieve their goals.
21. I try to achieve my goals by satisfying customers.
13. A good salesperson has to have the customer's best interest in mind.
2. I try to get the customer to discuss their needs with me.
5. I try to influence a customer by information rather than by pressure.
16. I offer the product of mine that is best suited to the customer's problem.
23. I try to find out what kind of product would be most helpful to a customer.
9. I answer a customer's questions about products as correctly as I can.
14. I try to bring a customer with a problem together with a product that helps him solve that problem.
15. I am willing to disagree with a customer in order to help him make a better decision.
1. I try to give customers an accurate expectation of what the product will do for them.
12. I try to figure out what a customer's needs are.

Stem-negatively stated items

19. I try to sell a customer all I can convince him to buy, even if I think it is more than a wise customer would buy.
6. I try to sell as much as I can rather than to satisfy a customer.
24. I keep alert for weaknesses in a customer's personality so I can use them to put pressure on him to buy.
3. If I am not sure a product is right for a customer, I will still apply pressure to get him to buy.
22. I decide what products to offer on the basis of what I can convince customers to buy, not on the basis of what will satisfy them in the long run.
20. I paint too rosy a picture of my products, to make them sound as good as possible.
7. I spend more time trying to persuade a customer to buy than I do trying to discover his needs.
17. It is necessary to stretch the truth in describing a product to a customer.
10. I pretend to agree with customers to please them.
4. I imply to a customer that something is beyond my control when it is not.
18. I begin the sales talk for a product before exploring a customer's needs with him.
11. I treat a customer as a rival.

NOTES: Item numbers are as they originally appeared in the Saxe and Weitz (1982) article.

SALESPERSON ADAPTIVE SELLING: ADAPTS
(Spiro and Weitz 1990)

Construct: Adaptive selling is defined as the "degree to which salespeople alter sales behaviors during a customer interaction or across customer interactions based on perceived information about the nature of the selling situation" (Spiro and Weitz 1990, p. 62). Five facets of adaptive selling were retained: (1) recognition that different sales approaches are needed for different customers, (2) confidence in ability to use a variety of approaches, (3) confidence in ability to alter approach during an interaction, (4) collection of information to facilitate adaptation, and (5) actual use of different approaches.

Description: The finalized version of the instrument consisted of 16 items which represent the five facets of adaptive selling listed above. Presumably, the items are scored on 7-point disagree-agree scales. Though five facets are specified, item scores are averaged over the 16 items for an overall ADAPTS score.

Development: Initially, the constructs domain was defined as consisting of six facets to assess adaptive selling. Items were generated for each facet and the initial instrument consisted of a total of 42 scale items. During the purification study, these 42 items were subjected to a principal component analysis and factor analysis. The pattern of loadings did not correspond to the conceptualized facets of adaptive selling discussed before. However, items representing five of the six facets did load highly on the first component. Therefore, one scale incorporating all of the facets rather than separate scales for each facet was developed. The final 16-item scale contained at least two items from five of the six facets. The original fourth facet, knowledge structure, was not represented in the final scale, because the items assessing categorization of sales situations were unrelated to the 16-items forming the final scale. Additionally, Spiro and Weitz (1990) discussed antecedents and consequences of the adaptive selling construct. The nomological validity of these measures was assessed by examining relationships of the adaptive selling measure to antecedents, consequences, and general personality measures of interpersonal flexibility.

Sample(s): A sample of 500 salespeople in 10 divisions of a major national manufacturer of diagnostic equipment was contacted. Pretest interviews confirmed that these salespeople continually encountered a wide variety of selling situations in which the practice of adaptive selling should be beneficial. Of the 500 questionnaires distributed, 268 were returned for a 54% response rate.

Validity: After the purification study item-to-total correlations ranged from .33 to .61. The reliability of the 16-item scale, calculated by using Cronbach's alpha, was .85. When the 16 items were subjected to a principal component analysis, the eigenvalues of the first two components were 4.59 and 1.12. Support for the nomological validity of the scale was found by correlating it with a number of constructs. Correlations of ADAPTS with measures of performance, self-monitoring, sensitivity to others, androgyny, social self-confidence, and interpersonal control were .26, .46, .41, .45, .36, and .42, respectively.

Scores: The mean response for the total scale (i.e., sum divided by number of items) was 5.51. The standard deviation was .66. Individual item scores are offered in Table 1 (p. 66).

Source: Spiro, Rosanne L. and Barton A. Weitz (1990), "Adaptive Selling: Conceptualization, Measurement, and Nomological Validity," *Journal of Marketing Research*, 27 (February), 61-69.

Other evidence: N/A

Other sources: N/A

References: N/A

SALESPERSON ADAPTIVE SELLING: ADAPTS
(Spiro and Weitz 1990)

1)	Each customer requires a unique approach	1
2)	When I feel that my sales approach is not working, I can easily change to another approach	3
3)	I like to experiment with different sales approaches	6
4)	I am very flexible in the selling approach I use	6
5)	I feel that most buyers can be dealt with in pretty much the same manner*	1
6)	I don't change my approach from one customer to another*	6
7)	I can easily use a wide variety of selling approaches	2
8)	I use a set sales approach*	6
9)	It is easy for me to modify my sales presentation if the situation calls for it	3
10)	Basically I use the same approach with most customers*	6
11)	I am very sensitive to the needs of my customers	5
12)	I find it difficult to adapt my presentation style to certain buyers*	2
13)	I vary my sales style from situation to situation	6
14)	I try to understand how one customer differs from another	5
15)	I feel confident that I can effectively change my planned presentation when necessary	3
16)	I treat all of my buyers pretty much the same*	6

NOTES: "*" denotes reverse scored items. The original 6 facets numbers are at the end of each item and correspond to the facets listed below. As previously stated, only five facets were retained (1-3 and 5-6 below).

1. A recognition that different selling approaches are needed in different sales situations.
2. Confidence in the ability to use a variety of different sales approaches.
3. Confidence in the ability to alter the sales approach during a customer interaction.
4. A knowledge structure that facilitates the recognition of different sales situations and access to sales strategies appropriate for each situation.
5. The collection of information about the sales situation to facilitate adaptation.
6. The actual use of different approaches in different situations.

INTER-INTRAFIRM ISSUES

SOCIAL POWER SCALES
(Swasy 1979)

Construct: An instrument to measure perceived interpersonal social power was developed based on the French and Raven (1959) conceptualization of six interpersonal power types. These included reward, coercive, referent, legitimate, expert, and informational (Swasy 1979). It is important to note that the power one individual (person A) holds over another (person B) is *perceived* and not necessarily absolute. Brief definitions of each power type are as follows:

Reward power - of person A over person B is based on the ability to mediate positive outcomes and to remove or decrease negative outcomes received by B.

Coercive power - rests on B's belief that A will punish him for not complying.

Referent power - results largely from a person B's feelings of identification with person A and the desire to maintain similarity with person A.

Legitimate power - stems from internalized values of person B which dictate that person A has the right of influence and that person B is obligated to obey.

Expert power - stems from person B's attribution of superior skills or knowledge to person A.

Informational power - stems from the "logic," "reasoning," or importance of the communication provided by the influencing agent (person A) and independent of the communicator.

Description: The final version of the instrument consisted of 31 items in a Likert disagree-agree format. Items are summed within factors to form total scores for each factor. Each item was scored 1 to 5 with higher numbers reflecting higher power. The author also suggested that using only the three highest loading items for each of the six power bases resulted in a scale of more reasonable total length and acceptable levels of internal consistency.

Development: After a review of the literature, 150 items which reflected different characteristics of a social power situation were generated. Six judges rated these items, resulting in 85 items having reasonably high interjudge consistency. Items were designated by the author as acceptable indicators if the following criteria were met: (1) a minimum of five of the six judges classified each item as an indicator for the same power type; and (2) each item also was not classified as an indicator in the other categories a total of 3 or more times (either within another category or over several categories). Two scenarios per power type were developed and subsequently rated by judges. The final situations were selected on the basis of being a clear representation of one social power type. Two scenarios depicting each power type were developed so that the scales would have some degree of generalizability. The final questionnaires were then completed by 321 students. Items reflecting each power basis were factor and item analyzed to determine the most reliable statements for the final scales. Reliability and predictive validity estimates were reported.

Sample(s): Six judges who were familiar with the French and Raven typology participated in the first phase of the study. Subjects were undergraduate accounting majors at UCLA. A total of 321 students were used in the final analysis of the scales.

Validity: Cronbach's coefficient alpha for each power component, as well as three-item versions of each component, were reported. The 3-item legitimate power scale had an alpha level of .59. (This low estimate was attributed to the rather unique nature of a scenario used for legitimate power.) The other alpha levels for the power types are as follows: coercive - .84 for the overall scale and .81 for a three-item version; expertise - .86 overall and .74 for a three-item version; referent - .83 overall and .79 for a three-item version; reward -.82 and .74 for a three-item version; and the three-item information dimension had an alpha of .74.

In addition, significant F-ratios based on mean scores for the three item versions of the scale across situations suggested that the scales were valid operationalizations of the power constructs.

Scores: Table 3 on page 345 of the Swasy (1979) article presents the results of a one way ANOVA and Newman-Keuls test of differences in social power scores across situations. These mean scores are based on the three-item versions of the scales and range from 5.03 to 12.17 across the six power dimensions.

Source: Swasy, John L. (1979), "Measuring the Bases of Social Power," in *Advances in Consumer Research*, Vol. 6, William L. Wilkie (ed.), Ann Arbor, MI: The Association for Consumer Research, 340-346.

Other evidence: N/A

Other sources: N/A

References: French, John R.P. and Bertram Raven (1959), "The Basis of Social Power," in D. Cartwright (ed.) *Studies in Social Power*, Ann Arbor, MI: Institute for Social Research.

SOCIAL POWER SCALES
(Swasy 1979)

REWARD

1) If I do not comply with A, I will not be rewarded.

2) The only reason for doing as A suggests is to obtain good things in return.

3) I want to do as A suggests only because of the good things A will give me for complying.

4) A has the ability to reward me (in some manner) if I do as A suggests.

5) If I do not do as A suggests I will not receive good things from A.

6) In this situation I am dependent on A's willingness to grant me good things.

REFERENT

7) In general, A's opinions and values are similar to mine.

8) Being similar to A is good.

9) I want to be similar to A.

10) In this situation my attitudes are similar to A's.

11) I would like to act very similar to the way A would act in this situation.

12) In this situation my behavior is similar to A's.

INFORMATION

13) The information provided by A about this situation makes sense.

14) The information A provided is logical.

15) I will seriously consider A's request because it is based on good reasoning.

COERCION

16) A can harm me in some manner if I do not do as A suggests.

17) If I do not do as A suggests, A will punish me.

18) Something bad will happen to me if I don't do as A requests and A finds out.

19) I had better do as A suggests in order to prevent something bad from happening to me.

20) A might do something which is unpleasant to those who do not do as A suggests.

EXPERTISE

21) I trust A's judgment.

22) A's expertise makes him/her more likely to be right.

23) A has a lot of experience and usually knows best.

24) A knows best in this situation.

25) A's knowledge usually makes him/her right.

26) I trust A's judgment in this situation.

27) In this situation I don't know as much about what should be done as A does.

28) A is intelligent.

LEGITIMATE

29) It is my duty to comply with A.

30) Because of A's position he has the right to influence my behavior.

31) I am obligated to do as A suggests.

NOTES: Items 1 through 3 represent the 3-item version of reward; items 7, 8, and 10 represent the 3-item version of referent; items 16 through 18 represent the 3-item version of coercion; and items 21 through 23 represent the 3-item version of expertise.

DEPENDENCE BASED MEASURE OF INTERFIRM POWER IN CHANNELS
(Frazier 1983)

Construct: The role performance of a firm in its primary channel responsibilities is assumed to drive the level of the other firm's dependence in a dyad. This dependence, in turn, determines the former firm's level of power over the latter firm (Frazier 1983, p. 158). Power has been consistently defined in the marketing channels literature as the ability of one channel member to influence decision variables of another channel member, and a potential for influence on another firm's beliefs and behaviors. However, the manner in which power has been operationalized has varied considerably in field studies. The measures proposed here assess auto dealer perceptions of manufacturer (or their boundary personnel) performance relative to industry average performance as reflecting levels of dealer dependence on their manufacturer. The assumption is made that role performance appears to be critical in explaining the level of another firm's dependence and goal attainment.

Description: Two versions of the scale are tenable. In one version, dealers indicate how well their manufacturer or boundary personnel perform in comparison with industry average performance on each of six elements (e.g., manufacturer generated demand for the make). Two elements (items) are designed to reflect corporate center performance and four reflect boundary personnel performance. Eleven-point scales ranging from -5, "very poor," through 0, "average performance," to +5, "very good," were used to evaluate performance. Though not specified, it appears that scores on this version are derived by summing and averaging over the items. The second version of the scale is an importance weighted measure of the first version. The importance of the six elements (i.e., the importance scores used in computing the weighted performance ratings) are operationalized using 11-point scales ranging from 0, "not important at all," to 10, "extremely important." Each element is weighted (i.e., multiplied) by its importance score for the second version of the scale (importance scores are not normalized prior to weighting).

Development: Development of the six items was based largely upon prior research involving channel power issues and a series of "prestudy" interviews. These interviews revealed two aspects of the manufacturer's organization where role performance is critical: the corporate strategic center and boundary personnel tactical center (Frazier 1983, p. 161). Items 1 and 4 (i.e., generation of consumer demand and high quality assistance) were felt critical for the performance of the manufacturer's corporate center. The remaining items were found to be critical to the role of the boundary personnel of the manufacturer. Tests of reliability and validity were performed.

Sample(s): Data were collected from 423 automobile dealer "principals" from an original sample of 944 dealers. Follow-up mailings and comparison data revealed that the sample was generally representative. Responses were obtained for the dealership's primary make of vehicle (Frazier 1983, p. 161).

Validity: Coefficient alpha was reported to be 0.81 for the weighted measure of role performance at the boundary personnel center and 0.83 for the unweighted measure (Frazier 1983, p. 162). The weighted and unweighted split-half reliability estimates for the two-item measures of performance at the corporate level were 0.66 and 0.70, respectively.

Discriminant validity was assessed by estimating a confirmatory factor model of the role performance elements, role performance at the corporate strategy level, and role performance at the boundary spanner level. The fit of this model and the variance explained (67% for the weighted version and 71% for the unweighted version) supported the discriminant validity of the power measure. The correlations between a measure of "chances of switching" suppliers and the unweighted and weighted dimensions of role performance and boundary personnel ranged from -.39 to -.55, offering evidence of convergent validity. Finally, correlations of the total weighted and unweighted versions of the scale with measures of dealer satisfaction ranged from .27 to .57, and for measures of manufacturer interests, corresponding correlations ranged from .32 to .50. These results offer evidence of nomological validity.

Scores: Overall means across the performance ratings for the six items were as follows: generated demand, 1.5; assistance, 2.1; car allocation and delivery, -.3; warranty claims, -.4; advice, -.2;

and cooperation, 1.3. For the same pattern of the six items, the mean overall performance ratings were: 8.4, 6.9, 8.9, 8.5, 6.8, and 8.0 (Frazier 1983, p. 163).

Source: Frazier, Gary L. (1983), "On the Measurement of Interfirm Power in Channels of Distribution," *Journal of Marketing Research*, 20 (May), 158-166.

DEPENDENCE BASED MEASURE OF INTERFIRM POWER IN CHANNELS
(Frazier 1983)

1. Manufacturer-generated demand for the make.

2. Cooperativeness of the manufacturer reps on interfirm issues.

3. Car allocation and delivery.

4. Interfirm assistance.

5. Quality of advice from the manufacturer reps.

6. Reimbursement for warranty claims and vehicle preparation.

NOTES: These are the six elements dealers rate their manufacturers on.

CHANNEL LEADERSHIP BEHAVIOR
(Schul, Pride, and Little 1983)

Construct: Channel leadership behavior is defined as activities carried out by a channel member to influence the marketing policies and strategies of other channel members for the purpose of controlling various aspects of channel operations (Schul, Pride, and Little 1983, p. 22). The focus taken here is on the leadership behavior of the franchiser (not franchisee).

Description: The channel leadership scale is composed of nine items, each scored on a 5-point basis where franchisees rate their franchisers from "completely agree" to "completely disagree" with the item. Furthermore, the scale has three dimensions (i.e., participative leadership, supportive leadership, and directive leadership) where three items reflect each dimension. Item scores can be summed within each dimension to form indices for each dimension.

Development: After a review of the organizational behavior literature and interviews with franchisees, 19 items were generated to reflect the construct. These items were administered to a sample of franchisees and trimmed to the final nine-item measure via factor analysis and coefficient alpha. Face validity of the items was also checked using 50 unstructured interviews. Lastly, the scale was administered to another sample and correlated with conflict measures and checked for validity.

Samples: For item generation, the sample size of the franchisees was not specified. A sample of 85 franchisees was used in trimming the scale to 9 items, and a sample of 50 was used to check face validity. Lastly, a sample of 349 franchisees responded to the main study where the scale was correlated with conflict measures.

Validity: Factor analyses supported a three-dimensional measure that represented the three dimensions of channel leadership. The three factors accounted for 82.53% of the variance in the scale items. Correlations among the three factors ranged from .35 to .52. Coefficient alpha for the three dimensions ranged from .80 for the directive leadership dimension to .92 for the supportive leadership dimension (n = 85). Face validity was also confirmed with the sample of 50. Canonical correlation of the three participative leadership items with a measure of administrative and product-service conflict within a channel was .49. The canonical correlation between the supportive leadership items and the conflict measures was .57, and the canonical correlation between the directive leadership items and the conflict measure was .45, providing evidence of nomological validity.

Scores: Neither mean nor percentage scores were reported.

Source: Schul, Patrick L., William H. Pride, and Taylor L. Little (1983), "The Impact of Channel Leadership Behavior on Intrachannel Conflict," *Journal of Marketing*, 47 (Summer), 21-34.

Other evidence: N/A.

Other source: N/A.

References: N/A.

CHANNEL LEADERSHIP BEHAVIOR
(Schul, Pride, and Little 1983)

In my franchise arrangement . . .

Participative Leadership

1)   Franchisees have major influence in the determination of policies and standards for this franchise organization.

2)   Good ideas from franchisees often do not get passed along to franchise management.*

3)   Franchisees are not allowed to provide input into the determination of standards and promotional allowances.*

Supportive Leadership

4)   There is a definite lack of coaching, support and feedback.*

5)   Once they've sold you the franchise, they forget all about you. . . except when your fees are due.*

6)   This franchise organization is highly interested in the welfare of its franchisees.

Directive Leadership

7)   I am provided sufficient guidelines and careful instructions on how to manage my franchise operations.

8)   The rights and obligations of all parties concerned are *clearly* spelled out in the franchise contract.

9)   I am encouraged to use uniform procedures.

NOTES: "*" denotes items requiring reverse scoring.

Items 1 through 3 comprise the participative leadership dimension, items 4 through 6 the supportive dimension, and items 7 through 9 the directive dimension. It is unclear as to if any items require reverse scoring. However, all supportive leadership items loaded negatively on the supportive factor, and item 7 loaded negatively on the directive leadership dimension.

CHANNEL MEMBER SATISFACTION: SATIND AND SATDIR
(Ruekert and Churchill 1984)

Construct: Channel member satisfaction is defined as the domain of all characteristics of the relationship between a channel member (the focal organization) and another institution in the channel (the target organization) which the focal organization finds rewarding, profitable, instrumental, and satisfying or frustrating, problematic, inhibiting, or unsatisfying (Ruekert and Churchill 1984, p. 227). Two operationalizations of the construct were presented. One is an indirect evaluation of the focal organization's beliefs. This scale is labeled SATIND. The other operationalization reflects a more direct approach to obtain the focal organization's evaluation of the target organization (i.e., satisfaction is asked for directly), and the scale is therefore labeled SATDIR. The dimensionality of each of the measures includes the following five components:

Social interaction - how satisfactorily interactions between focal organization and manufacturer are handled, primarily through the sales representative servicing the account.

Product - the demand for, awareness of, and quality of the manufacturer's products.

Financial - the attractiveness of the arrangement with respect to such matters as the focal organization's margins and ROI.

Cooperative advertising - how well the manufacturer supports the focal organization with co-op ad programs.

Other assistance - satisfaction with other promotional materials such as consumer promotions and point-of-purchase displays.

Description: Both the finalized versions of the SATIND, containing 21 items, and the SATDIR, containing 16 items, were designed for self- administration. A five-point Likert scale format was used for items in both scales, with possible responses ranging from "strongly agree" to "strongly disagree" for SATIND items, and "very dissatisfied" to "very satisfied" for SATDIR. Item scores can be summed within the 5 SATDIR and SATIND components to form dimension indices, or overall to form overall SATDIR and SATIND scores.

Development: Based on expert interviews and an extensive literature review, the construct's domain was originally defined as consisting of four components. Thirty-six items for SATIND and 16 for SATDIR served as the initial pool of items. The dimensionality of the SATIND measures was assessed via the following steps: 1) Item-to-total correlations were examined and any item that did not have a statistically higher correlation with the dimension to which it was hypothesized to belong was eliminated from the analysis; 2) the internal homogeneity of items belonging to each dimension was then examined via (a) coefficient alpha, (b) plots of the item-to- total correlations, and (c) principal factor analysis with oblique rotation. After these procedures were performed, 21 of the original 36 items remained for the SATIND scale. A final assessment of dimensionality (via LISREL) was conducted. The results of the confirmatory factor analysis showed that the items loaded as hypothesized on the five SATIND dimensions.

A set of similar procedures was applied to the 16 items making up the SATDIR scale. The subsequent factor analysis indicated that the SATDIR items reflect five dimensions of satisfaction. The five factors together account for slightly more than 67% of the total variation in the items. In summary, the evidence indicated that the SATDIR measure has five dimensions, and the labels are similar to the labels one would attach to those of the SATIND measure. In the confirmatory factor analysis though, one item from the SATDIR product dimension was switched to the other assistance dimension.

Additionally, the convergent, discriminant, and nomological validity of SATDIR and SATIND was assessed.

Sample(s): The research setting for testing the conceptualization was a field study of the perceptions of retailers and wholesalers toward the manufacturer of consumer batteries and ancillary products. After measures were developed, a total of 173 diverse organizations, representing 32% of the sample organizations, provided usable questionnaires. These organizations included both retailers and wholesalers. Also, four distinct lines of trade were represented, including food, drug, hardware, and mass markets.

Validity: The reliability of the 21-item linear combination for SATDIR was .89. Individual dimension alphas were .87, .76, .67, .56, and .73 for social interaction, product, financial, cooperative advertising, and other assistance, respectively. The reliability for a 15-item (though 16 items are specified) linear combination of SATDIR was .90, and dimension reliabilities were .70, .68, .79, and .75 for social interaction, financial, cooperative advertising, and other assistance. (Only one item was retained for the SATDIR product dimension.)

The correlation between the overall SATIND and SATDIR measures was .63, and the correlations between the overall SATIND and SATDIR measures and a single-item global satisfaction measure were .68 and .58, respectively, offering evidence of convergent validity. Nomological validity was assessed by correlating SATIND and SATDIR with various constructs. For example, the overall SATIND had correlations of -.52 and -.55 with measures of role ambiguity, and -.43 and -.46 with domain measures. SATDIR correlations with these constructs were -.58 and -.57, and -.39 and -.48, respectively.

Scores: Means scores and standard deviations were not reported in the Ruekert and Churchill (1984) article.

Source: Ruekert, Robert W. and Gilbert A. Churchill, Jr. (1984), "Reliability and Validity of Alternative Measures of Channel Member Satisfaction," *Journal of Marketing Research*, 21 (May), 226-33.

Other evidence: N/A

Other sources: N/A

References: N/A

CHANNEL MEMBER SATISFACTION: SATIND AND SATDIR
(Ruekert and Churchill 1984)

SATIND SCALE ITEMS

Social interaction

1) My manufacturer's sales representative isn't well organized.

2) My manufacturer's sales representative doesn't know his products very well.

3) Manufacturer's salespeople are helpful.

4) Manufacturer's sales representatives have my best interests in mind when they make a suggestion.

5) My manufacturer's sales representative is always willing to help me if I get into a tight spot.

Product

6) Manufacturer's products are asked for by our customers.

7) Manufacturer's products are a good growth opportunity for my firm.

8) Manufacturer's products are not well known by my customers.

9) My customers are willing to pay more for manufacturer's products.

10) I would have a difficult time replacing manufacturer's products with similar products.

11) Manufacturer's products perform much better than their competition.

Financial

12) Manufacturer's everyday margins are lower than industry margins.

13) Manufacturer provides very competitive margins on their products.

14) There is poor return for the amount of space I devote to manufacturer's products.

15) Some of the manufacturer's products aren't worth carrying because their margins are too small.

16) I am very happy with the margins I receive on manufacturer's products.

Cooperative advertising support

17) Manufacturer should have better cooperative advertising program.

18) Manufacturer should provide better cooperative advertising allowances.

Other assistance

19) Manufacturer conducts excellent consumer promotions.

20) Manufacturer provides adequate promotional support for their products.

21) Manufacturer provides excellent point-of-purchase displays.

SATDIR SCALES ITEMS

Social interaction

1) Personal dealings with manufacturer's sales representatives.

2) Assistance in managing your inventory of manufacturer's products.

3) Order handing by manufacturer.

4) Manufacturer's handing of damaged merchandise.

Product

5) The quality of manufacturer's products.

Financial

6) Income received from the sale of manufacturer's products.

7) Everyday margins on manufacturer's products.

8) Manufacturer credit policies.

Promotional support

9) Manufacturer's national advertising support.

10) Manufacturer's cooperative advertising support.

11) Consumer promotion support by manufacturer (coupons, rebates, displays).

12) Off-invoice promotional allowances.

13) How promotional payments are made.

Other assistance

14) Order handling by manufacturer.

15) Level of backorders of manufacturer's products.

16) Speed of delivery of manufacturer's products.

NOTES: Though not specified by the authors, items 1, 2, 8 12, 14, 15, 17, and 18 of SATIND seem to require reverse scoring.

HOLZBACH'S ATTRIBUTED POWER INDEX: API
(Comer 1984)

Construct: The primary purpose of Comer's research was to examine the properties of Holzbach's (1974) multi-item API in a sales manager - sales representative setting. Holzbach (1975) constructed a multi-item attributed power scale (API) as a measure of interpersonal power relations in an organizational environment. Specifically, the API measures the power of the sales manager. It is also important to note that the items not only reflect the sources of power, but the exercise of that power as well. This scale was predicated on the French and Raven (1959) power base model which included expert, reward, referent, legitimate, and coercive powers.

Description: Using Busch's (1980) single-item power scales as a point of reference, Comer (1984) examined the quality of Holzbach's multi-item attributed power index. The Holzbach scale, designed for self-administration, consists of 25 individual statements measuring aspects of the power bases of French and Raven. Items are scored on 7-point scales ranging from "extremely inaccurate" to "extremely accurate." Respondents are asked to circle a mnemonic ranging from EI (extremely inaccurate) to VI, I, ?, A, VA, EA (extremely accurate). Item scores can be summed within power dimensions to form indices of each dimension.

Development: A questionnaire was constructed for the purpose of evaluating the dimensions of sales representatives' jobs and their relationships with their managers, as well as surveying key demographic data. The survey included both the Holzbach scale and the five Busch power statements. Via factor, item, MTMM, and reliability analyses, the API's appropriateness to a sales setting was examined.

Sample(s):   Mail questionnaires were sent to sales representatives employed by three companies. Two companies were engaged in the sale of industrial products; the other sold consumer goods. Three hundred thirty-three questionnaires were sent; 207 were usable.

Validity: Cronbach's alpha was used to measure the internal consistency of the Holzbach scale in each company. The alpha values were consistent across power bases and companies. The alpha value ranges were as follows: expert .89-.90, reward .88-.90, coercive .69-.75, referent .75-.90, and legitimate .64 -.76. Both convergent and discriminant validity for the Holzbach scales were assessed by examining the API with Busch's measures via the multitrait-multimethod matrix method. Though the results failed to establish discriminant validity (i.e., some of the API power bases were too highly correlated to infer discriminant validity), four of the five convergent validity estimates (i.e., correlations of the API measures with Busch's measures) were significant, ranging from .29 to .71.

Factor analysis was used to explore the API structure. The factor loadings indicated that the reward, coercive, expert, and referent power results were similar to those found by Holzbach's (1974). That is, the items loaded as hypothesized on their respective factors. However, the legitimate power factor did not reproduce cleanly.

Nomological validity was assessed by correlating the API dimensions with the INDSALES satisfaction measure (Churchill, Ford, and Walker 1974). The correlation between INDSALES and expert, referent, and coercive power across the 3 subsample groups ranged from .69 to .72, .72 to .80, and -.18 to -.57, respectively. In summary, the API represents an improvement in the measurement of power-base utilization in sales manager-sales representative relationships.

Scores: Means and (standard deviations) were reported by Comer for each power dimension and were 26.09 (4.80), 25.05 (3.91), 21.80 (5.16), 25.54 (5.26), and 24.36 (5.25) for expert, legitimate, coercive, referent, and reward power, respectively.

Source: The original source of the scale is Holzbach (1974). However, since Holzbach's work is an unpublished dissertation, the API examined here is from:

Comer, James M. (1984), "A Psychometric Assessment of a Measure of Sales Representatives' Power Perceptions," *Journal of Marketing Research*, 21 (May), 221-225.

Other evidence:	N/A

Other sources:	N/A

References: Busch, Paul (1980), "The Sales Manager's Bases of Social Power and Influence Upon the Sales Force," *Journal of Marketing*, 44 (Summer).

Churchill, Gilbert A., Jr., Neil M. Ford, and Orville C. Walker (1974), "Measuring the Job Satisfaction of Industrial Salesmen," *Journal of Marketing Research*, 11 (August), 254-260.

French, John R. and Bertram Raven (1959), "The Basis of Social Power," in D. Cartwright (ed.) *Studies in Social Power*, Ann Arbor, MI: Institute for Social Research.

Holzbach, Robert L. (1974), "An Investigation of a Model for Managerial Effectiveness: The Effects of Leadership Style and Leader Attributed Social Power on Subordinate Job Performance," doctoral dissertation, Carnegie-Mellon University, Ann Arbor, MI: University Microfilms.

HOLZBACH'S ATTRIBUTED POWER INDEX: API
(Comer 1984)

Reward

(2) Gives credit where credit is due
(12) Recognizes achievement
(13) Willing to promote others
(16) Rewards good work
(23) Offers inducement

Coercive

(3) Rules by might
(11) Retaliative
(17) Overly critical
(21) Disciplinarian
(24) Strict

Legitimate

(7) Have obligation to accept his/her orders
(14) Duty bound to obey him/her
(15) Has authority
(19) Entitled to direct my actions on the job
(20) Authorized to command

Expert

(4) Skilled
(5) Knowledgeable
(8) Experienced
(10) Proficient
(22) Qualified

Referent

(1) Admire him/her
(6) Identify with him/her
(9) Respect him/her as a person
(25) Likable
(18) Friendly

NOTES: Item numbers are as they appeared in the Comer article.

POWER SOURCES IN A MARKETING CHANNEL
(Gaski and Nevin 1985)

Construct: Gaski and Nevin (1985) examined the concepts of perceived and exercised reward/coercive power in a dealer-supplier relationship (i.e., a channels framework). Specifically, perceived reward/coercive power is viewed as the dealer's perception of the ability of the supplier to mediate rewards and punishments (i.e., considered as "sources" of power). Exercised reward/coercive power is viewed as the actual granting of rewards and imposition of punishment by the supplier (cf., Hunt and Nevin 1974). Another power measure, based on the dealer's perception of the potential influence that a supplier has over the dealer's business, was also conceptualized. This power measure assesses the supplier's ability to get the dealer to do what he would not have done otherwise.

Description: In essence, Gaski and Nevin's power measure is composed of five separate indices: perceived reward power (a source), perceived coercive power (a source), exercised reward power, exercised coercive power, and a supplier's ability to potentially affect the dealer's business. The perceived reward power index is composed of 15 items scored from "no capability" to reward (0) to "very much capability" to reward (4). The perceived coercive power index is composed of 6 items also scored on the aforementioned 0 to 4 format. The exercised reward power index is composed of 15 items scored from "never" exercises the power (0) to "often" exercises the power (3). The exercised coercive power index is composed of 6 items also scored on the 0 to 3 format. The supplier's ability to affect the dealer's business is measured with 10 items scored from "not at all" (0) to "as much as they wanted" (3). Item scores within each index are summed to form an overall score for each power index.

Development: The initial pool of items for the indices was drawn from extant channels literature (e.g., Hunt and Nevin 1974; Lusch 1976). The items were screened, modified to fit the research setting, and checked for face validity. Then, with a large sample, the measures were assessed for reliability and validity.

Sample(s):   The large sample consisted of 238 dealers of heavy industrial machinery (i.e., dealers who handled the Melroe products of the Clark Equipment Company - the supplier).

Validity: Coefficient alpha estimates for the perceived reward power, perceived coercive power, exercised reward power, and exercised coercive power indices were .87, .69, .83, and .62, respectively. The alpha for the supplier's ability to affect the dealer's business index was .86. Discriminant validity was said to be evidenced by the fact that the correlations among indices were not as high as the lowest coefficient alpha of the indices. These correlations ranged from -.16 to .56. The power indices were used as independent variables to predict dealer satisfaction with the supplier, conflict with the supplier, and dealer performance. For dealer satisfaction, significant regression coefficients were -.12, -.30, .31, and .35 for perceived coercive power, exercised coercive power, perceived reward power, and exercised reward power, respectively. For conflict, significant regression coefficients were .19, .43, -.30, and -.37 for perceived coercive power, exercised coercive power, perceived reward power, and exercised reward power, respectively. For performance, only exercised reward power showed a significant regression coefficient (-.11). These results show support for the predictive validity of the power indices.

Scores: Neither mean nor percentage scores were reported.

Source: Gaski, John F. and John Nevin (1985), "The Differential Effects of Exercised and Unexercised Power Sources in a Marketing Channel," *Journal of Marketing Research*, 22 (May), 130-142.

Other evidence: N/A.

Other sources: N/A.

References: Hunt, Shelby and John R. Nevin (1974), "Power in a Channel of Distribution: Sources and Consequences," *Journal of Marketing Research*, 11 (May), 186-193.

Lusch, Robert F. (1976), "Sources of Power: Their Impact on Intrachannel Conflict," *Journal of Marketing Research*, 13 (November), 382-390.

POWER SOURCES IN A MARKETING CHANNEL
(Gaski and Nevin 1985)

Perceived Coercive Power (Source)

Please check (X) the appropriate space to indicate *how much capability* Clark Equipment has to take each of the following kinds of action in their dealings with your organization.

	no capability				very much capability
	___	___	___	___	___

Delay delivery
Delay warranty claims
Take legal action against you
Refuse to sell
Charge high prices
Deliver unwanted products

Perceived Reward Power (Source)

Please check (X) the appropriate space to indicate *how much capability* Clark Equipment has to take each of the following kinds of action in their dealings with your organization.

	no capability				very much capability
	___	___	___	___	___

Provide advertising support
Give trade allowances/incentives
Train personnel
Provide sales promotion materials
Grant favors (golf, lunches, etc.)
Give inventory rebates
Provide financing/credit
Furnish supplies
Give business advice
Provide service
Give pricing assistance
Give free samples
Provide ordering assistance
Provide inventory management assistance
Demonstrate products

Exercised Coercive Power

Please indicate (X) *how often* Clark Equipment takes each of the following kinds of action in their dealings with your organization.

	never			often
	____	____	____	____

Delay delivery
Delay warranty claims
Take legal action against you
Refuse to sell
Charge high prices
Deliver unwanted products

Exercised Reward Power

Please indicate *(X) how often* Clark Equipment takes each of the following kinds of action in their dealings with your organization.

	never			often
	____	____	____	____

Provide advertising support
Give trade allowances/incentives
Train personnel
Provide sales promotion materials
Grant favors (golf, lunches, etc.)
Give inventory rebates
Provide financing/credit
Furnish supplies
Give business advice
Provide service
Give pricing assistance
Give free samples
Provide ordering assistance
Provide inventory management assistance
Demonstrate products

Supplier's Ability to Influence the Dealer's Business

Please indicate (X) your response to each of the following.

	not at all	slightly	moderately	as much as they wanted
	____	____	____	____

If Clark Equipment wanted you to raise the prices you charge for their products, what is the maximum amount you would raise prices?

If Clark Equipment wanted you to lower the prices you charge for their products, what is the maximum amount you would lower prices?

If Clark Equipment wanted you to increase the quantity of their products you order, what is the maximum amount you would increase order quantity?

If Clark Equipment wanted you to decrease the quantity of their products you order, what is the maximum amount you would decrease order quantity?

If Clark Equipment wanted you to change the composition of your product line, what is the maximum amount you would change your product line?

If Clark Equipment wanted you to change the type of advertising and sales promotion you do for their products, what is the maximum amount you would change your advertising and sales promotion?

If Clark Equipment wanted you to change your customer service policy, what is the maximum amount you would change your customer service?

If Clark Equipment wanted you to change your inventory procedures, what is the maximum amount you would change your inventory procedures?

If Clark Equipment wanted you to change your customer credit policy, what is the maximum amount you would change your customer credit?

If Clark Equipment wanted you to change the way you display their products, what is the maximum amount you would change your display of their products?

BUYCLASS FRAMEWORK SCALES
(Anderson, Chu, and Weitz 1987)

Construct: The "buyclass framework" (Robinson, Faris, and Wind 1967) posits that different organizational buying approaches are required for different purchase situations. The different purchase situations can range from a "straight rebuy" to a "modified rebuy" to a "new task" purchase. These three buyclass decisions are defined and determined along three dimensions: 1) how much information the prospective buyer needs to make a good decision; 2) the seriousness with which the prospective buyer considers all alternatives; and 3) how familiar the purchase situation is to the prospective buyer. The "straight rebuy" is low on all three dimensions, the "modified rebuy" is in the midrange of all three dimensions, and the "new task" is high on all three dimensions (Anderson et al. 1987, p. 72). Anderson et al. (1987) construct measures that reflect the three dimensions.

Description: The buyclass scales are actually two sets (i.e., versions) of the same scale. Both versions are represented by two, rather than the original three, dimensions specified. One dimension is titled "NEWNESS + INFO," which reflects the original dimensions 3 and 1 above. The other dimension, "ALT," reflects dimension 2 listed above. All items are scored on 7-point scales ranging from "0%" to "100%" of the time (see instructions). Item scores can be summed within dimensions to form indices of each dimension.

Development: The academic and trade literatures were used to generate a large pool of items. Then, a sample of 12 sales managers, using a sequential editing process over several months, was used to refine and trim the items. A large sample of sales managers from a number of different electronic component firms responded to the items. Via factor analysis, reliability, and validity checks, Version 1 of the scales was derived. In a replication study, the procedures for scale development and validation were repeated with a variety of manufacturing firms, and Version 2 of the scale was derived.

Samples: For deriving Version 1 of the scale, a sample of 169 sales managers from 16 electronic component firms was used in the main study. For Version 2, a sample of 158 sales managers from a variety of manufacturing firms was used in the main study.

Validity: For the Version 1 sample (n = 169), factor analysis revealed a two-factor structure (i.e., "NEWNESS + INFO" and "ALT"). The NEWNESS + INFO factor had a coefficient alpha of .73, and the ALT factor had an alpha of .57. The correlation between these two factors was .14. Nomological validity was assessed by correlating the two factors with several buyer behavior statements. These correlations ranged from -.17 to .49 (in the predicted direction) for the buyer behavior statements and the NEWNESS + INFO factor, and -.05 to .18 for the buyer behavior statements and the ALT factor. These results offer evidence for the nomological validity of the NEWNESS + INFO factor.

For Version 2, factor analysis again revealed the two-factor NEWNESS + INFO and ALT structure. Coefficient alpha was .71 and .53 for these two factors, respectively. Nomological validity was again assessed by correlating the two factors with several buyer behavior statements. These correlations ranged from -.63 to .61 (in the predicted direction) for the buyer behavior statements and the NEWNESS + INFO factor, and -.18 to .18 for the buyer behavior statements and the ALT factor. These results are supportive of the nomological validity of the NEWNESS + INFO factor.

Scores: Neither mean nor percentage scores were reported.

Source: Anderson, Erin, Wujin Chu, and Barton Weitz (1987), "Industrial Purchasing: An Empirical Exploration of the Buyclass Framework," *Journal of Marketing*, 51 (July), 71-86.

Other evidence: N/A.

Other sources: N/A.

References: Robinson, Patrick, J., Charles W. Faris and Yoram Wind (1967), *Industrial Buying and Creative Marketing*, Boston, MA: Allyn and Bacon.

BUYCLASS FRAMEWORK SCALES
(Anderson, Chu, and Weitz 1987)

Instructions: The following statements describe circumstances which might exist when one of your salespeople is trying to make a sale. Please indicate *how frequently* the salesperson would face the situation described in the statement. This can be indicated by circling the number that most accurately indicates the percentage of sales situations that fit the statement. Each question is independent: your answers do not need to add to 100% or any other number.

EXAMPLE: It is hard to get an appointment to see the account.

Percentage of Situations

0%   10%   **30**%   50%   70%   90%   100%

This manager indicates that in 30% of the selling situations, the salesperson has difficulty getting an appointment. Notice that "account" means customer or prospect. Those 30% of selling situations that are difficult could be cold calls, follow-ups with a regular customer, or some combination of prospects and customers.

Version 1

NEWNESS + INFO items

1)   The account seldom purchases this type of product.

2)   The product is the first purchase of its kind for the account.

3)   The account has not dealt with this product class or requirement before.

4)   This is still a rather new purchase for the account.

5)   The account's requirements have changed since the product was purchased last.

6)   The account has complete knowledge about what product characteristics are needed to solve the problem.*

7)   The account knows exactly what is needed.*

8)   The purchase decision demands a lot of information.

9)   The account is willing to gather and consider a lot of information before deciding.

10) The account is willing to consider new information in making a decision.

ALT items

1)   The account is seriously interested in alternatives to the present supplier.

2)   The account wants to consider all the alternatives carefully.

3)   The account is interested in salespeople calling to propose changing suppliers.

4)   The account is open to suggestions for change in the current purchase pattern.

5)   The account has considerable experience with the product class but is considering new options, new suppliers, or new products.

NOTES: Items 1 through 5 of NEWNESS + INFO reflect the newness of the buying situation. Though five newness items are listed in the Appendix (see Anderson et al. 1987, p. 84), the text states that 4 items reflect newness.) Items 6 through 10 reflect the information items of the NEWNESS + INFO factor. All items are scaled such that higher values represent greater frequency of encountering new tasks and lower values reflect more routine purchases. Thus, items with an "*" require reverse scoring.

Version 2

NEWNESS + INFO items

1) The customer seldom purchases this type of product.

2) The customer considers the purchase decision to be routine.*

3) The customer has not dealt with this product class or requirement before.

4) The customer has routinized the purchase decision so that it no longer requires a lot of attention.*

5) The customer's requirements have changed since the product was purchased last.

6) The customer has complete knowledge about what product characteristics are needed to solve the problem.*

7) The customer needs a lot of information before making a purchase decision.

ALT items

1) The customer is seriously interested in alternatives to the present supplier.

2) The customer has considerable experience with the product class but is considering new options, new suppliers, or new products.

NOTES: Items 1 through 5 of NEWNESS + INFO reflect the newness of the buying situation. Items 6 and 7 reflect the information items of the NEWNESS + INFO factor. All items are scaled such that higher values represent greater frequency of encountering new tasks and lower values reflect more routine purchases. Thus, items with an "*" require reverse scoring.

DISTRIBUTOR, MANUFACTURER, AND CUSTOMER MARKET POWER
(Butaney and Wortzel 1988)

Constructs: Within the channels of distribution literature, power and power types have been defined in various ways. Butaney and Wortzel (1988, pp. 54-55) define and measure three types of power operative in channels of distribution:

Distributor power (DP) - the extent of the distributor's freedom in make marketing decisions about the manufacturer's product. Distributor power is considered a form of "exercised" power as it represents an outcome, the power successfully achieved by a channel member to alter the behavior of another channel member.

Customer market power (CMP) - is defined as those characteristics having the potential to affect the customer's power in the marketplace.

Manufacturer market power (MMP) - is defined as those industry characteristics or conditions having the potential to affect the manufacturer's power in the marketplace.

Description: The DP is composed of 17 items scored on 5-point scales (see next page). Item scores are summed to form an overall index of DP. CMP is a three dimensional scale. The dimensions are knowledgeable customers (CMS), large customers (CL), and customer switching costs (NCDS). There are 2, 3, and 4 items for the dimensions. CMS, CL and NCDS items are scored on 5-point scales and summed within dimensions to form CMS and CL indices. MMP is composed of two dimensions labeled manufacturer low concern for competition (NMI) and concentrated industry structure (MI). NMI and MI are composed of 4 and 2 items, respectively, scored on 5-point scales. Item scores are summed within dimensions to form indices for the dimensions.

Development: For the DP, an original pool of 27 items was generated. Using a panel of expert judges, this pool was trimmed to 22 items. The 22 items were then subjected to factor analysis and items with loadings greater than .40 on the first factor were retained, resulting in the final 17-item DP. For CMP and MMP measures, a pool of 40 items was generated and then trimmed to 21 after expert panel judging. These items were factor analyzed and reduced to the final CMP and MMP dimensions of 2 items for CMS, 3 items for CL, 4 items for NCDS, 4 items for NMI and 2 items for MI. For all scales, reliability and nomological validity were assessed.

Samples: The panel of experts used to trim the initial item pools was composed of members of an industrial electronic distributors association and 2 professors familiar with the channels literature. The main sample, with which the factor, reliability, and validity analyses were performed, was composed of 83 managers from the electronics components industry.

Validity: Coefficient alpha for the 17-item DP scale was .76. (Alpha based on a weighted DP scale, in which each item is also evaluated on an 11-point scale as to its importance, was .85.) Alphas for the CMS, CL, and NCDS dimensions of customer market power were .74, .55, and .57, respectively. Alphas for the NMI and MI dimensions of manufacturer market power were .58 and .56.

Using DP as the dependent variable and CMS, CL and NCDS as independent variables in a regression equation, only NCDS had a significant beta coefficient (-.28). With NMI and MI as predictors of DP, both variables had significant beta coefficients (-.34 and -.22, respectively). Thus, some evidence of nomological validity among the variables was provided.

Scores: Neither mean nor percentage scores were reported.

Source: Butaney, Gul and Lawrence H. Wortzel (1988), "Distributor Power Versus Manufacturer Power: The Customer Role," *Journal of Marketing*, 52 (January), 52-63.

Other evidence: N/A.

**Other
sources:** N/A.

References: N/A.

DISTRIBUTOR, MANUFACTURER, AND CUSTOMER MARKET POWER
(Butaney and Wortzel 1988)

Instructions and DP items: To market and distribute a product, several marketing decisions have to be made. In making these decisions, a distributor may have almost complete responsibility, or freedom to make a decision may be shared with the manufacturer, or the manufacturer may have almost complete responsibility. For each of the marketing decisions and activities listed below, please indicate the level of freedom or responsibility you have as compared to the selected manufacturer (in marketing the manufacturer's brand). Please check the appropriate response category where. . .

1 = manufacturer has almost complete responsibility
2 = manufacturer has more responsibility than myself
3 = manufacturer and I share equal responsibility
4 = I have more responsibility than the manufacturer
5 = I have almost complete responsibility

Distributor Power (DP)

1) Choosing geographic territories to sell in.
2) Setting sales targets or goals.
3) Setting selling prices to customers.
4) Determining distribution policies to customers.
5) Determining the training program for your salesforce to sell the product.
6) Keeping the manufacturer from selling direct in your territory.
7) Product return-related issues.
8) Choosing customers to sell to.
9) Determining pricing policies (e.g., quantity discounts to customers).
10) Deciding to join in cooperative advertising with the manufacturer.
11) Keeping the manufacturer's other distributors from selling in your territory.
12) Accommodating customer's request for product modification.
13) Margins allowed by the manufacturer.
14) Providing presale customer services (e.g., product information).
15) Attending sales meetings organized by the manufacturer.
16) Resolving customers' product-related technical problems.
17) Determining sales strategies/policies (e.g., frequency of sales calls to customers).

Customer market power items (CMP)

CMS dimension

1) The customers possess a great deal of market information.
2) The customers possess a good idea about the costs of the product to the distributor.

CL dimension

3) Customers are able to bargain the terms of the sale.
4) 20% of my customers account for 80% of my total product sales.
5) Most of my customers can buy the product directly from manufacturers.

NCDS dimension

6) Supplier's name and brand are not very important purchasing criteria for customers.
7) Customers' cost of finding and qualifying other suppliers is low.

8)   Customers' importance for the product quality in their purchasing criteria is low.
9)   The customers in the industry do not insist on buying a specific manufacturer brand.

Manufacturer market power items (MMP)

NMI dimension

1)   When one manufacturer reduces the product price, the other manufacturers do not reduce their prices.
2)   When the manufacturer increases price, the customers do not switch brands.
3)   Competition among manufacturers in the industry is not strong.
4)   The manufacturer possesses a great deal of industry information (e.g., trends, problems, competitive brands).

MI dimension

5)   Only a few manufacturers produce a large volume of the product in the industry.
6)   Industry sales are not equally distributed among the manufacturers.

NOTES: All CMP and MMP items are scored on five-point scales from strongly disagree (1) to strongly agree (5). Item 4 of the NMI dimensions had a negative loading on its factor.

MULTIPLE INFLUENCES IN BUYING CENTERS
(Kohli and Zaltman 1988)

Construct: Influence of an individual in a buying center was defined as the changes in purchase decision-related opinions and behaviors of buying center members as a consequence of the individual's participation in the decision making. This definition tapped the notion of how different buying center members' opinions and behaviors would have been if the individual had not been involved in the decision making. The definition provided for intentional as well as unintentional change resulting from the individual's participation (Kohli and Zaltman 1988, p. 198). Furthermore, the measure was designed to assess the influences exerted by an individual in a specific purchase decision rather than in purchase decisions in general.

Description: The buying influence scale consists of 9 items scored on 5-point scales ranging from "very small" to "very large." It is important to recognize that the measure was primarily designed to assess influence in final evaluation and selection phase of decision making. Item scores are summed to form an overall total score.

Development: After an extensive review of the literature, scale development proceeded by selecting the specific stage of the decision-making process for which the measure would be designed. The final evaluation and selection phase of the decision process was selected because it was felt that this phase was the richest with respect to group dynamics. A panel of academic judges was asked to critique the structure and content of the initial set of items designed to measure influence. The revised set of items went through several phases of pretesting. The final set of items contained nine items. Via factor, item, and reliability analyses, the final scale was derived and evaluated.

Sample(s): Five hundred randomly selected members of the National Association of Purchasing Management were surveyed. A total of 251 usable responses was obtained for an effective response rate of approximately 55%.

Validity: Alpha for the 9-item scale was .93. The dimensionality of the measure was assessed by performing a factor analysis. The general factor had an eigenvalue of 5.48 and accounted for over 60% of the variance, suggesting a unidimensional structure. Investigation of face validity, content validity and aspects of construct validity (including convergent, discriminant, and nomological validity) were also assessed. The results suggested support for convergent and discriminant validity. Also, findings were consistent with prior expectations on theoretical grounds and provided strong support for nomological validity of the influence scale. For example, the correlation between the scale and a single item measure of influence was .66, indicating convergent validity. Lower correlations were found with size, risk and time pressure measures, indicating discriminant validity. Lastly, nomological validity was provided by correlations of the scale with expertise (.45), reward power (.34) and coercive power (.25).

Scores: Mean scores and standard deviations were not cited in the Kohli and Zaltman (1988) article.

Source: Kohli, Ajay K. and Gerald Zaltman (1988), "Measuring Multiple Buying Influences", *Industrial Marketing Management* 17, 197-204.

Other evidence: N/A.

Other source: N/A.

References: N/A.

MULTIPLE INFLUENCES IN BUYING CENTERS
(Kohli and Zaltman 1988)

1. How much weight did the committee members give to his opinions?

2. How much impact did he have on the thinking of the other members?

3. To what extent did he influence the criteria used for making the final decision?

4. How much effect did his involvement in the purchase committee have on how the various options were rated?

5. To what extent did he influence others into adopting certain positions about the various options?

6. How much change did he induce in the preferences of other members?

7. To what extent did others go along with his suggestions?

8. To what extent did his participation influence the decision eventually reached?

9. To what extent did the final decision reflect his views?

NOTES: Items were scored on a 5-point scale ranging from "Very Small" to "Very Large."

*Reprinted by permission of the publisher from Kohli, Ajay K. and Gerald Zaltman (1988), "Measuring Multiple Buying Influences," **Industrial Marketing Management** 17, 197-204. Copyright 1992 by Elsevier Science Publishing Co., Inc.*

POWER AND INFLUENCE IN GROUP SETTINGS
(Kohli 1989)

Construct: There are a number of power and influence types operating in organizational buying, and purchase decisions in organizational buying are often greatly affected by these different types of influence and power. Consistent with existing literatures (e.g., French and Raven 1959; Gaski 1984; Kohli and Zaltman 1988), Kohli (1989, pp. 51-53) defines several sources of individual power and influence operating in organizational buying:

Manifest influence - refers to changes in purchase decision related opinions and behavior of buying center members that result from the individual's participation in a buying center.

Influence attempts - refers to the amount of effort exerted by an individual to influence a purchase decision.

Self-perceived influence - the influence an informant believes he or she exerted on a decision.

Reinforcement power - refers to the ability to mediate positive and negative reinforcements. In essence, reward and coercive power are components of reinforcement power, where *reward power* refers to an individual's ability to provide material and nonmaterial rewards to other individuals (generally in compliance to his/her requests), and *coercive power* refers to an individual's ability to mete out material and nonmaterial punishments to others.

Referent power - is the extent to which others like and identify themselves with that person and have regard for his/her personal qualities.

Legitimate power - refers to the extent to which others feel that they ought to comply with the wishes of an individual and derives from both formal and informal social norms.

Expert power - refers to the extent to which an individual is perceived by others as being knowledgeable about other issues.

Information power - refers to an individual's access and control over relevant information.

Departmental power - is the relative importance of a department in general to an organization.

The above definitions and their corresponding measures represent an extension of the Kohli and Zaltman (1988) manifest influence measures.

Description: For each of the above definitions, multi-item scales were developed. Across scales, all items were scored on 5-point formats (see next page). Item scores are summed within each scale to form an index for each power or influence type.

Development: Through an extensive literature search and existing measures, a pool of items was generated to reflect each type of power and influence. An expert panel of academicians was used to revise the items. The items were further refined via a three wave pre-test of personal interviews with managers involved in joint purchase decisions. Then, in a large study, the items were tested for factor structure, reliability, and validity. These tests resulted in the elimination of several items which resulted in the final versions of the scales.

Samples: Fourteen managers participated in the personal interviews to refine the items. A sample of 251 from the National Association of Purchasing Management was used in the study examining the scales' factor structure, reliability, and validity.

Validity: Factor analysis revealed a six-factor structure for the power measures reflecting the six power components defined above. Coefficient alpha estimates were .95, .86, .80, .85, .90, and .88 for reinforcement power, referent power, legitimate power, expert power, information power, and departmental power, respectively. Alpha estimates for manifest influence, influence attempts, and self-perceived influence were .93, .90, and .86, respectively.

Using manifest influence as the dependent variable, the six influence types and self-perceived influence as independent variables, the relationships among power and influence were examined. For the overall sample (214 of 251), 38% of the variance in manifest influence was explained by the predictor variables, with reinforcement power (beta = .33) and expert power (beta = .49) as the major contributors. The sample was also split into high and low groups across several contingency variables. R-square estimates across the groups ranged from .26 to .56. Furthermore, the correlations among the independent variables ranged from .03 to .48, suggesting low multicollinearity. These results show predictive validity for the measures.

Scores: Various mean scores were offered. A split of the large sample based on influence versions of the questionnaire as high or low (see Table 4, p. 58) offered mean scores as follows:

	Low influence		High influence	
	Mean	sd	Mean	sd
Scale				
Manifest influence	24.0	7.2	34.6	4.7
Self-perceived influence	19.0	3.7	18.5	3.7
Influence attempts	10.7	3.9	12.8	4.0
Reinforcement power	19.4	8.8	26.6	12.5
Referent power	16.2	4.1	16.4	4.7
Legitimate power	4.0	1.9	5.4	2.4
Expert power	13.8	3.6	16.6	3.5
Information power	9.8	5.2	9.8	5.1
Departmental power	12.1	4.1	13.0	4.3

Source: Kohli, Ajay (1989), "Determinants of Influence in Organizational Buying: A Contingency Approach," *Journal of Marketing*, 53 (July), 50-65.

Other evidence: N/A.

Other sources: N/A.

References: French, John R., Jr. and Bertram H. Raven (1959), "The Bases of Social Power," in *Studies in Social Power*, D. Cartwright (ed.), Ann Arbor, MI: University of Michigan Press.

Gaski, John F. (1984), "The Theory of Power and Conflict in Channels of Distribution," *Journal of Marketing*, 48 (Summer), 9-29.

Kohli, Ajay and Gerald Zaltman (1988), "Measuring Multiple Buying Influences," *Industrial Marketing Management*, 17 (August), 197-204.

POWER AND INFLUENCE IN GROUP SETTINGS
(Kohli 1989)

The final versions of the scale are as follows:

Manifest influence

1)   How much weight did the committee members give to his opinions?

2)   How much impact did he have on the thinking of the other members?

3)   To what extent did he influence the criteria used for making the final decision?

4)   How much effort did his involvement in the purchase committee have on how the various options were rated?

5)   To what extent did he influence others into adopting certain positions about the various options?

6) How much change did he induce in the preferences of other members?

7) To what extent did others go along with his suggestions?

8) To what extent did his participation influence the decision eventually reached?

9) To what extent did the final decision reflect his views?

NOTE: The above items are scored from very small (1) to very large (5).

Influence attempts

Relative to others. . .

1) . . . he spent more time to impress his views on the committee members.

2) . . . he tried harder to shape the thinking of others.

3) . . . he spent more energy to make sure his opinions were taken into account.

4) . . . he exerted more effort to make sure the final decision reflected his views.

NOTE: The above items are scored from strongly disagree (1) to strongly agree (5).

Self-perceived influence

1) How much weight did the committee members give to your opinions?

2) To what extent did you influence the criteria used for making the final decision?

3) How much effort did your involvement in the purchase committee have on how the various options were rated?

4) To what extent did your participation influence the decision eventually reached?

5) To what extent did the final decision reflect your views?

NOTE: The above items are scored from very small (1) to very large (5).

Reinforcement power

1) They believed he was capable of getting them pay raises.

2) They felt he could improve their standing in the organization.

3) They felt it was desirable to be approved by him.

4) They valued receiving recognition from him.

5) They felt that he could arrange desirable assignments for them.

6) They believed he was capable of getting them promoted.

7) They believed he was capable of interfering with their promotions

8) They felt he could take them to task.

9) They felt he could make life difficult for them.

10) They thought he could block their salary increases.

11) They believed he could arrange for them to be assigned to unpleasant tasks.

NOTE: The above items are scored from none (1) to all (5). Items 1 through 6 reflect the reward power component and items 7 through 11 reflect the coercive power component.

Legitimate power

1) They felt that the purchase decision should reflect his preferences because he had more at stake than others.

2) They felt they ought to comply with him because the purchase decision would affect him more than others.

NOTE: The above items are scored from none (1) to all (5).

Referent power

1) They disliked him as a person.*

2) They thought highly of his personality.

3) They shared his personal values.

4) They identified with him as a person.

5) They had a high regard for his personal qualities.

NOTE: The above items are scored from none (1) to all (5). Item 1 (*) requires reverse scoring.

Expert power

1) They felt he was knowledgeable about the organization's needs with respect to the product.

2) They thought he was competent to make an assessment of the various options.

3) They felt he knew exactly how the product would be used.

4) They felt he had the expertise to make the best decision.

NOTE: The above items are scored from none (1) to all (5).

Departmental power

1) The functions performed by this department are generally considered to be more critical than others.

2) Top management considers this department to be more important than others.

3) This department tends to dominate others in the affairs of the organization.

4) This department is generally regarded as being more influential than others.

NOTE: The above items are scored from strongly disagree (1) to strongly agree (5).

Information power

1) He served as a communication link between the suppliers and the committee members.

2) He was in direct contact with the suppliers.

3) He was responsible for obtaining information about suppliers for the committee members.

4) He held independent discussions with the various suppliers on behalf of the purchase committee.

NOTE: The above items are scored from strongly disagree (1) to strongly agree (5).

APPENDIX TO INTER-INTRAFIRM ISSUES

There are numerous articles that use multi-item measures to assess aspects of power, conflict, and influence strategies in the channels literature. Most of these measures, though, were derived for the specific research setting or product being studied. Application of these measures to other products and settings could be problematic, and thus, we have chosen not to summarize these types of measures here. However, the interested reader is referred to the following articles as a partial guide to some of these study/product specific channel measures.

Anderson, James C. and James A. Narus (1984), "A Model of the Distributor's Perspective of Distributor-Manufacturer Working Relationships," *Journal of Marketing*, 48 (Fall), 62-74.

Anderson, James C. and James A. Narus (1990), "A Model of Distributor Firm and Manufacturer Firm Working Partnerships," *Journal of Marketing*, 54 (January), 42-58.

Frazier, Gary, and John O. Summers (1984), "Interfirm Influence Strategies and Their Application Within Distribution Channels," *Journal of Marketing*, 48 (Summer), 43-55.

Frazier, Gary and John O. Summers (1986), "Interfirm Power and Its Use Within a Franchise Channel of Distribution," *Journal of Marketing Research*, 23 (May), 169-176.

Gaski, John (1984), "The Theory of Power and Conflict in Channels of Distribution," *Journal of Marketing*, 48 (Summer), 9-29.

Gaski, John (1986), "Interrelations Among a Channel Entity's Power Sources: Impact of the Exercise of Reward and Coercion on Expert, Referent, and Legitimate Power Sources," *Journal of Marketing Research*, 23 (February), 62-77.

Hunt, Shelby and John R. Nevin (1974), "Power in a Channel of Distribution: Sources and Consequences," *Journal of Marketing Research*, 11 (May), 186-193.

Kale, Sudhir (1986), "Dealer Perceptions of Manufacturer Power and Influence Strategies In a Developing Country," *Journal of Marketing Research*, 23 (November), 387-393.

Lusch, Robert F. (1976), "Sources of Power: Their Impact on Intrachannel Conflict," *Journal of Marketing Research*, 13 (November), 382-390.

SOURCES FOR CHAPTER 7

Anderson, Erin, Wujin Chu and Barton A. Weitz (1987), "Industrial Purchasing: An Empirical Exploration of the Buyclass Framework," *Journal of Marketing*, 51 (July), 71-86; Appendix A-E, pp. 84-85.

Behrman, Douglas and William D. Perreault, Jr. (1982), "Measuring the Performance of Industrial Salespersons," *Journal of Business Research*, 10, 355-370; Table 3, pp. 366-367.

Bush, Robert P., Alan J. Bush, David J. Ortinau and Joseph F. Hair (1990), "Developing a Behavior-Based Scale to Assess Retail Salesperson Performance," *Journal of Retailing*, 66 (Spring), 119-129; Table 2, pp. 129-130.

Butaney, Gul and Lawrence H. Wortzel (1988), "Distributor Power Versus Manufacturer Power: The Customer Role," *Journal of Marketing*, 52 (January), 52-63; Table 2, p. 56, and Table 3, p. 57.

Chonko, Lawrence B., Roy D. Howell, and Danny Bellenger (1986), "Congruence in Sales Force Evaluations: Relation to Sales Force Perceptions of Conflict and Ambiguity," *Journal of Personal Selling & Sales Management*, 6 (May), 35-48, Appendices A and B, 44-47.

Churchill, Gilbert, Neil M. Ford and Orville C. Walker, Jr. (1974), "Measuring the Job Satisfaction of Industrial Salesmen," *Journal of Marketing Research*, 11 (August), 254-60; Table 2, p. 258.

Comer, James M. (1984), "A Psychometric Assessment of a Measure of Sales Representatives' Power Perceptions," *Journal of Marketing Research*, 21 (May), 221-225; Table 2, p. 224.

Ford, Neil M., Orville C. Walker, Jr., and Gilbert A. Churchill, Jr. (1975), "Expectation-Specific Measures of the Intersender Conflict and Role Ambiguity Experienced by Industrial Salesmen," *Journal of Business Research*, 3 (April), 95-112; Appendix, p. 112.

Frazier, Gary L. (1983), "On the Measurement of Interfirm Power in Channels of Distribution," *Journal of Marketing Research*, 20 (May), 158-166, Table 2, p. 193.

Gaski, John F. and John Nevin (1985), "The Differential Effects of Exercised and Unexercised Power Sources in a Marketing Channel," *Journal of Marketing Research*, 22 (May), 130-142, Figure 4, p.135, and Table 3, p. 140.

Hackman, J. Richard and Greg Oldham (1975), "Development of the Job Diagnostic Survey," *Journal of Applied Psychology*, 60, 159-170.

Hackman, J. Richard and Greg Oldham (1980), *Work Redesign*, Reading, MA: Addison-Wesley Publishing Co., Appendix A 275-294.

House, Robert J. and Gary Dessler (1974), "The Path-Goal Theory of Leadership: Some Post Hoc and A Priori Tests," in *Contingency Approaches to Leadership*, James G. Hunt and Lars L. Larson (eds.), Carbondale IL: Southern Illinois University Press, Table 8, 46-47.

House, Robert, J. and John R. Rizzo (1972), "Role Conflict and Ambiguity as Critical Variables in a Model of Organizational Behavior," *Organizational Behavior and Human Performance*, 7, 467-505, Figure 3, p. 481.

Hunt, Shelby D., Lawrence B. Chonko and Van R. Wood (1985), "Organizational Commitment and Marketing," *Journal of Marketing*, 49 (Winter), 112-126; Table 3, p. 117.

Ironson, G. H., P. C. Smith, M. T. Brannick, W. M. Gibson, and K. B. Paul (1989), "Construction of a Job in General Scale: A Comparison of Global, Composite, and Specific Measures," *Journal of Applied Psychology*, 74, 193-200, Table 1, p. 195.

Kohli, Ajay K. (1989), "Determinants of Influence in Organizational Buying: A Contingency Approach," *Journal of Marketing*, 53 (July), 50-65; Appendix, pp. 62-63.

_____ and Gerald Zaltman (1988), "Measuring Multiple/Buying Influences," *Industrial Marketing Management*, 17, 197-204; Appendix, p. 203.

Mowday, Richard T., Richard M. Steers and Lyman W. Porter (1979), "The Measurement of Organizational Commitment," *Journal of Vocational Behavior*, 14, 224-247; Table 1, p. 228.

Rizzo, John R., Robert J. House and Sidney I. Lirtzman (1970), "Role Conflict and Ambiguity in Complex Organizations," *Administrative Science Quarterly*, 15 (June), 150-164; Table 1, p. 156.

Ruekert, Robert W. and Gilbert A. Churchill, Jr. (1984), "Reliability and Validity of Alternative Measures of Channel Member Satisfaction," *Journal of Marketing Research*, 21 (May),226-233; Table 1, p. 229, and Table 2, p. 230.

Saxe, Robert and Barton A. Weitz (1982), "The SOCO Scale: A Measure of the Customer Orientation of Salespeople," *Journal of Marketing Research*, 19 (August), 434-51; Table 1, p. 156.

Schul, Patrick L., William H. Pride and Taylor L. Little (1983), "The Impact of Channel Leadership Behavior on Intrachannel Conflict," *Journal of Marketing*, 47 (Summer), 21-34; Table 2, p. 26.

Schriesheim, Chester A. (1978), "Development, Validation, and Application of New Leadership Behavior and Expectancy Research Instruments," *Doctoral Dissertation*, College of Administrative Science, Ohio State University.

Sims, Henry P., Jr., Andrew D. Szilagyi, and Robert T. Keller (1979), "The Measurement of Job Characteristics," *Academy of Management Journal*, 19 (June), 195-212; Figure 1, p. 200.

Singh, Jagdip and Gary K. Rhoads (1991), "Boundary Role Ambiguity in Marketing-Oriented Positions: A Multidimensional, Multifaceted Operationalization," *Journal of Marketing Research*, 28 (August), 328-338; Appendix, pp. 337-338.

Smith, Patricia C., Loring M. Kendall, and Charles L. Hulin (1969), *The Measurement of Satisfaction in Work and Retirement: A Strategy for the Study of Attitudes*, Chicago: Rand McNally & Company.

Smith, Patricia C., Loring M. Kendall, and Charles L. Hulin (1985), *The Job Descriptive Index* (Revised Ed.), Bowling Green, OH: Department of Psychology, Bowling Green State University.

Smith, Patricia C., Loring M. Kendall, and Charles L. Hulin (1987), "The Revised JDI: A Facelift for an Old Friend," *Industrial Organizational Psychologist*, 24 (4), 31-33.

Spiro, Rosanne L. and Barton A. Weitz (1990), "Adaptive Selling: Conceptualization, Measurement, and Nomological Validity," *Journal of Marketing Research*, 27 (February), 61-69; Table 1, p. 66.

Swasy, John L. (1979), "Measuring the Bases of Social Power," in *Advances in Consumer Research*, Vol. 6, William L. Wilkie (ed.), Ann Arbor, MI: Association for Consumer Research, 340-346; Table 2, pp. 344-345.

Wood, Van R., Lawrence B. Chonko, and Shelby Hunt (1986), "Social Responsibility and Personal Success: Are They Incompatible?" *Journal of Business Research*, 14, 193-212; Appendix A and B, pp. 207-209.

ASSOCIATION FOR CONSUMER RESEARCH

The Association for Consumer Research (ACR) is a society of individuals who have a professional interest in consumer research. The objectives of this association are:

1. To provide a forum for exchange of ideas among academics and policy officials in business as well as government who are interested in consumer research.

2. To stimulate research focusing on a better understanding of consumer behavior from a variety of perspectives; for example, marketing, psychology, sociology, anthropology, consumer sciences, economics, etc.

3. To disseminate these research findings through publications and conferences.

For more information, please contact:

H. Keith Hunt, Executive Secretary
Association for Consumer Research
Graduate School of Management, 632 TNRB
Brigham Young University
Provo, UT 84602